Struggle for the City

Volume 8
SAGE SERIES ON AFRICAN MODERNIZATION AND DEVELOPMENT

Struggle for the City:
Migrant Labor, Capital, and the State in Urban AFRICA

FREDERICK COOPER
Editor

WITHDRAWN

SAGE PUBLICATIONS
Beverly Hills / London / New Delhi

Copyright © 1983 by Sage Publications, Inc.

For information address:

SAGE Publications, Inc.
275 South Beverly Drive
Beverly Hills, California 90212

SAGE Publications India Pvt. Ltd.
C-236 Defence Colony
New Delhi 110 024, India

SAGE Publications Ltd
28 Banner Street
London EC1Y 8QE, England

Printed in the United States of America

Library of Congress Cataloging in Publication Data

Main entry under title:

Struggle for the city.

   (Sage series on African modernization and development ; v. 8)
   Bibliography: p.
   Contents: Urban space, industrial time, and wage labor in Africa / Frederick
Cooper—Workers as criminals /
William Worger—Productivity and protest / Jeff Crisp—
[etc.]
   1. Labor and laboring classes—Africa—Addresses,
essays, lectures. 2. Cities and towns—Africa—Addresses,
essays, lectures. 3. Africa—Social conditions—Addresses,
essays, lectures. 4. Social Classes—Africa—Addresses,
essays, lectures. I. Cooper, Frederick,
1947-   . II. Title. III. Series.
HD8774.S87   1983   305.5'62'096   83-11196
ISBN 0-8039-2067-9

FIRST PRINTING

Contents

INTRODUCTION

1

URBAN SPACE, INDUSTRIAL TIME, AND WAGE LABOR IN AFRICA

FREDERICK COOPER

In 1920, the Municipality of Nairobi declared that anyone "lodging in any verandah, outhouse or shed, or unoccupied building, or in a cart, vehicle or other receptable," without a visible means of support, was a vagrant, subject to prosecution (cited in van Zwanenberg, 1972: 196). Having helped to build a society in which Africans might choose to live in an outhouse or a shed, the colonial state forbade them to do so. Likewise, colonial and postcolonial governments from South Africa to Senegal have periodically bulldozed squatter settlements that housed low-paid workers at little cost to the state, and they have arrested or harassed women who brew beer in urban locations, even though the women's efforts would seemingly dull the sensibilities of the poor. In trying to build cities on the basis of cheap migrant labor, states have had to face the difficult question of what kind of urban order they were likely to create.

Colonial officials, mining companies, and railway administrators built their cities, mines, and workshops, but not as they would have liked. The kind of society that emerged was not a natural derivative of

Author's Note: I am grateful to Sara Berry, Jane Burbank, William Freund, Peter Gutkind, Terrence McDonald, and Charles Tilly for help with this introduction.

a social category known as urban, nor was it a natural consequence of Africa's "dependent" position in the wider world. The types of housing in which Africans lived — and those from which they were excluded — the controls that limited how long they could stay in the city, the layout of urban services and transportation, and the nature of supervision in factories, workshops, and housing estates were all the objects of thought, planning, and execution in capitals and corporate headquarters. What the planners had to face was not merely the mobilization of labor power, but the control of human beings, of people living in societies and immersed in cultures. As workers sought to shape their lives as individuals and as members of collectivities, they too shaped the life of the city. The woman who brewed beer at night might refresh a downtrodden workforce for the benefit of capital, but she was a dangerously autonomous person, with too many ties to other people, with too few official eyes on her. The men who frequented her *shebeen* might dull their senses, but they also participated in an urban culture that was antithetical to hard work, that accepted forms of conduct that the state defined as criminal, and whose very cultural separateness made it at least a potential base for political organization. In some circumstances, the rough hostility of such a culture might be tolerable, but in others it might undermine the possibility of building a stable, more reliable work force. Harassing squatters, beer brewers, and prostitutes underlined the hegemony of the dominant class, whose orderly ways were made to appear legitimate, while the illegitimacy of lower-class life was rubbed in by the humiliation of police raids. Such an urban policy might also preclude other forms of control, cooptation, and legitimacy, and make more difficult the development of a hierarchy of privileges and incentives that would encourage a differentiated and "respectable" working class instead of a threatening urban mass.

Despite the contradictions of urban society, some scholars extol the virtues of self-help and entrepreneurship among urban slum-dwellers, while others insist that capitalism's quest to minimize wage costs explains the structure of labor and the city. Yet states — colonial and postcolonial — have shrunk back before the consequences of both maximizing entrepreneurship and minimizing wages. The ambivalence and inconsistency that run through the history of urban policy reflect the complexity of the issue of social reproduction. No society can go on producing, Marx wrote (1977: 711), without constantly reconverting part of its products into the means to produce more. The most elusive of the commodities capital had to renew was human labor power. Daily reproduction was one dimension: the rest, nourishment, and relaxation necessary to get workers back on the job the next day. So too was the raising of new generations of workers and care for nonworkers, and — most difficult of all — the renewal of the relationship of capitalist and worker, the development of predictable patterns of behavior, obedience, and effort. In the development of capitalism, workers' loss of access to the means of subsistence meant that the food, housing, and other goods necessary for the reproduction of the work force were themselves commodities produced by wage laborers (Marx, 1977: 724). Every act of alienating people from the means of production simultaneously created markets and the labor power to supply them, and the dialectic of production and reproduction pushed capitalism forward.

In Africa, some Marxist scholars now argue, capitalism's strength lies in the fact that it does not organize its own reproduction (Meillassoux, 1975; Wolpe, 1972). While the daily reproduction of labor power necessarily takes place near the mine or factory, the social cost of those not actually on the job is absorbed by the surviving precapitalist forms of production in rural Africa. The countryside is the locus of reproduction for capitalist production in the city. Such an argument appears to explain the ability of employers to pay low wages, the continued importance of back-and-forth migration between town and country, and the absence in Africa of the dialectic of market and labor that lent European capitalism its dynamism. Other scholars (Portes and Walton, 1981) argue that minimizing reproduction costs explains the internal structure of the city as much as its relationship with the countryside: Squatter settlements and the production and distribution of consumer items at low cost through the use of family labor subsidize capital's wage bill. The city, much as the countryside, preserves economic relationships distinct from those of capital to labor.

What these arguments do not explain are the ambiguities described above. They present capitalism without class struggle, and an urban order defined only by functions and categories. Work is work, a proletarian a proletarian.

However, work is not just work, and the necessity that drives a worker into a factory or mine only begins to explain how a capitalist converts the workers' time into output in the face of varying imperatives within the production process and of varying forms of resistance and manipulation by workers. Whether workers — individually and collectively — accept discipline each day, or acquiesce grudgingly, and whether their efforts at improving their own lot take place within or against the structure of work depends very much on how they are integrated and fragmented within a wider social order. These are questions of production and reproduction, of ideology, culture, and law, as much as food and houses. Could capital — whenever its own demands for productivity and order rose, and when it faced an increasingly experienced African work force with deeper roots in the city — obtain consent in the workplace without creating a social system in which commodities, property, and wage labor defined aspirations and relationships? Could capital continue its relentless drive to accumulate when it confronted workers for whom alternative modes of social organization were not memories or dreams but concrete realities, strongly rooted in their own urban neighborhoods and rural villages?

For capital, controlling laborers' working days and working lives entailed multifaceted struggles with workers trying themselves to shape the pattern of their own lives. The structure of production — in factories, mines, railways, and services — both reflected and affected the structure of space, and the principle of a market in land and buildings coexisted uneasily with the principles of land occupation and personal relationships that developed in the "irregular settlements" and "informal sector" that helped to reproduce the labor force. Production and reproduction were not abstractions, but processes directed by specific people and classes from the mine magnate to the owner of a house, and the question of what kinds of classes, with what kinds of relations to the working class, carried out these processes also helped to shape urban social order. This introduction will explore the struggles of capital, the state, and workers to define and transform the structure of time, space, and class relations. Running through it and the following essays are the questions of who shapes the city, in what image, by what means, and against what resistance. This book explores the ways in which the imperatives of capitalist production shape social processes, and the limits of those ways. It is a book about struggle, not so much the dramatic confrontations of strikes, riots, and revolt, but the daily struggles over the details of life in the workplace, the marketplace, and the residence. It examines the ways these small struggles affected large and elusive questions: the transformation of ideology and culture, the forging of vast spatial systems in which people carried out their efforts at survival, advancement, and struggle.

The book begins with William Worger's study of Africa's first mining town, Kimberley. He shows how difficult it was for mining capital to develop the institutions of compound, labor registry, and jail through which workers could be controlled on and off the job, and that these mechanisms, once established, not only moved Africans along a migratory pathway, but built a system of ideological control, drawing boundaries of permissible behavior. The book ends with Colin Murray's reassessment of South African migratory labor in the 1980s, when the use of systematic controls over movement and the mass expulsions from the cities had so transformed the countryside that rural slums became urban dumping grounds, hardly more self-sustaining than a city yard. In between, Jeff Crisp looks at another way — based on "scientific mangement" — of controlling mine workers, in a more recent era and in the context of effective challenges from workers in the Gold Coast after 1947. However, in the same time period in another place, as Jeanne Penvenne shows in the case of Lourenço Marques, capital might still try to define all African workers as criminals and thus bring about a quite different pattern of struggle in the workplace and city. Luise White stresses the ambiguous position of prostitutes, who both epitomized and in effect caricatured the values of a commoditized, accumulating society; who filled valuable roles in servicing a male, migratory labor force; yet who did so in such a way that they called into question the kind of city the colonial state wished to build and the kinds of property-owning classes that the state could allow to organize the reproduction of labor. Gérard Salem peers into the rarely glimpsed interior of what is often passed off as the "informal sector" and studies how small-scale entrepreneurs went about their struggles, with a narrow commercial system and with the workers out of whom a bit of surplus value could be extracted. Finally, Sara Berry puts the Nigerian city back into the countryside, arguing that class formation takes place in a single system embracing both and that the strategies of people at all social levels must be assessed in relation to this wider spatial system. From South Africa to Nigeria, the most basic social processes transcend the dichotomy of city and countryside.

URBAN TELEOLOGIES

Coming to grips with the processes that shaped the meanings of time, space, and class in urban Africa is an elusive task. It is made no easier by approaches to the social sciences that see history as moving forward toward ends the nature of which can be treated as a given, whether the process is called urbanization or proletarianization.

Urbanization

The very term "urbanization" suggests a self-propelled process. However, its roots in the classics of sociology are actually rather shallow. For Marx, Weber, and Durkheim, the city was a basic category of social life at a particular moment in history, when the tension between the distinct social forms in city and countryside led to the breakdown of feudalism. The forces this breakdown unleashed — however differently these writers conceived of them — ran through all of society, although perhaps more intensely in the dense environment of the city. When Marx wrote (1973: 479) of the "urbanization of the countryside" under capitalism, he was pointing out that the particularity of the urban was destroyed by its extension (Giddens, 1981: 148; Saunders, 1981: 11-47).

The human ecology school most prominent in the United States during the 1930s had a new perspective. Cities were big, dense, and heterogeneous, simple facts that, in Louis Wirth's famous formulation (1938), shaped a way of life distinct from that of rural areas. However, this school had trouble separating density, as a cause of social phenomena, from the other currents affecting city and countryside alike (Saunders, 1981). Urbanization theory became a "fetishism of space," treating social processes as if they were derivatives of universal laws of space (Tabb and Sawers, 1978: 12). Then, the so-called urban problem became a kind of natural disaster that could be solved by a "single army of boy scouts" (Castells, 1977: 186).

As Africans flocked into cities in ever greater numbers in the 1950s, the dualist approach to urbanization suggested that they were entering the mainstream of history. The key word in the urban anthropology of those years was "adaptation," and studies stressed how organizations from ethnic associations to trade unions eased the — inevitable — movement into an urban way of life.[1] The liberal affirmation that the African was becoming an urbanite was an affirmation of modernity.

Such studies, Bernard Magubane charged (1971), discussed everything except what really mattered. They placed colonial, racial, and class structures outside the realm of investigation, examining only individual responses to an implacable and unquestioned entity. Magubane protests too much. Such work as Mitchell's study (1956) of an African urban cult, which Magubane finds condescending, exotic, and trivial, point to ways in which African migrants established networks among themselves and sought, symbolically and ritually, to understand their world. Without this kind of investigation, analyses of African consciousness and action would be rooted in nothing more than colonialism itself, and resistance would be another teleology, not a process growing out of the social and cultural bonds Africans tried to forge (see Mayer, 1981).

The concept of urbanization, as Castells argues (1977), is less powerful as an analytic tool than as ideology: It defines a certain kind of social structure as inherently modern, inevitable, and superior. The authors of this book, in common with other recent writers (see Cahiers d'Etudes Africaines, 1982), are less sure than scholars used to be what urban means. Indeed, the types of spatial units discussed are more specific than the city: the mining compound, the native location, the rural slum. We have gone from an answer — urbanization — to a question: What is the relationship of particular kinds of space to particular social processes?

Dependency and Marginality

It does not take a very daring critique of the universalism of urbanization theory to distinguish Monrovia from Paris. For some scholars, the characteristics of urbanism are less a general description than a standard. The concept of "overurbanization," for example, expressed a belief that African cities have too many people supported by a too unproductive countryside; city dwellers produce too little of a too narrow range of goods; and they are forced into marginal economic and social roles. Yet this separation of the normal and the pathological is as simplistic as it is ethnocentric (Castells, 1977: 41-42). In dependency, underdevelopment, and world-systems theories, the problems of the "periphery" of the world economy are not a tropical disease, but an integral part of the strength of the "core" of the world economy. A worldwide division of labor consigns the periphery to primary production and relegates its cities to the task of organizing the drainage of commodities and surplus from farms and mines. Technical and social development in rural areas is frozen, while urban labor is divided into a foreign-dominated sector using capital-intensive technology — and hence providing few jobs — and a marginal sector, squeezed between the overpopulated, backward countryside and stagnant employment in industry. Marginals get by as hawkers, prostitutes, casual laborers, or small-scale artisans, but they get nowhere; their marginality lies in the fact that their roles are dead ends, not stepping stones to more lucrative and productive economic activities. The shanty where the marginals live is not a transitional phenomenon but a permanent part of the "dual circuit" characteristic of labor markets in the periphery (Santos, 1979; Quijano, 1974). Marginality has been no more reduced by the economic growth of Brazil than by the stagnation of Ghana.

The continued migration of workers to town is similarly seen as a response — but not a solution — to the dependence induced in rural Africa by the penetration of the world economy. As dependence created cash needs without rural development and as urban labor only partially met workers' needs over their lifetimes, workers oscillated between city and country, perpetuating old social structures, draining the countryside of adult male labor, and rendering Africa as a whole even more incapable of developing varied, complementary, and productive economic activities (Amin, 1974; Riddell, 1981; Gregory and Piché, 1978; Soja and Weaver, 1976).

These theories — with variations — thus connect marginality in the internal structure of cities, migration between city and countryside, and underdevelopment in the relationship of periphery and core. The apparent permanence of marginality and migration is a consequence of the apparently permanent underdevelopment of the periphery. Yet the dichotomy of core and periphery creates a new, grand fetishism of space.

Johannesburg is no more Monrovia than it is Paris. Once the spatial dichotomy breaks down, the question of what fosters or retards specific processes of capital accumulation, expansion of the forces of production, and mobilization and control of labor becomes the critical one.[2] Core-periphery theories have made the essential point that all such processes must be seen in a global context, but they have not got to the roots of the processes themselves.

The inadequacies of this group of theories are by now familiar (Brenner, 1977; Cooper, 1981). Discussions of marginality and migration in these terms suffer from a similar conceptual rigidity. The contention that a certain division of labor is functional for the world capitalist system substitutes for analysis of how forms of labor were created and resisted. The relationship of supposedly marginal workers to formal employment, as well as to rural areas, is in fact far more complex, fluid, and changing than theory suggests (Portes and Walton, 1981: 78-82; Perlman, 1976).

In South Africa, the African worker is at the center — not the margins — of capital's efforts at accumulation. Precisely for this reason, the South African state's attempt to control residence and migration have been so important. Elsewhere, too much marginality — a footloose working class — can be an obstacle to accumulation rather than a basis of it.

Proletarianization

If underdevelopment theory insists that world commerce determines African urban structure, another radical position emphasizes production; the growth of a working class in the African city shapes its structure and the conflicts that occur within it. This process has been seen in rather linear terms: African workers became concentrated in key mining and commercial centers; their experience in the workplace led them to a greater sense of collective identity and class consciousness; and they organized to challenge capital and the state (Sandbrook and Cohen, 1975; Gutkind et al., 1978).

This conception parallels, often explicitly, the title of E. P. Thompson's *The Making of the English Working Class* (1963) but pays less attention to the contents of this work. Thompson stressed the forms of work, association, and culture among workers before the rise of industrial capitalism, the unsuccessful struggle of workers *not* to be a class — defined solely by their homogeneous labor power — and the effects of these experiences on the subsequent action of workers as a class. Africanists are now beginning to take such early struggles seriously. Patterns of migration may have reflected as much African resistance to capitalist work rhythms as a cost-minimizing strategy of employers. Wage labor could be a strategy to gain resources for expanding agricultural production, not just a consequence of rural decay. Fleeing to a city could help to break down the dominance of rural patriarchies and oligarchies without necessarily bringing about subordination to urban employers (Marks and Rathbone,

1982: 15-20; Cooper, 1980; Beinart, 1982; Kitching, 1980). How the social networks, economic patterns, and cultural forms created during these early struggles affected the confrontations that later emerged in mines and dockyards remains to be examined. The confrontations themselves do not grow proportionately to numbers of workers or length of employment, but ebb and flow in more complex ways, as basic questions of restructuring the organization of work come to the fore (Cooper, 1981: 41-44).

If a kind of progressivism has influenced one tendency in African labor history, another — within structuralist versions of Marxism — has been oddly static. Capitalism does not revolutionize the relations of production in Africa as it did in Europe; instead, it "articulates" with precapitalist modes of production, sapping their autonomy without changing their internal logic, and draining adult male labor into wage employment without taking over the burdens of supporting women, children, and nonworking men (Meillassoux, 1975; Wolpe, 1972; Foster-Carter, 1978). These are the theories that focus attention on the symbiotic relationship of capitalist production and precapitalist reproduction.

Structuralist Marxism has come under strong fire (Thompson, 1978; Giddens, 1981). The logical necessity for a system to reproduce itself does not explain how specific classes act, or how concrete actions generate new contradictions. Applied to Africa, the structuralist position assumes that capitalism's imperatives caused agriculture to decay to just the right degree and that workers moved back and forth on cue. It fails to grasp capital's difficulty in obtaining steady, reliable work from laborers who retained access to land, the efforts of workers to bring resources back to the countryside or to devote them to petty trade or production in the city, and the serious challenges workers have posed to capital and the state. If there ever was a moment when labor came forth in sufficient quantity and worked sufficiently reliably and peaceably — perhaps during the period of low demand for labor during the Great Depression — it was short (Cooper, 1981: 40-41).

If the structuralists have put forth the relationship of production and reproduction more explicitly than any other school, they have created too stark a dichotomy between the two, too neat a geographical separation between the locus of each, and too weak a conception of how forms of production and reproduction affect each other. Only in some circumstances were the size and cost of a labor force all that concerned capital. Otherwise, it had to face the multifaceted confrontation of different ways of using resources and organizing social life,

a confrontation carried out in the arenas of production and reproduction.

In Europe, the long and complex development of capitalism
entailed the conquest of time and space, not just in pockets but within
a seamless web enveloping all of society. With the dominance of wage
labor, work time became starkly separated from leisure time as well as
from the flow of tasks shaped by the relationship between people and
nature; time became a commodity, divided into standardized units
that the proletarian had to sell and that any possessor of capital could
buy (Thompson, 1967). Space also became a commodity, and access
to land and buildings had to come through markets, which in turn
conditioned how time had to be sold: as regularly as space was
consumed. If in feudal society the relationship of exploiter and
exploited was specific and not easily transposed over space, under
capitalism, capital and labor power both became movable and detached. The relationship of employer and worker was fundamentally
the same regardless of the persons involved and whether the job was
in a city or in the country, in the workers' home town or a distant land.
In the process, the tension between city and country, so basic to the
society of feudal Europe, was transformed.

Europe was made over not simply by the working out of an
abstract social logic, but by specific classes confronting equally
specific cultivators and workers. Cities had already been built in
stone, and the symbolic meanings of urban and rural life could not
suddenly disappear. Capitalists and workers alike drew on their past
authority and past sense of social norms even as they struggled over
the new meanings of space and time.

Behind these new meanings lies the alienation of the means of
production. As Giddens (1981) reminds us, the power of Marx's
analysis lies in his stress on the specificity of capitalism, and it risks
being undermined by too glib an assumption of capitalist dominance
in areas where capitalism has not revolutionized production. Structuralist Marxists, like dependency theorists, rightly argue that
surplus can be drained through the relationship of capitalism to other
forms of production, but a surplus must be produced before it can be
drained, and capital's problematic control over the total process of
production and reproduction poses severe limits to the dominance of
capitalism.

Without the urbanization of the countryside, the city itself in
colonial Africa took on some of the dimensions of the precapitalist
city. It was a "crucible of power" (Giddens, 1981: 147), sometimes
originating as a garrison town, most often looking warily at rural areas

not fully under control. Europeans congregated in cities because the countryside frightened them, and firms concentrated in a single primate city or a small network of cities because markets for labor, services, and goods were so uneven. Arising out of the expansion of European capitalism, the colonial city was the kind of social bastion that European cities had long ceased to be. The colonial city, Anthony King argues (1976), deserves its own place in a typology of urban forms. The dominance of an imperial power over a conquered people defines the city, and dominance is underscored spatially and symbolically by the maintenance of social distance between the quarters of the conquerors and the conquered. King fails to appreciate that political control was less implacable than it seemed to be. The sprawling squatter settlement was as much a part of urban structure as the carefully planned commercial zone. If the colonial city was not fully capitalist, it was not fully colonial either.

Capital's inconclusive assault on Africa created a guerrilla army of the underemployed rather than the juxtaposition of disciplined troops and the reserve army of the unemployed characteristic of industrial capitalism. The guerrilla army frequently worked badly and cluttered up the city, while — in their simultaneous guise as farmers — the troops failed to produce enough food to feed the city. Capital and the state were forced to pursue ways of controlling time and space distinct from the forms of labor control they stressed where workers could only work, or else they had to take on the task of separating workers from rural life and socializing them to the proper culture for a working class. Workers, meanwhile, struggled to preserve or create their own ways of using space and time: "straddling" between country and city or between wage labor and petty trade, and moving between urban and rural squatting (Berry, this volume; Kitching, 1980; Cooper, 1981). Yet at the same time, the mine or the railway yard produced challenges to capital's control of labor remarkably similar to those generated by European working class.

TIME AND WORK

If the separation of producers from the means of production in capitalist development made the European working classes' time into a divisible, measurable, salable commodity, it also made time into a central object of struggle between capital and labor (Thompson, 1967). The battle over the length of the working day led to questions of the working year — vacation time versus work time — and the working life, in relation to childhood and retirement. In the world of the migrant worker, time is an equally critical issue, but its parameters are not the same.

In the early industrial revolution in Europe, capital fought to lengthen the working day and the "sanction of the sack" was its principal weapon. In early colonial Africa, employers' prime concern was lengthening the working year, and their stress on contracts and penal sanctions betrayed the unreliability of the sanction of the sack. As Worger and Penvenne show, reliance on compounds, flogging, jails, fines, and passes in South Africa in the 1870s and Mozambique in the 1950s reveals not only the need for coercive instruments to control time, but an attempt by the state to use the authority of the law to drive new notions of time, idleness, and discipline into culture (compare Ignatieff, 1978).

If the worker in a capitalist economy had nothing to sell but time, all an employer could buy was time. Time had to be made into effort, effort into output. The sanction of the sack gets us only to the beginning of the issue of control on the shop floor. The sanctions that the state and capital in different parts of Africa used to keep Africans in the workplace were not necessarily the means by which the delicate questions of what happened once they were there could be resolved. The heavy-handed system of control that van Onselen (1977) describes in gold mines — fines, corporal punishment, withholding rations, tolerance of beer brewing by favored workers — might meet some expectations of performance, but not others. Such questions became increasingly critical in the 1940s, when both the demands for intense and reliable production and the challenges of workers escalated sharply. The contrast between Penvenne's account of criminal sanctions in postwar Mozambique and Crisp's of scientific management in the postwar Gold Coast points to the critical alternatives for controlling time, and the troubles both labor systems faced remind us that neither crude nor sophisticated mechanisms necessarily work.

Marxist labor economists have lately tried to spell out different forms of the labor process under capitalism. Braverman (1974) stresses that proletarianization only got workers into factories: then, slowly, the position of skilled workers was eroded, work divided into ever more narrowly defined tasks, managerial power strengthened, undocumented aliens formed separate pools, so that the divisions of ethnicity and gender became actual parts of the labor process.[3] In Europe, guest workers enter a separate labor market, pushed into the harsher segments of the labor system. The boundaries of segments change with political struggles and the efforts of some groups to work their way into a better position, but legal and institutional mechanisms prop up barriers, help to divide the working class, and allow capital to shift between long-term stability and short-term cost minimization depending on its needs (Gordon et al., 1982).

At first glance, the lessons this literature seems to offer Africanists are the useful ones of contrast. The entire Third World workforce seems like a subordinate segment within a worldwide division of labor. So it might have been had African workers not had something to do with it. The shuttling mechanisms by which colonial states controlled workers' time produced a special version of the homogenization process that had stimulated class conflict in industrial countries. The combination, especially before the 1940s, of largely male migration, low wages and lack of social services, harsh supervision on the job, and the lack of regular channels for achieving advancement or respectability tended to make all African workers into so much interchangeable labor power. Moving in and out of jobs, between jobs and jails, and between city and country — failing to develop roots in a differentiated job structure — workers in the city became an urban mass. The dangers of an inchoate and volatile urban society, of the urban mob, were familiar parts of the history of capitalism in Europe, and the state had sought to contain such forces (Chevalier, 1973; Stedman Jones, 1971). But the growth of wage labor in colonial Africa threatened to create dangerous classes without also creating respectable working classes.

Anxiety about the unruly mass began at an early date, but fears became actualities during the wave of strikes and disturbances that swept across the West Indies and Africa from the mid-1930s to the early 1950s, the period of intensified production and inflation (Cooper, 1981, forthcoming). Strikes, riots, and shop boycotts — reflecting varying degrees of organization — overlapped; they seemed to racapitulate in a moment a hundred years of the history of collective violence in Europe, from the food riot to the industrial action (Tilly et al., 1975).

In the British Empire at least, the disturbances prompted a rethinking of the nature of colonial society (Lee, 1967), including the execution separated from conception, and, as a result, the nature of work was degraded. This view is overly linear. Some groups of skilled workmen defended their skills more successfully than others; new kinds of skill became necessary as others were eroded; and the struggles over the control of work took place not just in the workplace, but in other social arenas as well (Burawoy, 1978; Edwards, 1979; Crisp, this volume).

Gordon et al. (1982) see changing forms of labor control not in evolutionary terms, but in relation to class struggle, economic crises, and systematic attempts to restructure work. The problem was not simply to discipline workers within factories, but to contain and control the working class. The initial process of creating a proletariat also created a working-class movement. A second phase of capitalist development spawned oligopolies more capable of tackling the strengths of particular groups of workers, making the working class more homogeneous and interchangeable. Workers' time came to be increasingly controlled by technology — by machines or an assembly line that set the pace of work — while older patterns of direct supervision by foremen were modified by various organizational techniques, such as Taylor's scientific management. Outside the workplace, expanding educational facilities and other public institutions taught the working class the generalized skills capital now needed as well as the values of obedience and punctuality. Yet each form of labor control generated its own form of resistance. Sophisticated technology created vulnerability to action at key points in assembly; mass workforces fostered industrial unionism; and large-scale layoffs threatened massive social disruption. Capitalism moved into a new phase, characterized by the segmentation of work. In oligopolistic industries, where ensuring the long-term consent of workers to management control had become more important than minimizing wages, collective bargaining and grievance procedures mediated conflict and shop floor control was bureaucratized. Meanwhile, the state countered pressures coming from the era of homogenization with a wider range of measures to stabilize class relations. Yet at the very same time more competitive industries, much of the growing service sector, and agribusiness stuck to older patterns of direct supervision of foremen, harsh working conditions, low pay, and minimal long-term security. Labor segmentation theory argues that these two divisions (more in some formulations) drew on distinct labor pools. In the United States, in different periods, immigrants, blacks, women, and question of the urban mass. The alternative to the dangerous mass that slowly emerged in official minds was the differentiated labor force. However widespread the urban crises, the actual changes in work organization depended very much on the give and take of particular situations. In Mombasa, the unrest that bridged the general strikes of 1937 and 1947 led to a systematic transformation of dock work, altering the meaning of work-time and — or so officials hoped — of urban order. Casual labor on the docks had epitomized the separation of production and reproduction: The employer bought, quite literally, one working day at a time and ignored the rest of the social cost of labor. In Mombasa as much as in London, casual labor was both cheap and dangerous (Stedman Jones, 1971). Casual workers were too footloose to discipline properly: Because they worked a day at a time, the sanction of the sack did not touch them; because of their connection with nearby farming communities they could hold out without work for longer than workers fully immersed in markets; and because they lived and shared housing with both more regular workers and with idlers and criminals, their irregular ways contaminated the entire city. The strikes revealed to authorities an urban mass out of control.

A second concern developed as the strikes drove up wages: Without the incentives of a long-term career and with no progress in shaping a more tractable work culture among dockers, casual workers were not sufficiently productive (compare Crisp, this volume). Cheap labor was expensive. In fact, officials understood neither the actual nature of social relations in Mombasa — which was far more complex than the idea of a mass suggested — nor the determinants of productivity on the docks. They correctly perceived the fragility of managerial control and the social fluidity of the city. From the mid-1940s, they began forcing casual workers to register, then to work a minimum number of days per month, and then to work on monthly contracts. The companies accepted that such a work organization would mean higher wages for a more compact work force, and eventually conceded medical, pension, and other benefits. The municipality built family housing and other amenities aimed at regular wage workers. Dockers continued to struggle effectively for better wages and conditions but they had conceded the terrain of struggle: They had accepted industrial time, and made steadiness and life-time jobs the basis of their economic lives (Cooper, forthcoming).

To change work was to change the city, replacing the large floating population with a smaller and more differentiated one, with each industry calling into the city only the workers it employed and accepting — if grudgingly — the costs of reproducing the work force within the city itself. The changes implied a new attitude toward an African labor force, moving away from thinking of workers as so much anonymous labor power and toward fostering within each industry distinct patterns of recruitment, bargaining, and advancement. Within this framework, building trade unions in individual industries was acceptable, but the efforts of Kenyan workers to build a union of all workers were not and were duly repressed. The segmented city did not come to be as sharp a contrast to the urban mass as planners had hoped. The transition came from pressures within the city itself, and the absence of parallel developments in agriculture sent more people into the city. A differentiated work force was created, but the orderly, manageable city remains an elusive goal.

Similar relationships between strikes and efforts by capital to build a more stable, differentiated work force are evident in the Gold Coast (Crisp, this volume) and Zambia (Heisler, 1974; Chauncey, 1981). The same issue was broached in South Africa in the 1940s, but with opposite results — an escalation of controls over migration. The issue has not gone away.

The problem of time refuses to stay in the workplace. The relationship of work time, leisure time, and reproduction time is also a relationship of workplace, residential space, and reproduction space.

SPACE AND WORK

Just as capitalism's transformation of time into a commodity confronted the humanity of the people from whom capital bought time, the extension of capitalism confronted the physical actuality of the world. However capitalism transformed work, workers still had bodies, which took up space and required services; the universality of the market might cross the divide between town and country and link distant lands into a single system for the circulation of capital, but nothing circulated faster than the constraints of distance and communication permitted. If Marxist critics of urbanization theory have rightly attacked its tendency to treat social phenomena as derivatives of spatial relations, Marxist theory itself has to confront the fact that social relations exist in space; even as society shapes space, space shapes society.

The concrete obstacles of space to the universalizing tendencies of capitalism bring back the concept of the urban into Marxist theory. The city cannot be explained by the logic of capitalist production itself, which sweeps across industry and agriculture alike. Most theorists find the reasons why cities exist in capitalist society, why some develop more rapidly than others, and why cities take particular forms in the realms of circulation and reproduction. Whether those realms can be governed by the rules of capitalism — and still do what capital needs to have done — constitutes the most elusive part of the urban question. Firms need to exchange goods whether or not it pays a particular capitalist to run a railroad; capital in general needs to have workers housed and transported cheaply, even if it is in the interests of some capitalists to make housing and transport as expensive as possible; manufacturers, bankers, technicians, and lawyers need to get together; and the conflict over the control of time described above requires that capital worry about certain, not necessarily profitable, processes to socialize, stabilize, and appease workers. Essential aspects of infrastructure and consumption — schools, hospitals, roads, and parks — are basically collective in function; they are not commodities that individuals buy, use, and discard; they create a long-lasting built environment with large effects on future circulation of commodities and capital. If the abstract logic of capitalist production creates individualistic, impersonal, despatialized relationships, the logic of circulation and reproduction creates collective and concentrated spatial structures (Castells, 1977; Harvey, 1973, 1975, 1981; Lojkine, 1976; Rose, 1981; Pickvance, 1976).

If industrial capitalism is capable of producing all the toaster ovens and electric razors that the world can use, it is less clear that it can produce the housing its work force needs, in Liverpool any more than in Lusaka. The fact that space acquires a commercial value exposes it to the tension between the possibility for particular capitalists to profit by developing new resources and the profits to be gained by restricting access to resources. Space, unlike steel, is not a readily expandable commodity, and speculation, the differential values of particular locations, and monopoly all constrain the expansion of housing (Marx, 1981: 906-916). Moreover, buildings have special characteristics: They take a long time and much money to build, last a long time, and must be paid for slowly by people whose wages capital in general would like to keep low. Credit is a solution to the problem, but only by plunging the specific social problem of housing into the general cauldron of interest rates (Harvey, 1973; Pickvance, 1976). The most free enterprise-oriented states have intervened massively in housing, from opening credit to moderate-income people to undertaking large scale construction and town planning projects (Castells, 1977; Harvey, 1977). The alternative to confronting the high costs of built space is spreading out, and that shifts the burden from housing to transport, which shares many of the same limitations of private production as does housing.

How workers are housed has much to do with how they are integrated into a social order. In nineteenth-century London, as in other growing cities, market forces drove workers out of central districts and into dangerous association with the unrespectable poor, leading to government intervention in housing and transport (Rose, 1981). In the United States, the extension of individual housing to workers in the twentieth century (with heavy government assistance) was intended not only to put roofs over people's heads, but to lead workers to identify with the value of private property and to work steadily in order to keep it. However, as changing market forces made and remade urban space, the values of community — family, ethnic group, neighborhood — had to be defended not only politically but in real estate markets, "on capital's own terrain: that of the commodity" (Cox, 1981: 438; Harvey, 1973, 1975; Katznelson, 1979). The state faced pressures to foster accumulation in the city and to temper its effects on reproduction and social structure. State intervention not only contradicted an ideology that claimed that market mechanisms are supposed to work and created conflict with particular interests within the capitalist class, but forced the state to confront in piecemeal fashion the very pattern of speculation, interest rates, and production difficulties that gave rise to the housing problem in the first place. States procede from crisis to crisis, without altering the underlying contradictions of accumulation and reproduction (Castells, 1977; Harvey, 1981; Rose, 1981). Even so, the market and the state both fracture and reintegrate communities and classes across the city map, in differing patterns that help to determine the forms and effectiveness of urban social movements (Katznelson, 1979).

These paragraphs only suggest the importance of a growing body of theory. For Castells (1977), the city can best be understood in terms of the increasingly collective character of consumption under capitalism: It is above all the locus of reproduction of the working class. However, it is not clear why cities should be only that. Lojkine (1976) and Harvey (1975) instead emphasize the city's role in the circulation of capital and in the general process of accumulation. It is not clear, as Saunders has shown (1981), that these theories are actually urban theories, or why the authors are so eager for them to be urban.

Although the theories of Castells, Harvey, and others have had considerable influence on studies of cities in Europe and the Americas, they have had virtually none on African studies, even though the theorists' concern with the relationship of accumulation, community, and social movements is quite germane, in however particular a way, to African cities. Castells (1977: 39-63) and Harvey (1973: 232) themselves make only some underdeveloped remarks about "dependent urbanism," while Africanists most often discuss housing, poverty, and social movements as if they were a wholly distinct theoretical problem from housing, poverty, and social movements in industrial countries (Sandbrook, 1982; Sandbrook and Stren, 1982), or else they adopt a rather eclectic approach that could well be illuminated by (and illuminate) more theoretically precise forumulations (Cahiers d'Etudes Africaines, 1982). This essay can do little more than suggest a direction that a rethinking of the connection between spatial organization and capitalist penetration in Africa might take.

Two themes come to mind. One has been discussed already: The Marxist structuralist argument about the connection of production and reproduction — presented as the articulation of modes of production — is also an argument about space. It posits that the spatial meaning of reproduction in contemporary Africa is quite distinct from its meaning in industrial Europe: Reproduction space in Africa is rural, not urban, and its institutional basis is therefore very different. The second point seems at first to have little to do with the logic of capitalism. Yet of all the ways that space can be divided — class or racial segregation, or the divisions of workplace and residence, private and public space — one of the most critical in Africa is the division between legal space and illegal space. This is a distinction that reveals the uncertainty of who can define urban society and how. Discussion of these points will lead to a question: How are forms of space connected to forms of protest?

The separation of production space and reproduction space in the structuralist argument leaves a minimal type of reproduction to the workplace: getting a man through to the next day. Within the mining compound or the urban location in colonial cities, the spatial meaning of daily reproduction was often taken all too literally: The size of a man's body determined the space for reproduction. Even reformist concerns in the 1940s and 1950s often escalated the standard only from the bed space to the single room. If workplace reproduction was minimal, migratory space was elaborate, designed and policed by organizations like the Rhodesia Native Labour Association or the Bantu Administration of South Africa. In South Africa, the centrality of the jail and the courts for pass offenders within the spatial circuit points not only to the power of the state in connecting production and reproduction, but to the extremely limited degree to which workers' incorporation into a world of markets and commodities could provide a basis for obtaining consent in the workplace.

So an agglomeration like Kimberley, built around compounds, mines, labor bureaus, and jails for black workers and a wholly distinct set of institutions for the personal and collective consumption of white workers and bosses became a very distinctive kind of spatial structure. Such an urban form was at variance not only from the European mining town but from the "totalitarian" mining towns of Katanga, where the company kept reproduction under its own eyes (Fetter, 1973), or from the far looser organization of commercial centers in West Africa. However, the imperatives of production were not the only ones shaping urban forms, and the entrenched Coloured community of Cape Town gave that city a distinct structure that was to be the target of decades of assault from the South African state (Western, 1981).

The actual relationship of social process and city structure is masked, Castells argues (1977), by the concept of urbanism. However, the mask might be as important as the reality. Indeed, the tenuous nature of colonial control made the mask of city planning and urban architecture all the more important as a symbol of hegemony. Colonial planning served not to integrate — or even to give the illusion of integration — but to emphasize distinctiveness and domination. Writing about India, King (1976) shows that colonial architecture created its own hierarchy of dwelling units — the *landhy,* the labor line, the bungalow — and its own architectural vocabulary. Planning emphasized the creation of barriers to separate neighborhoods as well as distinctions in density, building design, and amenities. Metaphors of disease and contamination — the "sanitation syndrome" (Swanson, 1977) — served as rationales for racial segregation, and later for the purging of the poor from central cities (Marris,

1962). However, the price of symbolic dominance is that it precludes symbolic integration into a universal world of markets and commodities. Popular assaults on the modern, largely foreign quarter of Cairo just before Nasser's coup were a manifestation of the dangers of spatial symbols of power (Abu-Lughod, 1976: 209-210). The reproduction of urban culture remains a thorny issue.

When concern shifted to the city as a possible locus of cheap reproduction, it often ran into the nature of space as a commodity. In South Africa during the 1920s, growing but fluctuating demand for black workers in Johannesburg encouraged the government to tolerate African initiatives in housing in suburbs like Sophiatown, but speculative capital saw the same space as useful for real estate development for whites, and pushed its views through the Johannesburg city council. Meanwhile, African property owners and workers in the area of tolerated African housing saw the relative openness of such housing as preferable to closely supervised locations, and they slowly forged a new kind of urban neighborhood. Authorities saw the culture that evolved in this context as criminal and ultimately politically threatening. Black Sophiatown was tolerated at first, then, in the 1950s, destroyed (Proctor, 1979; Lodge, 1981). Since then a spatial counterrevolution has transformed countryside as well as city more by the massive urban expulsions than by the long-term decline of agricultural land (Simkins, 1981). "Rural slums," in Murray's tragically apt phrase, do not represent any meaningful economic basis for social reproduction; they represent instead the state's attempt to atomize workers into ethnically defined locations and to put distance and a bureaucracy between the slums and the very jobs that pay for reproduction and, most important, the visible and vulnerable terrain of struggle in the cities.

This is one direction of spatial change. The economic expansion that made Africans in cities an issue in South African politics in the 1940s pushed British policy in colonial Africa in an opposite direction at the same time. When the state began to address the issue of remaking time, it simultaneously had to remake space. Landhies and compounds could not house a work force that was to be socialized into a life of labor. Much attention was given to questions of family housing, construction of municipal housing estates, upgrading employer-provided housing, and whether the fuller meaning of reproduction was to be paid for by individual capitalists or by the state. In either case, housing policy emphasized a direct relationship between employment and residence and the direct authority of managers and bureaucrats over residential space (Stren, 1978; Cooper, forthcoming).

In saying this much, the bounds of an approach to space that stressed the linkage of production combined with minimal daily reproduction in the city with reproduction in rural areas have been transcended. The central flaw is close to that of theories such as Castells's theory: their functionalist conception of capitalist domination. If the state fosters a minimalist approach to reproduction or promotes fuller reproduction within the city, it is serving capital. By treating the conditions necessary for the reproduction of capitalism as a cause, the argument cannot be contradicted (Saunders, 1981: 207-208). As soon as one admits that the actions of noncapitalist classes matter, the determinant logic of capital comes into question: Might not the changing structure of the city — as with work — represent real concessions by capital and real gains by workers: better houses, water, a fuller family life? If capital can reassert itself through new forms of control over work and space, does that negate the importance of struggle in forcing the original concessions and might not the new structure lead to still newer forms of struggle?

What happens when reproduction within the city — as much as in the countryside — is not entirely organized by capital and the state? For some scholars, a functionalist answer suffices: Self-built housing and enterprises run by family and client labor also lower the costs of urban labor and hence wages (Portes and Walton, 1981: 87-106). The very processes that cheapen the *physical* reproduction of the workforce might make *social* reproduction — the extension of capitalist relations of production — all the more difficult, a question explored in these pages by White, Berry, and Salem. These issues are particularly acute in the housing question.

African entrepreneurs who take over vacant land or acquire it under customary law and allow workers to build houses on it or arrange for low-wage, unregulated builders to construct housing seem to be another vehicle for a minimalist approach to reproduction; their efforts cost the state and capital very little, the pain being born by workers who inhabit bad housing and by African entrepreneurs willing — like Chayanov's peasants — to exploit themselves for low returns. Arguably, this type of housing has done more to shape the form of African cities than the most vigorous efforts at urban planning (Haeringer, 1972). "Slums" as well as "squatter settlements" of the entrepreneurial or self-help variety housed 53 percent of Accra's population in 1968, 60 percent of Dakar's and Abidjan's, 48 percent of Nairobi's, 80 percent of Douala's, and 90 percent of Addis Ababa's (U.N. statistics cited in Salau, 1979: 331).

Alongside the aggressive, entrepreneurial approach to indigenous housing were the squatter invasions of Johannesburg, a communal variant along the lines of the long history of squatter invasions in Latin America (Perlman, 1976). In the 1940s, 60,000 to 90,000 people organized themselves, took over vacant land, and built their houses. They did for themselves what capital and the state would not do, and thereby reordered the map of Johannesburg in yet another way. Like "birds in the cornfield," they reappeared in a new spot whenever the police chased them away, and ultimately the state decided to tame what it could not suppress and the settlements became Soweto (Stadler, 1979). Eventually, gaining control of one social movement led to another, the rebellion of Soweto's youth.

Squatter settlements have been organized by entrepreneurs, religious groups, political leaders, and by slowly forming networks among migrants to the city or people expelled from city centers to suburbs (Vernière, 1978; Norwood, 1975; Peil, 1976; Jules-Rosette, 1981). They are rarely as anarchic as the terms used to describe them suggest — "irregular," "spontaneous," "illegal" — but their social order is not the social order of state hegemony. States have rarely seen self-help as the solution to urban problems. Instead, their efforts since World War II in the housing field largely parallel their uneven thrusts in the workplace: constructing housing estates and subsidizing and regularizing housing for the more stable and compact working class officials hoped to shape. Housing the urban poor was not, and most often still is not, the focus of attention; housing policy has been aimed at better paid workers and civil servants (Barnes, 1982: 7; Stren, 1982: 87-88; Hansen, 1982: 123). Ideologically, high housing standards, urban planning, and labor stabilization were of a piece: These policies attempted to fix a working class into a direct, long-term relation with capital and the state, to tie an urban population's access to space to regular participation in wage labor.

Faced with day-to-day realities, states have had to back site-and-service schemes and squatter upgrading programs that in effect recognized what African city dwellers had previously done for themselves. Even these programs have had income limitations that favor the top segments of the working class previously aided by employer and state supplied housing (Hansen, 1982: 127; Vernière, 1978: 31; Stren, 1982). Because the dangers that led to changed housing policies after the war, as with changes in the workplace, were specifically urban and because rural Africa remained such an intractable arena for state-directed change, this type of urban reform has been its own negation. More people have flocked to the city, and slum clearance in central cities has sent more people into irregular suburban settlements. Especially since independence, state policies that stressed ultra-modern standards most vigorously were the farthest removed from the realities facing most city dwellers and the most likely to give rise to sprawling and illegal settlements (Cohen, 1974: 33-34; Haeringer, 1972: 633).

While many foreign scholars and agencies have become admirers of self-help and private initiative in housing, African governments have usually been more ambivalent. This ambivalence is as critical a part of the question of space as any cost-benefit analysis of a site-and-service scheme. Much as the favelas of Latin America, the rude ways in which poor Africans house themselves have been lightening rods for elite hostility (Perlman, 1976).

Space is ideologically charged. For that reason, the distinction between legal and illegal space both reflects and affects the form of the city. The importance of this point has been emphasized in French scholarship (Cahiers d'Etudes Africaines, 1982: 10; Haeringer, 1972: 646; Vernière, 1978), but it is taken most seriously by African governments. Much space in African cities is illegal space: It is occupied space rather than owned space. A larger proportion in some cities is in a legal limbo: land tenure may be private or customary, deeds registered or not. In the most heavily populated neighborhoods, houses do not conform to codes; amenities do not meet established standards; and construction, local services, and other businesses in the quarter take place outside of labor, commercial, and tax regulations. The distinction is visible: The downtown is zoned and gridlike, the irregular settlement unzoned and a hodgepodge. Illegality, for the state, is a rationale for not providing water and other amenities, while for house builders, it is a reason to use cheap materials and to spread out rather than build vertically: The distinction thus affects the form and quality of housing, in some ways for the better, in others for the worse (Haeringer, 1972: 629, 647-649; Vernière, 1978). The illegal settlement is often less closely integrated into state-run urban structures — hospitals, police, and schools — but more fully integrated socially and economically than legal settlements into the surrounding rural areas (Vernière, 1978). In the legal zone, space is exchanged through real estate agents and lawyers; access to illegal space is allocated through diverse relations of affiliation and clientage. Life in legal and illegal space is hardly dichotomized, but the notion of legality is important to shaping the direction of a complex process.

Marxist historians (Hay et al., 1975; Thompson, 1975) have lately subjected the meaning of law to close analysis, suggesting that a capitalist class's need to place its own property rights under the rubric of universal principles as well as the state's need to temper the implementation of law in accordance with tensions and traditions meant that the rule of law was something more than a mere instrument of an accumulating class. Capital accumulation is not just grabbing resources, but a process of generalizing and legitimizing an economic and social system. Where the dominance of the capital-labor relation was most in doubt, the ideological importance of emphasizing the principles of law, property, and regular ways of doing things was all the greater.

The problem with illegal space in an African city was not that it failed to reproduce a work force quite cheaply, but that it reproduced the wrong work force for the postwar economy. Squatter settlements and self-built houses eased the housing crises of rapidly growing cities, but they gave rise to the wrong kind of city. The entrepreneurship that made such settlements work was closely linked to entrepreneurship in prostitution, brewing, and theft; irregular settlements were centers of such activity (Bujra, 1978-1979; N. Nelson, 1979; van Onselen, 1982). Illegal space was certainly not the only locus of illegal activity — government offices were the scenes of many crimes — but the association of criminality with a particular space defined alternative norms and ways of life as having their places within the city. However much illegal beer and sex contributed cheap services to male, low-paid workers, they both literally and figuratively infected the working class. The slums bred values antithetical to a work culture; they were ugly, and, with their goats, miniature garden patches, and wandering hawkers, symbolized a kind of social life that an elite conscious of its own modernity did not want to see. The spontaneous settlement undermined the symbolic value of urbanism as much as that of the law.

The diverse ties and economic activities brought together in the squatter settlement did little to socialize people into a world where labor and commodity markets determined access to resources. They taught that a better life lay not within the kind of respectable working-class culture that had slowly developed in European cities, but in using jobs as springboards into the rough urban world European reformers had tried to extinguish (Stedman Jones, 1971; van Onselen, 1982). And the settlements brought together workers, nonworkers, and sometime workers in potentially dangerous combinations.

Colonial and postcolonial rulers have manifested their dislike of illegal space in periodic binges of slum clearance, in the harassment of prostitutes and beer brewers, and in intricate regulation of businesses, houses, trade, and manufacturing and in purges of the unlicensed. In South Africa, the redefinition of space reached its logical conclusion with the labeling of most blacks as foreigners, without legal right to the entire country. In the colonial period, the Nairobi Municipal Council fine-tuned legal space, with regulations that specified when Africans could be in certain neighborhoods, and what kind of people could be in, own, or inherit a room or house (White, this volume). In much of former British West Africa, space was not so tightly regulated, and relatively loose building regulations enabled private housing and construction to expand, but the concept of legality was honored in extensive land litigation (Barnes, 1982; Peil, 1976). In Dakar, the government tolerates vast irregular settlements in suburban Pikine because its existence made possible the removal of slum dwellers from the prestige center of the city: three quarters of Pikine's population formerly inhabited Dakar (Vernière, 1973: 593, 1978). Legality can become a thorny political issue. In independent Nairobi, a city council closely linked to the representatives of international capital who made downtown so imposing seemed bent on extending the downtown's property structure to peripheral slums, but its bulldozers have been restrained by the clientelistic politics of those settlements (Chege, 1981; Norwood, 1975).

Much is at stake in the politics of the urban clean-up. The displacement of poor or moderately well off householders in central Lagos to suburban housing estates in the 1950s — done in the name of sanitation and prestige — broke up not only a residential neighborhood, but a pattern of social and economic life. It hurt women who traded in the city center and artisans who required a network of contacts; it helped some people escape the burden of relatives, but made the old more isolated (Marris, 1962). The spatial restructuring best fit a direct relationship of worker to employer rather than the complex interweaving of ties within a neighborhood. However, just those linkages are created in an irregular settlement like Pikine. If the alternation of removals, resettlement, and toleration of spontaneous settlement fractured communities and fostered a sense of powerlessness, fending off the bulldozers or invading new territory might have the reverse effect, especially when the seizure of space and the defense of community, as in pre-1973 Chile, was closely linked to political organizing (Castells, 1977: 360-375).

The editors of a recent issue of *Cahiers d' Etudes Africaines* (1982: 10) contrast the "legal city" with "real cities," and Vernière (1973: 604) suggests that it is the legal city that is truly marginal to the social life of the urban majority. The very reality of these cities has made the project of ruling classes to transform urban order more difficult, for they are confronted not only with the cost of regularized building and land policies, but the political networks of neighborhood patrons and landlords (Chege, 1981; Barnes, 1982; J. Nelson, 1979). Legal space does not yet define urban social structure, only an attempt to forge a hegemonic urban order. The continued tensions over squatting and prostitution, slum clearance and police raids remind us that an elite's idea of hegemonic urban culture exists in a close, uneasy relationship to other, quite viable, patterns of social relations and values. The culture that developed in working-class locations in South African cities was vigorous, innovative, and autonomous (Coplan, 1982; Mayer, 1981; van Onselen, 1982). The squatter community Jules-Rosette (1981: 38) studied in Lusaka became a "sacred space," defined by its religious bonds rather than by its place in a hierarchy of urban land values. The regulated capitalism that shapes, however imperfectly, the cities of advanced capitalist countries has in most cities of Africa shaped heavily patrolled enclaves, but has not woven workplace and residence in the city, let alone the countryside, into a web of commodities and wage labor.

Urban conflict does not lie at the end of a tunnel of proletarianization and urbanization. The struggle for the city is cultural as much as political, and it goes on every day, as well as bursting forth in periods when basic structures are at issue. When, for example, squatter invasions, bus boycotts, rent strikes, and industrial action erupted in South Africa in the 1940s and 1950s, they were not reflexive responses to urban problems, but concerted actions that grew out of community and class ties, political consciousness, and organization. These actions took place in particular kinds of space and they were attempts to alter space, to come to grips with an elaborate system for regulating workplace, residence, and movement (Stadler, 1979).

The relationship of spatial organization and collective action in Africa needs specific attention. Here, an example will serve to suggest the issues involved. In the late 1930s and 1940s, the wave of disorder that swept African cities was more widespread and more threatening to the colonial state than anything before or since. Conflict ranged from squatter invasions in Johannesburg to a railway strike in Senegal to general strikes in Kenya, Tanganyika, and Nigeria, to shop boycotts and demonstrations in the Gold Coast, to demonstrations of the unemployed in the Camerouns to mine strikes in the Gold Coast, South Africa, and Northern Rhodesia (Iliffe, 1975; Hemson, 1977; O'Meara, 1975; Jeffries, 1978; Cooper, forthcoming). The disorders involved very different forms of work and demographic patterns. Yet they were concentrated in a span of ten to fifteen years, and influenced and reinforced each other, above all because cities and mine towns in those years brought together, through migrant labor systems, different crises of reproduction in a single, demographically dense, socially connected locus.

A period of intensified production, acute pressure on urban resources, and severe inflation, with as yet unreformed migrant labor systems, set the stage. For some workers, the crisis took place within the confines of minimalist daily reproduction — a room or a meal became more expensive. For others, a more deep-seated strain on the total process of reproduction was critical, for many workers were spending an increasingly long time in urban labor, were striving to support a wider range of family obligations, and were seeking jobs that would provide increasing income as obligations grew. In Mombasa in the 1940s, for example, both testimony and statistical studies suggest convergent crises for the casual warehouse employee worried about the cost of bed space and a railwayman who had worked steadily for five years and had just brought his wife to live with him (Cooper, forthcoming). The problem with a city, especially Mombasa, where the state did not control space tightly, was that the two were very likely to talk to one another, or to listen to a politician. As in the labor process itself, the organization of space both integrates and fragments communities; the presence of people close together physically, and treated socially as a homogeneous mass of labor power, was potentially dangerous.

It is no coincidence that the wave of urban disorder occurred not in the Depression, much as people suffered, but in a period of expansion. The social crisis of the Depression was largely sloughed off onto rural areas. Rural Africa has itself been far from quiescent, but in the absence of a singular process of transformation sweeping through the countryside, each area has had its own conflicts separated by large distances. The crisis of the cities in the 1940s was also not a singular one, but the rapid build-up of concentrations of workers, the relatively small number and small size of the cities where production and communications were bunched, and the consequent inflation with drastic effects on all aspects of social reproduction brought the crises together.

We are led to a proposition simpler than that of the urban ecology school: The importance of density was not that it determined any particular social process, but that whatever social processes developed, happened near to each other. The specifically urban character of the turmoil in these years does not follow from the extent of urbanization, measured in numbers, but from the conjuncture of social processes in narrow spaces. Whether the urban cauldron that seemed to be coming to a boil in the 1940s would boil hotter or cooler in future years would not be decided by the rate of population growth, but by the complexities and contradictions of how the dangerous masses were integrated and fragmented into social structure.

It is not surprising, then, that in the aftermath of the wave of strikes and disturbances, colonial authorities did not look to a burst of initiative from African entrepreneurs to end the crunch on housing and other resources, even though shortages had contributed to the troubles. Housing estates, the linking of houses to jobs, and centralized planning and enforcement of regulations on the use of space were critical to gaining some leverage over the process of integration and fragmentation. Making the irregular settlement larger might solve the physical housing crisis, but not the crisis of the urban mass.

The temperature of the urban cauldron is especially critical because of the multiple processes that go on within it. The city is essential for the circulation of capital *and* for the reproduction of labor. The facilities for the one — railway yards, docks, warehouses, and workshops — are close to the facilities for the other — houses, retail stores, and schools. A crisis in the one can disrupt the other. The very narrowness of commercial pathways in colonial Africa and the timidity with which capital stuck to the locus of state power made the problem of disruption and the threat of bottlenecks all the more acute. So the problems of reproduction that arose in the late 1930s soon became crises of circulation and production in ports, commercial centers, and mines.

Colonial states responded to the crises of the urban mass by attempting to build more differentiated labor forces and to break up and reintegrate residential space. Pressures and responses varied, but never could the state completely control access to space or the kinds of community ties that workers brought with them or created. The political implications of differing patterns were important and persistent. In Kenya, relatively high wage differentials dating from the 1950s have been protected by trade unions in the midst of growing urban poverty, while in Ghana stagnation and inflation eroded much of the early gains of the most militant workers, producing a broader, populist coalition that linked skilled workers, job seekers, and small businessmen. Such coalitions have produced outbursts, like the general strikes of 1961 and 1971, and a widespread, if inchoate populist sensibility that strongly colors urban politics. However, in Kenya, the general strike of 1947 in Mombasa was the last strike that not only engaged specific segments of the labor force, but swept through the city's entire working class (Jeffries, 1978; Sandbrook, 1977, 1982; Cooper, forthcoming).

The South African state, on the other hand, has moved from a system that defined all African workers as criminals to one that defined the vast majority as aliens. To be sure, the state has used the notorious Section 10 rule as well as the provision of very unequal forms of state-controlled housing to draw lines within the urban work force (Wilkinson, 1981), but even the most privileged workers have families and friends who are cut off from them by the draconian control of residence and migration. Within cities, such as Durban in 1972-1973, dockworkers and manufacturing workers flung together by a social structure that transcends differences between workplaces have acted together as an urban working class. Cities are constantly being cleansed of nonworkers, only to extend the urban slum to the rural slum. So in developing a strategy that fragments workers regionally and ethnically — more than in terms of access to property within a city — South Africa's government may well be sewing a much wider web of connection among black South Africans than has yet existed. Mayer's recent (1981) reexamination of rural resistance ideologies he had studied two decades earlier suggests that these ideologies are no longer uniquely rural, but reflect a more self-confident identification of migrants with the working-class culture that has emerged in the segregated living spaces of South African cities. Should the turmoil that has engulfed South African cities in the past decade spread to the rural slums described by Murray, the regime will at last achieve in its own way the urbanization of the countryside.

MOBILITY, AUTONOMY, AND CONFRONTATION

Two recent analyses of the urban poor make diametrically opposed points in their titles: Peter Lloyd writes (1979), albeit with a question mark, of *Slums of Hope?,* while Peter C. W. Gutkind writes (1973) of a transition "From the Energy of Despair to the Anger of Despair." Lloyd has seized on the individualism of the urban migrant, whose very migration suggests initiative and who seeks to mobilize diverse personal ties in a quest for advancement. Gutkind belives that the energy that has gone into such strategies has been in vain, and that the urban poor have become increasingly conscious, collectively, of the wide gap and rigid barriers separating them from capitalists and rulers.

Lloyd's multiple ties only diffuse class formation if they actually produce results for the individuals who manipulate them, and his vision of a fluid city is developed in isolation from the forces that might decide whether hope is fulfilled. If not, the same networks that seem to cut across class lines might converge into a dense and dangerous network of bonds among workers, the self-employed, and job seekers, united by poverty and oppression. Gutkind's rigid city follows from a view of ruling classes as isolated from the masses and African economies as underdeveloped. However, those African economies experiencing the most — rather than the least — national development might be the ones to experience the crystallization of a capitalist class, that class's willingness to discard ties of patronage and affiliation, and the kind of class polarization and antagonism that Gutkind expects.

The alternatives of social fluidity and polarization come from models that put too much stress on static categories to explain dynamic processes. The ties of kinship, ethnicity, and clientage can either be a source of mobility or the basis of a dangerous autonomy — cultural as well as social — among the poor that ruling classes might contain but cannot penetrate.

Using categories of workers to predict political action has been a problem at two extremes, with migrants or casuals, and with the "labor aristocracy." Migrants, it might seem, have too diffuse affiliations to build up workplace solidarity; they are too easily replaced or coopted to stand firm in conflicts; and they are more likely to move on in the face of difficulty than to organize the workplace. The best paid, unionized workers, on the other hand, are often thought to be aloof, self-interested, and conservative (see discussion in Sandbrook and Cohen, 1975). All this is often true, but often false, and the question is how workers use their positions and connections in struggles. Migrants' access to rural resources can enable them to hold out longer in a strike, as in Namibia in 1972 (Moorsom, 1977), while unionized workers can be vanguards of wider working-class action (Jeffries, 1978). Casual and permanent workers struck together in Mombasa in 1947 and Durban in 1972-1973.

The contradictory meanings of mobility and autonomy emerge most clearly with that ill-defined and much-discussed social category, the petty bourgeoisie (Bechhofer and Elliott, 1981). Are these people truly bourgeois, only small, or actually an underclass, only too individualistic to know it? The term embraces people with differing positions in economic systems: the slum landlord, a small employer, the independent artisan, a trader, and a prostitute. It covers a range of prosperity and affluence. A worker may aspire to join the petty bourgeoisie by buying a small shop, while a job-seeker might find a refuge there as a small-scale trader. The imprecision of the concept, however, is its virtue, for these roles all share an ambivalent and unstable relationship to the division of capital and worker in capitalist society; they occupy what Wright (1980) calls a "contradictory class location." In Africa, the petty bourgeoisie's wide sphere of operations is the other side of the limited extent to which capitalism provides goods and services, as well as the limited ability of the state to do what is necessary for the reproduction of capitalist relations of production. The ownership of the means of production and the accumulation of surplus value do not explain, for example, how most citizens of Abidjan are housed. Instead, the seizure of a bit of land or intricate negotiations with traditional occupiers, the mobilization of community and patronage to protect access to land, and variously organized ways of building provide housing for many and profit for some.

The petty bourgeoisie boosts economic activity and eases social polarization in African cities because it is relatively easy to enter, but for just that reason competition is keen, profit margins low, and capital accumulation limited. The skills of the petty bourgeois in running small enterprises and manipulating personal relationships encourage the successful to diversify rather than expand. Large firms give the petty bourgeoisie so much space because their customers are poor and markets modest, but as soon as a small firm opens a strong market, big ones are likely to displace it (Gerry, 1979), and in any case large firms control access to tools and raw materials.

For a petty capitalist to cease to be petty is to make a qualitative as well as a quantitative change. Becoming a true bourgeois means transcending the personal or communal relations with workers that Salem and Berry describe, and which constrain discipline of the work force and management of the enterprise. It is also to jeopardize the relations of clientage, kinship, and community essential to urban fluidity. For a petty bourgeois to fail to advance beyond the urban poor is to create the conditions for the emergence of some form of populist ideology and the coming together of people in diverse economic niches through their shared subordination to monopoly capital, foreign capital, and the state. The petty bourgeoisie is in fact the line between Lloyd's fluidity and Gutkind's polarization.

So African cities seem poised between opposites, and the play for individual advantage and the building up of clienteles is sometimes interrupted by outbursts of popular rage. Amilcar Cabral (1969: 72) thought a petty bourgeoisie could move in opposite directions, toward pursuit of personal advantage or (less likely) toward leadership of a revolutionary struggle that would, if successful, eliminate the petty bourgeoisie as a privileged category. To distinguish opposites is to look at specific processes instead of static categories, but the contradictory position of the petty bourgeoisie should be no surprise. If the triumph in industrial Europe of the bourgeoisie — the ability of a class to monopolize the means of production, control labor, and act coherently in its own interest explains anything about social processes — so too should the inconclusive actuality of capital's assault on Africa.

By looking at the petty bourgeoisie we come back, in class terms, to an argument made about illegal space. For space to become a commodity is to create a class that owns it. What kind of class would this be, deriving its position from what social bases, and forming what kind of relations with other classes? On the surface, it is puzzling that all those interested in economic development have not applauded the efforts of the hard-driving entrepreneurs who organize urban space and animate small-scale production and commerce. Why should some development economists or the International Labor Office have to convince their fellows, as well as such capitalist-spirited officials as those who run Kenya, of the virtues of what they call the "informal sector"? Why indeed should informality be an economic variable? Some economists keep using this vague and euphemistic phrase instead of specifying what kind of economic structures exist in small-scale business, examining the limitations those structures pose for accumulation, and — most important — asking why the distinction between formal and informal means so much to policy makers.[4]

The more one learns about the informal sector the more its personnel and operations seem to overlap the formal one and the further its internal organization, however unique, seems from the anarchy implied by its title (Salem). The one definition that can actually be used simply accepts the criteria of local regulatory agencies: The informal sector is wherever the labor inspector, the buildings inspector, and the tax collector do not reach. As Salem points out, defining the informal sector by what it is not simply reinforces the state's notions of its own hegemony.

The legal and ideological significance of the idea of an informal sector makes more sense when we keep in mind the twin and partially contradictory tendencies in capitalist development: toward generalizing capitalist relations of production and ensuring their orderly reproduction. The kinds of enterprises that exist beneath the regulator's gaze are of course nothing new in the history of capitalism, although they used to be called sweat shops and tenements, but social reformers eventually came to see them as obstacles to developing a respectable working class (Stedman Jones, 1971). In late twentieth-century Nairobi the problem of order is as acute as in late nineteenth-century London, while the problem of socializing labor is even greater. The more the informal sector offered opportunities and the more the petty bourgeoisie bridged cleavages in the social structure, then the more "Today's wage-labourer is tomorrow's independent peasant or artisan, working for himself" (Marx, 1977: 936), a pattern some observers insist is at least an aspiration for African formal sector workers (Peace, 1979). The interplay of small workshop, rural village, and large factory creates alternative means of livelihood, alternative ambitions, and alternative relations of production to the subordination of labor to capital (see Berry, this volume). The most effective formal-sector workers, given such alternatives, might be the most likely to be dissatisfied with a promotion to foreman. At the same time, the Horatio Alger characters that a development-oriented ideology should support wholeheartedly are too close to Robin Hoods. The landlord in Mathare Valley derives his property rights from an act fundamentally antithetical to the value of property — seizure of land — and the hawker or workshop owner who ignores regulations flaunts a framework of legal and bureaucratic supervision of accumulation that fledgling states are trying anxiously to impose. Workers who are clients of their employers are in a sense not fully free; workers who are immersed in an environment filled with illegal beer brewers and prostitutes are not fully respectable (N. Nelson, 1979; Bujra, 1978-79).

The state, colonial and postcolonial, is caught up in these ambiguities, between today's profits and the structures that determine tomorrow's, between pressing needs and concern with the kind of society it is helping to forge. When a government tolerates squatter settlements, but insists that their status remain illegal and raids them periodically, it acknowledges that neither it nor capital can reproduce an urban labor force, but must pretend that they can.

In cities in advanced capitalist societies, the state buffers the conflict of community and accumulation, enhancing its own legitimacy in the process (Katznelson, 1979). In African cities, people are more likely to be buffered from the harshness of poverty and unemployment by social ties rooted in illegal space and the nonregulated economy, which only emphasize the impotence of the state. This in turn may draw the state into gestures of control that, whether effective or not, show the state's hostility to the poor's efforts at survival. Still, the very organization of community and patronage, as well as the widely held populism that the state's impotence and hostility fosters, creates political pressures that the state can only ignore at great risk.

White's study of Nairobi raises the possibility of looking at such contradictions historically. The Kenyan state cracked down on the women who were at the center of illegal space and illegal economy not so much because it objected to what they did — providing housing, sex, and other services — but because the people who sold such services were coalescing as a class and passing on property and establishing a pattern of relationships with each other and with the working class. The state hit hardest not at the most visible or outrageous practitioners of vice, but at the most respectable, at a time, the late 1930s, when they were beginning to reproduce themselves as a class and when the question of who would establish relationships with the working class was acute.

White's study also suggests that unrespectability in a petty bourgeoisie was closely linked to gender (see also Bujra, 1978-1979, and N. Nelson, 1979). And if a working class, as in Lourenço Marques in the 1950s, could not exactly attain respectability, at least men moved slightly upward in the constraining work structure; women did well merely to move in, to obtain dead-end jobs (Penvenne). How much women's roles in the illegal economy reflect the gender biases of the legal economy and how much the complex position of women in the patterns of social reproduction, rural and urban, that White begins to explore, are questions that need further attention (see also Vidal, 1977).

If the connection of an African petty bourgeoisie to a working class began to be a serious social problem in a colonial city in the late 1930s, ten years later, the threat was more likely to be seen in explicitly political terms, the danger that a petty bourgeois politician — a Nkrumah or even a not so petty bourgeois such as Azikiwe — might mobilize the dangerous masses in African cities. It was at this time that colonial states began to take seriously the question of making a respectable and ideologically acceptable petty bourgeoisie, as well as a respectable working class, a problem that proved impossible to contain within the structure of the colonial state.

Holding an African petty bourgeoisie rigorously in check could also lead to danger. In South Africa, blocked aspirations and economic circumstances barely ahead of a working class itself pressed by inflation led the petty bourgeoisie to join workers in the "militant agitation" of 1918-1920 (Bonner, 1982). Concessions to the petty bourgeoisie, for fear of its leading an urban mob into action, were made before that class's own fears of disorder actually quieted the situation. Again in the 1950s, property-owning Africans and Coloureds were among the main victims of the Group Areas Act (Western, 1981; Lodge, 1981), and O'Meara argues (1975) that this assault on the petty bourgeoisie helped to galvanize the previously petty bourgeois African National Congress into increasing identification with working-class issues and an increasingly radical stance.

Collective action is not caused by urbanization or by the grievances of the poor (Tilly et al., 1975). Social movements are not singular groups engaging in actions inherently characteristic of that group; they grow out of developing, deepening, extending relationships. Class relationships are formed where people live as well as where they work (Katznelson, 1979), and class formation is a political process even before clearly delineated classes engage in politics. Social movements — such as the combinations of bus boycotts, pass burnings, squatter invasions, student riots, and strikes in South Africa — extend the struggles of a working class into the realm of consumption as well as production, and they build a dynamic as they succeed and fail.

Struggles are won and lost, and old struggles create memories and cleavages that affect new ones. The struggle for the city has included huge events, the Mombasa general strike of 1947 or the Soweto riots of 1976, and the many small events described in these pages. Conflict over work discipline and housing, over what kinds of conduct would be legal or criminal, over what forms of social relations could develop in workplace, urban residence, and rural village, and over the values and cultures that could develop inside urban space all shaped the city and further patterns of struggle. These patterns do not lead to a single fate for all of Africa, either subordination determined by the world economy or to revolutionary triumphs following upon the creation of a proletariat. However, in the course of years and decades, the struggles over time, space, and class spell the difference between the escalating polarization and confrontation in South Africa, the cycles of populist outbursts and patronage politics in West Africa, the modest gains of dockworkers in Mombasa, and the misery of coerced laborers in colonial Mozambique. Day by day, they are the difference between hope and despair. The struggles continue.

NOTES

1. For summaries of the adaptation tradition, see Little (1965, 1974), and for a retrospective by a leading practitioner, see Epstein (1981: 34).

2. Wallerstein (1979) softens the dichotomy by putting the "semi-periphery" between the two. He explains its existence by saying it is functional to the world-system, not by explaining how any particular peripheral economy gets promoted. South Africa gets lumped with Zaire.

3. Segmentation theory, like marginality theory, stresses the barriers between different labor markets. However, it locates these barriers in terms of struggles for control of the workplace, not as implacable entities linked to position in the world economy. This theory also offers a new perspective on the tiresome debate over the relative importance of race and class in South Africa: race, in the process of capitalist

development, is transformed into a part of the labor process, a form of segmentation intrinsic to the domination of the capitalist class.

4. Some radical scholars have persuasively questioned this concept, but seem so concerned to establish that capitalism dominates informal as well as formal sectors that they have largely avoided the plunge into examining particular forms of economic organization within the informal sector and their implication for capitalist accumulation. See Gerry (1979), Moser (1978), and Scott (1979). For further discussion of related issues, see King (1977), Hart (1973), and Bujra (1978-1979).

REFERENCES

ABU-LUGHOD, J. (1976) "Developments in North African urbanism: the process of decolonization," in B. J. L. Berry (ed.) Urbanization and Counterurbanization. Beverly Hills, CA: Sage.

AMIN, S. (1974). "Introduction," in S. Amin (ed.) Modern Migrations in Western Africa. London: Oxford University Press.

BARNES, S. (1982) "Public and private housing in urban West Africa: the social implications," in M. K. C. Morrison and P. C. W. Gutkind (eds.) Housing the Urban Poor in Africa. Syracuse, NY: Maxwell School of Citizenship and Public Affairs, Syracuse University.

BECHHOFER, F., and B. ELLIOTT (1981) The Petite Bourgeoisie: Comparative Studies of the Uneasy Stratum. London: Macmillan.

BEINART, W. (1982) The Political Economy of Pondoland. Cambridge: Cambridge University Press.

BONNER, P. (1982) "The Transvaal Native Congress, 1917-1920: the radicalisation of the black petty bourgeoisie on the Rand," in S. Marks and R. Rathbone (eds.) Industrialisation and Social Change in South Africa. London: Longman.

BRAVERMAN, H. (1974) Labor and Monopoly Capital: The Degradation of Work in the Twentieth Century. New York: Monthly Review Press.

BRENNER, R. (1977) "The origins of capitalist development: a critique of neo-Smithian Marxism." New Left Review 104: 25-92.

BUJRA, J. (1978-79) "Proletarianization and the 'informal economy': a case study from Nairobi." African Urban Studies 3: 47-66.

BURAWOY, M. (1978) "Toward a Marxist theory of the labor process: Braverman and beyond." Politics and Society 8: 247-312.

CABRAL, A. (1969) Revolution in Guinea (R. Handyside, trans.) New York: Monthly Review Press.

Cahiers d'Etudes Africaines (1982) 81-83: Special issue on cities.

CASTELLS, M. (1977) The Urban Question: A Marxist Approach (A. Sheridan, trans.) Cambridge: MIT Press.

CHAUNCEY, G., Jr. (1981) "The locus of reproduction: women's labour in the Zambian Copperbelt, 1927-1953." Journal of Southern African Studies 7: 135-164.

CHEGE, M. (1981) "A tale of two slums: electoral politics in Mathare and Dagoretti." Review of African Political Economy 20: 74-88.

CHEVALIER, L. (1973) Laboring Classes and Dangerous Classes in Paris During the First Half of the Nineteenth Century, (F. Jellinek, trans.). Princeton, NJ: Princeton University Press.

COHEN, M. A. (1974) Urban Policy and Political Conflict in Africa: A Study of the Ivory Coast. Chicago: University of Chicago Press.

COOPER, F. (forthcoming) Urban Disorder and the Transformation of Work: The Dockers of Mombasa.

——— (1981) "Africa and the world economy." African Studies Review 24 (2/3): 1-86.

——— (1980) From Slaves to Squatters: Plantation Labor and Agriculture in Zanzibar and Coastal Kenya, 1890-1925. New Haven, CT: Yale University Press.

COPLAN, D. (1982) "The emergence of an African working-class culture," in S. Marks and R. Rathbone (eds.) Industrialisation and Social Change in South Africa. London: Longman.

COX, K. R. (1981) "Capitalism and conflict around the communal living space," in M. Dear and A. J. Scott (eds.) Urbanization and Urban Planning in Capitalist Societies. London: Methuen.

EDWARDS, R. (1979) Contested Terrain: The Transformation of the Workplace in the Twentieth Century. New York; Harper & Row.

EPSTEIN, A. L. (1981) Urbanization and Kinship: The Domestic Domain of the Copperbelt 1950-1956. London: Academic Press.

FETTER, B. (1973) "L'union miniere du Haut Katanga 1920-1940: la naissance d'une sous culture totalitaire." Cahiers du CEDAF 6: 1-40.

FOSTER-CARTER, A. (1978) "The modes of production controversy." New Left Review 107: 47-73.

GERRY, C. (1979) "Small-scale manufacturing and repairs in Dakar: a survey of market relations within the urban economy," in R. Bromley and C. Gerry (eds.) Casual Work and Poverty in Third World Cities. New York: John Wiley.

GIDDENS, A. (1981) A Contemporary Critique of Historical Materialism. Berkeley: University of California Press.

GORDON, D. M., R. EDWARDS, and M. REICH (1982) Segmented Work, Divided Workers: The Historical Transformation of Labor in the United States. Cambridge: Cambridge University Press.

GREGORY, J. W., and V. PICHÉ (1978) "African migration and peripheral capitalism." African Perspectives 1: 37-49.

GUTKIND, P. C. W. (1973) "From the energy of despair to the anger of despair: the transition from social circulation to political consciousness among the urban poor in Africa." Canadian Journal of African Studies 7: 179-198.

GUTKIND, P. C. W., R. COHEN, and J. COPANS [eds.] (1978) African Labor History. Beverly Hills, CA: Sage.

HAERINGER, P. (1972) "L'urbanisation de masse en question: quatre villes d'Afrique noire." Colloques Internationaux du C.N.R.S.: La Croissance Urbaine en Afrique Noire et à Madagascar. Paris: C.N.R.S.

HANSEN, K. T. (1982) "Lusaka's squatters: past and present." African Studies Review 25 (2/3): 117-136.

HART, K. (1973) "Informal income opportunities and urban employment in Ghana." Journal of Modern African Studies 11: 61-89.

HARVEY, D. (1981) "The urban process under capitalism: a framework for analysis," in M. Dear and A.J. Scott (eds.) Urbanization and Urban Planning in Capitalist Societies. London: Methuen.

——— (1977) "Government policies, financial institutions and neighborhood change in United States cities," in M. Harloe (ed.) Captive Cities. London: John Wiley.

——— (1975) "The political economy of urbanization in advanced capitalist societies: the case of the United States," in G. Gappert and H. Rose (eds.) The Social Economy of Cities. Beverly Hills, CA: Sage.

——— (1973) Social Justice and the City. Baltimore: Johns Hopkins University Press.

HAY, D. et al. (1975) Albion's Fatal Tree. New York: Pantheon.

HEISLER, H. (1974) Urbanisation and the Government of Migration: The Inter-Relation of Urban and Rural Life in Zambia. London: Hurst.

HEMSON, D. (1977) "Dock workers, labour circulation, and class struggles in Durban, 1940-59." Journal of Southern African Studies 4: 88-124.

IGNATIEFF, M. (1978) A Just Measure of Pain: The Penitentiary in the Industrial Revolution 1750-1850. New York: Pantheon.

ILIFFE, J. (1975) "The creation of group consciousness: a history of the dockworkers of Dar es Salaam," in R. Sandbrook and R. Cohen (eds.) The Development of an African Working Class. London: Longman.

JEFFRIES, R. (1978) Class, Power, and Ideology in Ghana: The Railwaymen of Sekondi. Cambridge: Cambridge University Press.

JOSEPH, R. (1974) "Settlers, strikers and sans-travail: the Douala Riots of 1945." Journal of African History 15: 669-81.

JULES-ROSETTE, B. (1981) Symbols of Change: Urban Transition in a Zambian Community. Norwood, NJ: Ablex.

KATZNELSON, I. (1979) "Community, Capitalist Development, and the Emergence of Class." Politics and Society 9: 203-37.

KING, A.P. (1976) Colonial Urban Development: Culture, Social Power and Environment. London: Routledge & Kegan Paul.

KING, K. (1977) The African Artisan. London: Heinemann.

KITCHING, G. (1980) Class and Economic Change in Kenya: The Making of an African Petite-Bourgeoisie. New Haven, CT: Yale University Press.

LEE, J.M. (1967) Colonial Development and Good Government: A Study of the Ideas Expressed by the British Official Classes in Planning Decolonisation, 1939-1964. Oxford: Oxford University Press.

LITTLE, K. (1974) Urbanization as a Social Process. An Essay on Movement and Change in Contemporary Africa. London: Routledge & Kegan Paul.

——— (1965) West African Urbanization: A Study of Voluntary Associations in Social Change. Cambridge: Cambridge University Press.

LLOYD, P.C. (1979) Slums of Hope? Shanty Towns of the Third World. Harmondsworth, England: Penguin.

LODGE, T. (1981) "The destruction of Sophiatown." Journal of Modern African Studies 19: 107-32.

LOJKINE, J. (1976) "Contributions to a Marxist theory of capitalist urbanization," in C. G. Pickvance (ed.) Urban Sociology: Critical Essays. London: Tavistock.

MAGUBANE, B. (1971) " A critical look at indices used in the study of social change in colonial Africa." Current Anthropology 12: 419-45.

MARKS, S. and R. RATHBONE [eds.] (1982) Industrialisation and Social Change in South Africa: African Class Formation, Culture and Consciousness 1870-1930. London: Longman.

MARRIS, P. (1962) Family and Social Change in an African City: A Study of Rehousing in Lagos. Evanston, IL: Northwestern University Press.

MARX, K. (1981) Capital, vol. III (D. Fernbach, trans.). New York: Vintage.

⸻ (1977) Capital, vol. I (B. Fowkes, trans.) New York: Vintage.

⸻ (1973) Grundrisse (M. Nicolaus, trans.) New York: Vintage.

MAYER, P. (1981) "The origin and decline of two rural resistance ideologies," in P. Mayer (ed.) Black Villagers in an Industrial Society: Anthropological Perspectives on Labour Migration in South Africa. Cape Town: Oxford University Press.

MEILLASSOUX, C. (1975) Femmes, greniers et capitaux. Paris: Maspero.

MITCHELL, J. C. (1956) The Kalela Dance. Rhodes-Livingstone Papers, 27. Manchester: Manchester University Press.

MOORSOM, R. (1977) "Underdevelopment, contract labour and worker consciousness in Namibia, 1915-72." Journal of Southern African Studies 4: 52-87.

MOSER, C. (1978) "Informal sector or petty commodity production: dualism or dependence in urban development." World Development 6: 1041-1064.

NELSON, J. (1979) Access to Power: Politics and the Urban Poor in Developing Nations. Princeton, NJ: Princeton University Press.

NELSON, N. (1979) "How women and men get by: the sexual division of labour in the informal sector of a Nairobi squatter settlement," in R. Bromley and C. Gerry (eds.) Casual Work and Poverty in Third World Cities. New York: John Wiley.

NORWOOD, H. C. (1975) "Squatters compared." African Urban Notes B (2): 119-132.

O'MEARA, D. (1975) "The 1946 African mine workers' strike and the political economy of South Africa." Journal of Commonwealth and Comparative Politics 13: 146-173.

PEACE, A. J. (1979) Choice, Class and Conflict: A Study of Nigerian Factory Workers. Brighton: Harvester.

PEIL, M. (1976) "African squatter settlements: a comparative study." Urban Studies 13: 155-166.

PERLMAN, J. (1976) The Myth of Marginality: Urban Poverty and Politics in Rio de Janeiro. Berkeley: University of California Press.

PICKVANCE, C. G. (1976) "Housing: reproduction of capital and reproduction of labour power — some recent French work," in J. Walton and L. Masotti (eds.) The City in Comparative Perspective. New York: Russell Sage.

PORTES, A. and J. WALTON (1981) Labor, Class, and the International System. New York: Academic Press.

PROCTOR, A. (1979) "Class struggle, segregation, and the city: a history of Sophiatown, 1905-40," in B. Bozzoli (ed.) Labour, Townships, and Protest: Studies in the Social History of the Witwatersrand. Johannesburg: Ravan.

QUIJANO, A. (1974) "The marginal pole of the economy and the marginalized labour force." Economy and Society 3: 393-428.

RIDDELL, J.B. (1981) "Beyond the description of spatial pattern: the process of proletarianization as a factor in population migration in West Africa." Progress in Human Geography 5: 370-92.

ROSE, D. (1981) "Accumulation versus reproduction: *The Recurrent Crisis of London* revisited," in M. Dear and A.J. Scott (eds.) Urbanization and Urban Planning in Capitalist Societies. London: Methuen.

SALAU, A.T. (1979) "Housing in Africa: toward a reassessment of problems, policies and planning strategies." Civilisations 29: 322-339.

SANDBROOK, R. (1982) The Politics of Basic Needs: Urban Aspects of Assaulting Poverty in Africa. London: Heinemann.

—— (1977) "The political potential of African urban workers." Canadian Journal of African Studies 11: 411-433.

—— and R. COHEN [eds.] (1975) The Development of an Africa Working Class. London: Longman.

SANDBROOK, R. and R. STREN (1982) "Policy issues in Third-World urbanization: a dependency perspective." Toronto: Canadian Association of African Studies Conference.

SANTOS, M. (1979) The Shared Space: The Two Circuits of the Urban Economy in Underdeveloped Countries. London: Methuen.

SAUNDERS, P. (1981) Social Theory and the Urban Question. London: Hutchinson.

SCOTT, A. MacE. (1979) "Who are the self-employed?" in R. Bromley and C. Gerry (eds.) Casual Work and Poverty in Third World Cities. New York: John Wiley.

SIMKINS, C. (1981) "Agricultural production in the African reserves." Journal of Southern African Studies 7: 256-83.

SOJA, E.W. and C.E. WEAVER (1976) "Urbanization and underdevelopment in East Africa," in B.J.L. Berry (ed.) Urbanization and Counter-urbanization. Beverly Hills, CA: Sage.

STADLER, A.W. (1979) "Birds in the cornfield: squatter movements in Johannesburg, 1944-1947." Journal of Southern African Studies 6: 93-123.

STEDMAN JONES, G. (1971) Outcast London: A Study of the Relationship between Classes in Victorian Society. Oxford: Oxford University Press.

STREN, R. (1982) "Underdevelopment, urban squatting, and the state bureaucracy: a case study of Tanzania." Canadian Journal of African Studies 16: 67-91.

—— (1978) Housing the Urban Poor in Africa: Policy, Politics, and Bureaucracy in Mombasa. Berkeley: Institute of International Studies, University of California.

SWANSON, M. (1977) "The sanitation syndrome: bubonic plague and urban native policy in the Cape Colony, 1900-1909." Journal of African History 18: 387-410.

TABB, W.K. and L. SAWERS (1978) "Introduction." Marxism and the Metropolis: New Perspectives in Urban Political Economy. New York: Oxford University Press.

THOMPSON, E.P. (1978) The Poverty of Theory and Other Essays. New York: Monthly Review Press.

—— (1975) Whigs and Hunters: The Origins of the Black Act. New York: Pantheon.

—— (1967) "Time, work discipline and industrial capitalism." Past and Present 38: 56-97.

—— (1963) The Making of the English Working Class. New York: Vintage.

TILLY, C., L. TILLY, and R. TILLY (1975) The Rebellious Century 1830-1930. Cambridge, MA: Harvard University Press.

van ONSELEN, C. (1982) Studies in the Social and Economic History of the Witwatersrand 1886-1914. London: Longman.

—— (1977) Chibaro: African Mine Labour in Southern Rhodesia 1900-1922. London: Pluto.

van ZWANENBERG, R. (1972) "History and theory of urban poverty in Nairobi: the problem of slum development." Journal of East African Research and Development 2: 167-203.

VERNIÈRE, M. (1978) Dakar et son double: Dagoudane-Pikine. Paris: Imprimerie Nationale.

—— (1973) "A propos de la marginalité: réflexions illustrées par quelques enquêtes en milieu urbain et suburbain africain." Cahiers d'Etudes Africaines 13: 587-605.

VIDAL, C. (1977) "Guerre des sexes à Abidjan. Masculin, feminin, CFA." Cahiers d'Etudes Africaines 65: 121-153.

WALLERSTEIN, I. (1979) The Capitalist World Economy. Cambridge: Cambridge University Press.

WESTERN, J. (1981) Outcast Cape Town. Minneapolis: University of Minnesota Press.

WILKINSON, P. (1981) A Place to Live: The Resolution of the African Housing Crisis in Johannesburg, 1944-1954. University of Witwatersrand, African Studies Seminar Paper.

WIRTH, L. (1938) "Urbanism as a way of life." American Journal of Sociology 44: 1-24.

WOLPE, H. (1972) "Capitalism and cheap labour-power in South Africa: from segregation to apartheid." Economy and Society 1: 425-456.

WRIGHT, E. O. (1980) "Varieties of Marxist conceptions of class structure." Politics and Society 9: 323-370.

THE CONTROL OF LABOR

2

WORKERS AS CRIMINALS
The Rule of Law in Early Kimberley, 1870-1885

WILLIAM WORGER

In the late 1860s, diamonds were found in South Africa. Within two years, the search for diamonds developed into a struggle between black and white for possession of the stones and control over the labor power of black men. The early white diggers and the mining companies that replaced them took nearly fifteen years to deprive blacks of access to the ownership of diamonds and to establish firm discipline over black mineworkers, and they did so only after the diamond industry had been drastically restructured and after the state intervened decisively to watch, discipline, and punish black workers on and off the job. The laborers had resisted the efforts of employers to cut labor costs: They broke contracts and "deserted"; they resisted wage cuts and harsher measures of discipline; they played employers off against each other; and — or so their employers felt — they displayed a distressing irreverence to the sanctity of private property by taking and selling diamonds themselves. By the time the owners of the mines gained firm control over their laborers, they had created the most basic institutions that were to shape the lives of black workers in South African cities: the labor registration office, the location, the compound, and the jail. Ideologically, the diamond capitalists came to define the black worker not as a legitimate part of an economic structure or of a growing city, but as a presumptive criminal. Institutionally, their efforts came to embrace not only the workplace, but the entire town. Above all, capital and the state shaped a pattern of movement for black workers, exercising tight control over how they went between work and rest, between jobs, between city and country, and asserting, slowly and with great difficulty, control over the space and time through which black workers moved. Thus Kimberley became, for black workers, a new kind of urban structure, built in the interests of labor control and sanctioned by the rule of law.

The concept of the "rule of law" in its classic nineteenth-century formulation embodied three principles: that "regular law" rather than arbitrary power reign supreme in the regulation of society; that there be equality for all before the law; and that the courts, rather than any abstract constitution, are the protectors of the rights of individuals (Dicey, 1885: 215-216). It is this concept that most scholars have in mind when they write of the rule of law and of its extension by the British throughout much of the world including South Africa (Dugard, 1978: 17, 37-49). Yet those who use this concept usually do not relate the development and application of law, particularly criminal law, to the economic and political development of a given society and thus fail to investigate its role as an instrument of class rule.

However, recent work by Douglas Hay and E. P. Thompson on the development of criminal law in eighteenth-century England has done much to illuminate the relationship between law and its function in society. Hay has pointed out that criminal law "is as much concerned with authority as it is with property" and has argued that in eighteenth-century England "criminal law was critically important in maintaining bonds of obedience and deference, in legitimizing the status quo, [and] in constantly recreating the structure of authority which arose from property and in turn protected its interests" (Hay, 1975: 25). The law, developed out of the productive relations of an agrarian society was used by the ruling class to institutionalize and legitimize its power and was exercised through the courts in a careful balancing of "Justice, Terror and Mercy" (Hay, 1975: 63).

Thompson has, however, added the cautionary note that law should not always be seen as a mere instrument of the ruling class, but could take on a life and a logic of its own. After all, if law is to have an ideologically legitimizing function it must be seen to be just and not purely a tool of one class. Thompson argues that while law mediates "class relations to the advantage of the rulers," it also mediates those relations "through legal forms, which imposed, again and again, inhibitions upon the actions of the rulers" (Thompson, 1975: 264). Yet Thompson has also noted that in a society with "gross class inequalities," as England was in the eighteenth century, "the equity of the law must always be in part sham" and has suggested that when that law was transplanted to "even more inequitable contexts" it "could become an instrument of imperialism" (Thompson, 1975: 266).

This chapter takes up the question of the transplantation of law into an inequitable context: the city of Kimberley during the two decades after the discovery of diamonds in Griqualand West. Kimberley during this period was in a state of political and economic flux. Before 1870, there had been little outside interest in Griqualand West but with the onset of the diamond rush in 1871 Great Britain annexed the territory over the rival claims of the neighboring South African Republic and Orange Free State. During the next decade, the state in Kimberley changed from a limited form of three largely ineffective civil servants to a more elaborate structure of colonial government under a lieutenant-governor from 1873 to 1875, followed by a series of administrators between 1875 and 1880. In 1880, the British finally persuaded the Cape Colony to take over Griqualand West. Thereafter, mining capitalists, who had risen to positions of wealth and power in Kimberley in the late 1870s and early 1880s, exercised an increasingly powerful influence, built on their economic strength, over the colonial state.

In the same period that the state underwent considerable changes, the diamond industry underwent a massive structural transformation. The industry changed from a system of petty production dominated by merchant capital in the early 1870s to one where, in the early 1880s, large companies representing the rise of industrial capital dominated, to the triumph of monopoly capital in the late 1880s in the form of Cecil Rhodes's De Beers Consolidated Mines Limited.

Throughout this period of flux there was one relative constant: the racial division of the ownership of property (whether of the mines, the claims, or the diamonds themselves); whites generally possessed and blacks generally labored. The maintenance of this division was essential to the profitability of the diamond industry, for industrial capital required above all a cheap and disciplined labor force. It was in the quest for such a labor force that the criminal law became the most important factor in the mediation of class relations in Kimberley.

The legal system played a crucial role in elaborating and maintaining the rule of inequality, of capitalist over worker, of white over black. White employers sought to discipline their black workforce through legislative means. Through the extension of state surveillance and regulation, and a pervasive ideological equation of black workers with criminals, the white employers split away an emergent white working class from the black. White workers, subject to a much less rigorous, although still oppressive, set of controls, contrasted their perceived respectability to the ascribed criminal tendencies of black workers. Mining capital, with increasing access to the state and its law-making functions, manipulated the fears and insecurities of the white workers and obtained dominance over labor through this split. By the mid to late 1880s, black mineworkers were, for all intents and purposes, ascriptive criminals, subject to laws restricting every aspect of their behavior and incarcerated within a series of regulatory institutions — jail, convict stations, and company compounds — for the duration of their stay in the industrial city.

PART ONE:
EARLY DEVELOPMENTS,
1870-1875

In the early period of development of the diamond fields two factors largely determined the relationship between capital and labor. Most important was the division of the nascent industry into very small units of ownership and production. Diggers, working their tiny portions of ground individually or in small partnerships, oscillated between fortune and penury, mostly the latter. Needing cheap and reliable black labor for their survival, they sought extensive legal controls over the workforce. Their success in achieving these goals was limited by the second major factor: the changing and ambivalent nature of the state. Each change, from free digging to British colony, from rule by commissioners to that by a lieutenant-governor, involved a steady reduction in local autonomy, paralleled by increasing digger reliance, with regard to the control of their black workers, on a state that they perceived as hostile, until a crisis in late 1874 led to armed insurrection and the eventual establishment of a new colonial government amenable to the interests of capital and antagonistic to those of labor.

For most claimholders, the great majority of whom were white, diamond digging was a gamble and one that usually did not pay off. They came to a barren and inhospitable environment where their success appeared to be dependent on a combination of luck and a supply of cheap black labor. At the dry diggings of Kimberley (which had soon exceeded the nearby alluvial diggings on the Vaal River in diamond output), diggers worked claims of either thirty or thirty-one feet square although most of these were soon subdivided into half, quarter, and eighth portions. The diggers oversaw the work of their black employees (who did most of the work involved in diamond digging), ever fearful that their workers would steal the diamonds. One of the earliest accounts of the diamond fields suggests that no more than five men out of a hundred would make their fortune, another five perhaps would pay their expenses, while the remainder would not even cover their initial investment much less their living costs (Algar, 1872: 54; Boyle, 1873: 367).

Diggers gradually decided that the root of their problem lay with their black labor — with its supply, its cost, its control, and its apparent prediliction to the theft of the object of labor, the diamond. First reports of the diggings had made little comment on difficulties with the workforce. At the river diggings in 1870 and 1871, black labor was cheap and in plentiful supply and the diggers expressed little concern about discipline or theft (Cape Monthly Magazine, 1870: 243, 1871: 310). Yet, when the commissioners argued in 1872 that the future prosperity of the fields depended on a "constant supply of native labor," they were already concerned that the supply was inadequate.[1] Moreover, the supply fluctuated throughout the year, creating further difficulties. In winter, when the temperature often fell below freezing, many laborers left the fields. They also left periodically to plant and harvest their crops (Algar, 1872: 48). Employers did not fully control their laborers' time.

Nor could they control its cost. The intense and unregulated competition for black workers resulting from the greater labor demands of the dry diggings drove up wages by 1872. Weekly wages averaged 10 shillings and food was provided in addition. A local newspaper estimated that at least £45,000 was paid out each month in wages and food to the 12,000 black workers registered at the fields (a number that represented approximately two-thirds of the diamond industry's workforce). Black labor, it continued, apart from being "the most expensive in the world" was also "the most unmanageable."[2] There was much local concern with the constant refusal of employees ("servants" in the popular and legal terminology of the time) to obey what were deemed to be the "lawful commands" of their employers ("masters"). Diggers were also more concerned, in 1872, at the extent to which their workers appeared to steal diamonds and attributed much of their own financial failure to the widespread nature of the problem. The diggers believed that in order to achieve economic success, measures would have to be taken to assist in the supply and control of labor: to lower its cost and to end its thieving.

In the first years of the fields, discipline was more a matter of diggers' violence than the rule of law. Flogging with a *sjambok,* or tent rope, or striking with the fists were common methods, but they had two major drawbacks. First, digger violence had a negative effect on labor supply. An abused laborer could easily "desert" his employer and find work with another digger without any difficulty, or could leave the fields altogether and so increase the competition for the remaining workers. The lieutenant-governor from 1873 to 1875 concluded that one of the major causes of the poor supply of labor in the early to mid-1870s was the legacy of violence of the first years.[3]

Second, in attempting to establish its authority over the fields, the British administration began to punish those who took the law into their own hands. In July 1872, a digger was convicted by a jury for having flogged two laborers suspected of diamond theft and then leaving them tied up outside one winter's night, causing the death of one of the men. Found guilty by the jury of common assault under "great provocation," he was sentenced to six months hard labor (without the option of a fine) by the magistrate. The relative severity of the sentence, in a community where crimes of violence against black workers had not previously been punished, shocked Kimberley's residents. A local newspaper, the *Diamond Field* (12 September 1872), claimed that the sentence had "done more to defeat the ends of justice than uphold the dignity of the law." It was becoming obvious that individual acts of violence, unsanctioned by the state, could do little to solve the problems associated with labor.

Digger combinations had hardly more success than individual acts in overcoming these problems. With so many diggers (approximately 5000 in 1872) competing as employers there was never any possibility that they could achieve and enforce consensus on labor policies. The main drawback to any policy of extending controls over the workforce was that in response to such efforts the laborers would leave. In the middle of June 1872, with a depressed economic situation, the diggers engaged in collective action to lower the rate of wages to six shillings per week, with monthly payments rather than weekly, and one week's wages always to be held in arrears to prevent "desertion." The diggers agreed among themselves to fine any one of their number who paid a higher wage. At a mass public meeting the diggers told their black workers that if they refused these new terms they would be driven from the fields. It was the middle of winter and food would be scarce on any homeward route.[4]

The scheme was a fiasco. Within one week of the announcement the demand for labor far exceeded the heavily depleted supply. Hundreds of laborers left the fields and the diggers had to return to a weekly wage of ten shillings, with further unspecified inducements, and the expectation that wages would almost certainly rise even higher (Diamond News, 17 July 1872). Digger combination had little chance of success so long as the units of production (the claims and portions of claims) remained small, numerous, and in competition for the same limited supply of labor.

The *Diamond Field* (28 December 1871; also 2 May, 25 July, 8, 22 August 1872) had earlier suggested a possible solution to these problems through the use of law to control the workforce. It had argued that "natives" had to live "under a kind of patriarchal system," otherwise they would become "loafers, thieves and drunkards." The relative freedom of the black laborers on the fields, in comparison with the strict controls of their own communities, made them disrespectful of the diggers. What was needed was a system of control as strict and authoritarian as that which it believed chiefs exercised in the men's home communities.

Diggers wanted laws that would regulate every aspect of the behavior of their workers. In March 1872, the residents of Kimberley presented a memorial to the commissioners that listed the legislative controls they wished introduced. Many of these were to become law.[5]

(1) No "Kafir or other coloured person" to hold a digging license unless supported by fifty white claimholders.
(2) All employers to have written contracts with their servants registered before a government official.
(3) No contracts of less than three months.
(4) On discharge of each servant the employer has to endorse the servant's ticket of service as to completion of contractual obligations.
(5) No unemployed native laborer to be permitted in the camp longer than 48 hours after discharge.

(6) All employers and constables to have the right to search servants at any time. Any "native or coloured person" found to have a diamond in his possession for which he could not "satisfactorily account" would be liable to a sentence of at least fifty lashes.

(7) Any person (who was not a registered claimholder) convicted of having purchased a diamond from a "native or coloured servant" would receive fifty lashes in public, be expelled from the diamond fields, and have his property confiscated.

(8) A fine of £25 or one month's imprisonment for anyone inducing a servant to leave his master.

(9) Police to patrol the countryside to check that servants were properly registered.

(10) All diamonds found on any "natives" leaving the fields to be regarded as the property of their last master.

(11) No liquor to be sold to servants except with the written permission of their masters.

(12) Any person caught stealing diamonds to be liable to up to fifty lashes and three years imprisonment.

(13) No "native" to be allowed to move about the camp after 8 p.m.

Over the course of the next few months the diggers pressured the commissioners to give their proposals legal force. When peaceful measures had little effect, the diggers took stronger action, burning the tents of black claimholders, attempting to lynch black men suspected of stealing diamonds, and, on occasion, rioting. In the face of increasing social disorder, and unwilling to go to the expense and trouble necessary to repress the agitation, the commissioners wrote most of these demands into law, although the Colonial Office, upholding the principle that no British subject should be legally discriminated against on the basis of color, eliminated the references to "natives" and used the term "servant" instead (Smalberger, 1976).

Government Notice 68 of July 1872 established a Servant's Registry Office and ordered the construction of a depot where all arriving black laborers would be required to register and obtain a daily pass while seeking employment. This pass, and another one given upon securing employment, had to be carried at all times and shown "to anyone who may demand it": failure to do so by the laborer would render him liable to arrest and conviction before the local magistrate. Upon leaving the fields, the notice required that the laborer obtain a third pass certifying that he had carried out his employment obligations satisfactorily. Workers were required to remain on their employer's premises after 9 p.m. Any employer who attempted to engage labor outside the registry system could be fined £10 or imprisoned for three months.[6] The administration, responding to the pressure of the diggers, had begun to shape what workers did at, and to, and from the workplace.

A month later the pass law was elaborated: All servants upon registering for employment at the Registry Office were to be given a certificate stating their contract period and the rate of wages they were to receive. They were required, under penalty of a £5 fine or two month's imprisonment, to produce this certificate to any "justice of the peace, field-cornet, police officer, constable, or registered holder of a claim" who asked to see it. Without the pass,

> any person who shall be found wandering or loitering about . . . may be arrested by any police officer or constable without a warrant, and taken beore the magistrate of the district, and shall be liable to be punished by fine not exceeding five pounds, by imprisonment with or without spare diet for any period not exceeding three months, or by corporal punishment in any number of lashes not exceeding twenty-five.

As the law looked at a servant's movements, it began to extend its surveillance to his person. Any master could search the person, residence, or property of his servants at any time without a warrant while they were in his employ, and within two hours after they left his employ. All diamonds found in the possession of any servant were to be deemed the property of his master or, if he were currently without work, of his previous master. Any servant found guilty of diamond theft could be flogged, up to a maximum of fifty lashes, and/or receive twelve months hard labor. Although this legislation was intended as a means to regulate the black workforce it, like Government Notice 68, did not use racially discriminatory language. Black workers were referred to as servants and not as natives and thus the law remained, in language at least, color-blind.[7]

Language was one thing, however, actions quite another. The police and courts took vigorous action to enforce the laws regulating worker behavior. The police patrolled the outskirts of the mining camps, checking that departing black workers had the requisite passes and often searching them for stolen diamonds.[8] Within the camps the police patrolled the streets checking blacks frequently for passes as they sought to discover deserters. In 1872, for example, the

Kimberley Magistrates Court dealt with 4760 criminal cases and the most common offense by far was "desertion of employment" by black workers. Those found guilty were generally flogged ten or twelve times with a cat-o'-nine-tails and then sent back to their employer. Typical cases included those of prisoner 4409, known as "Sunday," who was convicted in February 1873 of desertion and received twelve lashes, and prisoners 4523 and 4524, "Jacob" and "Buffalo," who each received eleven lashes for the same offense. For the lesser crime of being in camp without a pass, prisoners 4670, 4671, 4672, 4673 ("Jimmy," "Hans," "Jim," and "Boy") each received the option of a five-shilling fine or three lashes. Such sentences were general for these offenses.[9]

Most of the diggers, rich and poor, did not believe that the state's efforts at control went far enough. Although labor registration had been carried out on a large scale in 1873 with 51,000 men contracted, in 1874 the number registered dropped to 43,000.[10] Most whites believed, by the end of 1874, that registration — the basis of the system of labor control introduced in 1872 — no longer served their purposes.[11] Diggers argued that they did not register their servants because of constant desertion. Indeed, the diggers were particularly annoyed at having paid to register their employees and now having these men leave their service still in possession of the contracts allowing them relatively free movement on the fields. The laborers were finding new ways to evade the control of their time, and the digger complained that the police did little to enforce the law.[12]

At the same time, diggers remained obsessed with the theft of diamonds. In August 1874, a mass meeting of diggers complained of the presence of "swell niggers" on the fields who, they claimed, were profiting from illegal activities while they themselves, the "rightful" owners of the diamonds, were unable to work (Diamond Field, 14 August 1874; Diamond News, 18 August 1874). Diggers argued that blacks should be prevented from holding claims not simply because of a racist desire to avoid black competitors but because they perceived black diggers as undermining their control of black labor by acting as fronts for the fencing of stolen diamonds. Illicit dealers could later claim that they obtained their diamonds from black diggers. Implicitly defining a black digger, as much as a black worker, as a criminal, diggers objected to the administration's refusal to enact racially discriminatory legislation and accused it of being unduly influenced by the Aborigines Protection Society in London. Instead of conspiring to "elevate in one day the servant to an equality as regards the right to hold property with his master," wrote the *Diamond Field* (28 November 1874), the state should provide "class legislation, restrictive laws, and the holding in check of the coloured races till by education they are fit to be our equals."

Thus, it seemed to many of the diggers, having secured legislation to protect their interests, that the state, instead of coming to their aid at a time of economic hardship, was moving into opposition to their interests. Conflict came to a head in 1875. Dissident diggers armed themselves and drilled in public challenging Lieutenant-Governor Richard Southey's authority. Southey, in response, stated that he was ready to arm blacks to defend law and order. After much parading and mutual exchange of insults, the affair was finally settled with the arrival of British troops despatched from Cape Town. Although the rebels were disarmed, Southey's victory was pyrrhic for, after a short investigation, the Colonial Office decided to replace him and his administration with one more in tune with the community's interests. In November 1875, a much reduced level of government was established under the control of a military officer appointed as Administrator of Griqualand West (de Kiewiet, 1965: 49-59; Sutton, 1979: 40-61; Turrell, 1981: 194-235).

In sum, three factors prevented the successful extension of legal controls over the black workforce in the first half of the 1870s. First, and most important, the small-scale, mutually competitive nature of the units of production made them economically unstable and prevented the formation of effective combinations of employers over any extended period of time. Second, the state, in the form of the colonial administration, seemed to be acting indecisively, enacting legal instruments of labor control but blunting them in the name of abstract principles of the universality of law. Third, and closely related to the second factor, criminal sanctions could not be applied fully because of the physical weakness of the state apparatus. There were too few police, the courts were clogged, and there were not enough jails.

PART TWO:
A PERIOD OF TRANSITION,
1876-1880

In the second half of the 1870s, major changes took place in the diamond industry and in the nature of the state, changes that had considerable impact upon labor. In the industry, the unit of production became steadily larger as combinations of claims were brought into single ownerships. The owners and managers of these larger units, in order to protect their considerable investments in property and machinery, sought greater controls over labor. In this effort they were energetically assisted by the state, which, with a greater economic stake of its own, sought to protect the prosperity of the industry. However, complete labor control could only be approached, not achieved, during this period. Despite the support of the state, the industry suffered from internal contradictions that prevented the achievement of the degree of labor control that the mining capitalists desired.

During the latter half of the 1870s, ownership of the mines steadily fell into fewer and fewer hands largely as the result of the passage of legislation permitting the holding of blocks of more than ten claims. Whereas in 1873 there had been 1200 claimholders in the Kimberley Mine, and the number had dropped to 381 by 1875 (largely through the cessation of working in many claims), the most important reduction took place in the two years following the introduction of legislation in 1876 removing the restriction on owning more than ten claims. Although there were still 300 claimholders in 1877, by May of 1878 this figure had almost halved. By the end of 1879 there were only 130 separate claimholders in the mine, a mere 12 of whom were said to own nearly three-quarters of the claims.[13]

The large claimholdings used much greater amounts of machinery, particularly that driven by steam. They needed considerable amounts of investment capital to purchase this machinery, and, most important of all, the large claimholdings needed a regular and disciplined labor force so that the machinery could be worked efficiently and profitably. An example of one such large claimholding, typical of many at the time, was that of Solz and Company in the Dutoitspan Mine (Diamond News, 10 July 1879). Solz worked a block of thirty claims by means of several steam engines and a labor force consisting of an engineer, several white overseers, and 87 black laborers. The various operations of mining — excavation, removal of the ground to the margins of the mine, and the washing and sorting of this ground, all through a combination of man and machine power — had to be carefully coordinated. Further, machines were obviously worked more efficiently by men who knew what they were doing. Therefore, the company wished to cut down the high turnover of labor so common on the small claimholdings and retain experienced black workers, even if their skills were very limited, for the full period of their contracts. In addition, the enlarged scale of operations made it necessary for the claimholder to delegate some of his supervisory functions over black workers to a new class of employee: the white overseer. The latter were usually unsuccessful claimholders whose position in production had now changed from that of owner/employer to worker. Such a transformation introduced new tensions in the changing relations of capital and labor: relations that the state took a much more active role in regulating than it had in the past.

Diamonds, by 1876, were the largest item in the Cape Colony's exports and their discovery had been the major factor in allowing the Cape to recover from the depression of the early 1870s. More immediately, in 1875 the British administration purchased the Vooruitzigt farm, which contained the Kimberley and De Beers mines and the township, for £100,000. As Lanyon put it, the state was now the "proprietor" of the town and thus it was "very expedient" to facilitate the working of the mines "so as to induce as many workers as possible to remain, and thus to enhance the value of the property."[14]

The coincidence of interest of state and industry in black labor was given practical form when Lanyon established a commission in 1876 "to enquire into and report upon the Supply and Demand for Native Labour." The commission recommended the establishment of an elaborate administrative structure to control the supply of labor, including measures to provide safe passage for blacks coming to the fields, severe penalties for persons enticing servants to desert, and a stress on the need to enforce a strict vagrancy law.[15]

Before these measures could be introduced, however, the diamond industry was struck by a severe depression. In June 1876, the *Daily Independent* (29 June 1876) estimated that the costs of working the mines exceeded returns from diamond sales by at least one-third. Faced with the need to cut working costs, the diggers, large and small, decided in late June to combine and to lower the wages of their black workers. Wages were then running at ten shillings to twenty-five shillings per week with food and sixty shillings to eighty shillings without. The diggers believed that any check given to labor would help the industry overcome its two great evils: the high cost of production directly related to the rate of wages paid, and the problem of overproduction, which diggers believed was caused in large part by the flooding of the diamond market with stones stolen from them by their own workers. The diggers decided to cancel unilaterally the terms of the contracts they had with their workers, on the basis that "no principle of equity could bind them to pay ruinously high wages to servants they no longer required," and to lower the rate of wages to five shillings per week.[16]

As in 1874, the workers refused to accept the reduction and began leaving the fields. By mid-July, hundreds had left and very few were arriving to replace them. By the end of July, the labor force had been reduced by one-half, with over 6000 men having left the fields. Wages had risen to a minimum of ten shillings per week with food.[17] The shortfall was so great that *Diamond News* (29 July 1876) was reduced to editorializing bitterly that "they [the workers] have made their exit in such large numbers that with all our hatred and contempt for them as men and laborers we are driven to make the admission that we would rather have their company than their room." Despite the reduction in the number of separate holdings, digger combinations had still not destroyed the black laborers' readiness to refuse to accept unilateral wage reductions and to leave the fields if the conditions of employment did not suit them.

Unlike Southey's administration, Lanyon's was prepared to take a much more active role in using the agencies of the state to help control the labor market. An example of the new activism is supplied by the experience of one digger, H. Green of the Dutoitspan Mine, in May 1876. Green wrote to Lanyon complaining of the great difficulty he had in obtaining labor while numerous unemployed men were holding out for higher wages. Green made a simple request to the administrator. "Could not the police put a little gentle pressure on these gentlemen to oblige them to enter service?" Lanyon responded with a note to the inspector of police requesting that he make a series of raids to check for passes and to arrest the unemployed. The inspector agreed to make a raid the following Sunday, when the unemployed would be "loafing about," although he was somewhat concerned by the fact that the jail at Dutoitspan was already full and unable to accommodate any more prisoners.[18]

The size and level of activity of the police force increased dramatically in 1876 from 44 officers and men in January to 112 in September. Lanyon also contracted with the former head of the Durban municipal police for the supply of 50 Zulu policemen to act as jail guards and to detect crimes in the "kafir community."[19] In January 1876, the colonial secretary in Cape Town wrote to the Kimberley inspector of police ordering him to "be very particular for the future in strictly enforcing the law which obliges all natives to register and obtain a pass."[20]

Arrests increased dramatically. In the first six months of 1875, 1396 blacks and 131 whites were arrested; in the first six months of 1876 arrests rose to 3131 blacks and 384 whites. Most of the increase in white arrests was due to a greater number of individuals being charged with "lying drunk in the streets." With regard to arrests of blacks, the greatest increase was in the number charged with being "in camp without passes," from 95 in 1875 to 971 in 1876. Arrests for "neglect of duty to masters" increased from 99 in 1875 to 257 in 1876, for "desertion of service" from 174 to 300, for "lying drunk in the street" from 83 to 320.[21] Both Lanyon and his inspector of police considered that the greater number of arrests did not reflect a large rise in the amount of crime in Kimberley but rather was due to the new strength of the police force.[22]

Throughout the remainder of the decade, the police continued to harass black workers in Kimberley. They made constant checks on men in the street, requiring them to show their passes, and they made regular Sunday raids on areas with a large black population to make sure that no person was in Kimberley who did not have official permission to be there. These police actions by necessity were carried out on a random basis since it was physically impossible to check that every person had a pass. Yet the randomness of these mechanisms of worker control assisted the police in creating a climate of psychological insecurity and fear. The very arbitrariness of law enforcement contributed to the disciplining of the members of the first generation of a new working class.[23]

The courts adopted rapid procedures in determining guilt and passing sentence, essential developments considering the number of cases with which they were deluged. In a single day in January 1876, for example, 107 cases came before the Kimberley Magistrates' Court. On 5 November 1877, 115 cases were dealt with; on 28 January 1878, over 150 (Diamond News, 6 November 1877, 29 January 1878). In such circumstances, the time available to determine guilt or innocence was limited; the magistrates generally accepted the evidence of the arresting officers as adequate proof of guilt.

Sentencing was punitive. One magistrate, in attempting to decrease the number brought before him each week charged with pass offences, increased the penalty from a ten-shilling fine or two-weeks' hard labor to a twenty-shilling fine or one-months' hard labor (with eighteen days on a rice-water diet) and even considered doing away with the option of a fine (Diamond News, 6 November 1877). Yet, while increasing the burden on those arrested, this measure had little apparent effect on the number arrested.

The production-line techniques of the courts were refined in 1879 with the establishment of the Police Magistrates' Court, which dealt with all offenses against the pass and master and servant laws. In 1879, the first year of operation for the new system, only 952 cases came before the Kimberley Magistrates' Court, while 4359 came before the Police Magistrates' Court. As the name implies, it was essentially an institution for disciplining those brought before it, doing without a jury, and aiming at a rapid turnover of cases.[24]

Despite the repressive activities of the police and courts, the total control desired by the mining employers over their black workers remained as elusive as ever. While the energy of the police had resulted in a great increase in labor registration in 1876, employers remained dissatisfied. Indeed, by 1880 the registration system was generally regarded as useless as a means to regulate the supply and behavior of workers.[25] As the *Daily Independent* pointed out, this failure had more to do with the competitiveness of the employers and their inability to act in concert than with any shortcomings in the strict enforcement of the law. In practice, employers often ignored the legislation they had pushed for and attempted to obtain workers by other means, such as illegally encouraging men to leave the employ of competing mining companies for their own operations.[26]

The employers' readiness to evade the law themselves also reflected an awareness that its strict application could have a detrimental effect on the supply of labor. The problem was best summed up in an editorial in the *Diamond News* (3 November 1877). The courts were constantly crowded with blacks "arrested nominally for being without passes, but really because they were suspected of being deserters." The police had stationed men outside the registrar's office to arrest groups of black men who had come to get passes on the vaguest suspicion that they might be deserters. The process was a "burlesque of an extremely stupid order" since men were being arrested, knocked about by the police, and placed in a heavily overcrowded jail for the night, then allowed free the next day to search for employment again. These police practices, as the paper stated, not only took workers away from their employers for brief but annoying periods (as when men who had left their passes with their employers were arrested), but also suggested to these same workers that the law was unjust.[27]

The Kimberley correspondent of the Cape Argus (reprinted Diamond News, 20 April 1880) argued that the main problem with the rule of law in the town had become the contradiction between extremely restrictive laws and the inconsistent ways in which they were enforced. The police might make a raid on some area and arrest several hundred people for being without passes. But the legislation was so all-encompassing that there was no possible way that everybody not in compliance with the provisions of the laws could be punished. Some laws were laxly enforced, such as the 1879 regulation requiring employers to feed their employees within the work compounds. Yet the police strictly enforced a law preventing black workers from going to "Kafir eating houses" (which had been the main source of meals for workers in the past) out of fear that such places were centers of illicit dealing in diamonds. Therefore, he argued, the actions of the police seemed "capricious and tyrannical" to those affected by them rather than regular and just. The worker soon realized that in dealing with the law and its agents, the only lesson to be learned was not to get caught.

Such arbitrary application of the law combined with the constant failure of many employers to fulfill their contractual obligations to workers had a counterproductive effect on the supply of labor. For example, one of the leading mining capitalists at Kimberley, J.B. Robinson, reported (Diamond News, 23 October, 6 November 1879) that when he attempted to enforce the law and make his black workers eat on his company premises, two-thirds of them left and sought work with other employers who were not so ready to respect the law. The registrar of contracted servants reported to the colonial secretary that black workers were constantly coming to his office to complain of the nonpayment of wages by their employers. He cited the case of "John," a black laborer who had come to him with just such a complaint. Coleman noted that John had gone to court with his complaint, but that the case had become entangled in procedural delays. Therefore John, who had neither the time nor the money to pursue his case, "made up his mind to lose his money and quit the Fields in disgust . . . as many had done before him."[28] Thus black workers, in response to harassment from the police and employers, and subjected to courtroom practices that gave little heed to their concerns, took themselves and their labor away from the diamond fields.

In an attempt to ameliorate the worst effects of these pressures on the workers, and thus protect the supply of labor, Lanyon created in 1877 a new civil service position, that of Protector of Contracted Servants. Lanyon insisted that nonpayment of wages and ineffective court practices caused injury to the "good name" of the fields amongst the "tribes of the interior." The new protector's duties were

> to attend the Magistrates Courts every day [and] defend all cases in which natives are concerned, *except criminal ones* [my emphasis], to prevent their falling into the hands of [law] Agents who act unscrupulously towards them, and extort money from them and their friends outside, to investigate and settle all cases in dispute between master and servant, to enforce payment of wages and to look after the interests of the natives in every way.[29]

In short, the protector would act as a check on the actions of disreputable employers and the excesses of the courts.

The first protector — who was also the registrar — had some limited success. In October 1879, for example, he defended 79 men before the police magistrate and managed to have the charges dismissed in 29 of the cases. Amongst those discharged were Adrian who was given the opportunity to explain that he was "in camp without a pass" because he had come to attend the funeral of his child, and Hendrik, who explained that he did not have a pass allowing him to seek employment because he had only come to Kimberley to sell some sheep.[30] Such men had seldom been given the opportunity to explain their actions in the past before being convicted.

However, there were far too many cases for one man to deal with on a part-time basis. Indeed, the *Argus* correspondent (Diamond News, 20 April 1880), writing well after the appointment of the protector, concluded that the supply of labor was steadily decreasing in reaction to the practices of the police and the courts: "Everyone knows the extraordinary freemasonry and the rapidity of communicating information possessed by the Kafir race, and this source [of labour] is nearly dried up by the lugubrious reports which are daily being taken away by parties leaving the Fields." He cited two examples. First, the case of some Swazi who, after traveling hundreds of miles, turned back within sight of Kimberley discouraged by the reports of conditions which they received from departing workers. Second, the case of an old chief in Basutoland who, when approached by a labor recruiter, "absolutely refused [to supply any men], saying that never again would he send any of his tribe to the Diamond-fields, for all those who had been there came back maimed and useless in body, and corrupted in mind." Thus Lanyon's partial measures to ameliorate the harsh and arbitrary rule of employers and courts had not been sufficient to counter the detrimental effects of these factors on the supply of labor.

At the same time that the state was rigorously enforcing laws that had generally been introduced prior to the mid-1870s, the large claimholders and company men who grew in importance in the diamond industry after 1875 moved to protect their large investments and secure maximum profits by attempting to extend the compass of the law into further areas of the lives of their workers. They attempted to introduce a system of strip searching which would apply to all workers, white as well as black, and they pressed for closer regulation by the state of those parts of the urban area inhabited by blacks.

Mining capitalists led the agitation for searching. Julius Wernher, the manager of the largest mining company in Kimberley, argued that the diamond industry's profitability was severely undermined by theft. He claimed that at least three-fifths of the mines' production was stolen by workers and suggested that the problem could be totally eliminated only so long as all employees were searched each time they left the mines (Diamond News, 16 May 1878). His emphasis on the threat of illicit dealing provided a strong ideological argument that was to be used over and over again throughout the agitation for the introduction of searching. The *Diamond News* (4 May 1878) made a typical use of this argument when it claimed that no "honest man" would object to being searched "because any honest man, be he black or white, will heartily concur in any measure which will lead to the conviction of the guilty, even though at some personal inconvenience." As a result of the agitation of the mining capitalists, the state introduced Ordinance 11 of 1880 to establish a comprehensive system of searching at every mine.

The searching law was not enforced in 1880 for two reasons. First, there was the great shortage of black workers in 1880 due to disturbances in the two areas that supplied most of Kimberley's laborers, Basutoland and the Transvaal. No employer was going to put at risk his economic survival by the application of further punitive controls, which his workers had already made apparent they would not put up with.

The second reason for the nonenforcement of searching was the opposition of the white overseers. The conflicting needs of different claimholders and companies and the considerations of local politics had forced some claimholders to support the overseers' complaints. George Bottomley, a large claimholder, for example, had at first been an enthusiastic supporter of the searching scheme. However, while he owned large amounts of valuable property he was still a relatively small employer of white labor with perhaps no more than five to ten white men working for him, whereas Wernher's company employed well over fifty white overseers. The relationship between smaller employer and white employee was a more personal one, especially since both had the common experience of being or having been a claimholder. And the smaller operations, with none of the capital resources of the larger companies, could not afford to ride out a strike. In addition, the white workers formed a large proportion of the local electorate, an important factor in Bottomley's decision to change sides since he had considerable political aspirations (Diamond News, 29 July 1880).

In contrast, proposed regulations affecting only blacks failed to create any dissension among white capitalists and overseers. The proposals of mining capitalists for closer supervision of the urban dwelling areas of blacks and the establishment of municipal locations reflected a desire to extend the controls of the workplace throughout the urban community and to ensure a regular and disciplined movement of black labor within the town. The argument for such controls was familiar: All blacks were thieves. Throughout the later 1870s the press continuously claimed that there was extensive trafficking in illegal diamonds in those parts of Kimberley populated mainly by blacks.[31] George Bottomley used the argument of diamond theft when he suggested to the Kimberley Borough Council (Diamond News, 14 March 1878) that a municipal superintendent of locations should be appointed. This official could regulate areas in which blacks lived, maintain order, and ensure that only people employed through the Registry Office be allowed to remain in the town. This new form of regulation, claimed Bottomley, would check diamond theft and alleviate the labor problems of the industry: "natives would be restrained, and their habits and occupation known."

The logic of Bottomley's argument lay in his idea that ultimately all black workers in Kimberley, during every moment of their temporary residence in the town, would be under the control of either an employer, a civil servant, a policeman, a jailer, or a municipal officer. This control would ensure a regular and disciplined movement of the worker from first entry to the urban area, to the Registry Office, to an employer, to a location (while employed but not living on an employer's premises, or unemployed but with a pass permitting the worker to look for employment), to another employer, and then back out of the town once the period of contracted labor had been completed. Desertion would be prevented because there would be no unregulated area within the town to which to escape.

The bylaws of the Kimberley Town Council, drawn up in 1878, made provision for the appointment of a superintendent of locations. His duties included laying out the locations, numbering each and every hut, preparing a register of all location residents, and checking for passes to ensure that all the location inhabitants had an officially sanctioned means of earning a living. When the Cape government finally passed control of the existing locations, which had been largely unregulated, to the council in 1880, the superintendant strictly enforced these regulations. In his first six months in office he had 643 blacks arrested for transgressing location regulations. Still, he found it quite impossible to achieve the degree of control over location residents which the regulations made theoretically possible. For, with a shortage of labor, most employers ignored the labor registration system. The superintendent, for his part, was dependent on the registration system working effectively. He could not harass men for passes if their employers refused to give them any without causing further difficulties in the supply of labor. In addition, not all blacks were as yet forced to live in the locations. In short, the scheme could not work as effectively as planned so long as the competition for labor remained intense, but disgruntled employers still complained that "loiterers" always found refuge in the locations and thus escaped their "responsibility" to labor in the mines.[32]

By the beginning of the 1880s neither the repressive activities of state agencies nor the attempted extension of labor control beyond the workplace had succeeded in securing a system of regulation that satisfied the white employers who controlled the mining industry. This failure was due to a number of factors. First, despite the increasing penetration of the state into the workplace, the locations, and the town as a whole, the British Colonial Office was not prepared to sanction "class" (meaning color) legislation. Second, the mechanics of repression could not succeed so long as the demand for cheap labor exceeded the supply of men willing to work for the wages offered. Third, as long as the industry remained relatively competitive, if less so than in the early 1870s, workers could always play employers off against each other. That the schemes did not bring labor under strict control did not, however, stop them from being very oppressive to those workers summarily tried for loitering or not having a pass.

PART THREE:
INDUSTRY OFFENSIVE,
1881-1885

Changes in the structure of the diamond industry in the 1880s led to the extension by mining capitalists and the state of much greater controls over black labor. Within the industry a major crisis extending from 1882 well into the mid-1880s was resolved through the elimination of many of the smaller limited liability companies (which had only been formed in 1880-1881) and the increasing dominance of a few very large companies. Parallel changes in the nature of the state, with colonial rule largely replaced by representative government, allowed these large companies to gain greater access to Parliament and to use this access to extend their power in Kimberley and increase their control over both the black and the white workforces in the mines. At first this control was applied through greater police activity against blacks, but the total control desired remained elusive so long as there remained a shortage of cheap black labor and so long as all the company men could not agree on what policies to adopt. However, another product of the depression that hit the diamond industry in late 1882, apart from the bankruptcy of many of the smaller companies, was a reduced demand for black workers. Indeed, the number of black laborers employed in the industry was halved. The operators of the largest mining companies took advantage of this situation of labor surplus to introduce a new form of labor regulation that lay under their direct control: the establishment of closed compounds. The rigid control these institutions afforded over workers' residence was used in conjunction with continued reliance on the regulatory apparatus of the state: the police, the courts, the jails, the locations, and the newly established De Beers Convict Station. Mining capitalists, by the mid 1880s, were able, much as Bottomley had envisaged, to maintain their black workers in a continual round between compounds, locations, jails, and entry to and exit from the town. Criminal law and public and private institutions were integrated into a complex system of labor control.

The diamond industry suffered a severe structural crisis during the first half of the 1880s. Toward the end of 1880 and the beginning of 1881 the number of publically registered limited liability companies in the four mines had risen from 6 to 71 (Roberts, 1976: 197). Most of these new companies were formed in the atmosphere of a boom with claimholders joining their properties and selling shares in the newly established companies on the basis of highly inflated valuations of their claims. The promoters of these companies hoped to attract capital to the diamond industry from the rest of South Africa and from England and Europe both for their immediate profit and so that they could purchase the large amounts of machinery that were needed to work the mines more efficiently and profitably.

However, the majority of these companies suffered from a combination of often crippling constraints. First, there was always a great difference between the amounts of fixed and working capital they had. Claimholders took most of the invested capital for themselves in exchange for the value of their claims and spent the bulk of what remained on expensive machinery. Few companies kept any capital in reserve to pay for unexpected working expenses. Second, open cast mining was becoming increasingly difficult with so many of the companies working at different depths and undercutting each other's operations. Third, with increased production and problems in the European diamond market, the price of diamonds fluctuated considerably and was in a general decline from late 1882 through to 1888. The fourth constraint, and the one regarded as the most crippling at the time, was the continuing shortage of cheap black labor.

While most of the companies formed in 1880 and 1881 were relatively small, a number of significantly larger operations were established at the same time. These included the Griqualand West Diamond Mining Company formed by J. B. Robinson in September 1880 with a capital of £280,000, the De Beers Mining Company formed in April 1880 by Cecil Rhodes and C. D. Rudd with a capital of £200,000, and the Kimberley Central Diamond Mining Company formed in October 1881, by George Bottomley among others, with a capital of £576,860.[33] The founders of these companies, Kimberley's mining capitalists, believed that the fate of those companies that had failed, of which the small operations formed a disproportionately large number, could befall them if they did not act to eliminate the constraints on the diamond industry. However, only the fourth constraint, the supply of cheap black labor, did at least seem potentially within their control. Therefore, in 1882, the mining capitalists sought to implement new controls to discipline their black workforce and make it accept the industrial demands — such as regular attendance at work, and the fulfilment of contracts — that had been important in the past and were now critical to the financial success of mechanized production. Once again, mining capitalists sought to harness the state in this renewed attempt to control the space and time in which black workers in Kimberley survived.

In 1880, Griqualand West was annexed to the Cape Colony, the office of administrator was abolished, and the Cape Parliament became responsible for enacting legislation for the territory. While the British Colonial Office still exerted ultimate authority through the governor of the Cape, Kimberley was no longer under the direct jurisdiction of officials of the colonial service. The Cape Parliament now became the main forum in which Kimberley's residents expressed their concerns and sought political remedies.

Kimberley's first parliamentary election, in March 1881, centered on the problem of black labor. J. B. Robinson's election manifesto held out to the community the promise of properity, happiness, and civilization, but warned that the realization of this future was dependent on the supply and treatment of black labor. While black labor could be treated humanely and fairly without threatening the golden future, black workers still had to be taught "to respect the laws of *meum* and *tuum*" — to know their place — through the strict enforcement of existing legislation such as the pass and masters and servants laws. Robinson was elected to Parliament along with his fellow neophyte magnate, Cecil Rhodes.[34]

The problem of illicit diamond buying (IDB) was the first major issue brought to Parliament by the Kimberley members. Within a year of their election they sought remedies for this problem through the establishment of a select committee to investigate the issue and suggest legislative remedies.[35] The old beliefs that blacks were natural thieves and that they were grievously damaging the industry — allegedly stealing one-third to one-half of all diamonds — became more acute in the crisis of 1881-1882 and took on a new dimension with the restructuring of the companies. One witness before the select committee bluntly demanded "exceptional legislation" in the interests of the "special class who are now engaged in mining . . . a class [once] consisting merely of diggers; but now . . . [consisting of] the shareholders in the Joint Stock Companies." The witnesses wanted to force workers to submit to searches, to work naked, to be confined to compounds, and to be flogged if caught stealing. The select committee accepted most such recommendations and in 1882 Parliament passed the Diamond Trade Act.[36]

Under this legislation, those accused of IDB were presumed guilty until they could prove their innocence. The legislation provided for the establishment of a special court to try those accused of IDB, presided over by a judge assisted by two magistrates, and without a jury. People found guilty of IDB were to receive very severe punishments: whites faced prison terms of up to fifteen years, fines of up to £1000, and the possibility of permanent banishment from Griqualand West; blacks could expect to be flogged in addition to the preceding penalties.[37]

At the same time, the Kimberley police force was increased from the 73 white officers to which it had fallen to 105 by the end of 1882 and 150 in following years. An independent detective department was established — with a chief detective, three white detectives, and forty black detectives — to concentrate on IDB.[38] The detectives made considerable use of "trapping": officers or hired black "traps" offered stones to suspected fences.[39]

The result was an acceleration in police harassment, arrests, and convictions. As Table 2.1 shows, the number of people arrested in Kimberley reached extremely high levels in the early to mid-1880s, especially since the population was declining during this period. A comparative survey of arrest rates between several English cities and Cape Town, made in 1884 by the Cape Commissioners of Police, found that the average number of arrests made by each police officer ranged from 53 in Liverpool, to 45 in Cape Town, 43 in Newcastle, and 29 in Manchester. Kimberley, by comparison, had an arrest rate of between 114 and 160 persons per police officer in 1882 and remained close to this figure for the remainder of the 1880s. Moreover, the total number of arrests in Kimberley in 1882 amounted to almost half the total for Manchester, a city with at least four times the population. Even in a South African context the number of arrests in Kimberley was extraordinarily high: Cape Town, for example, a community of roughly similar size to that of Kimberley, recorded only one-third the

Table 2.1   Arrest and Conviction Rates, 1875-1889

Year	Total Arrests (A)	Summarily Convicted (B)	B as % of A
1875	1,527 (½ year)	867 (½ year)	56.7
1876	8,646	5,679	65.7
1882	2,012 (2 months)	1,329 (2 months)	66
1883	14,003	10,934	78
1884	14,144	11,195	79.1
1885	16,214	12,948	79.8
1886	16,359	13,129	80.2
1887	14,886	11,321	76
1888	13,520	10,494	77.6
1889	10,788	8,262	76.5

SOURCES: GLW 93(2770); CO 3575, 3605, 3631, 3656; CGHPP, G 77 1882, G 12 1885.

number of arrests as were made by the Kimberley police.[40] Many of these arrests made were during raids for pass law offenders. Often 30 to 100 people would be picked up in such a sweep: On one occasion later in the decade 286 were arrested in a single day.[41] Much of the cause of this high rate of arrests was attributable, as it had been before when Lanyon had first taken office, to the greater activities of the police rather than to any increase in crime.

Most of the arrests, as Table 2.2 reveals, were for relatively minor crimes: transgressions against the various laws that regulated black labor. While pass law offenses accounted for the single largest number of arrests, almost as many again were arrested under the categories of breach of the peace, municipal bylaws (generally relating to location regulations), committing a nuisance (usually urinating in public by blacks in a town that provided no public lavatories for them), and the other offenses listed in section II of the table. The penalties for these offenses were a considerable burden for those convicted: generally fines ranging from ten shillings to forty shillings (the latter well over the average weekly wage of a black worker) or the option of choosing a jail sentence of one week's to a month's hard labor.

Justice in the courts was generally summary for pass law offenders. They were arraigned in batches, sometimes containing up to fifty people, before the police magistrate, allowed to plead guilty, and sentenced *en bloc*. The superintendent of the Kimberley Gaol, who attended the court in his official capacity, reported that the longest trial he had witnessed had lasted no more than ten minutes.[42]

Table 2.2   Arrests by Crime 1875-1888

Crime	1875[a]	1876[a]	1882[b]	1884	1885	1886	1887	1888
Section I: Pass offenses								
Loitering without a pass	95	971	658	5337	6325	6274	6071	4105
Loitering without a special pass				819	229	127	94	189
Loitering after hours				54	47	136	–	148
Subtotal	95	971	658	6210	6601	6537	6165	4442
As a % of total arrests	6.2	24.2	32.7	43.9	40.7	39.9	41.4	32.8
Section II: Other offenses mainly relating to black labor								
Breach of the peace	246	386	135	300	298	–	–	–
Bylaws, municip.	–	–	25	560	817	950	554	654
Committing a nuisance	80	150	–	637	466	179	304	–
Desertion	174	300	–	402	–	–	–	–
Drunk	83	320	324	2248	2110	2488	2585	3287
Masters and servants	–	–	–	67	507	399	277	207
Neglect of duty to master	99	257	–	565	1245	1133	534	421
Searching regulations	–	–	–	59	108	124	161	132
Vagrancy	–	–	–	–	–	–	–	–
Subtotal	682	1413	484	4838	5551	5273	4415	4701
As a % of total arrests	44.6	35.2	24.0	34.2	34.2	32.2	29.6	34.7
Section III: Other offenses								
Assault	153	256	136	702	672	815	699	727
Murder	3	4	7	17	38	42	–	27
Theft	233	376	144	969	1324	1172	1093	1050
IDB related	66	105	43	203	244	206	181	202
Miscellaneous	295	882	540	1205	1784	2314	2333	2371
Subtotal	750	1623	870	3096	4062	4549	4306	4383
As a % of total arrests	49.1	40.5	43.2	21.8	25.0	27.8	28.9	32.4

a. First six months only.
b. First two months only.
SOURCES: GLW 93(2770); CO 3575, 3606, 3631; CGHPP, G 77 1882, G 12 1885.

The summary processing by the Police Magistrates Court resulted in a high rate of convictions. In 1882, 76 percent of all cases brought before the court resulted in conviction. The Kimberley Magistrates Court, by contrast, had a conviction rate of only 23 percent. In addition, the number discharged without conviction by all the courts in Kimberley was declining: from 35.5 percent of all cases in 1875 to 22.8 percent in 1882.[43] Essentially, enforcing summary punishment against those who were suspected of being recalcitrant workers, the courts acted as an adjunct to the employers.

Yet the severe application of state power in 1882 could not alone provide a complete system of labor control for much the same reason that it had failed in the past: many employers, competing desperately against each other for the same black workers, evaded the regulations and encouraged men to desert to their operations. Indeed, an attempt by a number of companies to collectively lower wages in late 1882 completely failed when other companies refused to participate.[44] After all, the small companies could not afford to put their labor supply at risk while those companies that worked at greater, and therefore more dangerous, depths also had problems in getting workers.[45] Black wages continued to rise rather than fall. And IDB, in the eyes of the mining capitalists, remained as prevalent as ever, although the only proof of this continuance was the limited number of arrests for illicit dealing that proved, according to those same mining capitalists that the law was ineffective rather than that the problem was less than what they had claimed. In sum, the expansion of state activity had largely failed by the end of 1882 to solve the problems of IDB and of the cost, supply, and disciplining of the black labor force.

The collapse of the European diamond market in late 1882, and the consequent fall in the price of diamonds, accelerated changes in the organization of the diamond industry. The dramatic fall in receipts from diamond sales — by 16 percent in the De Beers mine, 25 percent in Kimberley, and 36 percent in Dutoitspan and Bultfontein — sent most of the smaller companies into bankruptcy by 1883 and left the larger companies even more dominant than they had been before.[46] The De Beers and Kimberley Central companies, along with a number of other large operations, not only survived the crash but used their financial resources to buy up the properties of their ailing former competitors.

The structure of the black workforce also changed dramatically between 1882 and 1883. With fewer companies in operation and those still working cutting production, the average number of black men employed in the diamond industry in 1883 had fallen to half what it had been in 1881 (Table 2.3). Moreover, the composition of the black workforce changed with men who recontracted comprising a far larger proportion than they ad in the past. This change in composition did not reflect a lack of new workers but rather a preference on the part of employers for men who had already worked in the mines, learned some skills, and were amenable to the disciplinary demands of industrial labor. Thus, labor shortage was replaced by a relative, although still limited, labor surplus.

The conjunction of changes in the structure of the diamond industry and the black workforce, together with declining receipts and the continuing high cost of labor with regard to working expenses (running at 25 percent to 40 percent in 1882) led mining capitalists to mount another offensive against labor. This offensive, backed up by the state, took two forms: the establishment of a system of strip searching of black workers (and partial inspection of whites) in 1883, and the introduction of closed compounds in 1885.

The searching system, enacted into legislation by a proclamation of the governor of the Cape in early 1883, followed the recommendations made by mining men (especially George Bottomley and J. B. Robinson) for a set of rules "to establish a system of search in and around the Mines . . . with a view to the better control of the Native Population generally."[47] All workers below the rank of manager had to enter and exit the mines through a limited number of guarded entryways each with a search house (with separate ones for black and white workers.) Blacks had to strip naked each time and be prepared to undergo intimate and degrading body searches. Whites did not have to take off their clothes and only had to undergo a limited visual inspection. The search system was intended to eliminate theft by keeping all unauthorized people out of the mines and preventing anyone from exiting with diamonds concealed on his person, and to discipline the workers to the time requirements of their employers by making them enter the mines through the search houses at the same time and preventing them from leaving the mine at any time that they were not permitted to do so by their employer.

However, even with a relative labor surplus and a greater sense of cohesion among the large companies, the scheme did not succeed to the extent that its promoters wished. It was physically impossible for the limited number of searchers whom the employers hired to search

Table 2.3   Composition of the Black Workforce, 1881-1885

	1881	1882	1883	1884	1885
Average number of black workers, all mines	17,000	11,920	8,360	9,000	11,300
Kimberley and De Beers mines					
(1) New hands as a % of contracts	26.1	16.8	9.4	18.5	(16.6)
(2) Old hands as a % of contracts	73.9	83.2	90.6	81.5	(83.4)
Dutoitspan and Bultfontein mines					
(1) New hands as a % of contracts	40.8	42.4	(9.9)	(7.7)	(13.8)
(2) Old hands as a % of contracts	59.2	57.6	(90.1)	(92.3)	(86.2)

NOTE: Percentages in parentheses are estimates based on part-year returns.
SOURCES: CGHPP, G 33 1882, G 8 and G 34 1883, G 11 1890; NA 195, 198, 202, CA.

12,000 black workers twice a day (on leaving the mine for lunch and at the end of the work day). Nor did all the companies force the workers to wear the sack that had been earlier agreed upon as the common uniform for all black laborers. Indeed, some companies allowed their men a choice of uniforms — the most popular being flour bags — in an attempt to prevent disgruntled employees from deserting and to attract workers from other companies to work for them (Daily Independent, 2 March 1883).

Very few diamonds were ever found in the searching houses even though they were in operation throughout the rest of 1883 and into the mid 1880s.[48] Indeed, in late 1883 and early 1884, mining capitalists extended the practical requirements of the regulations in regard to white workers in a successful attempt to break the power of white labor oganization at the diamond fields and subject all workers, irrespective of race, to various levels of control.

Buoyed by their success in the struggle with white workers, mining capitalists in 1884 contemplated the introduction of a further measure of labor control for black workers: closed compounds.[49] By then, most companies already housed their black employees in compounds on their properties. The men, however, were free to come and go after working hours and to make their own way to and from work. On occasion companies would request the police to discipline their workers, as the French Company did in October 1883 when it asked the police to go to its compound and arrest the men there for being late for work, but such measures could never be carried out in a thorough and consistent manner (Daily Independent, 12 October 1883). Closed compounding, which promised total control over black workers through their incarceration in fenced and guarded institutions, seemed the ideal system to prevent theft and to discipline labor.

The government inspector of diamond mines argued in his annual report for 1884 that all workers should be compounded, although whites should be in "small detached cottages with gardens . . . and . . . a central mess and reading room" rather than barracks. All workers would be physically separated from the rest of society, and from each other, and would be thoroughly searched before being allowed to leave their confinement. The greatest benefits of compounding, he believed, lay in the regulation and discipline it would allow to be exercised on a day-to-day basis in the mines (Cape of Good Hope Parliamentary Papers, G 28 1885: 12).

> By establishing a regular chain of responsibility among the employees in dividing the Kafirs into nominal squads and placing each squad under a particular overseer, so many overseers under the direct control of a particular sub-manager or foreman, and all under the manager of the claims or floor respectively, a most thorough control or supervision of all their [employers'] servants would be provided.

> The squads of Kafirs could be marched to and from the mines or floors by their overseers in charge, who would also look after them at work, search them as necessary, and be responsible to the sub-manager or foreman for their presence and conduct at work and for their general well-being; the managers or foremen being in turn responsible to their own managers and those to the Company or employer.

In short, the mining industry should be thoroughly self-contained.

Four factors largely explain the great support among mining capitalists in 1884 for the introduction of a system of closed compounding. First, as mentioned above, the searching system had apparently failed to eliminate IDB. Second, three of the largest companies in the mines — the De Beers, Kimberley Central, and French — were moving over to deep-level mining. This type of production, with its sophisticated technology and large capital investment, required a regular and disciplined supply of labor so that the machinery could be worked efficiently and to capacity. Third, labor was then in a relatively weak position. White labor organization had been effectively broken by a combination of industry and state power in May when six white workers had been shot to death by company employees. With regard to black labor, the chairman of the European Diamond Company summed up the situation when he suggested that dealing with blacks was essentially "a question of supply and demand" and if the supply was plentiful, or at least adequate (as it was), then "you can do what you like with your boys" (Daily Independent, 21 October 1884). Fourth, by late 1884, the Kimberley and De Beers mines, the two most important mines on the fields, were under the complete control of the Kimberley, De Beers, and French companies. So long as these companies could agree to work together in introducing a new system of labor control they could ensure its successful implementation through the dominance they had over the labor market. There were few operations in Kimberley that these companies, or others that supported them, did not control and thus they had a virtual monopoly over the job market.

These three companies, along with a number of others, established closed compounds for their black workers in 1885. In January, the French Company placed 110 black laborers in a set of barracks, which they were not permitted to leave, except to go to work, for the duration of their six-month contracts. The Kimberley Central followed two months later with a compound for 400 employees and later in the year compounds were built by the De Beers and the Bultfontein Mining companies.[50]

Throughout 1883, 1884, and 1885 the state gave considerable support to the mining capitalists in their attempts to subject black workers to more restrictive controls. In June 1884, the Kimberley Commissioner of Police wrote to the men who managed the Dutoitspan Mine that he wanted to do "all in [his] power to assist the Mining Interest" and suggested that to eliminate the problem of Monday morning absenteeism, each company appoint an overseer "to accompany constables [to the locations] and point out . . . boys [absent from work], and have them arrested for . . . Neglecting their Master's Work."[51] Reference back to Table 2.1 shows the extent of the police's energy with the greatest number of arrests being made between 1883 and 1887, years when the laboring population was considerably smaller than it had been in the earlier period. Table 2.2 shows that the percentage of arrests for offenses mainly relating to black labor (sections I and II) increased from 57 percent of total arrests in 1882 to 78 percent in 1884 and then hovered around 70 percent for the next three years. The conviction rate also increased during the same period, with a 15 percent jump between 1882 and 1883 and a further rise over subsequent years.

By the end of 1885, state and capital had established an extensive system of labor control. Black workers were subjected to a mesh of criminal laws and a maze of institutional controls; for, along with the closed compounds, the jail remained a primary agent of worker control; locations were still strictly controlled; and in 1884 the De Beers Mining Company, in conjunction with the state, established a convict station to provide a constant supply of very thoroughly regulated black labor — whose often contradictory nature was well described by one visitor to Kimberley in 1885 (Farini, 1886: 27-28).

> The Kaffir cannot understand the mixed treatment to which he is subjected. Those interested in encouraging the illicit diamond-trade employ him as a purveyor of stolen goods. Those interested in putting down the illegal traffic employ him as a spy [or trap] to get innocent people convicted. And yet if a Kaffir happens to come into town looking for work, and knowing nothing of the white man's laws innocently enters the streets "naked, and not ashamed", he is immediately arrested and "fined" [then imprisoned for a month or two because he has no money and, when let out, if he does not find a master the same day, arrested again, this time as a vagrant, and put back in gaol for a day or two] . . . The poor wretch is bewildered, and falls violently in love with the white man and his customs, and takes care to get somebody to give him a piece of paper certifying that he is in a situation. He then goes to seek for some Kaffir friends of his at the mines, and finds his way into a compound. Arrested for being there without permission, or with "unlawful intent", he is charged, fined and eventually gravitates again to prison. Having served his time he will probably return to his "master", but finds that he has been away "without leave" for a week, his "occupation gone" and the joyous round of the police-station, court-house, and prisoner's cell begin once more.

This description exaggerates the passive and uncomprehending nature of black reactions to the institutions and controls with which they came into contact, since many black workers could and did take advantage of the situation of labor shortage to exercise a certain amount of control over their conditions of employment. Nevertheless, it does convey the extent to which regulation of every aspect of a worker's behavior had been achieved by the mid-1880s.[52]

CONCLUSION

Law in Kimberley was as much concerned with authority as with property. White diggers and mining capitalists, at different times but often in similar ways, sought the assistance of the state and its legal apparatus to acquire a monopoly in the ownership of claims and diamonds and a battery of laws enforced by the police and the courts to discipline their black workers. This assistance was increasingly forthcoming as the state acquired a greater stake in the profitability of the diamond industry and as mining capitalists secured a more influential role in government. Although the laws were not racially discriminatory in their language, they were enforced in a discriminatory manner reflecting the racial division of property ownership and classes in Kimberley. Moreover, the law had an important ideological function sanctioning this division. The very extent of the legislation, with its all-encompassing regulation of black behavior, reinforced as it was by popularly accepted beliefs in the white community, essentially had the effect of equating blacks with criminals.

Yet to return to E. P. Thompson's caution — that the law has a life and logic of its own and should not be seen as a mere tool of one class — this essay has shown the difficulties inherent in any attempt to use the law as a means of control by one class over another. Indeed, Kimberley was in such a state of flux during the decade and a half under discussion that there was no one ruling class throughout this period, nor did the state have an unchanging form. Thus the law could not be used simply as a repressive tool, not only because of black worker resistance, but also because there was no common agreement among the whites about what policies should be pursued. This lack of agreement resulted in the passage of laws that could not be enforced to the full extent the legislation provided. Obviously, arbitrary harassment was an important ingredient in the rule of law in Kimberley, but it was not effective enough to secure the goals of those who came to dominate the industry. It was only with changes in the structure of the industry in the mid-1880s that mining capitalists were able to introduce private forms of control, sanctioned by legislation and enforced by the police and courts, and so finally established their authority over their workers. The laws and the compounds, the passes and the jails, would long remain in Kimberley. By defining the African worker as a criminal, capital and the state ensured that only institutions built to control criminals could control workers.

NOTES

1. Commissioners to Colonial Secretary, Cape Town, 22 February 1872, Government House Archives (GH) 12/1, Cape Archives (CA).

2. *Diamond Field,* 4 July 1872; *Diamond News,* 5 December 1872, 15 February 1873.

3. Sir Richard Southey to Sir Henry Barkly, 26 April 1873, Griqualand West Archive (GLW) 180, CA.

4. *Diamond News,* 19 June, 3 July 1872; *Diamond Field,* 4 July 1872.

5. "Memorial of Residents of Colesburg Kopje (Kimberley)", 23 February 1872, enclosure to Commissioners to Colonial Secretary, 20 March 1872, GH 12/1, CA.

6. *Statute Law of Griqualand West* (Cape Town, 1882), pp. 63-64.

7. Ibid., pp. 26-32, Proclamation 14, August 1872.

8. For example, in December 1872 between 1100 and 1500 departing laborers were stopped and checked for exit passes. The 275 men who did not possess that document were brought back to the Registry Office so that officials could check that they had fulfilled their contracts. Most had not, for 250 were fined 2/6 each and another 18 received six lashes each as well. Registrar (W. Coleman) to Government Secretary (J. Currey), 4 March 1873, GLW 71, CA; *Diamond Field,* 9 January 1873; *Cape Argus,* 14 January 1873.

9. Sergeant Bradshaw to Secretary to Government, 27 October 1874, GH 12/4, CA; Criminal Record Books, January 1872-19 February 1873, Kimberley Magistrates Archive (1/KIM) ADD1/1/2/1, ADD1/1/2/2, CA. Imprisonment as a punishment was generally restricted to whites.

10. See statement of W. Coleman (Registrar of Contracted Servants), 29 July 1874, 22 and 24 February 1875, and that of J. E. Howse (Registrar, Dutoitspan), 24 February 1875, GLW 20, CA.

11. See the letters of the Registrar to the Government Secretary of 12 and 18 December 1874, GLW 71, CA. On 13 January 1875, the *Diamond Field* referred to registration as a "farce."

12. Registrar to Government Secretary, 18 November 1874, GLW 55, CA; *Diamond Field,* 7, 14 and 28 November 1874.

13. "Report of Lieut.-Colonel Crossman, R. E., on the Affairs of Griqua-Land West," June 1876, Colonial Office Confidential Print African No. 96; *Diamond News,* 24 April 1877, 4 May 1878, 10 July 1879.

14. Lanyon to Barkly, 25 June 1877, GH 12/8, CA. However, there were divisions within the state on the issue of labor regulation for, while Lanyon supported the introduction of racially discriminatory legislation (Ordinance 10 of 1876) the Colonial

Office again disallowed his proposals, as they had done those of the commissioners in 1872, with the argument that the law should not discriminate between British citizens (including blacks from the Cape) on the basis of their color.

15. "Report of the Griqualand Labour Question," Government Notice 102 (1876), enclosure in Lanyon to Barkly, 1 June 1876, GH 12/7, CA.

16. *Daily Independent,* 29 June 1876. The lower wage figures included accommodation as well.

17. *Diamond News,* 15, 18, 20, 29 July, 3, 8, & 24 August 1876.

18. H. Green to Lanyon, 2 May 1876, Lanyon to Percy (Inspector of Police), 16 May 1876, and reply of Percy, 17 May, GLW 87(1524), CA. J. Stanton, the man who had flogged his servant to death in 1872, also complained at the same time as Green about the nonregistration of laborers, Coleman to Percy, 3 May 1876, GLW 86, CA.

19. Percy to Chief Clerk, 15 September 1876, GLW 93(2770); Lanyon to Barkly, 26 February 1876, GH 29/1 Enc. 38; Barkly to the Secretary of State, 9 February 1876, and Barkly to Carnarvon, 10 April 1876, GH 25/1; Lanyon to Barkly, 15 June 1876, GH 29/2 Enc. 64, CA.

20. Colonial Secretary to Inspector of Police, 7 January 1876, GLW 80, CA. The only exceptions to the law were to be restricted to those blacks who held claim, debris, or cart licenses.

21. Most of these arrests took place in May and June at the same time as the employers were attempting to lower wages. "General Summary of Offences committed at Kimberley and tried at the Resident Magistrates Court during the half year ending 30th June 1875", and same for the half year ending 30th June 1876, enclosure in Percy to Chief Clerk, 15 September 1876, GLW 93(2770), CA.

22. Percy to Chief Clerk, 15 September 1876, GLW 93(2770), CA; *Diamond News,* 21 September 1876.

23. My thanks to Charles van Onselen for suggesting these points.

24. Criminal Record Book, Kimberley Magistrates Court, 1879, 1/KIM ADD1/1/2/27; Criminal Record Book, Police Magistrates Court, 1879, 1/KIM ADD2/1/2/3, CA.

25. *Diamond News,* 13 April 1876, 11 January 1877; *Daily Independent,* 13, 15, 18, 24 and 25 September 1880.

26. See the issues of the *Daily Independent* referred to in the previous note, and the *Diamond News,* 27 September 1877.

27. For further discussion of the drawbacks of police actions see George Champion to W. H. Ravenscroft (acting Government Secretary), 6 March 1877, and note attached by R. Scholtz, 20 March 1877, GLW 101(675); W. H. Bevan (Vicar) to Administrator, 28 January 1878, and reply of the Colonial Secretary, 9 February 1878, GLW 114(165); Coleman to acting Colonial Secretary, 17 April 1877, GLW 102(947), and 29 November 1877, GLW 111(2766), CA.

28. Coleman to acting Colonial Secretary, 28 August, 13 September 1877, GLW 107(1958), 108(2126), CA.

29. Lanyon to Bartle Frere, 14 September 1877, GLW 9(139); W. Coleman, "Minute on the "Protector of Natives" and "Native Registry Office" for the information of His Honour the Acting Administrator," 18 September 1880, GLW 163(2654), CA.

30. For these and other cases see the "Return of all cases tried in the Court of the Police Magistrate and defended by the Protector of Natives during the month of October 1879," GLW 147, CA.

31. See, for example, the *Daily Independent,* 29 June 1876, 2 May 1878, and the *Diamond News,* 17 July 1877, 7 May 1878, 9 December 1879, 3 April 1880.

32. "Bye-Laws of the Kimberley Town Council," 1878, Section VII Native Locations, GH 10/14, CA. For details on the actions of the Superintendent see the *Daily Independent,* 10 June, 15 July, 3 September and 28 October 1881. For complaints of idlers and vagrants see the same newspaper, 15 July and 23 September 1881.

33. "Articles of Association of the Griqualand West Diamond Mining Company Dutoitspan Mine Limited", 24 September 1880, Deeds Office Kimberley Archive (DOK) 3/4; "Articles of Association of the De Beers Mining Company Limited", 28 April 1880, DOK 3/2; "Articles of Association of the Kimberley Central Diamond Mining Company Limited", October 1881, DOK 3/5, CA.

34. *Daily Independent,* 19 February 1881. Two other men, neither of them with extensive financial interests in the industry, were also elected.

35. Cecil Rhodes chaired the "Select Committee on Illicit Diamond Buying in Griqualand West," while Robinson and another Kimberley parliamentarian were also members.

36. Evidence of H.J. Feltham (quoted), S. Marks, and Francis Baring-Gould, "Report of the Select Committee on Illicit Diamond Buying in Griqualand West", *Cape of Good Hope Parliamentary Papers (CGHPP),* A 9 1882, pp. 3, 6-8, 12, 20, 105. Marks, in fact, had his contracted labor work naked, pp. 20, 22, 24, 30, 31. For public comments on the problem of IDB see the *Daily Independent,* 16 February, 18 June, 1 and 15 July, 18 and 22 August, 1 and 4 October, 12, 16, and 23 November 1881, and 2 February, 10, 13, 14, 15, 21 and 27 April, 8 and 10 May, 20 July and 5 August 1882. The committee report is in Cape of Good Hope Parliamentary Papers (CGHPP). A 9 1882, pp. iii-iv. See also Act 48 of 1882.

37. Act 48 of 1882.

38. The police force reforms were based on suggestions made by an officer brought from Scotland Yard and sanctioned by the Cape Governor in 1882. "Reports on the Kimberley Police and Detective Department by Bernard V. Shaw", CGHPP, G 77 1882, pp. 7, 9, 15, 20-26. Detectives had been employed by the police since 1874 but this was the first time that a completely separate force was established. Shaw also reported on the Kimberley jail and the Cape Town police during his trip to South Africa. On the implementation of his recommendations, see "Report by Commissioners of Police for 1882", CGHPP, G 100 1883, p. 27. For later years see the following reports, G 51 1884, G 12 1885, G 11 1886, G 7 1887.

39. For a discussion of trapping practices see the memorandum of Captain Harrel, 30 November 1880, Colonial Office Archive (CO) 3344(98), CA.

40. The figures for the English cities are based on arrest statistics for 1881, the Cape Town figure on 1884 returns, "Report by Commissioners of Police for 1884," CGHPP, G 12 1885, p. 11. The 1882 figure is an estimate based on calculations from the inadequate data available for arrests during that year, see CGHPP, G 77 1882. In 1884, the arrest rate per officer was 114 persons while in 1886 it was 163. See CGHPP, G 12 1885, p. 29 and the *Daily Independent,* 15 February 1887. It is difficult to compare population size. Manchester had 354,000 inhabitants in 1884, Cape Town approximately 80,000. Kimberley, by contrast, had a population of only 20,000 (of whom about half were black) at any one time but had a constant procession of blacks moving into and out of the town as they sought work and completed their contracts. Therefore the population comparison has been based on the police's own estimate of the number of people they had to deal with — 70,000.

41. For details on police and court practices see the "Report of the Committee on Convicts and Gaols", CGHPP, G 2 1888, passim.

42. Ibid., pp. ii, 3.

43. See the documents referred to in Note 40 and see CGHPP, G 77 1882, pp. 17-19.

44. *Daily Independent,* 28 August 1882. For details on the scheme see A. W. Davis to Directors of the Eagle Diamond Mining Company of De Beers Limited, 18 August 1882, Company Records found in the High Court, Kimberley (CR) 6/4, CA. Similar schemes had failed in late 1881 and early 1882. See the *Daily Independent,* 10 October, 23 and 28 November 1881, 11 February 1882, and *The Griqualand West Investor's Guardian and Commerical Register,* 24 November and 1 December 1881.

45. For a discussion of the problems of different companies see the *Daily Independent,* 29 August 1882.

46. Board for the Protection of Mining Interests, *Returns . . . Imports . . . Exports . . . and Production of Diamonds . . . 1882-85* (Kimberley, 1886).

47. Proclamation 1, 1883. For Bottomley's role see the "Report of the Joint-Committee . . . and Draft of Searching Rules and Regulations," Kimberley, 19 May 1882, Smalberger Papers, University of Cape Town. For Robinson's role see the *Daily Independent,* 10 January 1883.

48. For complaints of lack of finds see the *Daily Independent,* 1, 10, 12, 21 and 23 October 1884.

49. The introduction of compounds had been widely discussed in 1882. See the reports of Inspector Shaw referred to earlier and CGHPP, A 9 1882.

50. *Daily Independent,* 27, 28 April, 7 September 1885; "Report of the Inspector of Diamond Mines for 1885", CGHPP, G 40 1886, p. 19; Smalberger, 1974: 411.

51. E. Christian to the Secretary of the Dutoitspan Mining Board, 20 June 1884, Letters Received November 1883-November 1884, Dutoitspan Mining Board Archive, De Beers Consolidated Mines Archive. The policy was effectively carried out. In one instance in February 1885, 297 men were arrested at the Bultfontein Location for having passes but not being at work (*Daily Independent,* 24 February 1885).

52. This is not to suggest that worker resistance ended with the introduction of closed compounds (see Worger, 1982).

REFERENCES

Much of the primary documentation in this essay is derived from records in Cape Archives, Cape Town. The most relevant material was contained in the following collections: Colonial Office (CO), Company Records Kimberley (CR), Deeds Office Kimberley (DOK), Government House (GH), Griqualand West (GLW), and Kimberley Magistrate (1/KIM). In addition, the De Beers Consolidated Mines Limited Archive at Kimberley held some relevant documents while the John Smalberger Papers in the University of Cape Town contained photocopied records from various sources.

ALGAR, F. (1872) The Diamond Fields: With notes on the Cape Colony and Natal. London.

Anon (1882) Statute Law of Grigualand West. Cape Town.

Board for the Protection of Mining Interests (1886) Returns . . . Imports . . . Exports . . . and Production of Diamonds . . . 1882-85. Kimberley.

BOYLE, F. (1873) To the Cape for Diamonds: A Story of Digging Experiences in South Africa. London: Chapman & Hall.

Cape Argus (1873) Cape Town.

Cape Monthly Magazine (1871) "The Diamond-fields from a Commercial Point of View."

——— (1870) "Two Days at the Diamond-fields, A Social Picture." Cape Town.

Cape of Good Hope Parliamentary Papers (1882) A 9, "Report of the Select Committee on Illicit Diamond Buying in Griqualand West."

——— (1882) G 77, "Reports on the Kimberley Police and Detective Department by Bernard V. Shaw."

——— (1883-1886) G 100(1883), G 51(1884), G 12(1885), G 11(1886), G 7(1887), "Report[s] by Commissioners of Police for . . . [1882-86]."

——— (1886) G 40, "Report of the Inspector of Diamond Mines for 1885."

——— (1888) G 2, "Report of the Committee on Convicts and Gaols."

CROSSMAN, R.E. (1876) "Report of Lieut.-Colonel Crossman, R.E., on the Affairs of Griqua-Land West," Colonial Office Confidential Print African No. 96.

Daily Independent (1876-1885) Kimberley.

DE KIEWIET, C.W. (1937) The Imperial Factor in South Africa. A Study in Politics and Economics. Cambridge: Cambridge University Press.

Diamond Field (1870-1871) Kimberley.

Diamond News (1872-1880) Kimberley.

DICEY, A.V. (1885) Lectures Introductory to the Study of the Law of the Constitution. London: Macmillan.

DUGARD, J. (1978) Human Rights and the South African Legal Order. Princeton: Princeton University Press.

FARINI, G. (1886) Through the Kalahari Desert. London: Sampson Low.

Griqualand West Investor's Guardian and Commercial Register (1881) Kimberley.

HAY, D. (1975) "Property, authority and the criminal law," pp. 17-63 in D. Hay et al. (eds.) Albion's Fatal Tree: Crime and Society in Eighteenth-Century England. New York: Pantheon.

MATTHEWS, A.S. (1972) Law, Order, and Liberty in South Africa. Berkeley: University of California Press.

ROBERTS, B. (1976) Kimberley: Turbulent City. Cape Town: D. Philip.

SMALBERGER, J.W. (1976) "The role of the diamond-mining industry in the development of the pass-law system in South Africa." International Journal of African Historical Studies 9, 3: 419-434.

——— (1974) "I.D.B. and the mining compound system in the 1880s." South African Journal of Economics 42, 4: 398-414.

SUTTON, I. B. (1979) "The Diggers' Revolt in Griqualand West, 1875." International Journal of African Historical Studies 12, 1: 40-61.

THOMPSON, E. P. (1975) Whigs and Hunters: The Origin of the Black Act. New York: Pantheon.

TURRELL, R. (1981) "The 1875 Black Flag Revolt on the Kimberley Diamond Fields." Journal of Southern African Studies 7, 2: 194-235.

WORGER, W. (1982) "The making of a monopoly: Kimberley and the South African diamond industry, 1870-95." Ph. D. dissertation, Yale University.

3

PRODUCTIVITY AND PROTEST
Scientific Management in the Ghanaian Gold Mines, 1947-1956

JEFF CRISP

Throughout the first half of the twentieth century, the profitability of mining companies in many parts of Africa was threatened by periodic shortages of labor. These companies, aided by colonial administrations, introduced a variety of labor recruitment strategies in an attempt to resolve this problem, and by the time of World War II, the mines were able to attract large numbers of workers. Getting those recruits to work hard and productively, however, was another question. Before the war, when wages remained very low, the mines were prepared to tolerate the inefficiency of the labor force. Now, as wages rose in response to unionization and collective action by the workers, the question of productivity became far more pressing. As this case study demonstrates, the efforts of mining capital to increase productivity through the reorganization of the labor process met with considerable success, but simultaneously they had the effect of reinforcing the growing militancy and solidarity of the workers.

Since the publication of Harry Braverman's *Labor and Monopoly Capital* in 1974, Marxist scholars have become increasingly in-

Author's Note: This chapter was first presented, in shortened form, to a conference of the African Studies Association (U.K.), Manchester, September 1980. Much of the data presented in this chapter are examined in more detail in Crisp (1980: 277-377).

terested in the nature of the capitalist labor process, the managerial strategies used to control and reorganize the labor process, and the implications of those strategies for the development of working-class consciousness and protest. In particular, this new body of literature has paid considerable attention to the subject of "scientific management," the set of productivity-boosting techniques devised and promulgated by the American engineer, F. W. Taylor, in the last two decades of the nineteenth century (Braverman, 1974: 85-138; Burawoy, 1978; Coombs, 1978; Elger, 1979; Palmer, 1975).

Scientific management, or "Taylorism" as it became popularly known, was designed to revolutionize levels of industrial productivity through the application of precise and scientifically determined criteria of efficiency to production processes, replacing individually and arbitrarily formulated standards of performance. In practice, this meant the introduction of a wide range of new techniques to the shop floor, including time study and work study, ergonomics, aptitude testing, planned preventive maintenance, and payment-by-results. Such techniques soon became a familiar feature of the industrial environment in North America, spreading in the early twentieth century to Western Europe and even to the Soviet Union, where Lenin was an eager advocate of Taylor's ideas. By 1923, Taylor's biographer was enthusiastically claiming that scientific management had "penetrated to every country where modern industry is established," and that "in these countries there is no person who has not in some degree been affected by it, however unconsciously" (Copley, 1923: xiii).

Much of the important and growing literature on the capitalist labor process has been flawed by two weaknesses. First, it is often pitched at an increasingly high level of abstraction, divorced from empirical examinations and lacking the clarity and humanism of Braverman's original work. Second, while Braverman has justifiably been criticized for his unwillingness to examine working-class responses to Taylorism (Burawoy, 1978: 276; Coombs, 1978: 82), very few authors have taken up the challenge to examine working-class perceptions and actions, empirically or theoretically. This chapter, which examines working-class responses to scientific management in the Ghanaian gold mines between 1947 and 1956, is intended to go some way toward a correction of these tendencies.

MINING CAPITAL IN CRISIS

Although Taylor's managerial strategies had been formulated in the 1880s and had gained international recognition in the interwar period, it was not until the 1950s that scientific management was first introduced to the Gold Coast mining industry. In order to explain the timing of this innovation, it is necessary to examine the acute set of problems confronting mining capital in that colony after World War II.

In the late 1940s, a serious crisis was encroaching upon the mining industry in the Gold Coast. Since the beginning of the decade, the profitability of the colony's British-owned gold mining companies had been eroded by a combination of rising working costs, increased levels of taxation, and a static gold price on the international bullion market. With the outbreak of war in Europe, confidence in the industry's future rapidly evaporated. Share prices slumped, investment fell sharply, and programs of capital expenditure designed to modernize the mines were either abandoned or held in abeyance. Worse was yet to come, for in an attempt to conserve stores and shipping space for the Allied military effort, in 1942 the metropolitan government ordered four of the colony's eleven producing gold mines to suspend their operations.

In 1945, the mines were allowed to resume full production, but there still appeared to be little prospect of arresting the steady decline of a once highly profitable industry. The mining companies had no control over the cost of imported stores and equipment, which continued to rise, yet they could do nothing to raise the selling price of their product. Before and during the war, the mining companies had expected to resolve this dilemma by using their considerable political influence within the metropolis to secure a substantial reduction in taxation levels. Now, with the election of a socialist government in Britain and the strengthening of anticolonial sentiments within the international political arena, even that hope had to be abandoned.

In the Gold Coast itself, mining capital was confronted with escalating labor costs, pushed up by apparently irresistable pressures. The rapidly rising cost of living during the war, coupled with the growing size and strength of the colony's nationalist and labor movements, forced the colonial government to grant wage rises to public employees. The mining industry, represented by the Gold Coast Chamber of Mines, had little option but to follow the government's lead, with the result that in the period 1940 to 1947, wage levels in the mines increased by between 30 percent and 46 percent.

Much to the consternation of mining capital, these increases did not satisfy the 37,000 mine workers, but simply whetted their appetite for further wage rises. In September 1947, the recently formed Mines' Employees' Union (MEU) threatened a general mines strike in support of a demand for a pay award comparable to one granted to public sector workers. The Chamber of Mines refused to take the threat seriously, and rejected the union's demands. As a result of its intransigence, the chamber precipitated a stoppage that halted production for 35 days, forced the mining companies to concede large wage rises and other costly benefits, and once again prevented the poorer, low-grade mines from implementing the investment programs they required to re-equip for expanded and more efficient production.

In the aftermath of the strike, the mining companies pressed the colonial government to introduce restrictive trade union legislation, but to their frustration and incomprehension, the government refused to do so. In September 1949, the leaders of the MEU, encouraged by the success of their strike and the liberal attitude of the government, submitted another large wage claim. Only a fortuitous rise in the price of gold allowed the Chamber of Mines to concede the demand and to avert the threat of a second crippling stoppage. This, not surprisingly, was to prove an expensive way of buying industrial peace, for it inevitably reinforced the mine workers' belief in the efficacy of the strike weapon, a weapon that was to be used to devastating effect throughout the next decade.

The MEU's successful campaign for higher wages had a major impact on the cost structure of the gold mining industry. Since the turn of the century, a plentiful supply of cheap, expendable migrant labor from the colony's Northern Territories and surrounding Francophone areas had allowed the Gold Coast mines to remain profitable in spite of the colony's low-grade ore deposits. Now, in the postwar period, the growing militancy of the mine workers was one result of the replacement of this cheap and transient labor force by one that was partially stabilized, that had higher expectations, greater solidarity, and an effective industrywide organization. Ironically, by ending their dependence on an irregular supply of transient labor, the mining companies had also eroded the traditional basis of their profitability.

Confronted with this dilemma, the mining companies had to look for an alternative means of reducing the labor component of the industry's total working costs. Their initial response to this challenge was to organize a new and more aggressive recruitment campaign in the Northern Territories, hoping that an influx of new migrant workers would create a labor surplus in the mining areas, forcing down wages and curtailing the bargaining power of the MEU. This scheme yielded few positive results, as the postwar boom in the Gold Coast had already generated a large demand for new workers, primarily in sectors of the economy offering higher wages and far better working conditions than the mines could hope to provide. Thus, by 1950, the mining companies discovered that they were actually confronted with a net loss of labor to other employers.

With the failure of the recruitment scheme, mining capital reluctantly recognized its inability to control the three principal determinants of the industry's profitability: wage levels, the cost of stores and equipment, and the price of gold. It had, therefore, to seek an entirely new solution, one that could be pursued independently of the international bullion market, the suppliers of stores, the metropolitan and colonial governments, and the MEU. Only one strategy for survival appeared to meet these stringent qualifications, and that was "to counteract the rising spiral of costs by means of increased productivity . . . and the elimination of waste in all its forms."[1]

The mine managers' experience over the previous decade had convinced them that there was ample scope for improvement in these aspects of the industry's operations. During the war, workers in the mines had responded to the declining purchasing power of their wages by reducing their effort and restricting their output. As a result, the tonnage of rock excavated per underground employee had slumped by 43 percent. As the mine manager at Ashanti Goldfields complained, "the African's attitude to his work is changing and he is no longer prepared to put his back into it as formerly."[2] This problem was not peculiar to the gold mining industry, nor indeed to the Gold Coast, for it was an essential feature of a labor crisis that prevailed throughout the African colonies at this time, and that, according to Cooper, derived from "the rising cost of reproducing urban labour in an era of expanding commodity production and rising prices, which both preceded and followed the special burdens of World War II" (Cooper, 1981: 312). Managerial and governmental responses to this crisis varied in detail, but not in purpose, which was to compensate for rising labor costs by increasing the productivity of the African labor force. In Kenya, for example, the 1947 Mombasa general strike was quickly followed by C. H. Northcott's "African Labour Efficiency Survey," and the decasualization of the dock labor force (Clayton and Savage, 1974: 313-328; Kitching, 1980: 379-388). In Zambia, the copper mines responded to the crisis by introducing a policy of labor stabilization, and by replacing expensive expatriate personnel with skilled local workers.[3] In West Africa, the Gold Coast government commissioned the "Enquiry into the Productivity, Supervision, and Control of Labor," while the Seers-Ross "Report on Financial and Physical Problems of Development in the Gold Coast" recommended a range of solutions, including the intensification of labor supervision, the introduction of task work, and the retrenchment of inefficient workers.[4]

In the gold mines, the postwar managerial responses to the problems of rising wages and declining productivity included mechanization; the use of more efficient mine layouts, tools, and techniques; the introduction of more European supervisors; and experimentation with more generous bonus schemes for African workers. These initial efforts to boost productivity between 1947 and 1950 met with considerable success, reversing the downward trend in per capita output, and stabilizing the labor component of total working costs. The mine managers had little doubt that further progress could be made, and it was at this stage that the mine managers, lacking the time, knowledge, and experience to effect the required improvement themselves, responded to the crisis by seeking the assistance of professional consultants who specialized in the application of Taylorist principles to industrial production processes.

THE INTRODUCTION OF SCIENTIFIC MANAGEMENT

Scientific management made a relatively late appearance in the world of gold mining. In the early years of the twentieth century, scientific management had been introduced with some success to coal mining in America and Europe, but its application to the less regular and repetitive operations involved in the mining of gold was not considered seriously until the 1940s, when severe labor shortages began to threaten the profit margins of mining companies in South

Africa and Southern Rhodesia. In 1943, a Transvaal mine manager, J. S. Ford, published the Taylorist handbook, *Underground Management* (Ford, 1943), which quickly became the bible of the South African mining fraternity. Two years later, an observer reported that "the expression 'scientific management' has almost become a catch phrase on the mines of the Rand" (Heywood, 1945: 959). These developments had not gone entirely unnoticed in the Gold Coast mines, which had always drawn a substantial proportion of their supervisory and managerial personnel from the mines of Southern Africa. In the aftermath of the 1947 general mines strike, representatives of the Chamber of Mines had travelled to South Africa to discuss the latest developments in "manpower efficiency," and in 1948, E. Kirkman, Native Relations Officer of New Consolidated Goldfields, had visited the Gold Coast and produced a report on the "supply, distribution, efficiency, and administration" of labor in the mines.[5] Encouraged by some successful experiments with the new techniques, in 1950 the majority of the Gold Coast mining companies contracted management consultants from South Africa and Southern Rhodesia to undertake a systematic examination and reorganization of their operations.

The consultants' investigations quickly identified the factors reducing productivity in the Gold Coast mines to a level only half of that achieved in the mines of Southern Africa. According to Rhodesian consultants Somerset and Fraser (1958: 287), labor in the Gold Coast was "periodically in acutely short supply," and the mine workers' trade union "had at times been difficult."[6] The workers themselves were "the most inefficient in the world."[7] They were "not well disciplined, well trained, nor of a physically high standard." Overmanning was rife, and gold stealing was "an occupational disease for which no certain cure has been devised" (Allen, 1957: 522). Employees refused to be transferred from one task to another, and worked at a self-determined rate that was well below their full potential. Thus one mine manager complained about his machine crews: "16 holes is not a standard laid down by the mine, but appears to be considered by the workers as a fair days work . . . 16 holes of the average depth required occupies approximately half a shift under normal conditions."[8] Corrective measures proved useless, since the men were "quick to resent efforts to improve their performance — the usual reaction being a simple refusal to accept changed conditions."[9] Absenteeism rates of between 15 percent and 25 percent, and labor turnover rates of 80 percent to 90 percent were described as "abnormal" and as reflecting the workers' "indifference to the obligations of employment."[10] According to one expatriate miner:

> Labour moves from mine to mine, or from mine to other work just for the sake of a change. Some will chop and change jobs under assumed names at the same mine. Two tribesmen will often work alternate days, or work on the same ticket. Some prefer to work two days out of three, some will lay off for three or four months, and so on.[11]

These obstacles to efficient production were reinforced by the "notoriously backward" character of management in the Gold Coast mines. European supervision in the mines was "extremely dilute because of the difficulty of attracting good men to the tropics." The Europeans who were prepared to work in the Gold Coast were "lacking in knowledge of Africans and unused to supervising men," and were therefore guilty of "laxity and lack of control."[12] The political environment in West Africa made the situation worse, since "labour was not compounded as elsewhere in Africa, and consequently neither feeding nor attendance could be controlled." Indeed, the politicolegal apparatus for the control of labor in the Gold Coast, was in every respect less extensive, less rigorous, and therefore less effective than the one which the mining companies of South Africa had at their disposal.

Finally, the consultants believed that management in the Gold Coast had unacceptably low expectations of the labor force. Thus "it was considered that the West African native could not be taught in the comparatively short time he was on the mine to carry out carefully planned standard instructions," and it was believed that he would not respond to incentive payments and bonus schemes. This was not an entirely unreasonable assumption, since a quarter of the mine workers eligible to earn bonuses regularly failed to do so on account of their low output and high levels of absenteeism. As the Chamber of Mines complained, "the mining industry would like the African employees to place on increased wages a value similar to that they place on the extra leisure gained from task work."[13]

With their experience in the more efficient and cost-conscious mines of Southern Africa, it was not surprising that consultants such as Somerset and Fraser should have been alarmed by the conditions they discovered on the Gold Coast. Nevertheless, "the initial reaction of the survey . . . was that these obstacles could be overcome, at least sufficiently to justify the cost involved". Before going on to describe precisely how the consultants attempted to remove these obstacles, their diagnosis of the mining industry's poor performance can be located within a Marxist analysis of the capitalist labor process.

SCIENTIFIC MANAGEMENT AND THE LABOR PROCESS

According to Marx, capitalists have one "determining, dominating, and deciding purpose," and that is "the creation of surplus value" (Marx, 1976: 990). To achieve this objective, capitalists must do three things. They must use their capital to purchase "subjects of labor," or raw and processed materials; they must purchase "instruments of labor or tools and equipment; and they must purchase "labor power," or the human capacity for work, and use it to apply the instruments of labor to the subject of labor. The capitalists have now initiated what Marx calls a "labor process," the product of which is "use values," or goods capable of satisfying human needs and desires.

Capitalists, however, are not interested in the labor process or use values per se. They are only interested in use values insofar as they have an "exchange value," and they are only interested in the labor process insofar as it can be transformed into a "valorization process." By this, Marx meant that the real concern of capitalists is to extend the labor process beyond the point at which the exchange value of the goods produced exceeds the cost of the labor power used to produce them. Once this point has been reached, valorization, or the creation of surplus value, can commence.

Even at this point, capitalists are not fully satisfied. Because capitalists have an inherent tendency to accumulate wealth, and because they must compete against other capitalists, their aim is not simply to create surplus value, but to *maximize* it. However, as Lazonick has suggested (1978: 3), the maximization of surplus value is obstructed by two factors: by "objective" factors, such as the physical and mental limitations of the workers employed and the level of technology and science available; and by a "subjective" factor in the form of the workers' ability to restrict the quantity and quality of the labor power they provide.

When capitalists purchase labor power, they are buying only a potential for work, and to maximize the amount of surplus value created they must realize the full potential of the labor power at their disposal. This is not just a technical problem, because as Marx explains, the interests of labor and capital are antagonistic, and that clash of interests gives rise to a struggle between the two classes that is fought out within the labor process itself:

> The directing motive, the end and aim of capitalist production, is to extract the greatest possible amount of surplus value, and consequently to exploit labour power to the greatest possible extent. As the number of cooperating labourers increases, so too does their resistance to the domination of capital, and with it, the necessity to overcome this resistance by counterpressure. The control exercised by the capitalist is not only a special function, due to the nature of the social-labour process . . . but is at the same time, a function of the exploitation of a social labour process, and is consequently rooted in the unavoidable antagonism between the exploiter and the living and labouring raw material he exploits [Marx, 1954: 313].

Labor resistance is an obstacle to the maximization of surplus value; capitalists must attempt to counteract it with various forms of labor control. In examining the way in which capital seeks to control labor, Marx makes a basic distinction between the "formal" and "real" subjection of labor to capital. The formal subjection of labor takes place when a worker's labor power is exchanged in the market for a wage. In this strategy, which is characteristic of the earlier stages of capitalist development, capitalists frequently take over an existing labor process, and seek to achieve their objective of maximum valorization by lengthening the working day of the labor force, thereby increasing the length of time during which surplus value is being created. This Marx referred to as the creation of "absolute" surplus value.

This strategy is ultimately unsatisfactory for the capitalists. Not only does it fail to realize the full productive potential of the labor power at their disposal, but it also provokes a disruptive struggle with the labor force over the length of the working day. Consequently, the capitalist turns to the real subjection of labor. This is a strategy involving the reorganization of the labor process in such a way as to increase the productivity of labor, thereby enabling each worker to produce an exchange value the equivalent of his or her wage in a shorter portion of the working day, and increasing the length of time during which surplus value is being created. This Marx referred to as the creation of "relative" surplus value.

In the final stage of his analysis, Marx examines the principal means whereby capitalists have pursued the real subjection of labor and creation of relative surplus value. First, he examines "cooperation," or the bringing together of numerous workers in a single productive unit under the central control of the capitalist. Second, he discusses the "division of labor," horizontally by status and authority and vertically by task, so as to increase productivity while producing a labor force dependent on the coordinating functions of the capitalist. Third, Marx examines the use of machinery, which minimizes the contribution of a worker's strength and skill to productive activity and allows the hiring of cheap labor such as women and children.

As the recent body of literature on the labor process has indicated (Friedman, 1977; Edwards, 1979; Burawoy, 1979), Marx's analysis of labor control was primarily concerned with the means whereby the capitalists might technically realize the full potential of the labor power at their disposal. However, cooperation, the division of labor, and machinery do not themselves eliminate the problem of labor resistance or ensure that workers act in a manner that is compatible with the maximization of surplus value. To achieve these aims, capitalists must exercise *authority* over the labor force, removing the workers' desire and ability to exercise independent control over their tasks. In Lazonick's words, "what the real subjection of labour to capital actually requires is that as much as possible the subjective will of the labourer conforms to the objective requirements of profit-making" (Lazonick, 1978: 3). This is precisely the objective of scientific management.

Taylor fully recognized the impact of labor resistance on industrial productivity and was determined to eliminate it. What particularly concerned him were not the more overt and irregular modes of resistance, such as strikes or demonstrations, but covert and everyday modes of resistance, which he described as "soldiering": absenteeism, restricted output, malingering, insubordination, sabotage, and bonus cheating.

According to Taylor, soldiering is "by far the greatest evil from which both workmen and employers are suffering" (Taylor, 1903: 32). Some soldiering is "natural," in that it derives from humanity's inherent tendency to "take it easy." Because this form of soldiering is done openly, it is relatively easy for an employer to suppress. Much more serious is what Taylor described as "systematic soldiering," by which he meant those modes of resistance that workers use to reduce the quantity and quality of their output and which are done in a way that is secretive, collective, planned, and deliberately designed to further the interests of the labor force at the expense of the employer. The task Taylor set himself was to find a means of "doing away with slow working and 'soldiering' in all its forms, and so arranging the relations between employer and employee that each workman will work to his very best advantage and at his best speed" (Taylor, 1911: 14).

Taylorism, then, is by no means a neutral, "scientific" means of increasing industrial productivity. Rather, it is a direct manifestation of the struggle between labor and capital, a means of intensifying the exploitation of the former by the latter, a form of managerial counterpressure that seeks to eliminate particular kinds of worker resistance and to deprive the worker of any autonomy within the labor process. As Braverman (1974: 86) says, scientific management starts

> not from the human point of view but from the capitalist point of view, from the point of view of the management of a refractory work force in a setting of antagonistic social relations. . . . It investigates not labor in general, but the adaptation of labor to the needs of capital.

SCIENTIFIC MANAGEMENT IN ACTION

From the diagnosis of the Gold Coast mining industry provided by consultants such as Fraser and Somerset, it is clear that soldiering, both natural and systematic, lie at the heart of the crisis confronting mining capital. As one enlightened expatriate had written in 1940, "it is fairly certain that the workers, faced by managerial unconcern and indifference, 'get their own back' by negligent work, poor attendance, and studied indifference on their own part" (Meek, 1940: 58). Given the political and financial constraints limiting the mining companies' freedom of maneuver, the only means of restoring the profitability of the industry was to launch a full-scale assault on the labor force to eliminate such forms of resistance, reasserting the authority of management, and thereby maximizing the potential of the labor power mining capital had at its disposal. This section of the chapter seeks to explain precisely how the consultants tried to achieve those objectives.

Taylorism is based upon the assumption that "what the workers want from their employers beyond anything else is high wages" (Taylor, 1903: 22). Given sufficiently attractive financial incentives, Taylor believed, workers would no longer soldier, but would become committed to a persistent improvement in the quality and quantity of their output. Thus, according to Fraser and Somerset.

> with primitive labour on simple daily pay . . . bad tools or bad working conditions are treated with complete indifference. Broken shovels, dull saws, faulty switches, are accepted with philosophical detachment.

However,

> When every workman is conscious of the necessity for, and has a pecuniary interest in maintaining the conditions which will enable him to take home a substantial increase in earnings, the task of management in discipline and organization is greatly simplified, and its hand is greatly strengthened.

Acting upon this assumption, the first strategy employed by the consultants after 1950 was the introduction of new incentive schemes, or "payment-by-results" systems. Bonus systems had been in use for many years on the Gold Coast mines, but they had never been applied to more than half of the industry's labor force, and had always been insufficiently generous to eliminate low ouput, absenteeism, and other expressions of the workers' autonomy. Consequently, the new systems were designed to give at least 75 percent of the labor force a direct financial stake in increased production and to provide a much greater incentive for each worker. Unlike the bonus systems used before 1950, they were based upon "scientific" calculations of the amount of work performed by an individual or labor gang. Time study analysts examined each operation in the mine, divided it into a number of constituent tasks, and assessed the time required to complete those tasks if the workers concerned performed at a "standard rate." This rate was "analagous to that speed and effort required to walk at a rate of three miles per hour along even, level ground."[14] A "rest factor" was added, and the final figure was termed the "100 percent performance," expressed in terms of the "standard minute":

> This is a unit of work analagous to a horsepower . . . used to describe the credits allowed a workman for the performance of specified tasks. . . . The relationship between the credits earned in standard minutes and the total minutes in the working shift indicate the man's percentage effectiveness.[15]

Bonuses could be earned by all workers whose tasks were quantifiable in this way, and were paid once a 50 percent or 75 percent "effectiveness rating" had been attained. Theoretically there was no upper limit to the amount of bonus that could be earned, but in reality of course, bonus levels were subject to constant manipulation by cost- and profit-conscious managers. As C. H. Northcott (1932) had indicated in a report on scientific management, Taylorist bonus schemes are only allegedly scientific and in reality are based upon arbitrary and subjective estimates of the amount of effort required to complete a given task. Thus, in practice, the consultants frequently set standards too high, in which case very few workers were able to earn bonuses, and the system failed to provide a realistic incentive. Alternatively, standards could be set too low, especially when workers deliberately slackened their pace during time-study investigations. In this case, bonus payments "ran away," and standards had to be upgraded to encourage the workers to strive after ever-increasing levels of productivity. Although basic wages were guaranteed, and once earned could not be forfeited on account of poor performance, they could be reduced or withdrawn as a penalty for absenteeism, insubordination, and other minor offenses. Thus the new bonus schemes, ostensibly a carrot to be dangled in front of a labor force committed to increased earnings, became a stick used to beat workers who were willing to sacrifice income for leisure.

Second, in order to assure that the mine workers expended their energy in the most productive manner possible, the consultants trained the labor force in the use of new working methods. Some of these innovations were of a primarily technical nature. For example, drilling efficiency was improved through the extended use of tungsten carbide steel, and mechanical locos, scrapers, and loaders were introduced wherever possible in place of manual operations. At the same time, the mines' existing equipment was used more effectively as a result of "planned preventive maintenance" schedules designed to eliminate mechanical breakdowns. Other improvements to working methods had a more direct impact on the labor force. Following Taylor's insistence on the "scientific selection of workmen," aptitude tests were introduced to match each employee with a task suited to his physical and mental capabilities. Then, employing a combination of time study and work study, the consultants ascertained the most efficient method of performing each task, and described this method in words and pictures in a "manual of standard practice." These manuals described "precisely how management requires operations to be done in any given set of circumstances," and encompassed "the detail of every activity from stoping to clerical returns, from sampling to grass cutting." Workers and supervisors alike were warned in their manual that "NO ALTERATION OR DEVIATION FROM THESE INSTRUCTIONS IS PERMISSABLE WITHOUT THE CONSENT IN WRITING OF THE GENERAL MANAGER." Anyone found trangressing this rule was liable to dismissal, suspension, or demotion. The consultants, like their mentor F. W. Taylor, insisted that the objective of these minutely detailed instructions was "not so much to increase the energy output of the labourers concerned, but to render more effective their normal energy output."[16] Significantly, this was not a view shared by all managers in the mines, who were clearly alienated by the consultants' obsessive concern for efficiency. In the words of one expatriate engineer:

If the standard minute was a true measure of work, and if, for instance, a trammer, under incentive conditions produced 480 standard minutes per shift as against a pre-incentive performance of 240 minutes, he would have done more work, and unless conditions were exceptional, would have put out more physical effort.[17]

Third, the mine managers were advised to introduce new methods of labor distribution. Using the standard minute as a unit of work, the consultants calculated the total number of standard minutes, and therefore the number of man shifts, required to complete an operation in a given time if all employees maintained a "70 percent efficiency rate." This procedure enabled management to reduce labor complements and eliminate overmanning, to transfer surplus service labor to more productive tasks, to ensure that all workers were kept fully occupied, and to dismiss individual workers and labor gangs who consistently performed at below the standard rate.

The distribution of labor was made the responsibility of new Labor Control Departments, which operated "a properly designed specific plan, by which the daily distribution of labour is controlled according to predetermined standards." The plan enabled management to hire, fire, and transfer labor according to changing conditions, to compile more detailed records of production and productivity, and to keep a much closer check on the location, task, and performance of any worker or gang. The latter objective was also facilitated by the physical and administrative reorganization of the mines. For political and economic reasons, the Gold Coast mines could not hope to introduce the rigorous controls over worker mobility that were such an important feature of labor control systems in Southern African mines. Nevertheless, within their own concession areas, the mine managers were encouraged by the consultants to intensify their direct control of the labor force. Shaft tops were sealed off, making it impossible for workers to come and go as they pleased, and new clocking-on and changing facilities, based on the South African Salex System, were introduced. By establishing an elaborate network of control points and clerical returns, such systems provided much quicker and more accurate information about absenteeism and overtime. Workers now found it much more difficult to arrive at the mine late or to leave early, or to linger in the mine after hours in order to steal gold. According to the mine manager at Ashanti Goldfields, "without this close control, it is virtually impossible to improve labour utilization and efficiency."[18]

The fourth strategy employed to boost productivity in the mines, and the one on which the other three strategies ultimately depended, was to improve the quality and increase the quantity of supervision. The ratio of European supervisors to African workers was increased from 2.4 percent in 1949 to 3.2 percent in 1954, and in view of the political and financial constraints on this policy, particular attention was given to improving the quality of African supervisors. Potential supervisors were selected from the ranks of ordinary workers, and after completing a series of aptitude tests, were given the training necessary to "fit them for more responsible posts." Such trainees were informed that "as a supervisor, a man is no longer simply a worker, he is an executive, he has improved his status." His task was to "undertake the skilled functions of directing, coordinating, and controlling the actions of other people," and like the ordinary workers, he was induced to perform such tasks as efficiently as possible by the provision of incentive payments of up to one-third of his basic salary. Ultimately, the supervisor's functions were dependent on a single attribute, *discipline*. In the words of the Ashanti Goldfields training manual:

> The value of a good headman to the mine is in direct proportion to his ability to maintain discipline. Discipline is the first essential quality required by supervisors, and can only be enforced if the supervisor is amenable to discipline himself.[19]

J. S. Ford (1943: 303) made the same point even more bluntly:

> At least 90% of a Shift Boss's duties, other than transporting his body from point to point, consist of *maintaining discipline*.

More specifically, supervisors were empowered to use a wide range of sanctions, including fines, dismissal, suspension, and demotion, in order to maintain discipline in five ways: to eliminate malingering and slacking, whether the result of accidental overmanning or deliberate work avoidance by the labor force; to prevent workers from "bonus cheating," falsifying returns or reducing the quality of their output in order to earn higher incentive payments; to impose "strict adherence to times, especially to the time of starting work and knocking off"[20]; to ensure that workers performed their duties in accordance with the detailed instructions provided by management; and to enforce strict security precautions, eliminating the theft of gold and company property. In this final objective, both management and supervisors were aided by a wide range of innovations introduced in the aftermath of the 1947 mines strike and the 1948 riots in Accra and Kumasi. Mining camps and key installations were surrounded by high fencing, while local police forces were provided with special posts on the perimeter fence, floodlights, riot shields, and tear gas. The mines' own security forces were reinforced, and put under the control of a security department led by an expatriate who enjoyed close links with the colonial police force. While such innovations may have had the intended effect of making life more difficult for "political agitators" and gold-stealing gangs, it also raised the suspicions of the more liberal members of the colonial administration, who resented the mining industry's anachronistic attempt to introduce new restrictions on the workers' mobility. Thus one committee of enquiry observed that "living in a mining compound for a labourer can at best be not far different from living in a barracks."[21]

SCIENTIFIC MANAGEMENT AND DESKILLING

Before going on to examine the impact of these four sets of innovations, it is necessary to examine briefly Braverman's contention that the principal aim of scientific management is to cheapen labor and to extend the real subordination of the labor process by "deskilling" the work force, and transforming it into an undifferentiated mass of compliant and replaceable detail workers (Braverman, 1974: 124-137). Braverman's argument is not without foundation. Taylor was evidently aware that skilled workers were more expensive to employ than unskilled workers, and that skilled workers and craftsmen were able to withhold the tricks of their trade from management, thereby frustrating the efforts of capital to maximize the amount of surplus value produced. Consequently, as Braverman indicates, Taylor laid a great deal of emphasis on the need to separate the planning and execution of work, the former being the responsibility of "trained experts possessing the right mental equipment" (i.e., managers), and the latter being the task of "men having the right physical equipment for their respective tasks, and being receptive of expert guidance in their performance" (i.e., unskilled workers) (H. R. Towne, in Taylor, 1903: 9-10). Thus, while Taylor frequently emphasized the importance of "industrial training," he was in fact merely referring to the process whereby unskilled workers are taught to perform routine tasks in accordance with specified detailed instructions.

Despite Taylor's undoubted approval of deskilling as a means of boosting efficiency, productivity, and therefore profits, Braverman's single-minded emphasis on the relationship between scientific management and the destruction of skill is open to criticism on both theoretical and empirical grounds. Theoretically, as Elger has argued, the skills to be found within modern industry are not necessarily incompatible with capital's ultimate objectives. Certainly, the skills of the independent craftsman represent an obstacle to those objectives, since they cannot be readily incorporated into the capitalist labor process. Braverman is wrong, however, to equate independent craftsmen with skilled workers in modern industry, whose specialized abilities are readily incorporated into the capitalist labor process, and once incorporated, can be subjected to a process of intensification. Drawing on case studies of European and American industries, Elger shows that in some sectors, deskilling did take place on a large scale, while in others, old skills were maintained and new skills created. Elger concludes that Taylorism "did not . . . create a simply homogeneous mass of deskilled labour on the shop-floor, but meant the elaboration of a complex, internally differentiated apparatus of collective labour which contained an uneven variety of narrow skills and specific dexterities" (Elger, 1979: 82).

Elger's critique is supported by data from the Gold Coast mines. Unfortunately, the absence of data on the occupational, skill, and wage structure of this mine's labor force in the 1950s prevents a systematic analysis of deskilling, but from the available nonstatistical data it seems clear that the introduction of Taylorism in this period actually coincided with an unprecedented effort on the part of mining capital to *increase* levels of skill within the labor force. For many years prior to the 1950s, the mining companies had rejected the government's sporadic efforts to encourage the establishment of industrial training facilities, claiming that such a venture would prove too expensive, and that once trained, skilled workers would leave the mines to find more lucrative employment in other sectors of the economy. With the introduction of scientific management, however, the Chamber of Mines agreed to assist in the creation of a technical training institute, to expand its existing apprenticeship scheme, to support the government's program of trade testing, and to cooperate with colonial officials and members of the ILO in the introduction of the American Training Within Industry program. Simultaneously, the mines made strenuous efforts to retain the skilled workers they had trained by offering them long-service gratuities and special housing privileges. Rather than deskilling, therefore, scientific management in the gold mines brought a move in the opposite direction.

Deskilling was never a realistic option for mining capital in the Gold Coast, for the simple reason that the labor force was aready a largely unskilled one, dominated by short-term migrant workers who were employed to perform menial laboring tasks. There was, of course, a hard core of skilled and relatively stabilized workers, including artisans, clerical staff, machine drivers, and winding engine drivers, but the skills of such men were essential to the operation of the mines, and they could not, like so many tasks in manufacturing industry, be readily displaced by means of mechanization. Moreover, once this hard core of workers had successfully established the MEU and used its bargaining power to gain higher wages for the whole of the labor force, the argument that unskilled labor was cheap labor could no longer be maintained. Thus the success of the union in putting an end to the long era of cheap labor in the mines had a decisive impact on managerial perceptions of labor training and utilization. If the workers were to receive higher wages, the managers thought, then the mines should make a virtue of this necessity and encourage the creation of a more skilled and stabilized labor force, capable of working more efficiently and productively as a result of some systematic training.

Other considerations reinforced this argument. Competition for skilled labor from the Tema Harbour and Volta Dam projects was now so intense that the mines were forced to build up their skilled labor force through the training of indentured apprentices. Such a strategy also promised the replacement of expensive expatriate engineers by much cheaper local men. Finally, the consultants in the Gold Coast recognized what Braverman failed to appreciate; namely that scientific management, a form of direct control over the labor process, could be pursued simultaneously with responsible autonomy strategies that seek to control the labor process by indirect means (Friedman, 1977: 78). Thus even J.S. Ford, the high priest of Taylorism in South Africa, was fully aware of the ideological importance of industrial training in that it encouraged the worker to develop a sense of loyalty and responsibility toward his employer. In Ford's words, "as much knowledge must be inculcated in him as soon as possible so as to make him feel that he is not merely used as a 'hewer of wood and drawer of water' but also that his skill and initiative are of the greatest value" (Ford, 1944: 880).

THE WORKERS' RESPONSE TO SCIENTIFIC MANAGEMENT

The introduction of Taylorism to the mines of the Gold Coast, then, entailed the use of a number of interrelated strategies, whose ultimate objective was to increase productivity, and thereby restore the profitability of the industry. How successful were these strategies? By any standards, they proved to be a remarkably effective means of making the "drastic improvement to working efficiencies" that were the declared target of consultants such as Somerset and Fraser. Between 1950 and 1954, overall tonnage per underground worker jumped from 185.87 tons to 265.80 tons, an increase of 43 percent. At one of the mines reorganized by Fraser and Somerset, productivity was improved by no less than 64 percent. The tonnage produced by the mine's 3500 workers in 1954 would have required 6000 workers to produce at 1950 levels of productivity, an improvement representing an annual saving to the mine of £250,000. At another mine, tonnage per labor shift increased by 65 percent between 1949 and 1954, although only an additional 5 percent of the rock face was worked. At a third mine, labor was reduced by 25 percent, while total tonnage increased by 30 percent, representing an 80 percent increase in tonnage per shift. Such substantial improvements to productivity levels successfully countered the rising level of wages. Thus between 1950 and 1954 earnings (wages, bonuses, and overtime) per shift increased by 59 percent, but overall expenditure on labor rose by only 19 percent. In the same period, expenditure on working costs other than labor increased by 27 percent.[22]

It would appear from these statistics that the mine workers responded positively, or at least passively, to the introduction of scientific management, and that they were therefore successfully induced to adapt their behavior to suit the needs of mining capital. Taylor himself always insisted that workers would respond in a positive manner to his ideas. A labor force earning the high incentive payments made available by scientific management would, he argued, inevitably be a contented labor force, disinclined to take part in strikes or other forms of protest. Only if management sought to cheat the workers of their bonuses, or if a trade union insisted on obstructing his innovations, could scientific management be the cause of industrial conflict (Taylor, 1903: 68-69).

In fact, both Taylor's own experience and the evidence from this case study disprove this confident assertion. Taylor admitted that the introduction of scientific management could indeed arouse considerable hostility amongst the workers it affected. At the Midvale Steel Works, for example, Taylor became involved in "a war which as time went on, grew more and more bitter" (Taylor, 1911: 49). Taylor was the target of "constant unpopularity, direct sabotage, and threats of personal violence," including at least one threat on his life (Urwick and Brech, 1951: 30). As a result of such opposition, Taylor resorted to "unscientific" strategies such as "discharging or lowering the wages of the more stubborn men who refused to make any improvement" (Taylor, 1911: 49-50). In other words, a new managerial system, which was purportedly based upon the active and willing cooperation of the labor force, ultimately depended on the old-fashioned use of coercion:

> It is only through *enforced* standardization of methods, *enforced* adoption of the best implements and working conditions, and *enforced* cooperation [sic] that this better work can be assured. And the duty of enforcing the adoption of standards and of enforcing this cooperation rests with *management* alone. (Taylor, 1911: 83).

Taylor's personal experience was repeated elsewhere. A major stoppage at the Watertown Arsenal prompted the U.S. Congress to conduct an extensive enquiry into scientific management in 1912, while a series of stoppages in Britain and the rest of Europe in the 1920s and 1930s caused the British labor movement to undertake a series of investigations into the new "efficiency systems" being imported across the Atlantic.[23]

This pattern of resistance to Taylorism, almost totally neglected by Braverman, was repeated in a dramatic way in the Gold Coast mining industry in the 1950s. While scientific management successfully boosted productivity by attacking the mine workers' informal resistance to the capitalist labor process, it simultaneously managed to provoke a "major confrontation with labor," which was expressed in the form of overt, collective, and organized protest.[24]

The resistance encountered by mining capital in its attempt to secure control of the workplace is most readily demonstrated by an analysis of strike statistics for this period.[25] Between 1948 and 1951, when the methods of scientific management first began to influence managerial policy in the Gold Coast, there were 26 strikes in the gold mines, involving 24,112 strikers (28 percent of the Gold Coast total), and totalling 70,752 man days lost (MDL) or 11 percent of the Gold Coast total. Strikes for higher wages accounted for just over 37 percent of all MDL in the gold mines, and approximately one-third of all strikers. A significantly higher proportion of the mine workers' collective protest activity derived from conflicts in the workplace that were directly related to the new strategies used by management to boost productivity and efficiency. Twelve strikes, totaling 29,903 MDL, were organized in protest against dismissals, suspensions, demotions, and fines imposed on workers guilty of offenses such as misconduct, insubordination, and faulty work. Three strikes (758 MDL) were undertaken by workers demanding higher bonus payments or different methods of bonus calculation. Four stoppages (4,384 MDL) took place in protest against retrenchments and transfer, and two strikes (4937 MDL) were organized to express the participants' dissatisfaction with the behavior of individual supervisors.[26]

In the following three-year period, 1951 to 1954, when the methods of scientific management were used in a far more thorough, systematic and vigorous manner to assert control over the labor force, the reaction of the mine workers was correspondingly more militant. In this period there were 44 strikes in the gold mines, involving 27,555 strikers (40 percent of the Gold Coast total), and totaling 117,885 man days lost (also 40 percent of the colony's total). This quantitative increase in the level of strike activity in the mines was matched by significant qualitative changes. The proportion of man days lost in wage-related disputes slumped from over 37 percent to a mere 4.3 percent of the total, while the proportion lost in disputes about managerial and supervisory authority jumped from 63 percent to over 87 percent of the total.

In order to relate the pattern of mine worker protest in this period more clearly to the managerial campaign for higher productivity, it is necessary to describe some of these strikes in greater detail. No less than 22 of the 44 stoppages between 1951 and 1954 were mobilized in protest against disciplinary actions taken by supervisors and managers to punish employees guilty of offenses that included insubordination and refusal to obey instructions, unauthorized absenteeism, drunkenness and sleeping on duty, failure to complete a full day's work, and refusal to use a new type of jack machine. At Ashanti Goldfields the entire labor force stopped work for eleven days when six workers were dismissed for "gross inefficiency" and "irregular conduct," while at the T and A mine, underground workers downed tools for a day when a colleague was suspended for using extra detonators, fuses, and dynamite in an attempt to blast more rock and thereby enable the machine crews to earn higher incentive bonuses.

Five stoppages in this period were the result of disputes over bonus payments. At Marlu, 130 workers went on strike when they discovered that they had failed to reach the standard set by management to qualify for a bonus, and at T and A 780 men stopped work when management changed its method of calculating bonuses. Two strikes over bonuses occurred at Amalgamated Banket Areas. In the first, 40 men struck for five days when bonus rates were reduced, and in the second, 21 workers went on strike to protest against the imposition of higher incentive standards following the introduction of tungsten carbide drills.

The mine workers participated in four strikes to protest against retrenchments, transfers, and the reduction of labor complements. In August 1951, a consultant's investigations revealed that some workers in the T and A drill shop were completing their daily workload in less than three hours. Six men were instructed to transfer to the Engineering Department, and all 87 drill shop employees went on strike to defend their colleagues. Two years later 747 underground workers at the same mine stopped work for four days when tungsten carbide drills were introduced and the second spanner boy in each machine crew was retrenched on grounds of "economy and efficiency."

Managerial attempts to introduce new working schedules and methods of labor distribution provoked four strikes between 1951 and 1954. In January 1954, there were two strikes at Abosso to protest against new shift arrangements, and in the same month 558 men at Ashanti Goldfields refused to work for two days after management had implemented stricter procedures for checking the work of underground employees. A similar stoppage had occurred two years earlier at T and A, when consultants discovered that machine crews were drilling holes 12 inches to 16 inches deep instead of the stipulated 42 inches in order to earn higher bonuses for less work. A pass system was introduced that prevented the men from leaving the mine until their work had been examined by the shift boss, and all 1700 underground employees stopped work for two days in protest against this imposition. Finally, three strikes in this period were organized to protest against the behavior of individual supervisors. The most important of these stoppages took place at Ashanti Goldfields in June 1952, when 2000 men went on strike for four days to demand the dismissal of a headman who refused to be a party to the workers' gold stealing, and who was believed to be a security informant for the general mine manager.

According to the Labour Department, the mine workers' strikes of 1951 to 1954 provided "serious opposition" to the introduction of scientific management.[27] However, the scale and impact of this resistance should not be exaggerated, for it was subject to three related limitations. First, the strikes described above were for the most part of short duration, lasting one or two days. None involved workers at more than one mine, and the majority were organized on a departmental basis. As such, they did not represent a systematic or sustained campaign of opposition to the intensification of managerial authority. Second, although these strikes expressed the workers' antagonism to the practical effects of scientific management at the point of production, the mine workers did not attack the underlying principles of Taylorism, as many European and American workers had done in earlier years. Third, the mine workers' resistance was short-lived. The wave of strikes ended abruptly in mid-1954, and in the following eighteen months there were only six stoppages in the gold mines. This period of relative peace was followed at the end of 1955 by a massive upsurge of militant action in the form of a 100-day-long strike supported by all 24,000 workers in the industry. This strike was not, however, the result of a dispute about productivity or managerial authority, but followed the Chamber of Mines' refusal to concede a demand for a 35 percent increase in basic wages. The remainder of the chapter seeks to explain these features of the mine workers' resistance, and does so by analyzing the impact of scientific management on the relationship between the mine workers and the MEU.

After the formation of the MEU in June 1944, the union's leaders were confronted with the task of securing and consolidating rank-and-file support. This proved to be extremely difficult, as the union's officials and its potential members were divided by serious socioeconomic and cultural barriers. At both national and local level, the MEU was run by clerks, artisans, and skilled surface workers from the southern Gold Coast. These relatively privileged employees had played a minimal part in the long history of protest in the gold mines, and only after the legalization of trade unions in 1941 had they emerged to assume their leading role in the struggle against mining capital. In contrast, the mass of unskilled and underground workers were illiterate migrant laborers from the colony's underdeveloped Northern Territories who experienced the worst of the industry's appalling working and living conditions. They had been participating in militant and frequently violent collective protest since the beginning of the century, and they were not easily persuaded to abandon a firmly established tradition of independent action in order to articulate their grievances through the unfamiliar and unproven machinery of trade unionism.

Two years after its formation, the MEU had failed to attract mass support, and its membership stood at 2050, a mere 5.6 percent of the labor force. Recognizing the urgent need to broaden the union's popular appeal, in mid-1946 the national leaders launched a campaign to extract substantial wage concessions from the Chamber of Mines. The union's aggressive negotiating strategy successfully dispelled the workers' mistrust of their nominal representatives, and within a year the union's National Executive Council was sufficiently confident of its rank-and-file support to issue the ultimatum leading to the general mines strike of September 1947.

The powerful alliance forged between union and workers in the course of the general strike was not easy to sustain. The wage rises gained by the stoppage were soon eroded by the rising cost of living, and subsequent increases negotiated by the MEU were insufficient to satisfy the newly aroused expectations of the 15,500 workers who had now joined the union. Membership began to decline, and the mine managers gleefully reported that the union was "losing ground," and "was not nearly so strong as it was."[28] More dramatically, at the Nsuta manganese mine a group of workers called "The New Order of Youngbloods" had seceded from the MEU and were fighting a violent war of attrition against the incumbent branch union officials.

The mine managers' initial efforts to improve productivity after the general strike placed an additional strain upon union/worker relations. At first, the MEU General President had supported these efforts believing that "since our cry is for better pay we must also put out our best and spend our energy to increase production."[29] However, it soon became evident that this policy could not be maintained at the local level. Branch union officials discovered that if the intensification of managerial authority went unchallenged by the MEU, the workers would simply ignore the union and protect their interests through independent action. Fearing a total collapse of popular support and a repetition of the events that had taken place a Nsuta, the union's local representatives rejected national MEU policy and gave official support to the strikes organized by the rank and file to defend their freedom in the workplace. Labour Department officials had no doubts about the motive force behind these strikes, and as one observed in early 1950, "the Northern Territories labourer could be a very obstinate individual, and he had evidence to prove that action taken by the so-called southern executives had very often been determined by the N.T. boys."[30] These strikes convinced the union's national leaders of the need to institutionalize the influence of the northern and underground workers, and the general president instructed the branch unions to coopt rank-and-file spokesmen into their executive committees.

By the beginning of 1950, therefore, the MEU had recognized the need to respond to rank-and-file discontent provoked by the intensification of managerial authority, and was adopting, somewhat reluctantly, a policy of tacit opposition to the mining companies' efforts to improve productivity. Management described the union's demand for consultation on all cases of dismissal and demotion as "an unnecessary and futile struggle to achieve authority and influence" that threatened to "deprive management of its disciplinary powers."[31] Within the next eighteen months this emerging relationship between union and workers was destroyed. This was the time when the mine managers' efforts to control the mine workers were reinforced by the introduction of scientific management, a strategy provoking a much greater degree of discontent amongst the rank and file. Just as the workers looked to the MEU to lead their struggle against Taylorism, the union's willingness and ability to respond to rank-and-file consciousness was cut short by a power struggle within the National Executive Council (NEC).

In 1950, a group of MEU officials who wanted the union to play a more active part in national politics instigated a campaign to oust the founding members of the union from the NEC. The campaign culminated in mid-1951, when the incumbent general secretary and president were deposed and their supporters in the branches were removed in "a series of quite bogus elections."[32] Unlike their predecessors, the new officials refused to respond to the workers' growing resistance to the introduction of scientific management, and even aided management by establishing "productivity and efficiency committees" that were responsible for discussing new methods of boosting output.

The unwillingness of the new leadership to articulate the workers' opposition to scientific management was determined by several considerations. The new officials were by inclination more autocratic than their predecessors. In order to further their personal and political ambitions the union's administration was centralized, and patronage networks were established that both tied local officials to the dictates of the NEC and gave them a guarantee of protection against dissident elements within the branch unions. Consequently the union became far less susceptible to rank-and-file pressures than it had been between 1947 and 1950. Underground and northern representatives were removed from the executive committees, and branch presidents and secretaries no longer felt obliged to give official support to strikes mobilized by the rank and file. As one branch officer remarked when warned about the dangers of losing touch with the rank and file, "they were the truck and could move without its trailer."[33]

This aloof and arrogant attitude was reinforced by external constraints on the union's responsiveness to rank-and-file discontent. The mine managers made no secret of their dislike for the new leaders and were adopting a hardened attitude toward the MEU, victimizing prominent union officials and encouraging the division between southern surface workers and northern underground workers. The Chamber of Mines warned that while it recognized the union's right to negotiate higher wages, it would not tolerate any attempts by the union to sabotage the campaign for increased productivity. Wishing to avert the threat of further retaliatory action against the union, the new leaders agreed to restrict their efforts to the issue of wages and standard conditions of employment.

The colonial government was also encouraging the MEU to pursue an incrementalist and productionist policy. In the aftermath of the politically motivated Positive Action strike organized by the Trade Union Congress in January 1950 and in accordance with overall African policy, the Labour Department launched an intensive program of "trade union education," designed to depoliticize the unions, to encourage them to settle disputes through peaceful negotiations, and to teach union officials that they had "a vital part to play in educating the Gold Coast workers that it does not pay to be lazy."[34] The MEU, which relied upon the Labour Department to defend the union from the attacks of the more reactionary mine managers, was a principal target of the government's educational endeavors, and was inclined to take notice of its advice. Thus, in June 1954, the president of the influential Abosso branch union told workers:

> I must make it plain to you that unnecessary strikes, lockouts and hold ups will do the union more harm than good. I attended the trade union school for ten days at Kumasi, and I am now telling you what had been taught to me.[35]

These constraints on the willingness and ability of the MEU to mobilize a campaign of resistance to scientific management could not, of course, prevent the rank and file from taking independent collective action to defend their interests. Thus, of the 44 strikes that took place in the gold mines between 1951 and 1954, only one was organized or supported by the union, and many were actively opposed by it. Nevertheless, the failure of the MEU to support the workers in their struggle did have serious consequences for the success of that struggle. Without the organizational backing of a national trade union, the scale and impact of the mine workers' resistance was critically limited, confined to an intermittent sequence of short and spontaneous strikes that could not unite workers in different mines, and which only occasionally brought workers performing different tasks together in common opposition to management. The small scale and adhoc organization of such strikes enabled management to suppress them without a great deal of difficulty. While they were a successful means of securing isolated concessions for the workers, these strikes could not present a serious challenge to the introduction of scientific management.

One question posed earlier in the chapter remains unanswered. Why did the series of strikes against the intensification of managerial authority end so abruptly in mid-1954, to be followed in less than two years by a major strike in support of a demand for higher wages?

Understandably, the failure of the MEU's new ruling group to take up the workers' struggle against the introduction of Taylorist techniques reopened the division between union and rank and file that the former leaders had tried with some success to overcome. Union membership, which had risen to over 45 percent of the labor force in 1948-1949, had slumped to 28.4 percent by 1952-1953. In times of conflict with management the workers not only ignored the union, preferring to articulate their own demands, but sometimes also expressed positive hostility toward it. For example, during a general strike at Ashanti Goldfields in 1952, the Labour Department reported that the branch union had been "overwhelmed by events" and "was not decided as to its stand." Eventually the union officials decided to oppose the strike and appealed for a return to work. The strikers ignored these appeals, and jeered the officials at a mass meeting:

> No executive of a trade union cut a more sorry figure at that stage than the local executive. The last-minute attempts to regain control received no response whatever from the men, not even the gong-gong appeal of the General President of the MEU.[36]

Similar events were taking place at other mines. After a spate of four unofficial strikes in less than three weeks, the District Labour Officer in Tarkwa reported that "it has been observed with grave concern that in each case there has been an attempt by the Northern Territories element to strike without consulting their branch union officers." The Labour Officer promised to help the MEU General Secretary bridge "the yawning gap between the branch union officers and the N.T. elements," but the most prominent rank-and-file strike leader refused to accept a subordinate position in the local MEU executive committee.[37]

At Bibiani the alienation of the underground and northern workers from the union had reached an even more critical stage. At this mine over 65 percent of the labor force was from the north, and a Northern

Territories Association (NTA) had been formed to represent their interests. The workers, said the mine manager, "looked to the Northern Territories Association for help and not to the union." Concerned about the future of collective bargaining at the mine, he stated that since 1952 he had "been well aware that the union has not got the unity of strength in membership that was desirable." Proof of this statement came in dramatic form. In February 1953 four northern workers were arrested for failing to pay local rates to the District Council, and the NTA organized a violent demonstration and strike that halted production at the mine for three days.[38]

Despite their entrenched position within the union, the members of the NEC could not afford to ignore the rising tide of rank-and-file disaffection, and looked for a suitable strategy to counteract the trend. Shop stewards were appointed to improve communications between union and workers, and in an attempt to reduce the provocative exercise of managerial and supervisory authority, the MEU and Chamber of Mines agreed that union officials should be consulted before any punishment was imposed on a worker. This procedure proved to be counterproductive, merely reinforcing the workers' suspicions that the union was in league with management. For example, in September 1953 union officials at Marlu agreed that a loco driver's wages should be reduced for failing to observe a signal. Other workers promptly "organized the masses to resist any punishment" and a six-day strike ensued. The Labour Department reported "there is little doubt that the strike was led by the loco drivers, who usurped power from the union executive."[39]

A far more promising means of recapturing rank-and-file support was to adopt an aggressive policy in pursuit of higher wages. This strategy had three important advantages. First, it had been employed with considerable success by the union's former leaders in 1946-1947, and there appeared to be no reason why it should not work again. In the words of the government's trade union advisor, "it had to be remembered that although the Northern Territories worker would not lend his support to any political agitation, he would support the union fully in any demand for better conditions."[40] Second, demands for higher wages could not be interpreted as a threat to managerial authority or an attempt to sabotage the campaign for increased efficiency, and so could be made without fear of retaliation from the mine managers. Third, wage claims could be pursued through institutionalized negotiating procedures and would not, therefore, be obstructed by the Labour Department.

In September 1953, the MEU leadership began its campaign to recapture rank-and-file support. It submitted a 35 percent wage claim to the Chamber of Mines and organized a series of mass meetings to mobilize popular support for the demand. The "difficult and cunning capitalists" who controlled the industry were vigorously denounced, and the rank and file were told that "employers of mine workers in this country were all the time fooling the country and the miners that they had no profits." They should, therefore, "know their obligations to the trade union and organize well, for the employers were fooling and cheating the workers too much."[41] Unconcerned by such threats, the Chamber of Mines rejected the 35 percent wage claim, and when the MEU resubmitted the demand in April 1954, the chamber refused to discuss it or any other proposal made by the union. The union delegation walked out of the negotiating meeting in protest, and in a public exchange of acrimonious correspondence, the NEU threatened that a general strike would be mobilized to secure the wage demand.

The militant stance of the MEU, the provocative response of the Chamber of Mines, and the resultant bitterness of the confrontation between the two bodies had a decisive impact on the attitude and behavior of the rank and file. The percentage of the labor force paying subscriptions to the union increased for the first time since 1948, and at mass meetings held to discuss the wage claim, the rank and file "responded heartily" to the union's call for united opposition to the Chamber of Mines.[42]

Most significantly, the workers accepted the advice of their union leaders to live economically and avoid local and sectional stoppages in order to prepare financially for a protracted nationwide strike. Thus in mid-1954 the wave of unofficial strikes provoked by the introduction of scientific management came to an abrupt halt, and the mine workers redirected their militancy toward the more tangible goal of a 35 percent pay rise.

Negotiations between the MEU and the Chamber of Mines continued throughout the next twelve months, but no settlement could be reached. The rank and file grew increasingly impatient. They had supported the union's wage demand and followed its advice to avoid unofficial strikes, but no benefits had been won, and real earnings had stagnated. The MEU executives were now reported to be seriously concerned about their "loss of face with their members, especially the N.T. element."[43] Recognizing the need to secure some immediate concrete benefits for the workers, in mid-1955 the MEU General President accepted the chamber's offer of a compromise settlement. This move merely aggravated the workers, who insisted that the union should continue with its original demand.

Before any further progress could be made in negotiations, the workers' patience was exhausted. On September 29, 1955, the 5000 men at Ashanti Goldfields began a fourteen-day strike in protest against the introduction of a new pay system, which required them to work for 26 shifts before receiving any wages. Whilst this strike was in progress, the entire labor force at Tarquah and Abosso stopped work for five days to protest against the dismissal of eight underground workers.

The union leadership now recognized that it could no longer restrain the actions of the rank and file, and feared that their workplace grievances were about to resurface in another wave of unofficial local strikes. Consequently, the day after the Ashanti Goldfields strike ended, the general president moved to reassert control over the situation, announcing that if the union's wage claim was not conceded, a general mines strike would commence on November 7, 1955. The Chamber of Mines refused to make further concessions, the ultimatum expired, and all 24,000 mine workers withdrew their labor. They did not return until March 23, 1956, by which time the mining industry's strategy for survival was in ruins.

Ironically, scientific management contributed toward the demise of an industry whose fortunes it was intended to revive. Before the end of the strike, the colony's oldest producing mine was closed down, and even a £200,000 grant from the government could not save two low-grade mines from closure. In 1960, three years after the Gold Coast attained Independence, Nkrumah's government intervened and purchased all the remaining mines except for the profitable Ashanti Goldfields Corporation.

These developments had a significant impact on relations between labor, union, and management, both in the workplace and at national level. After the 1955-1956 strike, most of the mines abandoned the attempt to restore the long-term profitability of the industry, and in pursuit of immediate returns on invested capital, the Taylorist assault on the workplace was abandoned in favor of the old, "unscientific" forms of management. This trend was reinforced by the creation of the State Gold Mining Corporation (SGMC) in 1960. Profits were no longer of paramount importance, since the prime purpose of the mines was now to provide employment and foreign exchange.

By the early 1960s, the workers had succeeded in reestablishing a high degree of autonomy in the workplace, and from this period on, their collective action focused not on disputes over productivity or wages, but on the competence of the MEU, which had been effectively coopted and intimidated by the state (Crisp, 1979, 1981). Nevertheless, the lessons learned in the early 1950s were not easily forgotten, and the sporadic efforts of the SGMC and Ashanti Goldfields to restore levels of productivity and efficiency were consistently and vehemently opposed. In 1965, for example, the SGMC Managing Director reported that "some workers had been giving false returns of the number of holes drilled."[44] To prevent this, he proposed the introduction of monthly rather than weekly bonuses in order to allow a closer check on the relationship between actual tonnage produced and the reported number of fathoms drilled. The workers' response to this innovation was initially a strike, then a mass resignation, and finally an underground go-slow. In combination, these actions forced management to withdraw the proposal. In the following year, a new military government urged management to reassert control over the labor force. This was also resisted, and in a series of violent strikes taking place between 1958 and 1971, disciplinary and supervisory personnel were amongst the principal targets of the workers' anger. The Labour Department reported that "with the recent disturbances in the background, one can be sure that in the direction of enforcing discipline, anything that smacks of regimentation will be vehemently opposed."[45] "Labour indiscipline, weakness of supervision, and hence failure to carry out standard practices . . . has followed inevitably from the strikes and disturbances of 1968-69."[46]

This situation persisted throughout the following decade. In 1977, a report by a firm of British management consultants bemoaned the level of efficiency in the mines, noting that bonus payments had "degenerated into an additional payment of wages" and that "activity levels" of between 25 percent and 30 percent had become an accepted norm. They observed that the Taylorist Manuals of Standard Practice introduced between 1950 and 1955 were still technically in use in the mines, but that it had taken management several hours to find a copy for inspection, and that when it was eventually found, it was coverless, ripped, and only partially complete.[47] Even Ashanti Goldfields, jointly owned after 1969 by the Ghanaian government and Lonrho, found it extremely difficult to make the labor force work any harder. A report made by the mine's general manager in March 1978 had distinct echoes of the report produced by Somerset and Fraser more than two decades earlier, and symbolized the failure of the Taylorist offensive in the industry:

> The General Mines Manager stated that the total [production] achievement for the month was actually 27% below the point where a bonus can be earned and 37% behind earning a full bonus. The cumulative rating of 66.3% was way behind the target set, and present signs indicated a worsening of the situation . . . it appeared so far that the poor performance seemed to have no effect on the labour. . . . A recent study report had revealed that the underground night shift in certain working places produced nothing for the whole shift. . . . This could not be attributed to lack of supervision because the ratio of Shiftbosses to the number of working places was better and higher than at any other many other mines. . . . Management was at present concerned about the increasing rate of absenteeism. Sickness which used to average 5% had now increased. . . . Also fewer people were turning up for work on Friday night, Saturday morning and afternoon when called to do so. . . . The General Mines Manager said there has been an alarming increase in the apparent theft of miners' boots on the mine. . . . The Chief Engineer pointed out that light bulbs issued free of charge with A.G.C. embossed on them had been purchased by a messenger sent to the village to buy bulbs for the Company. The number of bulbs being used was out of all proportion to actual requirements.[48]

CONCLUSION

According to Braverman (1974: 136), scientific management is a strategy that invariably facilitates the real subordination of labor by capital. While he recognizes that Taylorist techniques have been largely superseded by alternative methods of labor control, he rejects the suggestion that this can be interpreted as an indication of the failure of scientific management. For Braverman, Taylorism has proved to be an effective means of asserting the authority of capital within the workplace and of turning the industrial worker into an "animated tool of management."

The evidence from this case study casts considerable doubt upon Braverman's conclusion. When confronted with the imposition of scientific management the Ghanaian mine workers certainly became animated — not, however, in any attempt to improve their level of productivity or efficiency, but in a vigorous defense of their freedom and autonomy within the labor process. As Burawoy (1978, 1979) has suggested, scientific management contains the seeds of its own destruction. The dilemma of the capitalist is to exploit the worker to the greatest possible extent while simultaneously keeping the worker oblivious to his or her own exploitation. Scientific management offers no real solution to this dilemma, since although it undoubtedly provides a means of boosting the rate at which surplus value is being created and accumulated, it does so in a very open, transparent, and crude manner. If, as Braverman implies, workers were simply the passive victims of managerial initiatives, then this would pose no problems for capital. The truth is, of course, that labor is an active rather than a passive agency, capable of perceiving its interests, acting in defense of them when they are threatened, and forcing capital to make compromises and adjustments. In North America and Europe, the ruling class had been forced to make such compromises and adjustments by the growing militancy of the working class. In the workplace, capital moved steadily away from strategies of direct control such as Taylorism and in their place introduced responsible autonomy strategies such as those advocated by the human relations school of industrial psychology. Meanwhile, outside the workplace, the state was using education, the media, and the arts to create a hegemonic work culture in which a respectable working class could internalize the ideology of capitalism. In the Gold Coast, managerial and official perceptions of African society and the African personality prevented this kind of flexible response to working-class organization and action. In the African context there could be no industrial consensus, only a culturally divided workplace bound together by clearly exposed relations of power.

The precise form of the labor process within capitalist enterprises, then, like the level of wages and the length of the working day, is determined in the process of struggle between labor and capital. As Edwards (1979) suggests, the workplace is a "contested terrain" in which labor and capital are constantly striving to push back the frontier of control to their own advantage. In the Ghanaian gold mines, that terrain was contested in an extremely intense struggle between 1947 and 1956 as workers acted collectively to resist the Taylorist offensive launched by management. As a result of that action, the frontier of control was successfully pushed back, forcing mining capital not only to abandon its experiment with Taylorism but also to undertake a radical reappraisal of its whole future in the Gold Coast. Thus both the introduction of scientific management to the gold mines and its withdrawal were in direct response to the militancy and solidarity expressed by the mine workers.

NOTES

1. Ghana Chamber of Mines Archive, Minutes of the Meetings of the Gold Coast Chamber of Mines (GCM), 7 December 1950.

2. Lonrho Archive, Minutes of the Ashanti Goldfields Corporation Annual General Meeting, 18 May 1947.

3. Report of a Commission Appointed to Enquire Into the Advancement of Africans in Industry. Lusaka: Government Printer, 1948.

4. Report on Financial and Physical Problems of Development in the Gold Coast. Accra: Government Printer, 1952.

5. GCM, 2 April 1948.

6. All subsequent unidentified quotations are taken from this source.

7. Interview with R. D. Power, former consultant, P. E. Mining Services, and former Managing Director, Ashanti Goldfields Corporation.

8. Award of Arbitrator in the Matter of the Trades Disputes (Arbitration and Inquiry) Ordinance, 1941, and in the Matter of a Trade Dispute Between the Gold Coast Mines' Employees' Union and the Gold Coast Chamber of Mines (Gorman Award). Accra: Government Printer, 1947: 72.

9. Ashanti Goldfields Corporation Archive, Inward Correspondence (Mine Manager to Company Secretary), 10 October 1946.

10. Report of the Mines Labour Enquiry Committee. Accra: Government Printer: 21.

11. Prestea Welfare Officer, quoted by T. Hilton, "The distribution and density of population in the Gold Coast Colony." Ph. D. thesis, University of London, 1956: 216.

12. Interview with L. H. Bean, former Managing Director, Gold Coast Chamber of Mines.

13. Gorman Award: 74.

14. Report of the Gold Coast Mines Board of Enquiry. Accra: Government Printer, 1956: 127.

15. For a detailed description of the analytical procedures of scientific management, see Taylor (1903).

16. Report of the Gold Coast Mines Board of Enquiry: 127.

17. "Report of discussion at April 1958: General meeting." Transactions of the Institution of Mining and Metallurgy, 67 (7) 1958: 484.

18. Ashanti Goldfields Corporation Archive, Inward Correspondence (Mine Manager to Company Secretary), 10 December 1953.

19. Ashanti Goldfields Corporation Archive, "A. G. C. official learners scheme: Notes on supervision," n.d.

20. The poor punctuality of the labor force had been a problem for management in the mines ever since the beginning of capitalist mining in the colony. The first attempt to improve punctuality through the introduction of a time clock, in 1924, had led to a major strike. See Crisp (1980: 156).

21. Report of the Mines Labour Enquiry Committee: 25.

22. These statistics are derived from data in O. Somerset and H. Fraser, "Report on scientific management principles applied to West African mining, 1950-1957," Typescript, H. H. Fraser and Associates, 1957. A copy of the report is held in the library of the Institution of Mining and Metallurgy, London.

23. See, for example, two reports published in London by the British Trades Union Congress: The TUC Examines the Bedaux System of Payment by Results, 1933, and "Report on the Bedaux and related systems," 1932. Copies of both are held in the TUC library.

24. Interview with R. D. Power.

25. These statistics are calculated from data in the Annual Reports of the Gold Coast Labour Department.

26. The following paragraphs are based on the Annual Reports of the Gold Coast Labour Department, and correspondence in Ghana National Archive, Sekondi (GNAS), File LWR12, and Tarkwa District Administration Archive, File M20.

27. Labour Department Archive, Accra (LDA), File K93, "Office note on H. H. Fraser", September 1954.

28. GCM, 27 February 1948.

29. Private papers of J. Sam, former General President of the MEU, "Report on underground visits," n.d.

30. Labour Department Archive Tarkwa (LDT), File LT17, District Labour Officer to Commissioner of Labour, 22 August 1949.

31. GCM, 14 April 1950.

32. "Gold Coast labor," unsigned government report, July 1952. My thanks to Peter Greenhalgh for a copy of this document.

33. LDT, File LT7, District Labour Officer to General Secretary, MEU, 27 January 1953.

34. LDA, File K93, Labour Department Minute, 17 January 1954.

35. Ashanti Times (Obuasi), 11 July 1952.

36. GNAS, File C86, Kumasi Labour Officer to Kumasi Acting Senior Labour Officer, 13 June 1952.

37. LDT, File LT17, District Labour Officer to Acting Chief Labour Officer, 10 July 1953.

38. LDA, "In the matter of the Trades Disputes (Arbitration and Inquiry) Ordinance, 1941, and in the matter of a trade dispute between the Gold Coast Mines' Employees' Union and Messrs. Bibiani (1927) Limited, Board of Inquiry report," 1954: 15.

39. GNAS, File C81, Acting Chief Labour Officer to Principal Secretary, Ministry of Trade and Labour, 18 September 1953.

40. GCM, 17 February 1950.

41. LDA, File LAC010, Obuasi Labour Inspector to Kumasi Labour Officer, 6 September 1953.

42. GNAS, File LWR12, Tarkwa Labour Officer to Regional Labour Officer, 22 May 1954.

43. GCM, 17 May 1955.

44. LDT, File LT12, "Notes of a meeting held by the Managing Director of the SGMC," 30 July 1965.

45. LDA, File KL188, Western Region Labour Officer to Chief Labour Officer, 20 January 1969.

46. State Gold Mining Corporation Archive, "Technical operations report," n.d.

47. State Gold Mining Corporation Archive, PD-NCB Consultants Ltd., "Report on survey of productivity and assessment of training needs to government of Ghana," May 1977.

48. Ashanti Goldfields Corporation Archive, "Minutes of a sub-committee of the Mines Standing Negotiating Committee-Metal Mines of Ghana held at Obuasi on 17th March 1978."

REFERENCES

ALLEN, G. (1957) "Gold mining in Ghana." Transactions of the Institution of Mining and Metallurgy 66, 10: 505-526.

BRAVERMAN, H. (1974) Labor and Monopoly Capital. New York: Monthly Review Press.

BURAWOY, M. (1979) Manufacturing Consent. Chicago: University of Chicago Press.

——— (1978) "Toward a Marxist theory of the labor process: Braverman and beyond." Politics and Society 8, 3-4: 247-312.

CLAYTON, A. and D. SAVAGE (1974) Government and Labour in Kenya, 1895-1963. London: Frank Cass.

COOMBS, R. (1978) "Labour and monopoly capital." New Left Review 107: 79-96.

COOPER, F. (1981) "Peasants, capitalists, and historians: review article." Journal of Southern African Studies 7, 2: 284-314.

COPLEY, F. (1923) Frederick W. Taylor. New York: Harper & Brothers.

CRISP, J. (1981) "Rank-and-file protest at the Ashanti Goldfields Corporation, Ghana, 1970-1972." Labour Capital and Society 14, 2: 48-62.

——— (1980) "Labour resistance and labour control in the Ghanaian gold mining industry, 1870-1980." Ph.D. thesis, University of Birmingham.

——— (1979) "Union atrophy and worker revolt: labour protest at Tarkwa Goldfields, Ghana, 1968-1969." Canadian Journal of African Studies 13, 1-2: 265-293.

EDWARDS, R. (1979) Contested Terrain. London: Heinemann.

ELGER, T. (1979) "Valorisation and deskilling: a critique of Braverman." Capital and Class 7: 58-99.

FORD, J. (1944) "Scientific management, with particular application to a Witwatersrand gold mine." Papers and Discussions of the Association of the Mine Managers of the Transvaal: 875-893.

——— (1943) Underground Management. Johannesburg: Johannesburg Consolidated Investment Co. Ltd.

FRIEDMAN, A. (1977) Industry and Labour. London: Macmillan.

HEYWOOD, G. (1945) "Some aspects of mining practice." Papers and Discussions of the Association of the Mine Managers of the Transvaal: 959-989.

KITCHING, G. (1980) Class and Economic Change in Kenya. New Haven, CT: Yale University Press.

LAZONICK, W. (1978) "The subjection of labour to capital: the rise of the capitalist system." Review of Radical Political Economics 10, 1: 1-27.

MARX, K. (1976) Capital, vol. 1. Harmondsworth: Penguin Books.

——— (1954) Capital, vol. 1). London: Lawrence and Wishart.

MEEK, C. et al. (1940) Europe and West Africa. London: Oxford University Press.

NORTHCOTT, C. (1932) "The Bedaux system — a critical appraisal." Unity (May).

PALMER, B. (1975) "The thrust for efficiency, managerial views of labor, and working class rebellion, 1903-1922." Review of Radical Political Economics 7 (Summer): 31-49.

SOMERSET, O. and H. FRASER (1958) "Scientific management principles applied to West African mining." Transactions of the Institution of Mining and Metallurgy 67, 7: 285-348.

TAYLOR, F. (1911) Fundamentals of Scientific Management. Reprinted in F. Taylor, Scientific Management. New York: Harper and Brothers, 1947.

——— (1903) Shop Management. Reprinted in F. Taylor, Scientific Management. New York: Harper and Brothers, 1947.

URWICK, L. and E. BRECH (1951) The Making of Scientific Management, Volume 1. London: Isaac Pitman.

4

HERE EVERYONE WALKED WITH FEAR

The Mozambican Labor System and
the Workers of Lourenço Marques,
1945-1962

JEANNE PENVENNE

**In the decade and
a half following World War II,** international trends toward expansion,
increasing demand for intensive labor, and concentration of workers
in urban areas brought about important changes in southern
Mozambique. In Lourenço Marques the state and private sector tried
to adapt existing systems of mobilizing and controlling labor to the
new situation, but while the state eventually relinquished some of its
former authority in labor mobilization, it maintained its key role in
directing and disciplining urban workers throughout the 1950s. In
Lourenço Marques of the 1940s and 1950s, as in Kimberley of the
1870s and 1880s, the assumption that African workers were presumptive criminals shaped the legislation regulating their mobility, their
conduct as workers, and the essential nature of urban work. Furthermore, the legal and ideological constructs treating Africans as

Author's Note: Data for this chapter were gathered as part of doctoral
research sponsored by the Social Science Research Council, Fulbright-
Hays, and the Fundaçao Calouste Gulbenkian. Field work in Mozambique

dependent upon state tutelage in most economic matters set forth the state's role as paternal mediator between labor and capital. Whether labor relations built on such premises could control a work force in the context of rapid economic growth, upward pressure on wages, and the expansion of alternatives — legal or illegal — that the sheer demographic growth of the city provided was another story.

By almost any criterion Lourenço Marques experienced a period of rapid growth in the post-World War II era. The city's population increased from approximately 68,000 in 1940 to 184,000 in 1960, with most of the increase occurring in the 1950s. The white population alone burgeoned from a prewar 14,316 to 28,301 by 1956 and 56,085 by 1960 (Anuário Estatístico, 1940, 1950, 1956, 1960). Tonnage handled at the state-controlled port authority quadrupled between 1940 and 1962. Residential, business, and public works construction boomed; the state undertook a major investment in the expansion and construction of telecommunications, transportation, and waterfront facilities; and investment in manufacturing and industry increased in response to the improving urban facilities (Pereira de Lima, 1970: 7-16; Hance and van Dongen, 1957). The African labor force employed in the district's private sector alone grew from 47,400 in 1950 to 96,000 by 1962 (Rita Ferreira, 1971: 81, 84, 89, 108).

This chapter focuses on what rapid economic expansion meant for black people living, working, and coming to seek employment in Lourenço Marques. To what extent were workers able to anticipate, accommodate, and manipulate changing constraints? How did workers balance investment of their labor among the increasingly attractive urban alternatives in light of continuing efforts by the state and private employers to try to allocate, discipline, and cheapen black labor?[1] The chapter demonstrates that while the constraints could never quite edit out the alternatives, the state's legal and coercive power continued to dominate worker strategies in Lourenço Marques. The legal Lourenço Marques was not the only Lourenço Marques, but while most people worked within the system, and many

was undertaken with the kind permission and support of the following people: Reitor Fernando Ganhao, Archivist Maria Inez Nogueira da Costa, Directors Aquino da Braganca, Gabriel Mabunda, Serra Ventosa, and Grup Dinimizador Gaspar Guevende. Sampling, coding, and programing Lourenço Marques employment records were completed with the help of Jack R. Warner, David Sousa, Frederick Cooper, Robert Lucas, and Patricia Vail. I gratefully acknowledge their support.

Table 4.1   Tonnage Handled Through the Port of Lourenço
Marques, 1940 to 1970

Year	Metric Tons Handled
1940	1,777,638
1947	2,989,289
1949	3,304,852
1955	4,134,341
1958	5,627,646
1962	7,093,310
1965	8,815,193
1970	13,665,799

SOURCES: Pereira da Lima (1971, Vol. III: 60); U.S. Consular Despatches, 127 of 1955 and 170 of 1961.

carefully worked around it, the risks taken by those working in illegal Lourenço Marques were generally acknowledged to be considerable. The state's ability to intervene to discipline black workers in Lourenço Marques was so pervasive that many workers recalled: "Here everyone walked in fear."[2]

BACKGROUND

From the late nineteenth century the city's economy was molded by its role as an important port for the transshipment of goods to and from the Transvaal mining areas. The export of minerals and import of machinery and building materials — the so-called transit trade — soon dominated the economy (Newitt, 1972: 45-52; Penvenne, 1982: 28-36). Furthermore, the port's national hinterland increasingly developed as a labor reserve for Transvaal industry rather than as a productive area capable of supplying goods for local consumption or export through Lourenço Marques (Harris, 1959; Newitt, 1974). Eventually the relationship among Mozambican laborers, Transvaal industry, and the state-controlled port and railway complex at Lourenço Marques was formalized through international negotiations that balanced monopoly recruitment of Mozambican labor for Transvaal industry against a percentage of Transvaal foreign trade guaranteed to be shipped through Lourenço Marques. Through the resultant labor/transit conventions, the Portuguese colonial state acquired a steady and substantial source of foreign exchange (see First, 1977; Newitt, 1974; Vail and White, 1979; Clarence Smith, 1972).

Formalization of Mozambique south of the Save River (Sul do Save) as a labor reserve went hand-in-hand with increased Portuguese bureaucratic control over the African population. The Native Affairs Department was created at the turn of the century to funnel the independent flow of mine labor through the monopoly recruitment agency, the Witwatersrand Native Labour Association (WNLA), but also to conscript sufficient labor to build, maintain, and operate the port to enable it to handle the negotiated traffic quotas (Penvenne, 1982: 48-124; Harris, 1959).

Until the mid-1950s, and in some cases as late as the early 1970s, the state and some Portuguese firms in Lourenço Marques employed state-conscripted, minimum wage contract laborers, so-called *chibalo* workers,[3] to minimize production costs in construction and transit handling, and ultimately to cheapen and control the city's independent labor force through strike breaking with conscripted scabs (Penvenne and Manghezi, 1981; Penvenne, 1982: 455-472). Widespread employment of chibalo labor in private construction, public works, and transit handling also undercut urban entry-level opportunities for unskilled migrants. At the same time, political pressure from Portuguese immigrants tended to curb opportunities for upwardly mobile Africans, particularly during periods of rising white unemployment. By the mid-1930s such pressure had already resulted in a significant whitening of formerly black jobs in both the private and public sectors (Penvenne, 1982: 413-446).

Throughout the twentieth century, vulnerability to labor conscription in rural areas and the narrow parameters for entry and mobility in the urban labor market enhanced the voluntary flow of Sul do Save men into clandestine or contract labor in neighboring countries. Saul Tembe was born in 1924 in Catembe, just across the bay from Lourenço Marques, but he worked for fifteen years (1943 to 1958) on annual contracts to the Tongaat Sugar Mill in Natal rather than commute across the bay to work in Lourenço Marques. Tembe explained, "Africans were afraid to work here because of chibalo. Once you have worked for nothing you do not want to stay here. When you finished at school you would go to the foreign countries at the borders, Swaziland and South Africa."[4]

By mid-century, a typical employment pattern had emerged among the majority of adult males in Sul do Save: They spent their economically active years working a series of contracts to South

Africa interspersed with stints of chibalo labor on local plantations or public works during the required repatriation intervals (Fuller, 1955: 146; Webster, 1978: 165-167; First, 1977: 113-142; Penvenne and Manghezi, 1981: 23-36). This employment pattern reinforced the trend for rural women to assume the burden of many formerly male managerial tasks on top of their principal responsibilities for domestic tasks, child care, and food crop cultivation. Women also became increasingly dependent upon repatriated mine wages to purchase necessary consumer goods, emergency food stores, and to pay household taxes (Young, 1977).

In quantitative terms, male emloyment in the port placed a poor second to mine labor, and female wage labor was almost insignificant in comparison with the majority occupation of domestic agricultural production. In 1951, for example, approximately 106,500 men were contracted in Sul do Save for work in South Africa, while the entire black male population of Lourenço Marques in that year (including minors) was still only 37,852 (First, 1977: 25-26; Província de Moçambique, 1955). In 1940, the vast majority of women living in and around Lourenço Marques continued to work their food crops (Colónia de Moçambique, 1944). Beginning with the postwar economic revival, however, investment patterns began to change, and slowly employment patterns and labor relations in the south, particularly in Lourenço Marques, changed in response. In 1958, Saul Tembe finally decided that conditions in the city had improved enough for him to seek work at home and end his career as a migrant to South Africa.[5]

From 1926 to 1933 what came to be called the New State government in Portugal assumed political control, outlined its economic and labor policies, and created the machinery to implement them.[6] From 1933 to around 1945 it put its strongly protectionist and authoritarian policies to work in Mozambique: credit, immigration, capital investment, and both black and white labor were tightly regulated by the state. From 1945 to 1950, the slow and cautious pace diminished somewhat with respect to credit, investment, and immigration as the New State moved firmly to take advantage of growth opportunities in the revived regional economy and permitted some national firms to do the same. The liberalization of economic and immigration policies in the postwar era, however, was not mirrored in labor policy — quite the opposite.

Beginning in the late 1940s, state-sponsored white immigration soared. With the implementation of a series of state-financed six-year development plans and a boom in locally financed commercial and residential construction some of the capital accumulated during the previous half century of exploiting ill-paid, tightly controlled African labor and highly protected markets was finally reinvested locally. Key monopolies, such as beer brewing and cement production, experienced unprecedented growth, and by the late 1950s many local industries began to diversify their operations. Beginning around 1957 and culminating in the reform legislation of the early 1960s, labor controls were altered to accommodate both a developing labor surplus and changing patterns of production. Between 1945 and 1957, however, the state regularly intervened in most labor relations in its efforts to counteract the tendency for increased labor demand to bid up wages, to maintain worker discipline, and to guarantee continuing supplies of chibalo labor to handle state and municipal projects.

The liberalization of penalties and reform legislation of this period were also directly linked to the important transition in capital investment and production processes in the city. Portuguese conglomerates made their decisive move into the Mozambican market, and by the 1960s their investments in industry and manufacturing fueled the demand for better skilled, more permanent black workers that marked a transition from the historic reliance on extracting absolute surplus value from unskilled migrants (Torp, 1979: 124-127; Sousa Ferreira, 1975: 164-167; U.S. Consul, Annual Economic Report, 1961). At the same time Portugal's efforts to secure investment capital from the international community made it increasingly sensitive to pressure to bring its labor policy into line with International Labor Organization standards (Vail and White, 1980: 382-385; Harris, 1966: 14-27; Sousa Ferreira, 1975: 167).

By 1974, the Lourenço Marques District was the most heavily industrial region of the colony. Local industry came into its own between 1945 to 1960 and grew rapidly between 1960 and 1974 (Torp, 1979: 126; Rita Ferreira, 1971). Meanwhile, the formation of FRELIMO in 1962 transformed labor relations within the city — from wage hikes and promotions to workshop discipline — into political issues.[7] The new departures in capital investment and labor control — especially in the southern part of Mozambique — are still so little studied that this chapter will be restricted to the period 1945 to 1962.

CRIMINALITY AND MOBILITY IN THE WHITE MAN'S TOWN

The nature and extent of controls and sanctions at the disposal of the state and private employers revealed a great deal about labor relations in Lourenço Marques during the 1940s and 1950s. The *Regulamento dos Serviçais e Trabalhadores Indígenas* of 1944 and 1949[8] and the *Estatuto dos Indígenas das Províncias de Guiné, Angola e Moçambique* of 1954[9] each set a very straight and narrow legal path for Mozambican workers in urban areas. To begin with, it was a criminal offense for healthy males over eighteen not to sell their labor, or to sell their labor in a manner not sanctioned by the regulations. Unemployment in the city was a crime, and forced labor was a permitted and indeed common sanction for criminal offenses (*Estatuto, 1954,* Art. 26: 13). The link between the crime of unemployment and the punishment of chibalo was so direct that a logbook registering unemployed workers to be assigned to chibalo under various municipal, state, and even private employers during 1960 and 1961, for example, was first labeled *"Chibalo,"* but then the chibalo was crossed out and the word *"Desempregos"* (unemployed) superimposed.[10]

Transgressions of urban labor regulations were punishable by fines or forced labor. Throughout the 1950s all the following were considered transgressions: failure to register with the authorities within three days from arrival in town, failure to declare oneself unemployed, changing jobs without authorization, unauthorized self-employment, unregistered casual labor, absence from the municipal area without permission, and inciting coworkers to quit.[11] Between 1950 and 1962 fully 12 percent of the entire registered urban labor force worked at least one term of chibalo for transgression of municipal labor regulations.[12]

The labor control system thus regularly funneled workers into chibalo, allowing the state and municipality (the city's principal employers) to continue to organize transit handling, sanitation, and public works around unskilled, temporary cheap gang labor. In a system where unskilled gang labor was fundamental to production techniques, expensive, unproductive prisons were an anachronism. Chibalo incorporated the two basic elements of prison punishment: time and surveillance — although each in a milder form than commonly associated with prisons. Chibalo terms for contravention of labor regulations, for example, ranged from three to eighteen months, with the majority around three months.[13] Chibalo workers were generally fed and housed apart from other workers (in military or police barracks, jails, and compounds), and worked under minimal surveillance.

The obvious question is how the authorities were able to exploit chibalo labor without inordinate expense for security and surveillance, and the unhappy answer is terror. Terror was the hallmark of Portuguese labor policy as recently as the late 1950s. It was the fundamental underpinning of control over the urban work force, particularly for workers in positions of trust such as domestic servants, and it facilitated the management of gang labor with a minimum of surveillance.

According to the Municipal Curator for Native Affairs in 1950:

> The growing influx of natives into urban centers in search of employment creates a problem of social discipline whose resolution requires a rigorous control over the activity of the native population in these centers, not only to hinder . . . vagrancy and criminality . . . but also to correct the misconduct of . . . workers while carrying out their jobs.[14]

Despite public disclaimers, state confidential circulars advocated the use of corporal punishment throughout the 1940s and 1950s as an integral part of such "rigorous control."[15] In the 1940s, Governor General Tristão de Bettencourt explained the rationale behind such brutality:

> Sometimes a servant refuses to do a job or becomes defiant. An instructive reprimand, well-oriented and guided by a criteria more instructive than repressive . . . will, to some extent, improve the native's conduct, making him more adaptable to service and to living on intimate terms with European families [Tristão de Bettencourt, 1942: 48].

Municipal logbooks recording corporal punishment for domestic servants (1951 to 1957) testify to the essential normality of beating and fear as mechanisms of control over urban labor — confirming what recollections of experience over a longer period make clear, that Tristão de Bettencourt's euphemistic "instructive reprimand" was a *palmatório* beating.[16]

Between 1953 and 1957, for example, nearly 1000 domestics were beaten in varying derees of severity at the municipal headquarters; 72 percent of the beatings involved youths between fourteen and twenty whose offenses ranged from breaking a teacup or scorching a sheet while ironing to simple "disobedience" or "rudeness." Disobedience accounted for 75 percent of all recorded offenses, while petty theft, the only offense that could be considered punishable in any common legal sense, as opposed to simple grounds for dismissal, comprised only about 2 percent of all cases.[17] Between 1950 and 1962, nearly 5 percent of the entire registered labor force in the city received at least one *palmatório* beating.[18] Clearly, state enforcement of worker discipline through beatings and forced labor was not an aberration or a holdover from earlier times, but rather made up an integral part of the state's continuing role in keeping urban labor cheap and manageable.

While palmatório beatings were experienced most often by domestic servants and chibalo sentences most often served by recent migrants and unskilled laborers,[19] the entire spectrum of sanctions was always available to employers and always in the minds of workers.[20] Simple forms of evading the system, or a lapse in respectful demeanor toward whites could result in hideously disproportionate punishment. An old man working as a day laborer on the docks, for example, was brutally beaten for allegedly hiding in the port zone to avoid working.[21] A cook was similarly treated for trying to evade registration. The cook knew the authorities would resist allowing his new employer to pay him 325$ escudos per month because he had only worked as a cook for a short time.[22] White-collar workers also risked strict sanctions. An office worker earning the impressive salary of 1200$ escudos per month, for example, was summarily sentenced to twenty months of forced labor at 180$ escudos per month simply for "abuse of confidence."[23] The arbitrary nature of punishment fed the atmosphere of fear, which tempered workers' strategies for making a living in Lourenço Marques.

The atmosphere of terror was so pervasive that workers tended to accept punishment even if they were innocent of any wrongdoing rather than risk a more serious confrontation. One informant walked away from two months back pay rather than challenge the false allegation of theft by his employer, explaining, "Was I going to risk my hide for 690$ escudos?"[24] Others who were beaten and imprisoned on false charges similarly put the incidents behind them, considering themselves fortunate that their treatment had not been worse

(Penvenne, 1982: 396-398). The simple fact, as Marvin Harris (1966: 27) observed, that employers did not have to prove their allegations in a court of law — that an accused worker was presumed to be a criminal — further deterred employees from seeking justice.

The experience of Samuel Chipoco Miuanga demonstrated the relationship among labor regulations, beatings, and chibalo, and Miuanga's experience was not uncommon. In 1950, he became discouraged working for low wages in Lourenço Marques as a legally registered casual construction worker and decided to join his cousin and several others to seek employment for higher wages in South Africa. Instead of following the legal route, which would have wedded him to a WNLA contract for at least twelve months at an undetermined job, Miuanga and the others attempted to cross the border as clandestine emigrants to seek employment as free agents. Miuanga was apprehended by the Portuguese border police and for several days was intermittently beaten and sent to work in the fields of a nearby Portuguese planter. Eventually he and the others were marched back to Lourenço Marques and sentenced to a one-year stint of chibalo as roadworkers for the State Geological Survey team.

Miuanga soon noticed that many of the chibalo workers on the survey team who had been on the job longer than himself returned to eat and sleep at their own homes after each work day instead of returning to the barracks, jails, or compounds where the gangs were usually fed and housed. Clearly some agreement had been reached between those workers and the overseer enabling the men to eat and sleep in the comfort of their homes as long as they dutifully arrived at work at the appropriate hour daily and did their work. The arrangement also saved the state the expense of feeding and housing the men. When Miuanga tried it, however, the overseer sent him to the administrative headquarters where he was beaten so badly that his hands and feet became severely swollen and bled. The police then forced Miuanga to lie on the floor, arms outstretched, while they stood on his painfully swollen hands. He was sent back to work in that condition for the rest of the day. Surveillance and discipline on the job remained as before, but Miuanga did not risk any further incident.[25]

On one hand, arrest records and the incidents of beatings and chibalo demonstrated the extent to which the state coerced urban workers to comply with a pervasive legal system favoring the interests of employers over employees and whites over blacks. On the other hand, the same statistics revealed the extent to which workers

Table 4.2   Arrests for Contravention of the Código e Regulamento dos Serviçais e Trabalhadores Indígenas, Lourenço Marques, 1946 to 1963

Year	Total Arrests	Arrests as Percentage of Censused Black Population
1946	3494	
1949	7323	
1950	7307	13%
1956	7239	
1959	8462	
1960	6620	5%
1961	3706	
1962	1525	
1963	461	

SOURCE: Anuario Estatistico (1946-1964).

tried, however unsuccessfully, to work around the tight legal constraints. It is difficult to estimate the number of workers who successfully evaded the system, and obviously some evasions entailed more risk than others, but some trends emerged from interviews and the ACLM sample.

Employment and penal histories together with published arrest records demonstrated that arrests, forced labor, and fines increased in the immediate postwar era during the state's drive to secure sufficient labor to undertake its extensive transportation and communications projects.[26] Documents and interviews revealed that the state routinely carried out so-called *rusgas* (roundups or raids) in the suburban areas looking for people with document irregularities, tricking people into curfew violations and, in short, arresting men on any pretext they could muster in order to generate sufficient labor to carry out a priority or temporary project. In such cases men with steady employment could be easily set free by their employers in the morning, but the practice commonly netted a sufficient number of men without employers or patrons who would have to work a chibalo term.[27]

Arrests peaked in the mid-1950s at the height of an urban labor shortage caused by increased demand for labor from private and public construction, but then dropped off sharply into the early 1960s when a surplus of unskilled labor developed. While overall arrests peaked in the late 1950s, the sample data, which detailed the nature of punishment issued to those arrested, indicated that forced labor sentences peaked with the labor shortage but then declined rapidly. Palmatório beatings followed a similar pattern. After 1957, fines became the most common punishment for all offenders except for the continuing use of corporal punishment to discipline youthful domestic servants.[28]

To what extent was the record of punishment an indication of the seriousness of worker resistance? First, the high incidence of palmatório beatings was not a consequence of serious worker resistance. As we have seen, domestics were the most frequently beaten, and disobedience was their most common offense. Informants who had worked as domestics during this period stressed that beatings were very arbitrary, often in response to quite trivial incidents: "For any little thing we were beaten."[29] Disobedience often boiled down to a servant having dallied on his way to the bakery when instructed to go directly about his business bear in mind that the vast majority were teenagers.

Second, workers who posed any serious challenge to their employers, or who were accused of challenging the authorities, were few in the overall context. Their punishment was commonly deportation either to São Tomé or northern Mozambique. Workers, frequently alcoholics, who had a long history of arrests for petty offenses were similarly deported.[30] Beatings were more accurately a gauge of the state's use of arbitrary terror tactics to foster a climate of fear than of any significant, persistant incidence of direct resistance by an oppressed labor force.

The majority of arrests for contravention of labor regulations in Lourenço Marques fell into two broad categories: working casual labor without authorization and failure to report to the authorities when not legally employed.[31] Both categories reflected the efforts of individual workers to market their labor to maximize income and protect themselves from long-term, low-wage legal contracts. Informants generally recalled that workers who failed to find satisfactory employment within the brief grace period were "sold" by the authorities to employers whose wages and working conditions were too poor to attract volunteers.[32] The Municipal Curator for Native Labor was permitted to avail "unemployed" workers to private employers rather than repatriate them when state and municipal requirements were filled.[33]

Informants further agreed that healthy adult males could generally find casual work on construction or at the wharves throughout this period. Risks of being apprehended as an unregistered worker at such jobs was somewhat diminished by the fact that thousands were hired on a daily basis, and in such cases it was impossible for the authorities to do much more than spot check without greatly compromising production.[34] While many workers were apprehended for unregistered casual labor, both the sample and informants indicate that many more were not. Sentences for working unregistered casual labor ranged from three to twelve months chibalo, three for first offenders and more for workers with a history of evasion.[35] Since incomes of casual laborers were only a small cut above chibalo wages, and overtime opportunities similar for both, the sentences were not as threatening to unskilled new migrants as a stint of chibalo was to those who had secured better paying positions in the city. In short, while the incidence of arrests for contravention of labor regulations was high — about one in ten workers arrested at least once between 1950 and 1962 — the nature of their transgressions revealed a pattern of workers cautiously evading the system in an attempt to gain time to find a satisfactory legal niche for themselves in the legal city rather than any persistent on-the-job confrontation between labor and capital.

Given the illegality of unemployment and the limited range of legal employment in the city, workers holding attractive jobs had all the incentive they needed to walk softly: they had found a niche and wanted to keep their jobs. For this group the state-directed disciplinary tactics commonly used with domestics and casual laborers were scarcely necessary; everyone knew that a respectful demeanor and close attention to urban regulations were essential to keeping any so-called good job. Employment records revealed very little turnover and little apprehended resistance among workers in acknowledged good jobs.[36] Informants from all backgrounds emphasized that there was nothing to be gained by confrontation in the city; one would simply be bringing trouble on oneself and one's family. If a person decided to seek work in Lourenço Marques it made sense to stay close to the rules and "to make a way" (Penvenne, 1979a).

The key change in the reform legislation of the early 1960s was the abolition of the registration system. With the abolition of the whole body of legislation specific to persons formerly considered *indígenas* (natives), the so-called *indigenato,* the bureaucracy no longer stood between the majority black labor force and a job, and no longer legally held black workers to employers who mistreated them; for the first time since 1904 most blacks could legally quit! The reforms further undermined the state's ability to directly intervene in employment contracts to hold down wages in the private sector (Harris, 1966).

The stifling labor control system imposed in the 1940s was one parameter of the workers' struggle in Lourenço Marques during this period and the reform legislation permitting a greater measure of free market labor relations in the early 1960s was another. They were important, but an appreciation of the workers struggle must include an understanding of the workers themselves: their needs, their individual constraints, and the differences among them.

UNITY AND DIVERSITY IN
THE URBAN AFRICAN LABOR FORCE

Fundamental to an understanding of mobility and constraint within the urban African labor force is an appreciation of its diversity. An individual's potential for upward mobility and his or her perception of and experience with mobility and labor controls were only most broadly determined by race. Social differentiation within the work force should not be completely overshadowed by the distance between black and white workers. While the black community was united by a spectrum of racist constraints it was also distinguished by all the individual and group characteristics commonly determining social differentiation. Patterns of mobility and the nature of strategies to further personal and career goals varied greatly. Age, sex, social status, education, experience and health were all factors contributing to a person's earning power, but sex was the most fundamental determinant of all.

While wage gaps between similarly skilled whites and blacks were large — about ten to one for most categories — the range of wages among black workers as a group was also large — about seven to one between top and entry level jobs.[37] Within the black labor force the across-the-board differences between salaries paid to men and women in similar jobs — usually two or three to one — remained an important injustice throughout this period. Furthermore, men, regardless of their social status and education, moved up the wage scale as they grew older, more experienced, more skilled, and more familiar with successful strategies for mobility. Elderly males who were perhaps less able to do their former jobs were given lighter work at lower wages if they were not retired or dismissed.[38] Mobility among women, however, was quite a different situation. Regardless of social status, education, skill, and experience, women enjoyed precious little upward mobility.

Table 4.3   Retail Price Index in Relation to Port Authority Wages

Year	Retail Price Index	Servent Wage	Day Labor Wage
1939	100	300$ escudos/monthly	12$ escudos/daily
1944	144.92	unchanged	unchanged
1950	196.13	unchanged	unchanged
1956	204.99	unchanged	unchanged
1957	213.73	600$ escudos	15$ escudos
1960	213.55	unchanged	unchanged
1962	220.71	unchanged	25$ escudos

SOURCES: Anuário Estatístico (1944-1963): Província de Moçambique (1961), Salarios do Péssoal Assalariado do Quadro Permanente, Dip. Leg. 2046, 24 Dezembro 1960.

Analysis of the pace and character of wage increments for urban workers is greatly complicated by the diversity of the labor force, but several general points should be made.[39] First, wartime inflation took a big bite out of every worker's income, and while whites were able to force wage gains to accommodate for their falling real wages, blacks from virtually all sectors of the urban economy were not able to do the same. Between 1939 and 1950, the cost of living in Lourenço Marques increased by almost 100 percent, while wages for most African workers stagnated. Civil service salaried workers and casual labor at the port, for example, received exactly the same wages from the mid-1930s to the late 1950s.[40] The dramatic wage increases of the late 1950s only brought wages back to about 90 percent of the value of wages earned in 1939. The relative stability of the cost of living from 1950 to 1956, however, enabled workers with access to overtime incentives to recoup some of their real income.

Wages in domestic service, the occupation of about half the urban labor force throughout much of the twentieth century, remained at the bottom of the wage range, even when monetary equivalents of room and board are taken into account.[41] The low level of service incomes should be qualified since domestic service was a common bridging occupation for very young, inexperienced male migrants. Most of the youths who worked first as domestics soon moved out of their jobs to take more secure, better paid jobs.[42] Domestics frequently used their entry years to get a foothold in the city, to improve their language skills, and acquire more marketable education and experience.[43] Those who remained in domestic service commonly moved into more skilled, higher paid positions as professional cooks or gardeners, but all male domestics received annual wage increments in proportion to their growing experience and assumed family responsibilities.[44]

For women, domestic service tended to be a dead end rather than a bridge. Unlike their male counterparts, females did not receive annual increments commensurate with increased responsibility as experienced servants or parents. On the contrary, women who found it necessary to leave wage labor temporarily upon the birth of a child frequently re-entered at a lower wage than they formerly received, despite the fact that they were the sole breadwinners of the household.[45] While domestic service remained an ill-paid occupation for both men and women, the men earning low wages in 1945 were not the same men earning them in 1962; the category was replenished by young migrants. The fact that the proportion of males to females in domestic service dropped from thirteen to one to four to one during this period in part explains why wages for servants remained at the bottom of the urban wage range despite increased demand from the growing white community and broader choice of male entry occupations in construction.

The growing number of middle level occupations for blacks in industry, business, and civil service exhibited a striking range of wage patterns, but unlike the stagnant pattern for domestics, wages among middle level workers increased gradually between 1945 and 1957/1958, but then increased quite rapidly from 1958 to 1962. Men in most industrial jobs, for example, earned between 200$ and 500$ escudos per month in 1946 (depending upon job category, experience, and length of tenure), but the comparable range in 1957 was from 450$ to 700$ escudos per month, and by 1962 from 525$ to 1000$ escudos per month.[46] Wage increases in this category reflected new initiatives in industry, expansion of established industries, and the sustained demand for semiskilled labor from the construction industry.[47]

Finally, the best jobs for blacks paid between 900$ and 1700$ escudos per month in the late 1940s. Those salaries increased to between 1200$ and 2300$ escudos per month by 1958, but then topped off at 2500$ escudos per month in the early 1960s.[48] Only citizens, not so-called indígenas, were allowed to earn more than 2500$ escudos per month. Blacks hoping to earn more than the ceiling wage had to file for an *álvara de assimilação,* a legal procedure that conferred citizenship on persons formerly considered indígenas.[49] The gap between wages in middle-level, firmly black jobs and top-level jobs for indígenas narrowed by about 40 percent between 1957 and 1962.

The fact that wages at the top and bottom levels were slower to improve than intermediate ranges was attributable to a concentration of increased demand for middle-level workers from construction and industry, but also to the tendency for the legal minimum wages (particularly for women) and maximum legal wages for all noncitizens to curb the market's upward pressure on wages at the top and bottom.

MAKING IT IN LOURENÇO MARQUES

Some workers came to the city because it was the only place they could get what they wanted from a job. Others, those who had managed to acquire a skill or education for example, came to Lourenço Marques because the rural market for their work was very limited.[50] People looked for urban jobs that suited their age and stage in life within the parameters of their health, sex, abilities, social networks, and constraints placed upon them by the state bureaucracy. In the postwar era, as Mozambicans began to experience rapidly deteriorating conditions in Sul do Save agriculture, many looked to the city for an alternative. In the same period, the range and attraction of job opportunities in the city increased. Roberto Tembe, a lifelong resident of the port, explained,

At the time of the great war of the forties the city was still small. There were no big buildings and there were few jobs; but then the city began to grow faster, faster and faster, and there were more and more jobs until now.[51]

The impact of rapid economic expansion of the black labor force as a whole, however, was most aptly described by an anonymous informant speaking to Harris in the late 1950s: "Formerly the faucet was completely shut. . . . Now it is open and the water is flowing . . . drip . . . drip . . . drip" (Harris, 1966: 34). The state was able to temper pressures of economic expansion on wages and job opportunities. Its legislation hampered job seeking and switching and channeled labor into low-wage, long-term contracts. The growing influx of rural women who could no longer make a satisfactory living from the land bolstered the low-wage sector of the labor market. Higher wage

Table 4.4   Registered Unemployment in Relation to
             State-Sponsored Immigration

Year	Registered Unemployed Lourenço Marques	Colonos Entering Lourenço Marques
1955	347	978
1956	437	713
1958	486	1,364
1959	837	1,976
1960	817	2,292
1961	754	2,660
1962	1,011	1,214
1963	1,127	1,109

SOURCE: Anuário Estatístico (1955-1963).

sectors, meanwhile, were strongly affected by the relationship between the state and the rapidly increasing population of poor, unemployed Portuguese immigrants.

Portugal's policy was to strengthen its political hold on Mozambique through state-assisted settlement of *colonos* (Portuguese settlers) "to whom work must be guaranteed" (Compilation of Legislation, 1939: np). The growing problem of unemployment among recent immigrants convinced the state to intervene, even in the private sector, to place them in jobs. The majority of registered unemployed were white office workers, commercial workers, carpenters, and masons. They were increasingly placed before educated and skilled local blacks who formerly aspired to such positions (Penvenne, 1982: 447-455). The combined impact of these factors was to widen the preserve of white labor at the expense of upwardly mobile blacks, and to keep overall mobility within the black urban labor force to a controlled . . . drip . . . drip.

ACCOMMODATION AND MOBILITY: THE CASE OF WOMEN AND INDUSTRY

Although it is still one of the best-kept secrets of the literature on African labor history, African women made up an important minority in the wage labor force of many African cities in the twentieth century. At the turn of the century, women who spoke Portuguese earned top wages in familiar positions as wetnurse or child's nurse, but many other women worked for very low wages as hod carriers at the port (Noronha, 1895: 139; Jessett, 1899: 81). During the twentieth century, local women worked many of the city's ill-paid, unpopular jobs, but were particularly important as laborers in the waterfront timber yards where lighters were used for unloading. By the 1940s, men had begun to take an interest in displacing women in those jobs. The administration, which was simultaneously trying to displace male domestics with females in order to free up more male labor, alleged that timber work was both too heavy and inappropriate for women.[52]

Women, like men, had worked as convicts throughout the century. Female convicts, most of whom had been arrested for drunkenness, brewing, and prostitution rather than contravention of labor regulations, commonly worked alongside men on brush clearance, road building, and municipal construction until their visibility was judged to be incompatible with the increase in white tourism of the 1950s (Penvenne, 1982: 114-120, 455-460; Penvenne, 1979a: 25-26). By the postwar period, women were increasingly assigned to less visible chibalo jobs, such as gathering fodder and cleaning up after animals at the city's zoological gardens.[53]

From the late 1940s, however, women were increasingly incorporated into the city's growing industrial sector as cheap labor. While the total African labor force employed in the private sector jobs in the District of Lourenço Marques nearly doubled between 1950 and 1962, the number of women in these jobs increased nearly six and a half fold: from 1,920 to 12,669 (Rita Ferreira, 1971: 81, 84, 89, 108). The increase was more dramatic than the figures suggest since it was specific to two areas, the processing industries and domestic service. Between 1950 and 1962, the district's private processing industries labor force doubled, but the number of women employed in that sector increased twentyfold (Rita Ferreira, 1971: 81, 84, 89, 108).

The cashew shelling industry, *Cajú* (cashew), as it was popularly known in the city, was largely responsible for the increased employment of women in industry. Three-quarters of the 1672 persons employed by Cajú in 1956 were women, all but five of them so-called indígenas.[54] By 1958, Cajú employed 63.4 percent of all women employed in urban industry (Silva, 1960: 56-57).

As early as 1945, Portuguese authorities were alarmed by the rate at which Sul do Save women from certain *circunscrições* (subdistricts) were abandoning their food crops and fleeing to South Africa or Lourenço Marques.[55] Since the law prohibited women from leaving their circunscrições without written permission from their spouse, parent, guardian, or local administrator, many women left illegally.[56] By 1952, the majority of Mozambicans entering South Africa through illegal networks emanating from Lourenço Marques were women.[57] The influx of rural women into the urban job market was, in part, a reflection of deteriorating social and ecological conditions due to the cumulative impact of land alienation, long-term male migration, the ravages of forced cotton cultivation, and the vagaries of Sul do Save's rainfall patterns; and in part, a response to the increasing availability of secure, if ill-paid, wage labor as an alternative to ever-precarious food crop cultivation (Penvenne, 1982: 411-413; Young, 1977).

Drought was a particularly important threat to cultivators in Sul do Save in the postwar era. In spring of 1947, a prolonged drought brought famine to many marginal agricultural areas.[58] Seasonal drought from 1950 to 1953, and again in 1956, was sufficient to require emergency food relief.[59] During lean years the population typically relied on repatriated mine wages to purchase emergency food supplies until the next growing season, but women who did not have menfolk in the mines or towns whom they could turn to for cash became desperate (Young, 1977; Silva, 1960: 56). Furthermore, women from periurban areas such as Bobucuana, Marracuene, Matola, and Machava increasingly looked to wage labor as residential and industrial construction pushed into their garden areas.[60]

Prior to the development of the cashew industry, only a few hundred African women worked in urban industry. At least as early as the 1920s, African, Afro-European, and Goanese women were employed as cigarette packers and rollers at the city's tobacco processing plants (Santos Rufino, 1929: vol. IV). By midcentury, tobacco plant workers were largely skilled local women who had been with the same firm throughout their careers. City industries, including tobacco processing and clothing manufacturing, employed women, typically in positions requiring manual dexterity, at minimum wages legally set at 55 percent of minimums for males throughout the period.[61] In 1956, for example, 25 percent of the African labor force at the city's tobacco processing plants were adult women involved principally in packing.[62] Because the cashew shelling industry's relied on manual dexterity, it emphasized employment of women from the outset.

While some women working skilled jobs, such as cigarette rolling and packing of machine stitching, were able to increase their incomes through piecework and overtime incentives, most women in urban industry did not have such options. Women at the *Fábrica de Malhas* and *Empressa Industrial de Tobacco* earned 500$ to 800$ escudos per month through piecework, but Cajú workers normally received only the legal minimum of 240$ escudos per month.[63] Wages for Cajú workers were raised by 5$ escudos per month in 1958 and then to 330$ escudos in 1961. For the period 1957 to 1961, however, Cajú women received merely 20$ to 25$ escudos per month more than chibalo workers who had the added benefit, such as it was, of receiving free food, housing, clothing, and medical assistance as well as periodic overtime income on top of their minimum monthly salary.

Finally, while many women in the tobacco and clothing industries enjoyed relatively high pay on a piecework basis, and Cajú women earned minimum wages, the two groups of women nonetheless shared some important characteristics. Both groups were predominantly heads of households and many supported minor children. All the women were markedly steady workers (Silva, 1960: 56; ACLM sample). In 1958, 75 percent of the stitchers at the Fábrica de Malhas were heads of households and 58 percent of that group supported their minor children. In the same year, 86 percent of Cajú women were also heads of households, with 62 percent supporting minor children (Silva, 1960: 56). There is less detailed information available on cigarette packers for that year, but in the early 1950s assimilation records indicated that all female cigarette packers registered as assimilados were single, locally born women.[64]

In the late 1940s, the Curator of Native Affairs in Lourenço Marques complained to his superiors that the criteria for setting minimum wages for women — the assumption that African women in the city lived with a wage-earning male — was blatantly ill-conceived. The fact was, he argued, that "hundreds of women working in Lourenço Marques industry do not have husbands" and he insisted that the unreasonably low wages for women were "one of the principal reasons for widespread prostitution which exists among natives in the *conselho*."[65]

Despite the acknowledged inadequacy of Cajú's wages, city employment records illustrated that women nonetheless registered to work at Cajú year after year. Between 1950 and 1962, 42 percent of all women registered to work in Lourenço Marques worked exclusively at Cajú, and the average tenure of all women who ever registered to work at Cajú in that period was six and a half years.[66] Part of the reason women opted to remain at Cajú was the limited, risky, and otherwise unattractive nature of their legal or illegal alternatives. Industries other than Cajú paid minimum wages and had fewer openings. Those industries offering piecework incentives to skilled labor experienced very little personnel turnover, and those openings that arose seldom reached the open market.[67]

While domestic service was a common occupation for women, interviews, municipal surveys, and employment records demonstrated that women, on the whole, preferred the low wages, regular daytime hours, and independent living arrangements as Cajú workers to equally ill-paid, live-in, around-the-clock work as domestics (ACLM sample: Silva, 1960: 55, 57; Álves, 1961: 117-119). In contrast to employment patterns among Cajú employees, women employed in domestic service experienced a pattern of ineffectual instability. Women changed domestic service jobs very frequently, but the changes seldom brought about any appreciable wage increase, some indeed were accompanied by wage drops.[68]

The state's claim to encourage employment of women in domestic service to better incorporate unsophisticated rural women into the ways of so-called civilized society (Tristão de Bettencourt, 1945: 47-48) was particularly ironic in light of a common complaint by women employed as domestics. Women suffered from all the job-related hardships of domestic service experienced by males — long hours, tiresome and exacting tasks, arbitrary discipline, low pay, inappropriate accommodations, and unjustified pay discounts — but in addition they frequently complained of sexual harassment by male members of their employer's household. Harassment of female servants contributed as well to the reluctance of European women to hire women rather than men as servants.[69] While the ratio of female to male servants increased in this period, the increase reflected a diversification of entry-level opportunities for young males without a parallel diversification for women. As noted by the Municipal Curator above, women who faced an unreasonable situation in legal Lourenço Marques were often forced to seek illegal alternatives to make or supplement a living.

Much more research is necessary before we have a full understanding of opportunities for women within the city's clandestine economy. The relationship between illegal sexual liaisons and capital accumulation in the postwar era, along the lines explored by Luise White for Nairobi, remains to be sorted out for Lourenço Marques. In early twentieth-century Lourenço Marques there was a clear link between legal and illegal sexual liaisons and proprietorship, with many of the city's prominent female proprietors coming from a background as prostitutes, brothel madams or as wives and mistresses of wealthy European landowners (Penvenne, 1982: 58-64, 255-294). By

1954, women made up more than two-thirds of the tiny portion of economically active blacks in Lourenço Marques earning a living from rents, but their origin and role in this period remains obscure (Santos, 1959: 70).

While the common illegal urban occupations associated with women, brewing and prostitution, doubtless remained lucrative, they involved a strong element of risk. Women apprehended for brewing commonly served from six to twelve months chibalo.[70] Prostitutes were often sentenced to three months chibalo or summarily repatriated.[71] Despite several administrative crackdowns on police, soldiers, administrators, and women involved in brewing and prostitution, in the late 1940s and early 1950s in particular, both businesses survived in areas where concentrations of single males provided a ready market: the Malanga intransit miners compound, the police and military barracks in Polana and Malangalene. Prostitutes and brewers obviously risked prosecution, but they also risked physical abuse from their customers. Assaults on women, while not necessarily limited to the Malanga and Malhangalene areas, were much more common there (Penvenne, 1982: 462-465).

While it may initially seem incongruous that African women returned year after year to work at Cajú, their choices appear more reasonable in the overall context of employment opportunities for women, legal or illegal. Given the deteriorating conditions in Sul do Save agriculture, and the narrower margins for mobility and earning power among women, employment at Cajú enabled many women to earn a secure and steady income, a quality not to be taken lightly at the margin of subsistence.

COMING TO TERMS: MALE CAREERS IN THE WHITE MAN'S TOWN

Men clearly enjoyed a broader range of opportunities and were much more successful at translating, increased experience, education, and skill into higher wages than were women. To the extent that men had good health and a basic facility with the Portuguese language, they could choose from an increasingly broad scope of employment opportunities to suit their career aspirations in Lourenço Marques. Some men came seeking a career, some a semiretirement, some an opportunity for short-term capital accumulation and some a temporary toehold en route to a mine contract in South Africa.

The attraction of any job depended in part upon the aspirations of the job seeker considering the position. Virtually deadend civil service *servente* jobs, for example, were sought after by middle-age Mozambican males because they offered steady, secure income without the strenuous manual labor commonly required in many designated black jobs. Since black people who were not legally exempted from the "moral obligation to work" — an exemption usually issued only with documented proof of terminal illness or disability[72] — were vulnerable to chibalo conscription for the crime of not being employed in registered wage labor, the willingness of "tired" middle-aged men to take such jobs made sense.[73]

Youths frequently came to the city to seek entry-level jobs to earn tax money, cash for clothing, and as an alternative to the low-wage, less attractive alternative jobs in rural areas. Typically, however, youths had to move on to a mine contract in order to accumulate a bridewealth.[74] Men who decided to work in Lourenço Marques, whether as a stepping stone to the mines, as an adult career, or a semiretirement, had to come to terms with the state bureaucracy that stood between them and the workplace. The rapid expansion of legal middle-level designated black jobs in the city in this period certainly made accommodation less painful for many workers.

Africans committed to making a career in Lourenço Marques, however, could enjoy some success within the tight parameters of legal Lourenço Marques. Apprenticeships in manual arts, for example, could lead to a well-paid career, but they involved an element of risk. Mobility and earning power depended upon an apprentice's chosen field of endeavor, his skill, and, in large part, upon the goodwill of the teacher/employer. Shoemaking and tailoring, for example, were relatively easy to enter, but competition with Indians and Europeans was strong and, once trained, it might be difficult for Africans to secure a license for self-employment, thus effectively forcing them to continue to sell their labor in Indian or European shops. That was indeed a common fate for Africans in those fields.[75]

Apprentice shoemaker Afonso Malumane's experience was typical. Malumane earned 345$ escudos per month as an apprentice, and 475$ escudos per month when he qualified as a shoemaker in 1955. By the early 1960s, however, he was still employed in an Indian-owned shop earning 750$ escudos a month, comparable to the income of a fully employed hodcarrier, but no better.[76] Apprentice shoemakers tended to become stuck in apprenticeships, or if successfully qualified, to be unable to secure licenses for independent shops. Many, therefore, moved to other endeavors after several years of apprenticeship.[77]

Alexander Mahite of Zavala and Fernando Sozinho of Manhica both made successful careers in Lourenço Marques through apprenticeships.[78] Mahite began as a casual laborer in Paulino Santos Gil's lumber and furniture manufacturing firm earning 14$ escudos daily. In 1954, he qualified as a cabinetmaker and received a raise to 435$ escudos per month. Mahite was doubtless aware of Santos Gil's reputation for exploiting cheap black labor, and in 1955 he applied for a position as cabinetmaker at Empressa de Madeiras and was hired. By 1955, he was earning 1200$ escudos per month, and in 1960, after one more change of employer, he reached 1350$ escudos per month. He had tripled his salary in less than six years, and during a period of low inflation that brought with it a genuine improvement in living standards.

Fernando Sozinho managed a similarly impressive salary increase, but within the same firm. He trained as an apprentice upholsterer at a Portuguese firm, apprenticing at a modest 350$ escudos per month. In 1959, he earned 2300$ escudos per month — a sevenfold increase over his apprentice salary — making him one of the best-paid black workers in the city. While skilled artisans enjoyed a certain prosperity in comparison with the majority of the black labor force, they also faced the bitter reality that they worked with an indeed even trained white workers who earned more and were promoted beyond their own reach.[79]

Success hinged upon the ability to come to terms with oppressive legislation and practice. All black workers grew accustomed to bribing petty officials at municipal labor offices for all kinds of things, most commonly for their consideration in getting workers through the endless lines to register or pay taxes. Workers who did not show appropriate "respect" could anticipate wasted time in line while "respectful" workers were accommodated before them.[80] Hopeful artisans had to contend with the further complication of licensing. All self-employed artisans were licensed by the municipal curator. They had to demonstrate both that they had the skill and experience to do the job — which necessitated cultivating and preserving good will among former employers — and that there was a need for their services within the city. On the latter point many found their license petitions opposed by Indian and European artisans fearful of African competition. Some licenses were granted contingent upon the petitioner's shop being located far from the most promising markets.[81]

According to the *Regulamento dos Serviçais Indígenas,* which remained in effect until the abolition of the indigenato, so-called *biscates* (odd-jobs, moonlighting) were illegal.[82] Artisans and businesspeople had to be either fully licensed as self-employed or be contracted employees, in which case they were only able to sell their services to their employer.[83] While there were some positive aspcts of legislation prohibiting employment of Africans for work other than that for which they were legally hired, such as preventing employers from forcing cashiers in retail outlets to carry out tote and haul labor commonly done by carriers, the practical impact of much of such legislation was to prevent workers from marketing their skills to their best advantage. People apprehended for biscates were usually warned, but then faced steep fines and chibalo labor regardless of their former incomes.[84] While some informants successfully worked evening and weekend biscates in the suburbs for years, they were aware that the risks were substantial.[85]

Common laborers had to cope with registration and taxation; artisans and business people had the added burden of licensing, but Africans who aspired to white-collar positions knowingly entered the realm of mobility through patronage. Workers who sought employment in what were commonly referred to as "the offices" had to have all the basic credentials: a fourth-class certificate; proficiency in Portuguese; and a diffident, courteous, so-called *bom rapaz* (good boy) posture. A fourth-class certificate represented an important investment of time and money by the graduate and his or her family, but in itself was insufficient for promotion within the civil service — the bastion of the offices — without the intervention of a powerful and loyal white patron.[86] Wage increments accompanying each classificatory promotion in the offices were so substantial and promotions so limited that services and gifts rendered in the quest for patrons were seen as genuine investments in future earning power. Getting a good job meant getting a good patron. Several patrons indeed had to be courted at any one time since whites frequently returned to Portugal for leave or for good, and workers could not afford to put all their eggs in one basket and risk having the basket transferred to Lisbon (Penvenne, 1982: 209-255).

Ultimately, legal constraints made it either necessary or most expedient for Africans in the offices to petition formally for the *álvara de assimilação*. Salary levels and key fringe benefits were tied to civil status; thus Africans who reached the black ceiling salary, or who wished to qualify for substantial family bonuses, either had to petition for assimilation or accept the fact that they had reached a dead end in their careers.[87] Assimilation, or the "status of nonnative," as it was somewhat awkwardly called in this period, became a requirement for some jobs. Africans who were unable to muster the requisite paper work and certificates of "good comportment" — submitted by sponsoring citizens — were ineligible for such jobs, and Africans already holding such positions when the requirement went into effect could be deemed "irregular," demoted to a designated black job, and have their wages reduced to a level appropriate to their civil status.[88]

Simply filing for the status of nonnative was an expensive procedure and there were no guarantees. Of the 646 petitions filed between 1932 and 1954, 156 were denied.[89] Furthermore, persons who successfully attained the status could subsequently be investigated — by the Native Affairs Department of course — and if found to be lacking the requisite material and social posture, returned, to the status of native.[90] The shoe was sometimes on the other foot. Certain jobs were reserved for so-called natives, and in order to secure an attractive black job, particularly in the period of the late 1950s and early 1960s when white pressure on top black jobs was strong, assimilados sometimes concealed their civil status or requested a return to native status (Ehnmark and Wastberg, 1963: 146-151).[91]

The underlying aspect of social control and manipulation embodied in the entire concept of assimilation was as clear to the African who petitioned for the status as it was to the dominant classes that created it to suit their needs, but so too were the material gains to be had in exchange for cooperation with the system.[92] The manipulatory aspect of assimilation was crassly stated in a wartime editorial advocating wage hikes for assimilados:

Assimilados are our comprador class. . . . They are our office boys, headmen, interpreters, nurses aids and police. Wartime inflation hits their needs. Rice, shoes and clothing prices are very high. We created and encouraged those needs. Assimilados are reliable; they do not question or challenge, but remain in their accustomed docility. Good parents look to the needs of their child before their own needs. We have a paternal obligation to our assimilados.[93]

Given the wage differential between assimilados and the majority African labor force, and the fact that mobility among workers in high-wage jobs entailed courting white patrons, it is hardly surprising that many common laborers felt they had little in common with assimilados except their color:

> People were afraid of them. When you looked at them you were looking at a bossman. They didn't speak to us, they only spoke to the whites. [Ordinary] people did not count for anything with them.[94]

Unskilled workers seldom had occasion to speak with whites, much less cultivate a white patron. They dealt with a black headman or perhaps an Afro-European overseer, but the white bossman was often a distant figure.

Common laborers also had a narrower range of opportunities to improve their legal income — most depended upon standard annual wage increments, piecework incentives, and overtime. Annual wage increments were typically granted to male workers in private commerce, industry, and domestic service. Wages for casual port labor — railyard, wharfside, and stevedoring alike — were fixed by the state and basic rates remained unchanged from 1933 to 1957; thus port workers' incomes depended upon the availability of overtime.

Port wages were so much higher after hours that day-shift production almost inevitably suffered so that workers could stretch the load or preserve their strength for overtime pay. Slow-downs were so prevalent among chibalo teams that the headmen and production managers developed an informal piecework system to accommodate the pattern and diminish tension at the workplace.[95] Discipline and diligence were not necessarily synonymous, and while overt worker indiscipline routinely brought harsh sanctions, those who worked at a distance from whites — particularly gang laborers — could manipulate conditions at the workplace without challenging authority. Unlike the case described by Jeff Crisp, a measure of inefficiency was one of the built-in costs of controlling workers whose wages provided little incentive for productivity.

Chibalo workers at the port could significantly improve their income through overtime work.[96] Their contract wages were paid upon repatriation; thus chibalo workers depended upon overtime earnings for cash while in the city. They had strong incentives to work overtime, and since the state had to provide them with room and board whether they worked eight or twelve hours a day, the state did not resist the strategy.

Chibalo gangs were worked on a quota basis — so many cars to be loaded or unloaded per shift — rather than having overseers simply drive the gangs through their shifts. Once the quota was completed, workers were free to rest on the worksite, return to the compound, or work on handcrafts until overtime became available.[97] Port zone directors were aware of the practice, but ignored it as long as production kept pace with traffic.[98]

Volunteer hod carriers and stevedores similarly paced their work with one eye on the clock, but they were more frequently sanctioned for obvious slowdowns.[99] Binge patterns were common among volunteers in the early 1950s. Ten to twelve men worked together as a gang for two or three days running. They worked and slept in shifts, with eight to ten men on and two to four men off.[100] One around-the-clock binge counted six half-shifts, with four of the half-shifts tabulated at overtime rates. Overtime rates were pegged to the nature of the job, and both volunteers and chibalo received the same rates in addition to their regular daytime half-shift pay (6$ escudos for volunteers and 3$ escudos for chibalo). In the early 1950s, for example, volunteers in cold storage work earned 6$ escudos per regular daytime half-shift, and each overtime half-shift paid an additional 5$ escudos, bringing the total to 11$ escudos per overtime half shift. Overtime at the caustic mineral wharves paid an extra 2$50 escudos and all others an extra 1$50 escudos per half-shift. By working one around-the-clock binge at cold storage, volunteers could earn almost a full week's regular pay.[101]

With the completion of the rail link to Southern Rhodesia in 1955, traffic at Lourenço Marques increased dramatically, and the state was determined to see that handling kept pace. Roberto Tembe and Joaquim da Costa, tally clerks at the port since the 1920s, had painful memories of workers trying to keep pace with the added traffic; their overtime income cost all too many lives and limbs in work accidents.[102] They told of workers being crushed to death when locomotives, under which they had hidden to grab some much-needed sleep, started up without warning.[103]

In 1953, safety measures were proposed to guarantee protection for those working in toxic materials, caustic minerals, and cold storage, but the Port Authority objected to the cost of recommended protective clothing and increased rest and shower periods. The proposals were suspended while less expensive measures were considered.[104] Right into the 1960s workers continued to pay the price for no protection.[105]

In conclusion, the impact of postwar economic expansion on the African labor force of the city was uneven. Competition for semiskilled, productive workers from the fast-developing industrial and manufacturing sectors, from the mid-1950s in particular, fostered a steady improvement in wages and work conditions for those in the position to take the jobs. State intervention to funnel labor to the least desireable jobs diminished by the period 1957 to 1962, and ultimately many of the constraints on urban blacks were alleviated by the reform legislation of the early 1960s. For many workers, therefore, the drip . . . drip . . . drip . . . was better than the closed faucet.

African women made very little headway improving their situation as urban wage laborers in this period, but the expansion of the cashew shelling industry eased the transition of unprecedented numbers of women from rural agriculture to urban wage labor by providing additional legal, entry-level jobs. The single group in the urban black community to find the faucet actually closing up over this period was the elite. The state's commitment to guarantee work to the ever-increasing colono population robbed educated, ambitious, skilled blacks of their chance to benefit in proportion with growing demand for the skills they worked so hard to attain. While the black elite had suffered a cumulative decline in socioeconomic status with respect to whites since the late 1920s, during the postwar era they even lost their edge over middle-level black workers.

Working overtime binges, courting white patrons, and working patiently and cautiously along in the best available niche were among the many quite undramatic strategies to emerge from interviews and employment records. The bom rapaz posture among aspiring office workers, the low-key slowdowns among common laborers, and the persistence of Cajú women developed in an overall context of pervasive and oppressive constraints on African mobility and economic activity. They were among the limited options tolerated in legal Lourenço Marques.

Beginning with the late 1950s shift in state-directed labor sanctions from forced labor and beatings to fines and culminating with reform legislation in the early 1960s, market relations began to supercede the state's strong-arm tactics in recruitment, distribution, and discipline of urban workers. While the state continued to meet any direct challenge by black labor with brutal force, day-to-day relations were less based upon terror. By 1962, there was less cause for workers to walk "with fear," but they certainly continued to walk softly.

NOTES

1. To allow a fuller examination of employment strategies, the equally important question of the struggle for business, residential, and leisure space in the city and its implications for African economic mobility are largely ignored.

2. Saul Tembe, 7 June 1977, Tape E. Camera Municipal de Maputo (CMM); see also Penvenne (1979a).

3. The exceptional patterns of workers volunteering for chibalo contracts are discussed in Penvenne (1982: 158-166, 357-362).

4. Tembe, 7 June 1977, Tape E, CMM.

5. Ibid.

6. The following paragraphs on New State policies draw heavily on statistics from the *Anuário Estatístico, Estatística Industrial,* and on the U.S. Consul's Annual Economic and Annual Labor Reports for Mozambique (see also Clarence Smith, 1972; Sousa Ferreira, 1975).

7. For FRELIMO'S impact on local labor relations see Mite Baza, 15 June 1977, Porto, Caminhos de Ferro e Transportes de Moçambique, Secção dos Cais (cais); Samuel Chipopo Miuanga, 19 July 1977, CMM.

8. *Portarias* 5,565 of 12 June 1944 and 7,798 of 2 April 1949.

9. *Decreto-Lei* 39,666.

10. Administracao de Conselho de Lourenço Marques, ACLM, "Registo de Chibalos/Desempregos," 1960.

11. ACLM Circular, 23 October 1959.

12. This chapter draws on a 5 percent systematic sample of the employment records for the entire urban labor force for the period 1950 to 1962. Employment records at the Administração de Conselho (ACLM) contained the following information on each registered worker: name, home area, sex, nature of each job held, wage and tenure of each job, authorized home visits and other outmigrations, transgressions of both labor and criminal legislation, punishment received, miscellaneous sanctions, and reasons for leaving an employer and returning to rural areas. Points made on this data base are noted as ACLM sample.

13. ACLM sample.

14. ACLM to Chefe, Gabinete da Governo Geral, 11 December 1950, 1197 B/15.

15. ACLM to Posto Administrativo de Munhuana (PAM), Circular Confidencial 3,363/B/6, 9 November 1943; Circular Confidencial 187/b/5, 30 June 1947; Circular Confidencial 428/B/5, 27 January 1947; Secretaria Geral to ACLM, Confidencial 1,139/B/11/1, 22 August 1951; ACLM logs 328/184, 390/206, 448/226.

16. A *palmatório* is a mallet used for beating. ACLM logbooks 328/184, 390/206, 448/226.

17. ACLM logbooks 328/184, 350/206, 448/226.

18. ACLM sample.

19. Ibid.

20. See Silvestre José Zuana: "Yes Sir! was all anyone in their right mind would say to a white person," and Daniel Tene Nhangumbe (pointing to his mouth), "this was your beak, not your mouth. It was not up to black people to say anything." Zuana, 17 June and Nhangumbe 1 July 1977, both CMM, Tape J.

21. ACLM registration record, ficha 10161.

22. Ibid, ficha 23041.

23. Ibid, ficha 12061.

24. Gabriel Mabunda, 10 June 1977, Tape F, cais.

25. Samuel Chipoco Miuanaga, 19 July 1977, CMM.

26. For example, Secretaria Geral to ACLM, Urgent 1110/B/15/3, 2 September 1947; ACLM to Secretaria Geral, 23 September 1949.

27. For rusgas during labor shortages see ACLM caixas R and B; and Gabriel Mabunda, 10 June 1977, Tape F, cais.

28. ACLM sample.

29. Pedro Faleca, 7 July 1977, CMM. See Penvenne (1982: 396-400).

30. For examples of chronic offenders, workers inciting others to quit, or serious labor challenges ending in deportation and beatings, see the following labor registration files: fichas 45141, 44161, 44201, 24661, 25421, 25581, 25381, 1001, 4821.

31. According to "Livros de Registo de Presos Judiciais e Administrativos" from 1951 to 1961 and the ACLM sample, common offenses were unregistered unemployment, leaving a contract without just cause as recognized by ACLM, casual labor without authorization, self-employment without authorization, and travel outside the city without authorization.

32. Vicente Mainga, Arquivo Histórico de Moçambique (AHM); Gabriel Mabunda, 12 June 1977 and joint interview José Cossa, Timoteu Comiche, Eugénio Langa, and Njone Macaringue, 18 June 1977, all cais.

33. ACLM to RCNI, 3 August 1950, 782/B/9; RCNI to ACLM, 23 August 1950, 2805/B/15.

34. The majority of informants who came to the city as uneducated, unskilled adults first worked as casual laborers on construction sites or at the wharves.

35. ACLM sample.

36. Ibid.

37. Entry occupations in permanent sector civil service jobs in 1961, for example, paid 300$ escudos and 3000$ escudos per month for blacks and whites respectively. Among adult black males 250$ escudos was the most common lowest wage in 1952, and 1700$ escudos was a common top wage. ACLM sample and Direcção dos Serviços dos Portos, Salarios de Pessoal Assalariado do Quadro Permenente, Dep. leg. 2046, 24 December 1961: 4-9.

38. ACLM sample.

39. Wages were computed from interviews, ACLM sample, and "Álvaras Industriais, Insalubrias, Incómodos, Perigosas, ou Tóxicas," 1939 to 1949.

40. ACLM sample and cais interviews.

41. ACLM sample.

42. Ibid.

43. The tendency for migrants to pick up the Portuguese language while working as domestic servants, working *no quintal* (in the backyard), as domestic service was called, is reflected in the expression *"Português do quintal,"* backyard Portuguese or pidgin Portuguese (Penvenne, 1979b: 4-11; *Brado Africano,* 20 November 1943 and 2 August 1947).

44. ACLM sample.

45. Ibid, especially fichas 5721, 5741, 5821, 35001.

46. ACLM sample.

47. Ibid.

48. Ibid.

49. U.S. Consular Despatches 151, 29 March 1955; 105, 15 December 1960; 146, 6 February 1961; U.S. Consul to Secretary of State, telegram, 73, 31 January 1963.

50. Interviews with carpenters Cirilo Capitine, 6 July and António Gabriel Tembe 6 and 11 July 1977, CMM and school teacher Timoteo Comiche, 18 June 1977, cais, Tape F.

51. Tembe, 16 June 1977, cais.

52. Ibid; *Brado Africano,* 10 December 1932; 28 October 1933; 23 May 1949.

53. Tembe, 7 June 1977, CMM, fichas 29601, 35001, 6221; Chibalo folder 1944-1949, ACLM.

54. *Estatistica Industrial* (1956, 1959: 79).

55. Circular 338 and 339/B/17/1 Direcção Provincial de Administração Civil (DPAC), 26 August 1946.

56. By 1946, carriers found to be transporting women without requisite permission to leave their circunscrição were heavily fined; "Aviso," ACLM, 24 June 1950, B/17.

57. ACLM to RCNI, 388/B/17/1, 19 September 1952.

58. *Brado Africano,* 22 March, 26 April 1947.

59. Droughts were detailed in U.S. Consul, Annual Economic Reports: 142, 6 April 1951; 151, 13 March 1952; 141, 27 January 1953; 131, 6 March 1956.

60. *Brado Africano,* 22 March 1947, 24 December 1945; Penvenne (1982: 177-307).

61. Anotarem os visitas feitas aos empregadores de mão de obra indígena de Conselho de Loureço Marques, ACLM document 293/171.

62. *Estatistica Industrial,* 1956, 1959: 132, 136-137.

63. ACLM document 293/171 and ACLM sample.

64. Livro de Processos de Justificação da Qualidade de Não Indígena, ACLM document 1517/1).

65. ACLM to RCNI, 29 September 1949, 50/B/8.

66. ACLM sample.

67. Amélia Alfredo Muiane, 13 September 1977, CMM; ACLM document 293/171 and ACLM sample.

68. ACLM sample, see fichas 12341, 13281, and 39721.

69. Amélia Alfredo Muiane, 13 September 1977, CMM; Lídia Felizmina Tembe, 2 November 1977, Matola; *Brado Africano,* 23 May 1942, 11 March 1950; Silva (1960: 55, 57), Alves (1961: 117-119).

70. See fichas 29601, 35001, 6221.

71. ACLM sample.

72. Fichas 34281, 14081, 20521, 19461.

73. Francisco T. Chondela, 14 July; Pedro Palechane Faleca, 7 July; Alberto Nhalivilo, 7 July; Sechene Uinge, 8 July, and Felizberto Zavala, 13 July — all 1977, CMM.

74. For discussion of the limits of urban employment for accumulation of bridewealth see Fausto C. Mondlane, 4 July; Ernesto Muianga, 4 July, Zagueu Muianga, 1 July, all 1977, CMM, and group interview with José Cossa, Njone Macaringue, Eugénio Langa, Timoteo Comiche, 18 June 1977, cais, Tape F.

75. ACLM sample.

76. Ficha 801.

77. ACLM sample; Samuel Chipoco Miuanga, 19 July 1977, CMM.

78. Fichas 3181 and 17361, respectively.

79. Antonio Gabriel Tembe, carpenter-cabinetmaker, 6 and 11 July 1977, CMM.

80. Salamão Nhaca, 11 October 1977, Arquivo Histórico de Moçambique (AHM) Maputo.

81. Correspondence on commercial licensing for 1946 to 1962 is contained in files D/7 throughout ACLM.

82. Chapter VI, Art. 40-44.

83. ACLM to Chefe da Gabinete, 11 December 1950, 1197/B/15.

84. ACLM sample.

85. Vicente Mainge, clandestine barber, 11-12 November 1977, AHM.

86. For discussion of family financing of education expenses see Bandi Albasini Chibindji, 16 June, and Manuel João dos Santos Tembe, 18 June, both 1977, Cais, tapes F and J.

87. U.S. Consular despatch 105, 15 December 1960.

88. DPAC to ACLM, 18 March 1946, 994/B/15/3; ACLM sample.

89. ACLM doc. 1517/1.

90. PAM to ACLM, 24 August 1949, 153/M3; Bento Navesse, 1 June 1977, Alto Mahé; Joaquim da Costa and Roberto Tembe, 24 August 1977, cais.

91. ACLM to PAM, 13 March 1944, 338/I/7/2; Basil LeMay and David Spence, 9 May 1977, Maputo.

92. Manuel João dos Santos Tembe, 18 June 1977, cais.

93. *O Diário,* 18 April 1943, reprinted in *Brado Africano,* 1 May 1943.

94. Inácio dos Santos Jeque, 3 July 1977, CMM.

95. Timoteo Comiche and José Cossa, production managers, 18 June 1977, cais.

96. Relatório dos Agentes do Curador e Delegacia de Saude, 141, 1952.

97. Comiche and Cossa, 18 June 1977, cais.

98. Francisco Guilherme de Brito, Chefe de Zona, 27 June 1977, cais.

99. ACLM sample.

100. U.S. Consular despatch 105, 9 February 1951.

101. Relatório dos Agentes do Curador e Delegacia de Saude, 141, 1952.

102. While going through logbooks recording work accidents in Lourenço Marques for this period I noted that virtually all accidents occurred at the waterfront, but since I failed to keep a tally of the accidents I cannot corroborate Tembe and Costa's recollections with statistics.

103. Costa and Tembe, 16 June 1977, cais.

104. U.S. Consul, "Annual Economic Reports," 1954, 1955, 1957.

105. Guilherme de Brito, Chefe de Zona, 27 June 1977, cais.

REFERENCES

ALVES, J. M. (1961) "A destribalização da mulher negra em geral com alguns apontamentos sobre o problema vivido em Moçambique." Estudos Ultramarinos 2: 99-129.

CLARENCE SMITH, W. G. (1972) "South Africa and Mozambique, 1960-1970." Societies of Southern Africa in the 19th and 20th Centuries 3: 174-188.

EHNMARK, A. and P. WASTBERG (1963) Angola and Mozambique: The Case Against Portugal. London: Pall Mall Press.

FIRST, R. et al. (1977) The Mozambican Miner: A Study in the Export of Labour. Maputo: Instituto de Investigações Científicas de Moçambique.

FULLER, C. E. (1955) "An ethnohistorical study of continuity and change in Gwambe culture." Ph. D. dissertation, Northwestern University.

HANCE, W. A. and I. S. van DONGEN (1957) "Lourenço Marques in Delagoa Bay." Economic Geography 33: 238-256.

HARRIS, M. (1966) "Raça Conflicto e Reforma em Moçambique." Política Exterior Independente 1, 3: 9-39.

——— (1959) "Labour emigration among the Mocambique Thonga: cultural and political factors." Africa 29: 50-66.

JESSETT, M. G. (1899) The Key to South Africa: Delagoa Bay. London: T. Fisher Unwin.

NEWITT, M. D. D. (1974) "Migrant labour and the development of Mozambique." Societies of Southern Africa in the 19th and 20th Centuries 4: 67-76.

——— (1972) "Land and labour in early twentieth century Moçambique." Iberian Studies 1, 2: 45-52.

NORONHA, E. (1895) O Distrito de Lourenço Marques e o Africa do Sul. Lisbon: Imprensa Nacional.

PENVENNE, J. (1982) A History of African Labor in Lourenço Marques, Mozambique, 1870 to 1950. Ph. D. dissertation, Boston University.

——— (1979a) "Attitudes toward race and work in Mozambique: Lourenço Marques, 1900-1974." African Studies Center, Boston University Working Paper, 16.

——— (1979b) "The streetcorner press: worker intelligence networks in Lourenço Marques, 1900-1962." African Studies Center, Boston University, Working Paper, 26.

——— and A. MANGHEZI (1981) "Chibalo e Classe Operária, Lourenço Marques, 1870 á 1962 e O Trabalho Forcado por quem o Viveu." Estudos Moçambicanos 2: 9-36.

PEREIRA DE LIMA, A. (1971) História dos Caminhos de Ferro de Moçambique Lourenço Marques: Edição da Administração dos Portos, Caminhos de Ferro e Transportes.

——— (1970) "Para um Estudo da Evolução Urbana de Lourenço Marques." Boletim Municipal 7: 7-16.

RITA FERREIRA, A. (1971) Evolução de Mão de Obra e das Remunerações no Sector Privado em Moçambique desde 1950 á 1970: Análise da Situação Cambial de Moçambique. Lourenço Marques:Comissão Coordenadora do Trabalho de Análise de Situação Cambial da Província de Moçambique.

———— (1967-1968) "Os Africanos de Lourenço Marques." Memória do Instituto de Investigações Científicas de Moçambique Serie C, 9: 95-491.

SANTOS, R. M. (1959) Uma Contribuição para a Análise da Economia de Moçambique. Lisbon: Editorial Império.

SANTOS RUFINO, J. (1929) Albuns Fotográficos e Descritivos, Colónia de Moçambique. Hamburg: Broschek.

SILVA, M. (1960) "As Missões Católicas Femininas." Estudos de Ciências Políticas e Sociais 37: 49-77.

SOUSA FERREIRA, E. (1975) "Portugal and her former African colonies: prospects for a neo-colonial relationship." Ufahamu 5, 3: 159-170.

TORP, J. E. (1978) "Industrial planning and development in Mozambique: preliminary considerations and their theoretical implications." Mozambique: Proceedings of a Seminar Held in the Centre of African Studies. University of Edinburgh.

TRISTAO DE BETTENCOURT, J. (1945) Relatório do Governador Geral de Moçambique. Lisbon: Agência Geral das Colónias.

VAIL, L. and L. WHITE (1980) Capitalism and Colonialism in Mozambique: A Study of Quelimane District. Minneapolis: University of Minnesota Press.

———— (1979) "The struggle for Mozambique: capitalist rivalries, 1900-1945." Review 3, 2: 243-275.

WEBSTER, D. (1978) "Migrant labour, social formations and the proletarianization of the Chopi of Southern Mozambique." African Perspectives 1: 157-174.

YOUNG, S.J. (1977) "Fertility and famine: women's agricultural history in southern Mozambique," in R. Palmer and N. Parsons (eds.) The Roots of Rural Poverty. Berkeley: University of California Press.

GOVERNMENT DOCUMENTS: MOZAMBIQUE

Colónia de Moçambique (1944) Censo da População em 1940. Lourenço Marques: Imprensa Nacional.

———— (1939) Compilation of Legislation Affecting Labour, Unemployment, Immigration and the Control of Foreign Immigrants in the State Administered Territory of the Colony of Mozambique. Lourenço Marques: Government Printing Works.

Província de Moçambique (1961) Salários do Pessoal Assalariado do Quadro Permanente, Dip. leg. 2046, 24 Dezembro 1960. Lourenço Marques: Imprensa Nacional.

———— (1959) Estatística Industrial, 1956. Lourenço Marques: Imprensa Nacional.

———— (1955) Recenseamento Geral da População em 1950. Lourenço Marques: Imprensa Nacional.

———— (1940-1963) Anuário Estatístico. Lourenço Marques: Imprensa Nacional.

5

A COLONIAL STATE AND AN AFRICAN PETTY BOURGEOISIE

Prostitution, Property, and Class Struggle in Nairobi, 1936-1940

LUISE WHITE

What one group of prostitutes says about another is not generally considered significant historical data. In cities like Nairobi, Kenya, however, with a labor force of single males packed into substandard dwellings, housing shaped sexual relations and one type of sexual relation — prostitution — shaped housing in its turn. Housing policy was the means by which the state tried to determine African rights within the city — whether or not Africans could remain there at all, and where, how long, and with whom they could live. In such cities, what one group of prostitutes said about another is crucial to any full understanding of the struggles over whether or not the state could, in fact, determine the place of Africans in the city.

This chapter concentrates on a few years in the late 1930s and on two separate series of events. First, the social policy of the state underwent a substantial change during the 1930s, manifesting itself most dramatically in the demolition of one illegal African village and the construction of its legal replacement between 1936 and 1938.

Author's Note: The author gratefully acknowledges funding from the Jan Smuts Memorial Fund of Cambridge University, the assistance of her interpreters, Margaret Makuna and Paul Kakaire, and advice from John Lonsdale and Frederick Cooper. Interviews are deposited in the Institute for African Studies, University of Nairobi.

Second, a new form of prostitution developed in the official African Location of Pumwani as early as 1935, and the conduct of prostitution there profoundly altered between then and early 1940s. The relationship of these two trends points to the most basic questions about a city in flux: Would the state, or an African petty bourgeoisie — a class composed largely of Muslims, half of whom were women, and prostitutes no less — restore a male labor force each day? Would that petty bourgeoisie — under the hallowed principles of private property and the market — be allowed to accumulate capital and pass property to heirs, thereby developing a partly autonomous economic base, around which a sense of continuity, a sense of place in the city, and a sense of collective identity might, over generations, emerge? How would the growing number of workers after the mid-1930s be affected by its intimate contact with this class that owned property, but was never quite up to the standards of utility, morality, and legitimacy of the colonial state? Could, in short, a respectable working class retain its purity when in contact with an increasingly unrespectable petty bourgeoisie?

Prostitution in Nairobi, like prostitution anywhere else, is domestic labor. All Nairobi prostitutes were self-employed; there is no evidence, oral or written, of anything that could be even vaguely construed as pimping. These women sold domestic tasks, individually or as a set, which reproduced male labor power. In exchange for a portion of a man's wage, prostitutes routinely sold bedspace (few laborers owned beds themselves), cooking, bathwater, companionship, hot meals, cold meals, beverages, sexual intercourse, and an ideology of sexual relations in which women were unfailingly deferential, polite, and interested. In those forms of prostitution that offered the most extensive set of domestic services, women managed to charge cumulatively for the tasks they performed (White, 1983). Thus, throughout Nairobi's history, when a man spent the night with a prostitute and received breakfast, he paid one-sixth to one-third more than men who were not given breakfast.[1]

Prostitutes provided the support work that enabled the male labor force to return to work at least slightly replenished. This, it would seem, served the needs of the colonial administration admirably. In Kenya, rural African household production subsidized Africans in formal employment well into the 1950s, so that working men could not afford to diminish their incomes by encouraging their wives to abandon farming and join them in town. Colonial officials knew full well what kinds of social relations emerged within the resulting demography and how much money it saved the state. In 1938, the Municipal Native Affairs Officer (MNAO) reported,

> 25,886 males employed and living in Nairobi have only 3,356 female dependents in the town . . . a proportion of just over 1 to 8. A demand arises at once for a large number of native prostitutes in Nairobi. . . . The immigration into Nairobi of young Kikuyu girls is continually mentioned by the Kikuyu Local Native Councils urging that steps be taken to stop it. The position there again is aggravated by the lack of proper native housing; whereas the needs of eight men may be served by the provision of two rooms for the men and one for the prostitute, were housing provided for these natives and their families, six rooms would probably be needed [Davies, 1938: 3-4].

First, it is clear from the above that the Kikuyu Local Native Councils (LNCs) complained more about prostitution than did the MNAO. Second, it is clear that the city provided very few rooms: Housing was under the control of private African landlords. However, Nairobi prostitution was as much a function of available housing as it was of the ratio of the sexes. The plastic spaces in which people lived — and the conditions under which they came to live there — literally shaped their social relations. Because of the rigid racial segregation of the colonial city and the perpetual shortage and insecurity of legal and illegal housing, prostitution in Nairobi evolved labor forms — ways of organizing the sale of a woman's labor power — that were determined by the woman's relationship to her place of residence. There were three forms.

The oldest, the *watembezi* form, is as old as Nairobi, which was founded in 1899; it is translated as "streetwalker," and comes from *kutembea*, the Swahili verb "to walk." In the watembezi form, the contract for the sale of domestic labor is made somewhere other than the woman's place of residence. Obviously, it is the only form of prostitution available to homeless women, and thus many young women practiced the form when they first arrived in Nairobi. However, this is not to say that homeless women abandoned the form as soon as they found accommodation. In watembezi prostitution, the amount of domestic services a woman sold was frequently negotiated in advance. This form was characterized by high profits over a short period of time, much as streetwalking was in most places.

The *malaya* form takes its name from the proper, dictionary Swahili noun for prostitute. This term was first used to describe the type of prostitution that emerged in the official African Location of Pumwani in about 1922 or 1923. In the malaya form, the woman stayed inside her room and the men came to her: The first and all subsequent contracts for the sale of domestic labor were made inside the woman's place of residence. This form, predicated on the fact that the woman had a room to which a man might also purchase access, provided the most extensive set of domestic services for sale. Malaya women's earnings tended to be slow but steady; in times of very high employment, however, they earned more than twice what semiskilled male laborers earned (White, 1983: ch. 3).

The *Wazi-Wazi* form in Pumwani gets its name from its historical association with Haya women from the Bukoba District in northwest Tanganyika, who were called Waziba, the Ganda term for them. It may also derive from the intensive form of the Swahili noun meaning "open" or "bare." This form emerged in Pumwani between 1935 and 1938, and seems to have been originated by non-Kenyan women, many of whom were Haya. The Wazi-Wazi prostitute made all contracts for the sale of domestic labor while sitting outside her room or on the verandah of the house in which she had a room. As in the malaya form, women had to have rooms, and the men solicited them. Wazi-Wazi women seem to have kept the sale of nonsexual domestic tasks to a minimum, and as a result they often did voluminous business in short-term sexual relations. Wazi-Wazi women called out their prices to men passing by; this, together with their visibility, earned them a reputation for open soliciting that shocked the Muslim malaya women of Pumwani; it also seems to have undercut malaya women's profits during the high employment years of the late 1930s.

PROSTITUTION AND HOUSING IN PUMWANI, 1922-1935

Nairobi was founded in 1899. The pre-World War I city had five well-organized and predominantly Muslim villages, each said to contain between 150 and 200 huts which served as lodging houses. In

1921-1922, three of these villages were razed to force the occupants into the first Native Location, which immediately became known as "Pumwani," Swahili for "resting place," to its harassed population. The remaining two villages, Kileleshwa and Pangani, were scheduled for demolition as soon as possible: in the case of Kileleshwa, possible was 1926, when its land came under municipal control; for Pangani, the state's inability to replace tenants' accommodation and compensate the householders made physical demolition impossible until 1936. Until the 1940s, Nairobi was checkered with several short-lived illegal squatter settlements filled with the huts the state called lodging houses, and these were sporadically dealt with by the structural method long favored by the Nairobi administration: Settlements were evacuated and burned out, and their owners sent away, impoverished, to build anew somewhere else.

Landlords from the demolished villages were offered paltry incentives to build new houses in Pumwani, since this would allow the government and private employers to house their labor force for free. The Nairobi Municipal Council (NMC) also invited those Africans who could afford to build lodging houses in the official location, and this enabled many women who had prospered from World War I watembezi prostitution to become Pumwani householders (Bujra, 1972: 9-13, 1975; White, 1983: ch. 2, 6).[2]

Thus, almost half of Pumwani's first property owners were women, and those women made up almost 80 percent of Pumwani's Muslim householders. Similar and more detailed figures obtained in Pangani: There, where the state had been unable to legislate against multiple house ownership, 312 houses were owned by 293 Africans, of whom 124 (42 percent) were women. Women in Pangani constituted just over 50 percent of the settlement's 247 Muslim home owners in 1933 (Kenya Land Commission [KLC], 1934: I, 1124; Bujra, 1972: passim; White, 1983: ch. 6). While it seems likely that Islam offered a tolerant religion with strong community ties to Nairobi's prostitutes (see Bujra, 1975), I think it is essential to see the Islamicization of single women in Nairobi as part of a larger trend in which male and female immigrants converted to Islam in Nairobi in the years before 1935 (see Bujra, 1972: 48; White, 1983: ch. 3).

The original plans for Pumwani, drawn up at various intervals between 1911 and 1914, were designed to control Africans' social and

sexual relations in the name of sanitation. According to the Director
of Public Works, the Committee on the Native Location believed

> that if they arrange to remove excrement and supply . . . potable
> water they have done all that the most exacting of natives could
> possibly require. As a matter of fact we do more than this for draught
> oxen in the PWD stables. Anything in the way of the ordinary
> human liberties and privileges which non-criminal sections of the
> population ordinarily enjoy in civilized communities are to be re-
> stricted wholesale in the interests of "proper organization" . . . and
> "thorough sanitary conditions."[3]

The committee also wrote bylaws that included a "good character"
clause that threatened immediate removal for anyone found to be
otherwise, and a rigid curfew that not only maximized the number of
hours Africans could spend in European employment but effectively
curtailed the mobility and interracial associations for which watembezi women had become well known. Thus, it was an offense for any
African who was not a domestic servant to be outside the Location
between 10 p.m. and 5 a.m., while non-Africans could not enter the
Location between 7 p.m. and 6 a.m. The idea that employers be
allowed to build lodging houses was dropped after World War I, but
the bylaws limited African landlords to one house each.[4]

Under municipal regulations Pumwani landlords held the
properties they built in usufruct; they could be transmitted to designated heirs but not bought or sold. Plot sizes were set by the same
committees that wrote the bylaws, and the average Pumwani house
was divided into between six and eight rooms, each room generally
measuring eight feet by eight feet. All but a very few houses were
constructed of mud and poles, and all had pounded dirt floors and
thatched roofs (in a preinsecticide epoch) and exceptionally poor
ventilation. Landlords lived in one room and rented out the rest
(White, 1983: ch. 6).

The city council planned for communal areas in Pumwani —
places for women to cook and do laundry, public latrines, and
churches for what was then Pumwani's nonexistent Christian population — but these were rarely used. They had been designed without
regard to African or Muslim realities.[5] Instead, the combined weight
of the Pumwani bylaws and the conditions of housing there drove
residents even further indoors, to far greater isolation than they had
experienced in the older villages.

By 1923, it became obvious, even to colonial officials,[6] that many single women living in Pumwani had adjusted to the lack of physical mobility the creation of the Location had forced upon them, but had done so in a way that turned the isolation of life in Pumwani to their advantage, and minimized the tensions of a community hastily thrown together.

Malaya women offered the men who came to them the short-term lease of whatever was in the woman's room: food, utensils, water, bedding, and the woman herself. From the earliest 1920s, malaya women insisted that they did not ask to be paid until the man was about to leave;[7] this enabled the woman to charge for all the tasks she had performed and the commodities that had been consumed. In this way, moreover, the woman did not immediately define herself as a prostitute, an important consideration when that prostitution took place in 64 square feet of living space.

Malaya prostitutes did not solicit men. "When I was young," said a woman who came to Pumwani in about 1924, "we'd stay in our rooms and the men came to us; they would knock on the door and ask if I was free to go with them."[8] This practice was scorned by watembezi women of the same epoch — "Those women in Pumwani, they stayed like wives"[9] — but it nevertheless made the malaya form exceptionally well suited to the needs of women householders and their female tenants. A woman who had come to Pumwani in about 1925 explained how men knew to come to her room:

> They knew that the house belonged to a woman who never had a husband, so they knew it was a safe place to come because the owner had no husband to beat them. If a man saw me and liked me, then he would come to my door and ask to come in. . . . The best way to find men was for them to come to your room and you talk, you make tea for them, and you keep your house clean, and you keep your bed clean, you have sex with him, and he gives you money. . . . I didn't go openly looking for men, and men came to my house with respect, no one could tell that they were my boyfriends and not my husband just from looking.[10]

Here we see the dominant features of the malaya form, the sale of domestic labor, and the firm belief that malaya prostitution was conducted "in secret," that no one could tell "who was a prostitute and who was not."[11] The interaction of these two features accounted for the slow but steady profits of malaya women.

In the malaya form, the value of sexual intercourse was roughly equal to the value of other domestic tasks. During Nairobi's first construction boom, 1926-1929, when 80 percent of the city's male Africans were legally employed, malaya women became available for daytime visits either for sexual relations and perhaps a snack, or for food and conversation only. These visits amounted to the sale of individual domestic tasks, and were profitable because of the sheer number of waged men in Nairobi. One woman who first practiced the malaya form in Pumwani after 1926 said,

> if you spoke to these men, and told them about yourself, and kept your house clean, and gave them bathwater after sex, he would give you a few more pennies, and if he liked you he would come again, and if he came again, even to greet you, you would give him tea, and if he came again for sex you would also give him tea, and then he would have to give you even 75 cents. . . . If a man knew you and came to you regularly, he would give you as much as a shilling, but if he was a stranger to you it would be 25 cents.[12]

During the 1920s, malaya women generally received between Shs. 1/ and Shs. 3/75 from the men who spent the night with them. These high prices were made possible in part by high money wages and low rents in Pumwani and Pangani. Prostitutes' earnings, like Nairobi's labor requirements, were seasonal, but malaya women insisted that three night-long visitors per week were fairly common in the 1920s. This would be a monthly income of about Shs. 24/. However, assuming a much more conservative estimate of one night-long visit per week and ten daytime visits totaling Shs. 2/50, a woman might earn as little as Shs. 18/. Given that in the late 1920s an unskilled laborer earned about Shs. 12/ and his rare but skilled counterpart might earn Shs. 28/, we can see how prosperous malaya women became. The woman quoted above, for example, purchased two houses in Pangani in 1930 for Shs. 600/ cash. During the Depression, laborers left Nairobi, and landlords raised rents mercilessly to recoup their losses, so that working men's buoyant money wages were eroded by their increased individual expenditure on rent. As a result, they had less to spend on prostitutes, and the night-long price paid to malaya women dropped to between Shs. 1/ and Shs. 2/50. Skilled workers, however, began to visit malaya women more frequently as prices dropped, and malaya women became available for short visits well into the night, and many claimed to have increased their profits by volume. Between

1930-1935, most malaya women earned between Shs. 15/-Shs. 22/ per month (White, 1983: ch. 2-6).

When malaya women described their work, however, they stressed relationships, not money. Malaya women from the late 1920s claimed that by making domestic labor continually available they were creating social relationships from which they themselves could profit. In both watembezi and malaya prostitution there is evidence that customers occasionally became permanent boyfriends[13] but in my research only malaya women spoke of this happening as though it had been planned.

It was the secrecy of the malaya form, however, that reveals the most about its relationship to the larger community. Secrecy, according to malaya women, helped to reduce residential tensions and their real or imagined potential for violence in early Pumwani: It limited the risks for men who were seeking women, and it brought capital into the community without involving nonprostitutes in anything that might appear to be, either to neighbors or administrators, illegal or dangerous. It also isolated malaya women from each other. The secrecy of the form guaranteed that if anyone was to be in danger, it was the woman herself.

For example, malaya prostitutes of the 1920s said that they did nothing if a man refused to pay them, a risk inherent in asking the price last. One woman said " If a man didn't pay me, I wouldn't do anything because I wouldn't want anyone outside to know what was happening,"[14] while another woman was more explicit:

I couldn't do anything like start a quarrel because then your neighbors would know that you are really a prostitute and you were supposed to be doing your work in secret. I mean that my people, the Muslim people here in Nairobi, often knew that a woman is a prostitute but she will have their respect so long as she doesn't bring this to their attention. If she has boyfriends, she must do it in such a way that she does not cause her neighbors to be ashamed that they live near her. So if a man refused to pay a woman, she really can't do anything to him because she wouldn't want to shame herself in front of her neighbors, and she wouldn't want to be made to leave her house because of fighting. And what if a woman did fight, and was beaten up very badly? She would be hurt, and it would be her neighbors who had to pay for the taxi to the hospital. In Pumwani woman were supposed to be prostitutes in secret, and no one liked it when a woman was open about being a prostitute.[15]

The speaker here herself is a property owner; she and her late sister inherited a stone house in Pumwani from their mother: Her tenants would have been delighted had she done something that would have allowed them to put her in their debt. However, the vitality and the legitimacy of the malaya form within Pumwani came from its articulation of (and with) the needs of urban tenants. The requirements of the malaya form were the requirements of tenants in a highly competitive housing market, and this determined the conduct of malaya prostitution more than an individual woman's property ownership did. Nevertheless, many malaya women were, or became, property owners, and by 1933 over 40 percent of Pumwani's and the soon-to-be-demolished Pangani's 700 householders were single women (Bujra, 1972: 29, 53; KLC, 1934: vol. 1, 1124).

African private landlords built, owned, and operated African housing in Nairobi. The Location of Pumwani was based on a pre-existing system in which landlords were autonomous, a system the British were only too willing to graft onto their own. Landlords chose the rents they charged; rents varied from between 15 to 300 percent of a semiskilled laborer's monthly wage during the period under discussion. Nairobi's landlords evicted the poor and reduced money wages at monthly intervals, something the Pass Laws could not do at any point in their operation (White, 1983: ch. 6).

In addition to all this, Muslim landlords, male and malaya alike, served the state by socializing the labor into the norms of urban life: This may not have made these men better laborers once they arrived at their worksite, but it kept public and private order in Pumwani and Pangani according to the most rigid standards. Muslim landlords, for example, frowned on drunkenness among their tenants. Malaya landlords were perhaps even more exacting: They actively discouraged any activity — whether it be drunkenness, receipt of stolen goods, and, as we shall see, infanticide — that might bring them under police surveillance, and thus demanded and received obedience to the law from their tenants. Moreover, malaya women, whether landlords or tenants, did everything in their power — including moving — to keep peace where they lived, because "men didn't like to come to a house where women were quarrelling."[16]

Malaya prostitution in the 1920s and 1930s was not frowned upon in the community it served and often housed: "In those days it was not dangerous to be a prostitute, any woman could be a prostitute, that was our job, to go with men to get money."[17] Pumwani in the interwar years was not a world divided into rigid categories of prostitute and respectable women; indeed, it is possible to argue that prostitute/householders were the respectable women; they were certainly the richest.

Who were the malaya women of this era? With almost no exceptions, women whose rural families engaged in subsistence production became malaya prostitutes. These women came to Pumwani, chose a form of prostitution intrinsic to urban African locations (see for example Southall and Gutkind, 1957: 79ff.), and accumulated their earnings as independent heads of households. As a woman who came to Nairobi in about 1925 said, "At home, what could I do? Grow crops for my husband or my father. In Nairobi I can earn my own money, for myself."[18] Even Pumwani-born malaya prostitutes echoed these sentiments, "I decided that even if my father had property it was not mine . . . so I came to Mathare to find my own property."[19]

The circumstances of the woman's natal family seems to have determined the form of prostitution she chose and what she then did with her earnings. The circumstances and the frequency with which women acquired urban property in Nairobi varied throughout the colonial era, but those circumstances were directly related to the agricultural production of the woman's natal family. Women from subsistence farming households were most often those who retained control over their urban incomes and used them to build or purchase real property with which they entered Nairobi's African petty bourgeoise (a class at least half-founded by women like themselves). Other women, whose families cultivated cash crops and at different times constituted a rural petty bourgeoise themselves, did not on the whole acquire personal wealth in the city, and most often returned home where their earnings came under patrilineal control or where they acquired property that was eventually inherited by their patrilineages. Those women who acquired real property in Nairobi and also subsidized or expanded their parents' farms were from households that mixed a small amount of cash cropping with subsistence cultivation (White, 1983: ch. 5).

Urban African property owners transmitted their property either to patrilineage or to their own households whether or not they had offspring themselves. Among Nairobi's African petty bourgeoise, childless women invariably designated heirs for their houses, mostly young women they had sheltered in town or those they had brought from their rural homelands years before (Bujra, 1975: 225ff., White, 1983: ch. 3-4). I know of no cases where the designated heirs of childless malaya women's houses were males. Malaya women effectively kept their own property independent, or at least outside the control of pre-existing patrilineages. Significantly, women whose urban property was acquired through profits from watembezi prostitution often designated a brother's son as their heir, transmitting their property back into their patrilineages.[20]

Thus, not every single woman's house in Pumwani and Pangani was a step toward urban class formation, but a good many were. During the 1920s and 1930s colonial officials knew this. It would be a mistake to say that the state tolerated exceptionally capable landlords who also happened to be prostitutes; on the contrary, the state tolerated prostitutes who also happened to own property. The state's primary objection was to urban property ownership, not prostitution. For all the peace-keeping reasons that made malaya women such ideal landlords, they were also the most dangerous: They actively formed relationships, and they enforced the rules by which their community lived. Doing this, they usurped some of the peace-keeping functions of the state.

In the 1920s, the demolition of urban property had required little more than a Medical Department recommendation and a bulldozer. By the mid-1930s, the rationale for destroying African property had shifted from the medical to the social. Houses were to be razed because of the purposes to which they were put. Thus one official justification for the destruction of Pangani proclaimed that "retired prostitutes have set up lodging houses which are also brothels and refuges for the criminal classes."[21] Historically, the issue that had dominated Nairobi's African policy, whether petty-bourgeoise prostitutes or the state should house the African labor force, had masked the more salient issue, which group — urban accumulators or migrant laborers — should be allowed to form classes. These issues intersected time after time in the events of 1936 through 1940.

PANGANI, SHAURI MOYO, AND THE MANUFACTURE OF THE UNRESPECTABLE PETTY BOURGEOISIE

Historians of Western Europe have for some years stressed the importance of the distinction between the respectable and unrespectable poor in nineteenth-century cities. They have noted the characteristic vocabulary, drawing on metaphors of disease, pollution, and corruption, with which officials and reformers described the unrespectable. The most important metaphor of all was contamination, and it became more salient as a more respectable working class — accepting much of the structure of property and production even as they strove for better wages and working conditions — emerged from the cauldron of class conflict. The danger of allowing casual labor, sweated trades, and all the forms of self-employment of the "residuum" — begging, theft, and prostitution — to continue in cities was that this residuum might contaminate the respectable, legal working class (Stedman Jones, 1971: 13-16, 188-183, 289ff.; Swanson, 1977: 387-409).

In most of early colonial Africa, this distinction seemed irrelevant. No African worker was likely to become respectable; getting him to work was difficult enough (Clayton and Savage, 1974: 108-152; Stichter, 1982: 41-59), and all workers went home when their labor contracts expired. In urban Kenya, the state certainly complained about the disease and corruption of the areas where Africans lived, but the state's own feeble attempts at housing Africans had proved so disastrous that these conditions were attributed to specifically African qualities, not to who owned the property. The state basically turned a blind eye to most illegal African property ownership between the establishment of Pumwani in 1921/1922 and 1930, the same period in which the state patronized the legal African property owners. During the 1930s, just as the owners of legal and illegal properties were becoming more entrenched in the city, the situation of the labor force was changing. By the late 1940s, the issue of building a respectable working class in African cities was to become very serious indeed (Cooper, 1981: 41-42), but as early as 1930, the issue was already being joined.

During the Depression, a substantial exodus of workers from Nairobi and other cities took place; the rural areas — scattered and disparate — were taking up the burdens of the economic crisis and dissipating the dangers of urban discontent. Nairobi's African population declined from 32,000 in 1929 to 28,000 in 1930 and descended steadily to 23,000 in 1933; it increased slowly back to 28,000 by 1936 and then skyrocketed to 38,000 in 1937 (White, 1983: ch. 4). Thus, with the reduced African population of early 1930s, the state could imagine itself in the role of landlord, a role at which it had failed dismally in the late 1920s, having been unable to rent out the 460 beds of its Quarry Road Estate in 1929 (Hake, 1977: 45). After 1936, employment in Nairobi revived and there was a new influx of male workers. The growth of the urban workforce brought back with renewed vigor the question of how to reproduce a labor force that seemed eager to leave the increasingly weakened rural agricultural systems as soon as the city presented opportunities. It was in the light of this new step in the development of a migratory working class that the question of class formation among the people who had historically performed the functions of reproduction in the city — the landlords and the prostitutes — came to be considered anew.

Even before colonialism was firmly established in Kenya, the British were aware that many rudimentary townships had settled populations dominated by property-owning "loose women." At least one administrator took advantage of their prosperity by taxing them at three times the earliest official rate.[22] During the formative years of colonial rule, however, there were debates within the administration over the right of Africans to remain in the towns where they had lived for some time. The supporters of urban Africans' fragile rights argued that "toil and age" and often years of service to the British Imperial East Africa Company had rendered them "homeless and disorganized . . . detribalized, demoralized, and decentralized" so that it was only natural for them to congregate around administrative centers.[23] In other words, this view held that the colony's earliest urban Africans were hapless victims of progress and should be allowed to stay in towns as a charity. This view obscured the fact that they were a class: They had property and heirs. This was obscured because the urban Africans were needed: As experienced soldiers, government servants, prostitutes, and traders, they were especially well suited to house and influence and monitor the young migrant laborers, for whom urban wage labor was often a way "to avoid tribal control."[24]

This meant that from the early part of this century there were two urban policies, one for the property owners and the other for the migrant laborers, the "absconding offspring."[25] In Nairobi there were fleeting periods when property owners and the administration worked willingly together, such as in the allocation of plots in Pumwani and in the more extravagant aspects of the 1931 Pass Laws, which were color coded to protect permanent residents from being forced to leave town (van Zwanenberg, 1972: 198). In the early 1930s, when the exodus of workers from Nairobi enabled the state — a nascent if unsuccessful landlord that housed 3.5 percent of Nairobi's African population in 1930 (White, 1983: ch. 6)[26] — to reevaluate its two urban policies. The result turned them inside out, as the state moved to legislate the African petty bourgeoisie out of existence.

Between 1930 and 1939, over 300 African property owners were made homeless and illegal by the official demolition of Pangani village (although squatters periodically occupied Pangani well into the 1940s,[27] and the construction of Shauri Moyo. Pangani, one of the oldest pre-World War I villages in Nairobi, had been first scheduled for demolition in 1919, but it was not until 1930, when the African population was declining, that a small number of evictions and demolitions were ordered by the NMC. By then, Pangani was the largest and most prosperous African community in Nairobi; it had more stone houses than Pumwani and considerably fewer prostitutes, as many young women had moved to Pumwani to be closer to laboring men.[28] The actual removal of Pangani's population was postponed while compensation for householders was debated and fixed and then was delayed further when a series of ill-advised evictions in 1936 brought complaints from the Colonial Office. The NMC, which had waited vainly for private employers to accommodate their own workers in Nairobi,[29] was finally forced to follow a 1934 recommendation that it provide housing for the evicted Pangani residents.

In 1936 the NMC borrowed £46,000 from the Kenya Government to build the Pumwani Extension. Consisting of 175 four- to six-room stone houses, before it was completed the new estate became known as *Shauri Moyo,* idiosyncratic Swahili for "my own business," referring to the protracted and painful debate among Pangani householders over whether or not they should accept the NMC's parsimonious offer of relocation there.

Between 1930 and 1936 there had been a number of fanciful plans over what to do with dispossessed Pangani householders, including moving them to the estate the municipality could not fill.[30] Although a few Pangani property owners had cut their losses and moved to Pumwani in the early 1930s,[31] only a few could have afforded to do this. In 1937, the NMC offered Pangani landlords the choice of either lifetime leases in Shauri Moyo or £50 compensation, this at a time when the materials for a four-room mud and pole house "of good design . . . intended . . . for lodging" was estimated at £78.[32] Many landlords took the £50 and went to build houses in nearby illegal squatter settlements, showing their disdain for the entire rehousing scheme, or indeed, for the state's notions of legality. But 175 (out of 293) Pangani landlords, all but a very few single women, accepted the lifetime leases in Shauri Moyo. They were thus permitted to live there at reduced rents for their own rooms, select the other tenants, collect and keep the rents they charged in all but one-third of the houses (where the NMC set rents), but they could neither transmit nor sell the properties in which they lived (Davies, 1938: 8-9; White, 1983: ch. 6). Thus, by giving self-selected householders lifetime leases on the new stone houses, the state guaranteed that the social controls of Nairobi Islam would be carried over to the new estate. The state had allowed the most compliant of Pangani landlords a means to accumulate some capital, but not to pass urban property to their heirs.

With the allocation of housing in Shauri Moyo in 1938, the central contradiction of urban policy in this era appeared to be resolved: The state needed private landlords but could not countenance the fact that they were making themselves into a class by the same mechanism with which they were housing the state's workforce. The cost of this resolution, however, was over 120 Pangani householders building elsewhere, swelling the ranks of the illegal landlords, the invisible petty bourgeoisie that the state periodically had to bulldoze out of existence.

The evidence is clear that private landlordism itself was not under attack: class formation was. Whereas in the early colonial era documentary sources referred to the vulnerability of the urban African propertied classes, by the mid-1930s, the only people speaking of the difficult situation of the landlords were the landlords themselves.[33] As early as 1930, landlords were seen as furnishing corruption to a suddenly industrious and respectable migrant labor force. In the words of Dr. A. R. Patterson, Kenya's veteran Director of Medical and Sanitary Services,

> Times have changed since 1924 and even the casual labour of today is not the red blanket savage of 1923. The boys . . . even the poorest of them, have now some ambition to be clean. Many are endeavoring to read and write. . . . As it is, however, they must sit among bugs and stale posho in filth and squalor.[34]

While few administrators ever described the Nairobi workforce in such glowing terms, most subscribed to and embellished the notion of contamination from the top down. Soon there were resounding attacks on the children and heirs of African landlords and of prostitutes. In 1931, Nairobi's district commissioner complained about the Nubian settlement at Kibera, which occupied Crown Land on the outskirts of the city, land that was then sought as a potential golf course (KLC, 1933: 182): "The old Nubian is a man to whom the colony owes much, but the second generation and the hybrids arising from mixed unions are degenerate."[35] He also blamed prostitutes for creating a generation corrupted by town life:

> All over Nairobi there is a race of detribalized natives, born to prostitutes, who cannot be sent home as they do not know to what reserve they belong, or have lost all desire and even the means to live in the reserve to which their fathers belonged.[36]

A year later, the district officer began to undermine the legitimacy of the landlords themselves, pointing out that not all landlords were former government servants and that many were lazy and opportunistic:

> Pumwani and Pangani thrive on the lodging system. You get a perfectly decent boy who has been a houseboy for some time and who has lost the art of living in the reserve, and he will probably buy a little house and let out lodgings at the rate of Shs. 10/room. It is really a little gold mine [Hoskings, quoted in KLC, 1933: vol. 1, 1151].

In 1933, the state's official "expert" on Pangani landlords bluntly wrote that the children of African property owners were contaminated by their urban environment:

> If they [the householders] go back to the reserves the chances are that their children will grow up decent people. If they continue living in town there is little hope of that [Carr, in KLC, 1333: vol. 2, 1123].

In other words, the heirs of African property owners were seen as growing up polluted.

In 1936, when the acting deputy governor was under fire for demolishing 36 houses in Pangani without providing any accommodation for the evicted occupants, he easily defended himself by combining the rhetorics of aged and increasingly corrupt landlords and corrupted youth. He informed the Colonial Office that Pangani had a "respectable nucleus" of "old men and widows, strict Muslims . . . detribalized, deruralized, and obviously incapable of being accommodated anywhere but in or near a town" but surrounded by the sort of young Africans who "live by their wits and on their fellows" who "prefer the amenities of town life which also gives them greater scope for their criminal proclivities."[37]

These words sealed Pangani's fate; there had never really been any question of whether or not it would be demolished, but the events and complaints and correspondence of mid-1936 served to establish when it should be demolished, at what rate, and under what conditions. The memorandum quoted above gave the state's case against African class formation succinctly and placed it in historical perspective: The old householders themselves (most of whom had owned property in Pangani since before World War I) had a right to be there, but they were too old to continue to be effective agents of social control; their young heirs were out of control, degenerate, and dangerous. Whereas previously administrators had seen a dialectic between one respectable class — landlords and then, suddenly, the labor force — and an unrespectable one, the acting deputy governor identified two indolent groups. Among the opportunistic Africans who had recently acquired urban property were the "retired prostitutes" who "set up lodging houses" that harbored "the criminal classes" from which the city had to be kept safe.

After Shauri Moyo was completed in 1938, the most direct prohibition on legal African property ownership was imposed. Despite strenuous objections from the Kenya government hierarchy, the director of Medical and Sanitary Services, the most influential voice in urban policy from the 1920s on (see White, 1983: ch. 3), managed to ban Africans from legally building mud and pole lodging houses. Only stone houses were to be allowed, and the estimated cost of a four-room house in stone was £250, five times the Pangani compensation figure, and more than three times the cost of an equivalent mud and pole structure.[38]

Thus, in 1938 the state presented proud evidence that stone structures were in fact doing the work of social control: Less than six months after the Railway Landhies opened 48 family dwelling units, they were praised for having lowered the number of venereal disease cases by an incredible 67 percent.[39] During the wildcat strikes of 1939, private landlords were seen as totally contaminating: It was their high rents, "this profiteering," that caused the "considerable native unrest" of that year.[40]

Between 1936 and 1940, the state successfully assaulted Nairobi's African petty bourgeoisie. How was this attack seen in Pumwani, by 1938 the last place African property ownership was legal? Specifically, how did malaya women, architects of independent accumulation for petty bourgeoise status and, as tenants and as landlords, ideologues of the proper conduct of the urban community, respond to the state's crackdown on their colleagues in Pangani? While many malaya women thought that the women who accepted housing in Shauri Moyo were "stupid," they tended to think that the evictions and temporary homelessness were one of life's misfortunes, part and parcel of being African in Nairobi (White, 1983: ch. 4). They did not name the state as the assailant. But in those same years, it was in the area of work that malaya women clearly understood and articulated that their position as laborers and as a class was being undercut and eroded. It was in the daily conduct of prostitution within Pumwani that they identified class conflict.

WAZI-WAZI PROSTITUTION IN PUMWANI, 1934/1936-1940

This section deals primarily with the ideas about Wazi-Wazi prostitution that were popular in Pumwani, and as a result, it is difficult to establish a precise chronology, especially when stereotypes seem to have piled on stereotypes year after year. My data suggest that while some women may have been practicing the Wazi-Wazi form as early as 1934, and that some of these women may have been Haya, the conduct of Wazi-Wazi prostitution that forms the bulk of this section developed after 1936, when the number of Nairobi's African workers soared.

In situations of dense overcrowding and high male employment, the Wazi-Wazi form had many advantages for women and men. Wazi-Wazi women sat outside their doors waiting for men, and they thus gained visibility without risking police harrassment, since they could do many things while waiting — watch children, prepare food, and sew (as increasing numbers of Christian women, veterans of mission homecraft classes, became prostitutes in Nairobi) — without inviting suspicion. By 1937, the form allowed women to establish new relations with male wage laborers new to town, many of whom may have been hesitant to go door to door in Pumwani asking for women. As the price in most Wazi-Wazi transactions was negotiated in advance outside the woman's door, the form may have been especially appealing to men whose real incomes were reduced by high rents. Indeed, Wazi-Wazi women were reputed to have called out their prices from where they sat, particularly on pay days. Their prices ranged from Shs. 0/25 to Shs. 1/00, and this seems to have brought down the price for brief sexual liaisons in this period.

Such conduct made the form especially well suited to what was called "short time in Nairobi, and this made the form especially convenient to women with small children and no nearby kin; they did not have to arrange for childcare, which they could be called upon to reciprocate, if they were only going inside for a few minutes. This was prostitution without bathwater. Perhaps just as important, Wazi-Wazi prostitution was ideal for women who shared rooms, for it allowed them to alternate their labor time while they reduced their individual expenditure on rent (White, 1983: ch. 5).

From almost all accounts, Haya women were associated with the Wazi-Wazi form. In fact, Haya women have been identified with the more aggressive and frequently lowest-priced prostitution in East Africa (Southall and Gutkind, 1957: 82-83; Little, 1973: 90-91). To understand why, we must look at the Haya before they became immigrants to towns. The Haya come from Bukoba District in northwest Tanganyika. In the early years of German rule, coffee was introduced to all the Haya chiefdoms and became a major cash crop. In the years after World War I, landowning Haya Lutherans formed a wealthy rural petty bourgeoise whose manual labor was performed by migrants. Their wealth had inflated the Christian brideprice to as much as Shs. 600/ or Shs. 700/. Unlike many African peoples, the Haya permitted divorce and the complete return of brideprice, and this traditional custom carried over into modern times. Thus, when the world price of coffee fell 90 percent in 1930, men needed cash to pay their debts and laborers and had one recourse: divorce.

> Men had to find money, and the obvious means was to divorce a wife and get the brideprice back in full. The fathers suddenly had to find Shs. 600/ or Shs. 700/ to return to sons-in-law. That meant ruin. Then the women found a solution. They had been taught during the "fat" years that they had a cash value. The lake steamer brought them in their hundreds to Nairobi and Kampala, and returning home years later, with bicycle and syphilis and umbrella, they were hailed as the economic saviours of their families [Sundkler, 1945: 253-258].

Young Haya men entered wage labor in large numbers at the same time (Southall and Gutkind, 1957). As we shall see, the way that women conducted their prostitution indicates that many were voluntary workers on their families' behalf. Despite the apparent modernity of cash cropping and aggressive forms of prostitution, the forces that sent Haya women into the cities of East Africa were very traditional: The basis for marriage was the father's accumulation, and the basis for divorce was the husband's accumulation, or lack thereof. In Haya society, women were the vehicles through whom cash was redirected into patrilineages. In marriage and divorce and in prostitution and after, Haya women of the Great Depression behaved as daughters, and this, I suggest, set them and their prostitution apart from the malaya women in Pumwani who condemned them as shameful, aggressive, and above all, public.

Forty years after the Haya had become widespread in Pumwani, malaya women described the Wazi-Wazi form with a passion and an awe and detail that I had never heard applied to other prostitutes before. Wazi-Wazi prostitutes were seen as interlopers, women with no commitment to the values of community and household cooperation. One woman said that if a man refused to pay a Haya prostitute,

> they would fight, and then the woman would start screaming for help, saying this man doesn't want to give her any money. The Waziba [Haya] women were the ones who started this screaming, saying that the man had to give them cash. And they would also start doing shameful things when a man tried to cheat them, they would start to abuse that man, and they would ask their neighbors to come, and they would fight in front of everyone. . . . Because it was this money that she depended on . . . and a woman would risk her blood to get her money.[41]

This is a far cry from malaya women protecting their neighbors from their work. Haya women did not make any attempt to follow the conventions of Muslim Pumwani life, and this scandalized malaya women. I know of no conversion to Islam by a Haya woman. They made no attempt to settle in Pumwani. As prostitutes, however, Haya women were described as having intense cooperation and substantial solidarity with each other, especially when it is compared to the comraderie of women who insisted that "no one could tell who was a prostitute and who was not."[42] Haya women remained their fathers' daughters, accumulating for their patrilineages, but in Pumwani they acted like sisters:

> In those days it was the Waganda and the Waziba women who were rich and they didn't buy any plots here in Pumwani. If one of those women died here by mistake in Nairobi her neighbors and friends who had come with her to Nairobi would take her clothes and money and her body and go straight to her home. Those Mziba women wouldn't have graves here in Nairobi, they'd go straight back to their own country. These women . . . they were sending money back to their own countries every week, and when they died they would be buried at home too, no matter where they died. When an Mziba woman died a neighbor would take the body and all the property to her father's house.[43]

Here again, we see the Haya as urban agents of the rural economy, earning money in town only to send it home.

Haya women cooperated as friends and as prostitutes. Their cooperation as workers was in that aspect of Wazi-Wazi prostitution most appalling to malaya women of the same era: that they called out the price — one that was low, and in theory, nonnegotiable — to men passing by. In doing this, Haya women were acting by consensus to establish price boundaries, to ensure that no individual woman could or would undersell the others, while enabling a prostitute to earn her subsistence without circumventing the revenues her neighbors might earn.

Malaya women of the mid- and late-1930s passionately condemned Haya prostitutes. They were said to be rich, shameful; they demanded cash in advance; they fought; they did all the things malaya women never did, and they profited from it at the expense of the profits of malaya women. One Pumwani-born woman clarified local objections to the practices of Wazi-Wazi prostitutes:

> Ziba and Nandi women, those were cruel women, they used to sit outside their rooms and sell their bodies without caring who saw them. . . . They used to call to men in the road, "Come here, come here," and some of them became very rich, but most of them got beaten up very badly, and they let their babies die. The Nandi and the Ziba were the first women to throw their babies away. . . . They would kill those babies as soon as they were born, and leave them in the toilets. Sometimes the police would come and ask us if we knew who the mothers were, but we could never say for sure.[44]

Wazi-Wazi behavior was shameful to malaya women, and it was dangerous: While the labor form itself was disrespectful, it was Wazi-Wazi women's visibility, the beatings, and the infanticide that invited the police to the doors of respectable women in Pumwani.

But, by 1937, respectable malaya women were already under attack from the state, not other prostitutes. By 1937, the state was in the process of making illegal the very things that enabled malaya women to function as a class: legal property-ownership. Seen in this way, the animosity and the fear and the censure malaya women had for Wazi-Wazi women was not merely an expression of class conflict; it was class conflict. The criminalization of African property ownership and the urban petty bourgeoise could have only been seen by malaya women as the state's tacit approval of the Wazi-Wazi form, which it was. If the Nairobi administration was going to countenance accumulation in the back alleys of Pumwani, they preferred that the cash thus accumulated flow directly to the rural petty bourgeoisie of other lands, as far away as possible. The demolition of Pangani and, to a much greater extent, the allocation of housing in Shauri Moyo, provided the Kenyan state with a way to undermine urban class formation without ever directly acting against prostitution.

It was only during the early years of World War II that the state actively interfered with prostitution, at a time when that prostitution subsidized an increasingly potent cycle of rural class formation in Kenya, particularly among squatters in Rift Valley Province and Kikuyu smallholders. In the late 1930s, the presence of these farmers' teenage daughters on the streets of Nairobi had been noted by European and African observers alike, and the Kikuyu Local Native Council had complained to the MNAO about it (Davies, 1938: 3-4).[45] Between 1937 and 1938, however, juvenile watembezi were not considered a problem (Davies, 1938: 3-4), and they went about their business unmolested, during which time they earned substantially less than Wazi-Wazi women did in Pumwani (White, 1983: ch. 5). During the early years of World War II, however, when all the factors that had contributed to the success of Wazi-Wazi women were multiplied by thousands of men living outside Pumwani and Shauri Moyo, juvenile watembezi began to become wealthy on the thoroughfares near Nairobi's military bases. Starting late in 1939, the MNAO ordered these teenagers arrested as often as his overtaxed police force could manage: his analogy was revealing, "it was like street sweeping."[46] The youth of these girls was only cited as a grounds for arrest when they began to earn a lot of money. The MNAO was determined to get these women off the streets as a way to remove their wealth from the cycle of rural class formation.

CONCLUSION

Malaya women had underestimated the colonial state. They seem to have believed that if they practiced the malaya form's deference and service to men with discretion and respect, if they strictly policed themselves and the community they sometimes housed, the truly radical fact that they were single women earning money for themselves and transmitting it as they saw fit might go unnoticed. For malaya women, the most conservative behavior in Nairobi prostitution accompanied class formation by people who were forbidden to have property in their own societies. Wazi-Wazi women, on the other hand, for all the aggressive behavior that accompanied their prostitution, were in fact prostituting themselves as daughters, doing over and over again for their fathers what they had once done through marriage: exchanging their labor power to subsidize their patrilineage.

The contradictions that follow from the most visible prostitutes being the most conservative family members, and the most circumspect malaya women being the most independent of East Africans are fascinating, but the contradictions did not confuse the colonial state. They knew that Wazi-Wazi women calling out prices — which would eventually be realized as stone houses in Bukoba — were less disruptive to the new directions of colonial rule than malaya women earning money for breakfast and bathwater that one day might be realized as stone houses in Pumwani.

In Pumwani and Shauri Moyo, the state achieved a retrenchment in the services malaya women were willing to provide for their paying customers. Without any legislation affecting prostitution, the state was able to guarantee that a large proportion of the late 1930s and early wartime workforce would have sex quickly, without prolonged contact with women who had a strong and frustrated commitment to urban community and property ownership. Women who had first practiced the malaya form in Pumwani during the mid-1930s requested the price in advance, regardless of how many services they provided for the men.[47] But women who first practiced the malaya form in Pumwani after 1937-1938 did so with no expectation of relationship or knowledge, or even very much money (White, 1983: ch. 5). When asked which group of men paid the best, one such malaya woman said: "I can't tell you what kind of men. It was like when someone is hungry, he eats. The men came, they asked me the price, we went together, they paid me, and they left."[48] Outside Pumwani, however, where illegal property ownership by women was a thriving enterprise — such as in the Mathare Valley and Eastleigh — the malaya form flourished in the 1940s with all the services and companionability that had characterized its conduct in 1920s Pumwani (White, 1983: ch. 7).

NOTES

1. Men's Price Sheets (MPS) 1977, compiled by Paul Kakaire and Luise White, Nairobi.

2. Kenya National Archives (KNA) MD 40/443, MacGregor Ross to Chief Secretary, Committee on Native Locations, PW 37/108, February 10, 1912.

3. Ibid.

4. KNA, MD 40/443, Native Location Committee By-Laws, 1914.

5. KNA, MD 40/1131, Housing of Africans in Nairobi, 2 vols., 1923, unpublished letter to Habari complaining about Pumwani.

6. KNA, MD 40/854/8/77, Confidential Memo on Prostitution, 11 October 1923.

7. Interview, Amina Hali, Pumwani, 4 August 1976; Miriam Wageithiga, Pumwani, 11 August 1976; Mwana Himani bint Ramadhani, Pumawani, 1976; Mama Abdullah Saidi, Pumwani, 2 March 1977.

8. Bint Ramadhani, 1976.

9. Wambui Murithi, Pumwani, 14 December 1976.

10. Kayaya Thababu, Pumwani, 7 February 1977.

11. Fatuma Makusidi, Pumwani, 20 May 1976; Rehema Monteo, Pumwani, 10 August 1976; Hali, 1976; passim.

12. Hali, 1976.

13. Wageithiga, 1976; Hali, 1976; Makusidi, 1976; Murithi, 1976.

14. Tamima binti Saidi, Pumwani, 15 March 1977.

15. Zaina binti Ali, Calyfonya, 21 February 1977.

16. Thababu, 1977.

17. Makusidi, 1976.

18. Thababu, 1977.

19. Tabitha Waweru, Mathare, 13 July 1976.

20. Murithi, 1976.

21. Public Records Office, London (PRO) CO/533/462/28005/B, Demolition to Pangani Village, Wade to Ormsby-Gore, 1936.

22. Rhodes House, Oxford (RH), Mackinder, geographical expedition, 1899; RH.MSS.Afr.r.29.

23. PRO, CO 533/130/12081, Ainsworth, PC Nyanza, "Memo regarding the question of Swahilis, Sudanese, and Other Africans presently residing in townships and newer stations, 592/1910, 9 June 1911.

24. PRO Ainsworth, 1911.

25. Ibid.

26. Nairobi Municipal Archives (NMA), NMC file, "Native Statistics."

27. NMA, Medical Officer of Health, Annual Report, 1948.

28. Miriam bint Omari, Pumwani, 25 March 1977; Hawa binti Musa, Pumwani, 1 December 1976; Thomas Colchester, London, 8 and 12 August 1977.

29. KNA Lab 9/1707/70/251, DC to Labour Officer, Nairobi, 1 March 1932; NMC Native Affairs Commission, Minutes, 1932-1937: 4 June 1937.

30. NMC Native Affairs Commission, 1 February 1932.

31. Binti Musa, 1976.

32. KNA MD 1131/63, 1940.

33. See, for example, Malim bin Hamis in KLC, Evidence, I, 1934, 1167.

34. KNA MD 40/1131, 1930.

35. KNA CP 9/15/3, DC E. B. Hoskings to Commissioner for Lands and Settlement, 1931.

36. Ibid.

37. PRO, CO 533/462/38005/38005/B. 1936.

38. KNA MD 40/1131/63, 1938-1940.

39. KNA PC/CP/AR, 1938.

40. PRO 533/513, Brooke-Popham, Governor to MacDonald, 1939.

41. Margaret Githeka, Mathare, 2 March 1976, see also Juliana Jacob, Pumwani, 25 Feb. 1977.

42. Makusidi, 1976.

43. Ibid.

44. Githeka, 1976.

45. Gathiro wa Chege, Mathare, 9 July 1976; Githeka, 1976; Murithi, 1976.

46. Zeitun Ahmed, Pumwani, 14 June 1976.

47. Miriam Musale, Pumwani, 18 June 1976.

REFERENCES

BEINART, W. J. (1982) The Political Economy of Pondoland. Cambridge: Cambridge University Press.

BUJRA, J. M. (1975) "Women 'entrepreneurs' of early Nairobi." Canadian Journal of African Studies 9: 213-234.

——— (1972) Pumwani: The Politics of Property, a Study of an Urban Renewal Scheme in Nairobi, Kenya. SSRC Report. (typescript)

CLAYTON, A. and D. C. SAVAGE (1974) Government and Labour in Kenya, 1895-1964. London: Frank Cass.

COOPER, F. (1981) "Africa and the world economy." African Studies Review, 24, 2/3: 1-86.

DAVIES, E. St. A. (1938) Some Problems Arising from the Conditions of Housing and Employment of Natives in Nairobi. (typescript)

HAKE, A. (1977) African Metropolis: Nairobi's Self-Help City. Sussex: Sussex University Press.

Kenya Land Commission [KLC] (1934) Evidence (3 vols.). London: His Majesty's Stationery Office.

—— (1933) Report. London: His Majesty's Stationery Office.

LITTLE, K. (1973) African Women in Towns. Cambridge: Cambridge University Press.

SOUTHALL, A.W. and P.C.W. GUTKIND (1957) Townsmen in the Making: Kampala and its Suburbs. Kampala: East African Institute for Social Research.

STEDMAN JONES, G. (1971) Outcast London: A Study in the Relationship between the Classes in Victorian London. Oxford: Oxford University Press.

STICHTER, S. (1982) Migrant Labor in Kenya. London: Longman.

SUNDKLER, B.G.M. (1945) "Marriage problems in the church in Tanganyika." International Review of Missions 34, 134: 253-266.

SWANSON, M.W. (1977) "The sanitation syndrome: bubonic plague and urban native policy in the Cape Colony, 1900-1909." Journal of African History 18: 387-410.

WHITE, L. (1983) "A history of prostitution in Nairobi, Kenya, c. 1900-1952." Ph.D. dissertation, Cambridge University.

van ZWANENBERG, R.M.A. (1972) "History and theory of urban poverty in Nairobi: the problem of slum development." Journal of East African Research and Development 2, 2: 165-203.

6

DE LA CALEBASSE À LA PRODUCTION EN SÉRIE
Les Réseaux Commerciaux Laobé au Sénégal et en France

GERARD SALEM

This chapter explores what the concept of the informal sector conceals. Laobé wood-carving enterprises could hardly be more highly organized. Based on the traditional divisions of the Laobé, social networks link rural areas of Senegal with particular artisanal shops in Dakar and then to Laobé sellers in Europe. Hemmed in by large-scale capital and the state, and facing strong competition, the proprietors of these shops rely on largely unpaid labor from apprentices trying to break into the craft and into the system of social relations governing production and distribution. The proprietors' ability to control access to residential space in particular neighborhoods of Dakar as well as to make use of relationships of kinship and marriage underlies their ability to obtain and control labor. This control becomes the basis of a detailed yet flexible division of labor within the workshop — as each piece is passed from worker to worker — and of complex commercial systems that tie several European cities into the Senegalese system. The chapter examines in detail the structure of the Laobé networks in the production and marketing of wood carvings and thus becomes a study of the connection of space, kinship, and production.

Author's Note: Je tiens à remercier Michel Sivignon, professeur de Géographie à l'Université de Dakar, qui a bien voulu relire et corriger ce texte.

Comme les autres pays africains, le Sénégal a connu dans les trois dernières décennies un mouvement d'urbanisation accélérée. Les spécialistes de la ville — géographes, urbanistes, sociologues, économistes, anthropologues — soulignent chacun à leur manière la complexité des formes d'insertion des néo-citadins à la ville et à l'économie urbaine. Chaque individue est confronté, à travers son groupe social d'origine, aux problèmes vitaux du logement, de la nourriture, de la santé, de la solidarité, etc. . . . ce que nous définissons comme les constituants élémentaires du "struggle for the city."

Notre première hypothèse est que, pour répondre à ces nécessités, chaque group d'individus procède à une interprétation et une réinterprétation des règles qui assurent leur fonctionnement, règles économiques, familiales, matrimoniales, etc.: ils définissent ainsi les moyens d'une stratégie d'intégration/utilisation à/de la ville. C'est à l'échelle où se définissent ces stratégies que la recherche doit être menée, échelle sociale et échelle spatiale: L'échelle sociale représente le niveau où le groupe-ethnique, lignage familial, castè, confrérique, plusieurs niveaux se superposant — trouve sa cohérence. Une démarche anthropologique s'impose à ce niveau d'étude. L'échelle spatiale représente l'aire sur laquelle le groupe imprime sa stratégie: milieu rural, villes secondaires, capitales régionales, pôles d'immigration internationale. Une démarche géographique prenant en compte les fonctions de ces différents espaces est alors nécessaire.

On définit ainsi un système résidentiel, plus ou moins large et d'une plus ou moins grande épaisseur qui ordonne la circulation des personnes (migrations, installation en ville, retour en milieu rural, accueil des parents, mariages, etc.) et des biens (distribution de l'argent, repartition des investissements, etc.).

Notre deuxième hypothèse est que ces stratégies sont fondées sur le triple problème du logement et de la propriété, de l'emploi et des revenus et des rapports avec le milieu d'origine.

Le problème du logement et de la propriété: les politiques urbaines suivies en Afrique, faites de déguerpissements et de constructions pour les classes moyennes ne touchent de façon positive qu'une infirme partie de la population dont la préoccupation majeure reste l'accès au logement et à la propriété foncière. Cela est particulièrement vrai pour les habitants de l'agglomération de Dakar-Pikine qui est passée de 132 000 habitants en 1945 à 236 000 en 1955, 514 000 en 1970 pour attendre environ 1 000 000 habitants en 1982. La ville a connu dans l'immédiat après guerre une prolifération de bidonvilles (carte 6.1) qui ont été systématiquement déguerpis vers une ville

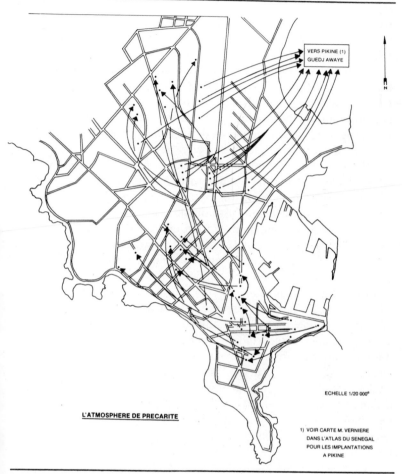

VERS PIKINE (1)
GUEDJ AWAYE

ECHELLE 1/20 000°

L'ATMOSPHERE DE PRECARITE

1) VOIR CARTE M. VERNIERE
DANS L'ATLAS DU SENEGAL
POUR LES IMPLANTATIONS
A PIKINE

Carte 6.1   Zone d'Accueil des Déguerpis à Dakar Centre

périphérique, créée ex-Nihilo, Dagoudane-Pikine, (Vernière, 1977; carte 6.2), dépourvue d'équipements collectifs et surtout privée d'emplois.

Dans cette atmosphère générale de précarité, la maison bien durable et rare constitue le seul gage de securité, assurance sociale et assurance vieillesse, relativement accessible aux pauvres. Convoitise des néo-citadins — M. Vernière parle avec bonheur de "la longue quête de la propriété" — la maison constitue la base matérielle qui permettra de "taller" l'installation des nouveaux venus. C'est dire

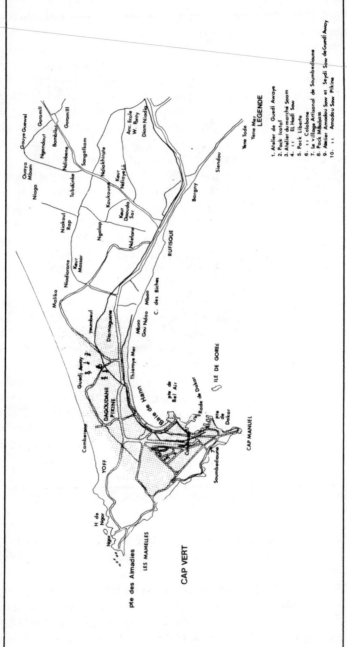

Carte 6.2   Urbanisation du Cap Vert: Localisation des Ateliers Laobé

LEGENDE

1. Atelier de Guedi Awaye
2. Pack Icolaf
3. Atelier du marché Saam
4.   ''   El Hadif Saw
5. Pack Liberte
6.   ''   Colobane
7. Le Village Artisanal de Soumbedioune
8. Pack Mbaao
9. Atelier Amadou Saw et Seydi Sow de Guedi Away
10.   ''   Amadou Saw Pikine

tout l'intérêt présenté par l'étude des maisons et des stratégies résidentielles (construction, occupation, partage, etc.). Il faut signaler dès maintenant que l'occupation de la maison et son héritage sont au centre des interprétations/réinterprétations faites par les groupes. On ne trouve pas en effet d'équivalent, en milieu rural, au bien indivisible et à la valeur marchande qu' est une maison. Selon quelle(s) règle(s) d'héritage un bien devenu marchandise se transmettra-t-il?

L'emploi et le revenu constituent le second souci majeur des citadins: le décalage entre le nombre de migrants et un marché de l'emploi des plus reduits confine cette population dans les petites activités de commerce et d'artisanat. Selon leur patrimoine spécifique, chaque groupe opère ainsi des spécialisations. Mais s'il est de notoriété publique que les harratines ont un quasi-monopole du commerce de l'eau, les Peul-Fouta du charbon de bois, etc. On sait peu de chose sur l'histoire et l'organisation interne de ces activités: en ville, quels types de contrat lient deux individus, comment le travail (notamment celui des enfants) est-il remuneré, à quelle(s) logique(s) répond(ent) la distribution des revenus, etc.?

C'est notamment dans les rapports entretenus avec le milieu d'origine que la rationalité des systèmes mis en place se revèlent. Les rapports règlent en effet le sens des échanges (famille restée au village, alliances matrimoniales, autorités confrériques, etc.) et créent les filières de migrations et d'emploi.

Dans le cadre d'une étude sur le système commercial sénégalais en France (Salem, 1981b), touchant à l'ensemble des activités de vente animées par des sénégalais, nous avons été amené à nous intéresser de plus près au groupe des artisans Lawbé, boisseliers de différentes ethnies. Ces artisans, principalement originaires des régions de Diourbel et Louga (carte 6.3), ont, chassés par la sécheresse de 1943 (Sarr, 1973) reconverti leurs activités de boisseleries traditionnelles (pilons, calebasses, mortiers) en production destinées aux touristes et à l'exportation.

Ils sont à l'origine de la commercialisation de ces produits en Europe, principalement dans le Sud de la France, dans les années 70. Rapidement rejoints par des commerçants mourides (Salem, 1982), les Lawbé ont vu simultanément le marché qu'ils avaient ouvert en France se couvrir par d'autres qu'eux (carte 6.4), et les commandes de produits fabriqués dans leurs ateliers dakarois se multiplier.

Le présent article s'attache à analyser les stratégies élaborées par les Lawbé collaborant d'une façon ou d'une autre avec le système commercial établi en France.

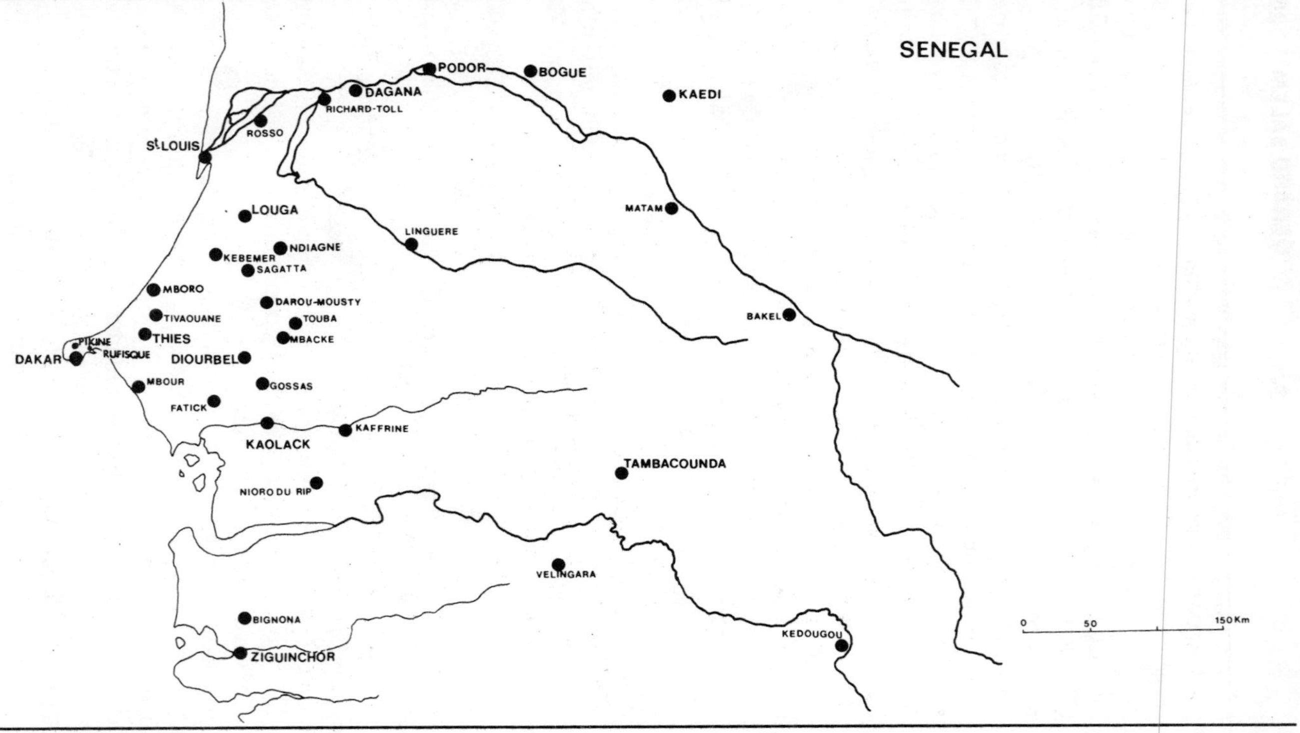

SENEGAL

KAEDI
BAKEL
MATAM
BOGUE
TAMBACOUNDA
PODOR
DAGANA
RICHARD-TOLL
LINGUERE
VELINGARA
KEBEMER NDIAGNE
DAROU-MOUSTY
SAGATTA
TOUBA
LOUGA
MBACKE
GOSSAS
KAFFRINE
ROSSO
TIVAOUANE
DIOURBEL
KAOLACK
KEDOUGOU
S.LOUIS
MBORO
THIES
FATICK
NIORO DU RIP
BIGNONA
ZIGUINCHOR
MBOUR
RUFISQUE
DAKAR

Carte 6.3   Sénégal

200

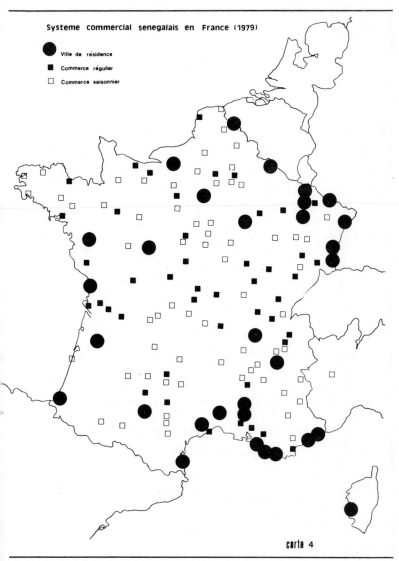

Carte 6.4   Système Commercial Sénégalais en France (1979)

LE GROUPE DES LAWBE

Une origine incertaine et une place originale dans la société sénégalaise. Même si ce n'est pas l'objet principal de cet article, il est nécessaire d'indiquer brièvement l'origine, selon la tradition orale, des Lawbé. Les mythes permettent en effet de mieux comprendre la place originale de ces boisseliers dans la société sénégalaise contemporaine.

Djibril Ly (1938) raconte ainsi l'origine des Lawbé:

> Il est raconté, mais Allah sait seul distinguer la vérité du mensonge.
>
> Dans le temps où l'état social n'existait pas et où les métiers n'étaient pas connus, vivaient dans le pays du Fouta trois frères: l'aîné Amady, le cadet Samba et le plus jeune Demba. Une grande famine s'étendit sur le pays et les plus riches même en souffraient; les trois frères encore en bas âge, ramassaient du bois qu'ils échangeaient contre des poignées de mil, leur seule nourriture.
>
> Un jour, dans la brousse, tandis qu'Amady et Demba cherchaient du bois ensembles, Samba resté seul rencontra un koumène auquel il fit part de sa triste situation et de celle de ses frères. Le koumène eut pitié de lui et lui remit une corde et un morceau de bois, lui conseillant de revenir à la tombée de la nuit, d'allumer un grand feu, d'y jeter le morceau de bois, il verrait alors sortir une vache du fleuve, elle s'approcherait de lui, il devrait l'attacher avec la corde et aurait soin de se coucher auprès d'elle pendant toute la nuit; en suivant ces conseils, il aurait ainsi de quoi nourrir ses frères et subvenir à leurs besoins.
>
> A la tombée de la nuit, Samba suit les conseils du koumène, allume le feu, voit sortir la vache qu'il attache et reste à côté d'elle. Toute la nuit la vache mugissait et à chague mugissement d'autres vaches sortaient du fleuve en grand nombre et se groupaient autour de la vache de Samba. Chacune avait un veau ou une génisse; au lever du jour Samba possédait ainsi un grand troupeau. Ses frères, inquiets sur le sort de Samba, le trouvèrent occupé à construire une petite case en paille au milieu d'un beau troupeau de vaches laitières, ils s'installèrent avec lui et furent heureux; mais il leur manquait des calebasses pour recueillir leur bon lait; heureusement, l'aîné, Amady, eut l'idée d'aller au village voisin chercher une hache avec laquelle il façonna dans le bois des calebasses pour les besoins de leur ménage.
>
> Les femmes du village voisin venaient souvent voir les trois frères pour obtenir un peu de lait et quelquefois de la viande de leur troupeau; trois d'entre elles s'unirent avec eux et ils en eurent une nombreuse descendance.
>
> Demba, le plus jeune, avait une très belle voix et chaque fois qu'il chantait, le campement se groupait autour de lui pour l'écouter.

A la mort des trois fréres, leurs enfants prirent chacun le métier de leur père.

Les enfants d'Amady continuèrent à travailler le bois, à façonner calebasses, pilons et mortiers, ce furent les Lawbé (bûcherons), au singulier Labbo.

Les enfants de Bamba se livrèrent à l'élevage du bétail et à la garde des troupeaux. Ce furent les Peuls ou Foulbé (au singulier Poullo).

Les enfants de Demba continuèrent à charmer les habitants du campements, par leur chant, ce furent les Wambâbé (au singulier Bambâdo).

Depuis ce temps-là, Peul, Wambâbé et Laobé sont toujours voisins.

Le beau récit de Djibrill Ly (1938) établit, sans jugement de valeur particulier sur un des groupes, le lien ancestral qui lie le pasteur peul, le Bambado, et le Laobé. Les Lawbé tiennent un discours sensiblement différent (récit de Abdou Sow):

Les Loabé sont d'origine peul. Trois Peul conduisaient un troupeau, tous trois étaient frères.

Les rivières se sont taries et, comme il fallait abreuver les bêtes, le plus fort des trois frères a été désigné pour abattre l'arbre qui était là, un kad. Il a abattu l'arbre avec une hache et l'a découpé en morceaux de deux mètres. Pendant ce temps, les deux autres frères continuaient à chercher de l'herbe pour les boeufs, un des deux ramassait les feuilles des arbres. Une fois les tronçons découpés et creusés, le frère qui avait coupé l'arbre a expliqué qu'ils pourraient, à partir de ce moment, se servir des vases pour faire boire les bêtes. Le plus jeune des frères a alors demandé au cadet (la bûcheron) — après l'avoir félicité — de lui découper des morceaux de 30 cm pour en faire plus tard des instruments de musique. Ils ont égorgé un agneau et le plus jeune s'est fabriqué des cordes pour la guitare. Un quatrième Peul est arrivé et s'est étonné de voir l'arbre abattu et les abreuvoirs. Il a demandé au Peul bûcheron de lui en faire un. Le marché a été conclu en échange d'un boeuf ou d'un mouton, le boeuf a été donné.

Le premier frére Peul, qui était resté berger, était jaloux de voir son frère obtenir un boeuf contre un abreuvoir et regrettait de ne pas être le seul à avoir un abreuvoir. Il a pris les bêtes et les a emmenées dans la prairie.

Un Peul qui passait par-là a vu l'abreuvoir et en a demandé un. Ils sont partis trouver le bûcheron. Ce dernier avait choisi comme lieu de travail un arbre entouré de lianes rampantes, il voulait les rencontrer.

En Wolof une plante qui rampe s'appelle LAONA (littéralement "ça a rampé"); pour désigner le lieu on a rajouté bé. Alors le Laobé c'est lá où les plantes rampent et c'est le Laobé. Le frère cadet, le Laobé, s'est consacré à la sculpture et au travail du bois.

Le benjamin, le plus chétif, après avoir fabriqué sa guitare, a fait le chant de l'ingéniosité du Laobé. Le Laobé flatté lui a donné un mouton. C'est ainsi que l'autre s'est transformé en quémandeur.

Les deux frères sont allés voir le troisième dans la brousse. Ce dernier leur a dit que dorénavant ils ne partageraient plus les bêtes, car les deux autres avaient d'autres moyens de vivre. D'où les expressions peul: Poulo dicco (le Peul aîné), le berger, Malaw Labo (le Laobé cadet), le sculpteur; Samba Bambado (le benjamin griot), le grit.

Un autre Laobé ajouta,

Quand le Peul a constaté qu'il pouvait vivre avec ses bêtes, il a trahi. C'est delà qu'on dit que le Peul a la trahison dans le sang.

Contre l'acte de trahison du Peul, le Laobé a décidé de tout vendre aux Peul "Je te vendrai le vase pour le lait, l'abreuvoir pour le boeuf. Je ne ferai jamais rien gratuitement pour toi."

Ces deux récits, au-delà de leur différence, illustrent la place un peu marginale du boisselier: véritable frère ennemi du Peul et du griot, il s'attache à lui une image d'individualisme et d'indépendance. En outre, les Lawbé distinguent en leur sein: deux sous-groupes, les Yett (sculpteurs) et les Dioula (commerçants Dioula).

LAWBE YETT ET LAWBE DIOULA

La distinction entre Lawbé Yett et Lawbé Dioula est rarement faite dans la littérature ethnologique ce qui est d'autant plus étonnant que les rapports entretenus entre ces deux groupes sont complexes et vivaces: les Yett ne manquent jamais une occasion de souligner la différence qui existe entre eux — travailleurs, artisans et pieux — et les Dioula — vagabonds, voleurs et païens — tandis que les Dioula revendiquent avec véhémence la parenté qui les lie au Lawbé Yett.

Cette opposition marque très profondement la nature des liens commerciaux qu'entretiennent ces groupes. Pour certains, cette opposition est due à la colonisation, d'autres considèrent qu'elle est d'origine magique:

> Deux frères Lawbé (Yett) sont partis chercher du bois en brousse. Quelques temps après leur départ, deux génies qui avaient pris leur apparence, sont venus voir les femmes des Lawbé et les ont emmenées dans la case. Deux enfants sont nés, ce sont les deux premiers Dioula, enfants de yett et de génies. . . . Quand les deux frères sont rentrés, ils ont compris ce qui s'était passé — jamais un Dioula ne dira cela, il est même dangereux de le rappeler.

On comprend mieux dès lors la difficulté qu'ont ces deux groupes à établir des relations commerciales. Ce d'autant qu'une rancune politique se surajoute à cette tension.

> Quand les colons sont arrivés, on pouvait voyager sans danger. Les Dioula se sont mis à vendre de la pacotille et du tabac contre du mil et des animaux. Quand ils n'avaient rien à vendre, ils volaient des ânes qu'ils revendaient dans d'autres villages. C'est delà qu'ils ont leur reputation de voleur d'ânes: voler c'est dans leur nature, c'est eux.
>
> Les Dioula aimaient l'argent, mais nous (les yett), on avait pas confiance; eux se servaient des pièces de cuivre fabriquèes par les colons, nous on préférait le troc. Chez les rois les yett et les dioula, c'était pas pareil. *Les Dioula étaient étrangers à tout.* Les yett, ils étaient là. Ce n'était pas guerriers. Ils préparaient des lotions, des liquides faits avec les arbres et les racines. Ils ordonnaient aux guerriers de se laver avec. Les Yett sont les seuls à connaître ces secrets. . . . Tout le monde craint les Laobé, parce que le Laobé ne craint personne sauf Dieu [récit de S. Dembele].

De fait, le Laobé yett, qu'il soit bûcheron ou sculpteur, doit affronter les arbres, sièges traditionnels des raab et des djinn. Faut il

voir dans ce contact intime avec les génies les rapports ambigus
qu'entretiennent les non laobé avec les Laobé? Méprisés et craints,
ils connaissent les secrets des arbres, les plantes médicinales et ont la
réputation de porter chance. De nos jours, quand on connaît un
Lawbé, il est dans le jeu de lui voler un vêtement ou un objet, ce qui
portera chance; pour la même raison, les jeunes lawbé sont des
partenaires sexuels très recherchés.

Ils s'attachent malgré tout à ce group une image négative: réputés
voleurs, mauvais musulmans, bruyants et toujours à la recherche de
querelles, on ne conclut une affaire avec un Lawbé qu'avec la plus
extrême prudence. Comme le dit Amar Samb (1973): "le lawbé se
révèle habile artisan, courageux bûcheron, ânier par excellence.
C'est le gitan sénégalais. Il est très doué, même dans les affaires et les
transactions, d'une finesse extraordinaire, dans le négoce."

L'ORIGINE GEOGRAPHIQUE DES LAWBE

Pour finir cette présentation grossière du group Lawbé, il nous
faut indiquer les grands sous-groupes de Lawbé-Yett. Sekhou De-
mbelé, ancien secrétaire de l'Association des Lawbé du Sénégal, les
présente ainsi:

> Les Lawbé sont divisés en quatre groups.
>
> (1) *Les Lawbé Ndiambour,* e'est le groupe le plus authentique
> parce qu'ils ont toujours été des sculpteurs sur bois et qu'ils
> n'ont jamais cultivé. Il existe même une légende qui interdit
> aux Lawbé de cultiver la terre sous peine de sécheresse . . .
> Les Lawbé devaient s'occuper à fournir les utensiles pour
> piler le mil, c'est pourquoi, dans un discours, j'ai dit que les
> Africains n'ont pas eu besoin des moulins pour avoir de la
> farine, grâce aux Lawbé.
>
> Ils ont été à l'origine de l'art sur bois parce que les rois
> avaient besoin de statues. Ils ne savaient pas photo-
> graphier, pas dessiner. Ils ont toujours été des artistes, des
> artisans. L'origine est le village de Ndiagne.
>
> (2) *Les Lawbé Sañaxor,* ils viennent de Pire. C'est toujours des
> Lawbé, parce que nés Lawbé, mais ils ne s'occupaient pas

seulement du bois. Ils défrichaient, mais il ne faisaient pas d'art. Deuxièmement, c'était des vendeurs de bestiaux et surtout d'ânes. Ils sont souvent métissés avec des Peul.

(3) *Les Lawbé Mbuki.* Ce sont ceux qui habitent entre le Saloum et le Baol. L'origine est le village de M'Boro. Ils sont métissés de Sérère et de Lawbé. On les trouve maintenant dans la région de Kaffrine. Eux aussi cultivent mais, quand il y a la sécheresse, ils font le travail du bois et aussi l'élevage. Leur travail se limite à la fabrication de pilons et de mortiers, pas d'art. Mbuki çà veut dire hyène. C'est les Peul qui one avancé le terme pour montrer que les Lawbé peuvent se transformer en hyènes. C'est vrai, mais c'est des hyènes inoffensives.

(4) *Les Lawbé Guet.* Ils sont originaires de Darou Mousty, Sagatta et Mbacké. Ce sont les Lawbé un peu à part. Ils étaient cultivateurs et bûcherons. C'est des mourides.

On ne peut comprendre le fonctionnement des réseaux commerciaux mis en place sans prendre en compte ces subdivisions. La carte synthétique au système commercial sénégalais en France (carte 6.4) cache en effet des réseaux, correspondant à des groupes très précis (cartes 6.5, 6.6, 6.7, et 6.8). Ces groupes ne se fréquentent guère, chacun a mis en place son propre système d'approvisionnement, de distribution, d'hébergement, de transports, etc.

En Amont du Système, la Production des Marchandises et la Vente en Gros

Nous avons systématiquement enquêté les ateliers de production Lawbé de l'agglomération du Cap-Vert, et étudié leurs rapports avec les ramifications commerciales en France.

Le Grand Atelier de Guedj-Awaye: La Coexistence de Groupes Differents

A la suite de divers déguerpissements, 70 artisans Lawbé venus de cinq endroits différents se sont retrouvés groupés dans un *pack* (lit-

Cartes 6.5-6.8   Des Circuits Parfaitement Organisés

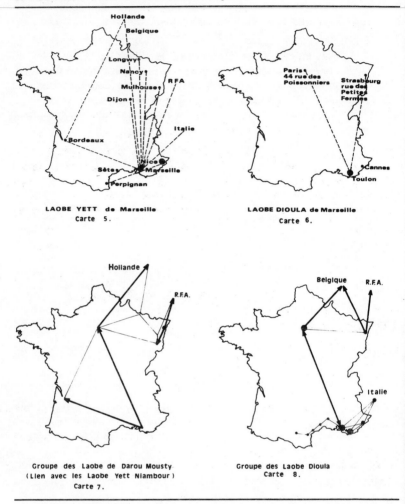

LAOBE YETT de Marseille
Carte 5.

LAOBE DIOULA de Marseille
Carte 6.

Groupe des Laobe de Darou Mousty
(Lien avec les Laobe Yett Niambour)
Carte 7.

Groupe des Laobe Dioula
Carte 8.

téralement le lieu, l'atelier). Les divisions qui existent à l'intérieur de l'atelier n'apparaissent pas à la première visite, on observe simplement un regroupement d'apprentis autour d'un maître sculpteur. Regroupés, ces cinq groupes ne se sont pas pour autant fondus, chacun a gardé ses filières d'approvisionnement en bois et ses réseaux de distribution.

Le premier atelier est composé de Lawbé Guet regroupés autour de Nar Sow — originaire de la ville de Touba, la capitale du mouridisme. Il a la charge de l'apprentissage de plusieurs jeunes Lawbé, parents lointains, venus récemment de leur village. Nar s'occupe de l'approvisionnement en bois de l'atelier, organise la production des marchandises et assure leur commercialisation. Cet atelier est en contact direct avec le pack mbabass animé par les correspondants des commerçants mourides de Paris qui assurent l'acheminement des marchandises de l'atelier de Guedj-Awaye aux Lawbé Guet disseminés en France. L'importance de cet atelier ne nous est vraiment apparue que lors de notre séjour à Bordeaux: chargé de rédiger l'avis de décès d'un jeune Lawbé, nous avons pu nous rendre compte de l'étendue des ramifications de ce réseaux.[1]

L'adhésion à la confrerie mouride, facteur de cohérence décisif du groupe, ne gomme pas l'identité sociale des taalibé (fidèles) et si l'aval du réseau est marqué par la persistance des facteurs de caste[2] l'amont l'est encore plus: les Lawbé Guet mourides assurent la tâche spécifique de coupe de bois et de sculpture des marchandises (souvent faites sur les lieux même de l'abattage ou dans le village familial).

Le second atelier, composé de Lawbé Sañaxor, est dirigé par El Hadj Ousmane Sow, correspondant de son cousin croisé Bara Sow grand commerçant de l'avenue touristique de Dakar William Ponty et de Sébastien Tine qui centralisent les expéditions vers la France au Pack Sérére. El Hadj Ousmane part avec ses apprentis, tous Lawbé Sañaxor, couper du bois en Casamance et sculpter ses produits au Pack. Il travaille à la fois pour Sébastien Tine qui lui transmet les commandes des commerçants mourides parisiens, et pour ses cousins, commerçants à Lille et en Belgique, à Nice et en Italie.

Le troisième atelier est composé de Lawbé Seigne qui vendent individuellement leurs productions au Pack mbabass ou les écoulent au village artisanal de Soumbedioune par l'intermédiaire d'un cousin propriétaire d'un emplacement. Ces Lawbé se sont spécialisés dans la fabrication de saladiers en teck et en kad.

Le quatrième atelier, le plus important, est animé par plusieurs compagnons Lawbé Ndiambour qui utilisent les services de nombreux apprentis. Leur production est à la fois "traditionnelle" (pilons, calebasses, etc.) et "moderne" (biches, masques sénoufo, etc.). Les produits destinés à la consommation des ménages dakarois sont, le plus souvent, faits à la commande, tandis que les sculptures vendues aux touristes ou acheminées en France passent par un réseau extrêmement complexe de relais, familiaux du village artisanal de Soumbedioune et de l'Avenue Ponty. Notre attention fut attirée par l'extrême mobilité des compagnons et apprentis que nous retrouvions d'une année sur l'autre dans des ateliers différents (notamment dans l'atelier Colobane), voire dans certains points de vente aux touristes. Cette circulation constitue, comme nous le verrons, l'originalité profonde du système mis en place par les Lawbé Ndiambour.

Enfin, l'atelier accueille également quelques Lawbé dont l'activité se limite à la production de pilons, de tablettes coraniques, de mortiers, etc. Ils semblent disposer de la clientèle fixe de Pikine et Guedj-Awaye et n'utilisent que rarement les apprentis pour la vente au porte à porte.

A ces cinq groupes, qui ne se distinguent pas au premier abord, correspondent donc une organisation de travail spécifique et des circuits commerciaux particuliers.

Il aurait fallu mettre en place un dispositif d'observation très lourd pour juger le volume des marchandises qui sort de chaque atelier. Il faut tout de même souligner que l'extrême degré d'organisation de cette production artisanale n'aurait pas manqué d'être masqué par une approche strictement statistique.

LES ATELIERS DE LAWBE GUET

L'Atelier de Pack Icotaf à Pikine.

L'atelier de Lawbé de Pack Icotaf à Pikine est composé de huit cases dont sept sont occupées par des Lawbé Guet. Les ateliers produisent tous les types de marchandises ("Traditionnelles" et "modernes") sans que cela affecte de façon évidente les relations maître sculpteur-apprenti. Par contre, les formes de commercialisation présentent de nombreux cas de figures.

(a) *Les productions traditionnelles.* Trois maîtres sculpteurs, Demba Sow, El Hadj Amadou Sow, et Thiofdo Sow, entourés d'une dizaine d'apprentis, consacrent entièrement leur travail à la production de pilons, mortiers, et de tam-tam vendus au porte à porte par les apprentis. Ces derniers, recrutés sur des bases familiales, sont, le plus souvent, des migrants récents et ne touchent aucune rémunération. Logés et nourris par leurs hôtes, ils sont intégrés dans des réseaux d'échange familiaux et ne disposent que d'un faible pouvoir d'initiative.

(b) *Les productions mixtes.* Les ateliers des trois premiers jouxtent ceux de Malick Sow, Amadi Sow, et Magatte Sow, proches

(text continues page 218)

Photo 6.1   Le grand atelier de Guedj-Awaye

Photo 6.2 Le pack Mbabass: les merchandises pour la France

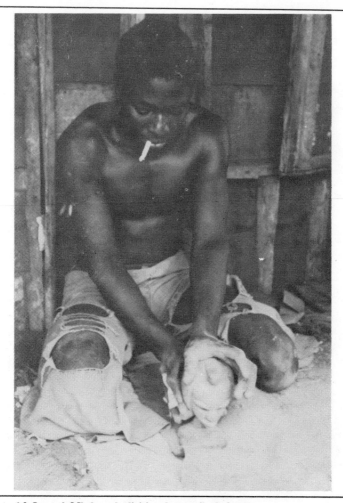

Photo 6.3 Le pack Mbabass: la division du travail—le fonçage

Photo 6.4 Un élément essentiel de rentabilité: le travail gratuit des enfants (Pack Liberté)

Photo 6.5   Le pack Mbabass: la division du travail—la teinture du bois

Photo 6.6   Elhadje Sadio Sow, le doyen des Laobé

Photo 6.7   Les productions Laobé au milieu des marchandises de toutes origines (Marseille)

cousins, dont la production est mixte: aux produits traditionnels s'ajoutent souvent les commandes de sculptures modernes confiées par des artisans spécialisés qui les sous-traitent. La commercialisation des produits traditionnels se fait toujours au porte à porte, tandis que l'écoulement des marchandises destinées à l'Europe passe par les commanditaires. Pour beaucoup d'apprentis, c'est-là l'occasion d'opérer une future reconversion dans des activités artisanales plus lucratives et, qui sait, d'espérer être un jour commerçant à part entière.

(c) *Les productions modernes.* L'essentiel de l'atelier est occupé à la production de masques et de biches. Deux maîtres sculpteurs, Ndiaga Sow et El Hadj Alioune Sow centralisent les commandes et distribuent le travail à une vingtaine d'apprentis. Le premier est en contact avec son oncle, Demba Sow, commerçant au village artisanal de Soumbedioune et avec le Pack mbabass; le second travaille exclusivement avec les correspondants des commerçants mourides résidant à Paris qui font parvenir des marchandises aux Lawbé Guet résidant à Mulhouse. Un troisième artisan, More Sow, travaille avec deux compagnons, Moussa Sow et Amadou Sow. Tous trois sont déjà allés en Europe (le premier dès 1973, le deuxième en 1975, le troisième en 1976), chargés de plus d'une demi-tonne de marchandises fabriquées dans l'atelier de Pikine. Mais il semble que cette formule ne soit guère rentable. La rentabilité des activités artisanales est trop faible pour permettre à ces artisans de financer un nouveau voyage en Europe; l'effet est paradoxal, tout se passe comme si la multiplication des intermédiaires et la spécialisation en aval des fonctions de grossistes assuraient le développement des débouchés (et par-là, du travail des ateliers), tout en interdisant à ces mêmes sculpteurs une chance de sortir de leur condition. Il est important en effet de souligner que tous les artisans rencontrés subviennent juste aux besoins de leur famille et que la rentabilité de leurs activités semble, comme nous le verrons plus loin provenir en grande partie du travail gratuit des apprentis. Enfin, cinq jeunes citadins de toutes origines sociales — on compte des bijoutiers toucouleur, un paysan sénoufo et deux Soninké — après des tentatives individuelles infructueuses d'intégration à l'économic urbaine, se sont greffés sur la vie de cet atelier. Ils bénéficient des circuits d'approvisionnement en bois de l'atelier, mais assurent individuellement la commercialisation de leurs marchandises. Seuls les deux artisans Soninké trouvent un débouché régulier au village artisanal de Soumbedioune par l'intermédiaire de quelques parents propriétaires d'une case.

L'atelier du Marché Saam

De jeunes Lawbé Guet, tous parents proches, en fin d'apprentissage, ont refusé de s'installer avec les autres Lawbé au grand atelier de Guedj-Awaye et ont crée un petit pack au coeur du marché Saam de Guedj-Awaye. Spécialisés dans la production de masques et de biches, ils achètent le bois aux artisans bûcherons du pack Wakhinane et ont établi individuellement leurs contacts avec le pack mbabass. Trois compagnons ont déjà réussi à financer leur voyage en Europe (Hollande); cinq restent, qui vendent des produits non finis à des artisans de passage ou à El Hadj Thierno D., employeur des jeunes Sérère (Lawbé mbucki) de Pack Sérère. Souvent, ces jeunes artisans confient des marchandises brutes à des "finisseurs" — dernière phase du travail, longue mais qui demande le moins de qualification — moyennant une rétribution à la pièce. Tous affirment leur volonté d'abandonner les activités artisanales pour se consacrer au commerce: la division du travail, progressivement instituée, constitue peut-être le premier pas.

Notre attention n'avait pas été attirée, au moment où ces enquêtes ont été réalisées, par la puissance organisatrice des dahira mourides. Nous devions apprendre par la suite que *tous* les Lawbé Guet étaient taalibé de Sérigne Samb Mbacké — comme ceux du Pack Guedj-Awaye — marabout mouride de Ndoulo influent entre tous dans la hiérarchie confrérique et auprès de l'Eat. Ainsi, certaines des questions les plus importantes restent elles en suspens. Il est certain qu'une structure de dahira, formelle ou non, se greffe sur le mode de fonctionnement de Lawbé Guet: dans quelle mesure ces liens interviennent-ils dans l'organisation du travail, quelle est l'importance des prêts maraboutiques dans le financement des départs en Europe, etc.?

L'ATELIER D'EL HADJ SOW, LAWBE SAÑAXOR

El Hadj Sow est propriétaire d'une grande remise sur la route des Niayes de Pikine. Il a depuis longtemps abandonné toute activité artisanale pour se consacrer à l'organisation du travail de ses nombreux apprentis et à l'approvisionnement de ses correspondants en France. Six apprentis, quatre lawbé et deux jeunes Sérère confiés par leurs parents à El Hadj Sow, travaillent à tour de rôle sur les masques et biches confectionnés: les deux premiers neveux coupent des tronçons de bois d'une cinquantaine de centimétres et ébauchent les grandes lignes du masque, les seconds façonnent les détails tandis que les jeunes Sérère sont chargés du masticage, du polissage et du maquillage des produits.

L'originalité du système mis en place réside dans le fait que les apprentis-neveux *sont retribués* pour leur travail (50 F CFA par tâche), et vivent dans leur famille. Les jeunes Sérère qui assurent les tâches ingrates ne sont pour leur part payés que 30 F CFA la finition. El Hadj Sow dispose ainsi d'une production suffisante et peu coûteuse pour approvisionner:

— Ousmane Sow, son jeune frère, commerçant en Corse;

— Mamadou Sow, fils de la seconde épouse de son père, commerçant a Longwy dans l'Est de la France;

— Bakakar Gadiaga, un cousin Lawbé lointain, commerçant à Perpignan qui travaille avec Abdou Fall Sow, son neveu.

LES ATELIERS DE LAWBE NDIAMBOUR

L'essentiel de la production acheminée en France est fabriqué dans les deux grands ateliers de Lawbé Ndiambour. Le premier se situe à Grand-Dakar (Cinéma Liberté), le second dans la Médina (marché Colobane). Il est difficile d'isoler l'activité de ces ateliers des formes de commercialisation proprement dites tant les chaînes mises en place par le groupe des Lawbé Ndiambour constituent un tout. Ce chapitre se limitera donc à l'examen de la production des marchandises, laissant à l'analyse des stratégies familiales la mise en articulation des différents bouts de réseaux.

Le Pack Liberté (Grand-Dakar)

Le Pack Liberté adossé au "Cinéma Liberté," appartient à El Hadj Thiawa Sow, Président de l'Association Nationale des Lawbé du Sénégal.[3] Ce pack abrite quatre ateliers qui entreteinnent des rapports originaux. Le premier, le plus important, est animé par Samba Sow qui est entouré de quatre compagnons et de deux apprentis, tous parents proches. "Chef d'atelier," les prérogatives de Samba Sow semblent très réduites: c'est lui qui enregistre les commandes de grossistes et qui les répartit entre les artisans. Il est à Pack Liberté le représentant d'El Hadj Thiawa Sow, propriétaire du terrain.

Les deuxième et troisième ateliers sont également animés par des Lawbé, mais dont les liens de parenté apparaissent plus distendus, sans doute s'agit il d'anciens captifs. Enfin, le quatrième atelier est occupé par de jeunes Sérère spécialisés dans les tâches de finition. Les rapports entre les quatre ateliers sont multiformes. Pour l'approvisionnement en bois: Samba Sow réceptionne le bois, parfois acheté par les commerçants grossistes, et organise le partage entre les ateliers. Plusieurs cas de figure sont possibles:

— Le propriétaire du bois (grossiste de Mbabass, parent Lawbé ou parfois artisan) peut demander à un sculpteur de travailler le bois brut pour en faire une marchandise déterminée. On peut considérer dans ce cas que seule la façon est payée.

— Souvent le propriétaire du bois cède quelques tronçons à un artisan en échange du travail de débitage (pour un tronc de 4 mètres, découpé en 8, l'artisan reçoit un ou deux morceaux). Les morceaux deviennent alors sa propriété et il est libre d'en faire ce qu'il veut. Ce travail est la prérogative traditionnelle des captifs.

— Enfin, le bois peut être directement vendu aux sculpteurs, parfois par le grossiste qui rachètera les produits finis. Cette dernière solution est la plus prisée des artisans parce qu'elle leur permet de vendre les petits bois de coupe comme bois de chauffage (20 F. la bassine) aux ménagères.

Les trois premiers ateliers assurent l'essentiel du travail, le gros oeuvre est assuré par les sculpteurs les plus vigoureux, le façonnage par les sculpteurs confirmés et la finition par les apprentis. Ces derniers réalisent également de petits objets — petites figurines représentant les sept jours de la semaine, ou petits tam-tam avec le bois acheté au maître sculpteur (ce bois est parfois cédé gratuitement). Le produit de la vente leur appartient.

Quand les commandes dépassent la capacité de travail des trois ateliers, il est fait appel aux jeunes Sérère. Payés à la pièce, ces jeunes artisans achètent, quand ils le peuvent, la sculpture non finie afin de la revendre directement aux grossistes: le travail de finition est payé 200 à 300 F CFA, tandis que la différence entre le prix d'achat d'une statuette brute et la vente du produit fini est de l'ordre de 7 à 800 F.

Il existe une concurrence extrêmement vive entre "finisseurs"; si chacun est, théoriquement, libre de venir travailler quand il l'entend, rien n'oblige un artisan à lui fournir des marchandises. J'ai observé, entre 1976 et 1978, une tendance à la baisse des rémunérations de cette catégories d'artisans.

Comme les apprentis, ils occupent le maillon de la chaîne d'où une plus-value importante peut être directement extraite. Ils n'ont aucune chance de devenir un jour maître sculpteur, la seule promotion sociale possible est de devenir commerçant. Mais la faible rémunération de leur travail rend, de fait, cet espoir illusoire.

Le Pack Colobane

La première impression, quand on rentre dans le Pack Colobane, est celle d'une très grande activité. Une soixantaine d'artisans de tous âges sont répartis en "4 tentes" disposées en angle et déploient une activité fébrile, tandis que le centre de l'atelier est occupé par les artisans chargés de creuser les tam-tam,[4] une des spécialités du Pack. Il m'a fallu plusieurs semaines avant de comprendre le fonctionnement de cet atelier: tous parents, les artisans du Pack semblent pourtant mener des activités disjointes. Les quatre chefs d'atelier sont Yoro Sow, Samba Sow, Aliou Sow et Pathé Dioum. Yoro est le plus ancien; il a succédé, à la tête de l'atelier, à son frère Amady Sow qui fut un des premiers à partir en France. Ce dernier offre les plus larges débouchés aux productions de son jeune frère et de ses apprentis, l'essentiel des marchandises part en France. Toutefois, quelques apprentis utilisent — dans les mêmes conditions qu'au Pack Liberté — les petits morceaux de bois pour leur propre compte.

Samba Sow est le chef du second atelier, secondé par ses demi-frères Amadou et Pathé.[5] Samba est le frère cadet de Seidy Sow, commerçant important de l'Avenue William Ponty qui est en étroite relation avec El Hadj Thiawa Sow. De même, Aliou Sow et Pathé Dioum, les deux autres chefs d'ateliers, disposent de débouchés commerciaux en France et Avenue William Ponty par le relais de parents proches.

Les quatre ateliers fonctionnent donc sur le même modèle. Le chef d'atelier est entouré de compagnons: chacun développe, dans les filières de son groupe, ses activités propres en faisant éventuellement appel aux autres artisans, mais surtout en utilisant le travail des apprentis.

Le recours à ce travail quasiment gratuit semble être la condition d'une accumulation minimum. En effet, quels que soient l'atelier et la marchandise produite, la rémunération du travail des artisans semble constante, de l'ordre de 500 F. par jour. Un tam-tam, fabriqué en deux jours, est vendu 3 000 F., la pièce de bois coûte 1 000 F., la finition 800 F., la place sur le marché 200 F. (100 F. par jour): les deux journées de travail (environ 7 h/jour) sont donc payées 1 000 F. Les calculs réalisés dans les autres ateliers donnent des chiffres semblables. Le calcul fait par les artisans est un calcul élémentaire d'économie; si certaines dépenses sont incompressibles (matière première et taxes) ils ont la possibilité de jouer sur le prix de la finition et surtout de multiplier le travail non rétribué des apprentis. Ainsi un artisan qui dispose de 10 apprentis (qui ne lui coûtent, rappelons-le, que le bol de riz et le gîte) peut espérer constituer un stock de marchandises suffisant pour partir en France (cas peu fréquent) ou quitter les activités artisanales pour le commerce (tout en gardant des apprentis).

Le cadre familial lawbé, trop étroit pour réaliser l'accumulation nécessaire, s'élargit, comme les anciennes corporations en Europe au Moyen Age. L'ancien système (encore illustré par les ateliers de fabrication traditionnelle) ne visait aucune accumulation; il avait pour simple fonction de permettre la reproduction du groupe. Dans la nouvelle logique, l'accumulation ne peut se réaliser que par des extorsions de travail non payé. L'originalité du système mis en place réside dans le fait que l'appel à une nouvelle main d'oeuvre continue de se faire dans le cadre familial; il reste à comprendre comment s'effectue cette "mobilisation," selon quels critères et pourquoi des inégalités aussi importantes apparaissent entre les différents artisans-commerçants.

Le Village Artisanal de Soumbedioune

Le village artisanal de Soumbedioune est à la fois un lieu de production et un lieu de vente aux touristes. Créé par l'Office Sénégalais de l'Artisanat, ce village avait pour vocation de regrouper, en un lieu, les différents corps de métiers et de les organiser afin de promouvoir l'artisanat national. Toutes les corporations sont organisées en coopératives à l'exception des artisans Lawbé qui ont opposé aux autorités une très grande force d'inertie (on peut se demander quel est le besoin d'organiser selon des schémas préétablis des activités on ne peut plus structurées). La dizaine d'artisans Lawbé Ndiambour qui s'est installée à Soumbedioune a, d'emblée, utilisé ce village dans sa propre logique, en gardant son organisation interne.

En fait de promouvoir la production des petits artisans, le village n'a fait que renforcer la position des plus gros réseaux. Presque toutes les cases appartiennent à des grossistes Lawbé, qui disposent souvent d'un autre point de vente au "plateau" et qui, pour des raisons déjà évoquées, font produire leurs marchandises ailleurs: le village artisanal n'est qu'un maillon de la chaîne et les ventes réalisées sur place ne constituent qu'un revenu secondaire.[6] Ainsi, ces cases abritent-elles souvent plusieurs compagnons, membres d'une même filière, avec leurs apprentis que nous avons eu l'occasion de rencontrer dans les Pack de Guedj-Awaye et de Dakar. (Cet aspect sera traité dans le chapitre consacré aux stratégies familiales.)

Le village n'en est pas moins un lieu de haute concurrence entre artisans Lawbé d'une part, mais aussi avec les boisseliers Soninké et Toucouleur. Ces derniers, un temps spécialisés dans la production et la vente de petites pirogues, font de plus en plus souvent appel aux ateliers disséminés en ville (notamment Pack Icotaf et Mbabass) dont l'organisation stricte du travail diminue les coûts. De même les artisans Lawbé, parfois originaires du Ndiambour, qui ne disposent pas d'une solide infrastructure familiale, font appel aux productions du Pack Mbabass et de l'atelier d'El Hadj Sow.

Le Pack Mbabass

"Ce n'est pas même dans le sein des anciennes corporations que la manufacture a pris naissance. Ce fut le marchand qui devint chef de l'atelier moderne et non pas l'ancien maître de corporation" (Marx, 1960).

Le Pack Mbabass est composé de deux ateliers, le Pack Sérère et le Pack Lawbé. Le terrain de Pack Sérère appartien à Abou Beye, deuxième Imam de la mosquèe tidjane du quartier de Grand-Dakar. Il est loué par El Hadj Thierno D. qui, en contact étroit avec les commerçants parisiens, l'a installé. Cet atelier est entièrement consacré aux tâches de finition des sculptures et à la préparation des colis à destination de la France. La division du travail y est extrême, chaque jeune Sérère n'effectue qu'une tâche très précise pour laquelle il est rémunéré à la pièce. N'importe quel artisan ou commerçant peut s'adresser à ces jeunes. Ces derniers, jeunes ruraux saisonniers de la région de Thiès, sont précisément disponibles dans la période qui précède la saison touristique en Europe. Locataires de la "Cité Bissap," quartier de Grand-Dakar, (Salem, 1981a) où sont regroupés de très nombreux jeunes Sérère, ils ont mis en place leurs propres filières migratoires. Un jeune finisseur, bien introduit auprès des pourvoyeurs de marchandises, peut espérer gagner 300 ou 400 F CFA par jour, mais un système de sous-traitance s'est spontanément mis en place: les plus anciens centralisent les commandes et les distribuent, moyennant une confortable commission, aux jeunes parents nouveaux venus. Là encore, l'objectif est de "court-circuiter" le plus grand nombre possible d'intermédiaires pour réaliser soi-même toutes les "étapes bénéficiaires." Quelques anciens finisseurs de Mbabass ont ainsi réussi à créer un débouché propre à Nice et Cannes. C'est dire toute l'importance des stratégies de groupes: isolés, les jeunes sont tenus d'intégrer un groupe dynamique, à moins d'être réduits aux rôles les plus ingrats et les moins rémunérateurs par les groupes dominants.

Il est essentiel de noter que cet atelier a été crée par les commerçants mourides installés en France qui, après s'être appropriés le marché français, mettent en place une structure en amont qui les rende moins dépendants des Lawbé et surtout qui leur assure le contrôle des prix et de la nature des marchandises. Les Lawbé ont beau dire que les produits qui sortent de cet atelier sont de mauvaise qualité, ils n'en sont pas moins battus sur leur propre terrain et de plus en plus souvent contraints par les lois du marché d'acheter ces marchandises moins chères. Ils sont, de la même façon, de plus en plus dépendants en France des filières mourides d'approvisionnement en produits fabriqués au Maroc, et Italie et en R.F.A.

Encore une fois, notre attention au moment où les enquêtes ont été réalisées, n'était pas centrée sur l'importance des facteurs confrériques dans les liens que peuvent entretenir deux partenaires commerciaux. Cela est d'autant plus regrettable que nous nous sommes rendu compte, en relisant les questionnaires réalisés, que presque tous ces jeunes Sérère étaient mourides. . . . Par contre, le "débauchage" des jeunes Sérère est animé par de jeunes Lawbé de toutes origines qui, payés eux aussi à la pièce par les commerçants —

effectuent le gros du travail. Ces jeunes Lawbé, directement dépendants d'El Hadj Thierno D. pour les fournitures de bois, sont étonnamment éloignés de leurs familles.

Comme en France, les différents réseaux ne sont pas totalement étanches. Un des problèmes essentiels reste celui de l'expédition des marchandises vers la France et il est fréquent de voir un transitaire Lawbé (le plus souvent El Hadj Thiawa Sow) assurer le départ de colis destinés à des commerçants mourides et vice-versa.

La description des différents types de Pack fait apparaître une organisation du travail diversifiée qui varie non exclusivement avec la taille de l'atelier mais selon sa plus ou moins grande dépendance au capital détenu par les commerçants qui contrôlent le marché français, extérieurs aux productions traditionnelles. On observe une double division du travail:

— Celle qui ventilent les différents types de production entre ateliers et à l'intérieur de chaque atelier: on passe ainsi de packs d'artisans reproduisant grosso modo les rapports de clientèle ruraux en ville à des ateliers totalement dépendant des débouchés détenus en France par d'autres qu'eux.

— Celle qui, pour la production d'une marchandise assure la productivité et l'extorsion de plus value (principalement sur le travail des enfants).

Cette situation est étonnament proche de celles décrites dans les classiques du marxisme. L'originalité profonde de la situation présente est que le système mis en place (à l'exception du Pack Mbabass) évolue par une interprétation faite par les Lawbé eux-mêmes des règles sociales les liant. Une analyse précise de quelques stratégies familiales s'imposait donc à ce stade du travail: c'est ce qui a été entrepris jusque sur les lieux de résidence.

LES STRATEGIES FAMILIALES DES LAWBE NDIAMBOUR

L'étude rapide des ateliers de Lawbé Ndiambour fait apparaître la très grande intrication des liens familiaux avec la production et la commercialisation des marchandises. Les liens de parenté entre compagnons, entre maître sculpteur et apprenti ne m'apparaissaient jamais évidents, dissous sous le vocabulaire français frère, cousin, père, etc. En fait de "solidarité traditionnelle," souvent évoquée, les liens et les règles de parenté paraissent servir de base à la définition de stratégies familiales. La première clé explicative semble résider dans les règles matrimoniales.

Les Règles Matrimoniales des Lawbé

Le mariage Lawbé se conclut entre deux chefs de famille et se déroule en trois étapes.

(1) Le Njamal, les fiançailles. Les deux jeunes gens sont promis l'un à l'autre, le future marié est alors apprenti dans un atelier de sculpture de sa propre famille. Ce "prémariage" constitue la sanction ou l'amorce d'une alliance commerciale entre les deux chefs de famille. Si le jeune garçon continue à habiter dans sa famille, il n'en tombe pas moins déjà sous la coupe de sa future belle-famille: il peut, à l'occasion, changer d'atelier et entretenir des rapports de dépendance avec son futur beau-père.

(2) Après la demande de confirmation de la promesse de mariage (*Namdittadé*), vient le mariage proprement dit, le *Ndifftingu*. La période de Kal commence alors, période où le jeune marié vit chez son beau-père, travaille dans l'atelier ou le commerce de celui-ci (comme pour mieux le souligner, on dit chez les Lawbé que c'est l'homme qui se marie et non la femme). Cette période correspond, le plus souvent, à la fin de la période d'apprentissage du jeune marié qui a, en fait, conquis petit à petit une relative indépendance financière. Le beau-père bénéficie alors de la quasi-totalité de travail de son gendre et l'intègre dans son propre réseau. La période de Kal est de durée variable mais ne dépasse jamais la naissance du premier enfant.

(3) Le jurtugu: le jeune couple rejoint le domicile de la famille du jeune homme (c'est à la femme de formuler la demande. Elle dit à son mari; "Fais ce que tu dois faire pour m'emmener." C'est l'occasion pour les femmes de chanter le *Leng gourou*. Au plan commercial, les relations entre le jeune marié, son beau-père, son père continuent.

Quand une mésentente entre les époux intervient avant le jurtugu, le divorce fait l'objet de négociations: si le jeune homme est a l'origine de la séparation, il perd le bénéfice des années passées chez son beau-père; si c'est la femme, ses parents sont tenus à dédommagement. Pour exprimer la chose, les Lawbé disent "Kou dié ke diou, ki ba tia," que l'on pourrait traduire littéralement par "C'est le premier qui sort qui perd tout." Ce mariage en trois étapes permet au jeune marié de payer progressivement la dot (au moment des enquêtes, les dots étaient de l'ordre de 300 000 F CFA, plus les frais de trois fêtes); quand le prétendant est déjà marié, la dot est beaucoup plus importante et surtout doit être payée en une seule fois.

Enfin, les traditions de lévirat sont très fortes chez les Lawbé *(le keito)*. Un individu est souvent tenu de prendre en charge la femme de son frère *(Kanko aîta tamou,* c'est lui qui doit l'hériter). Cet héritage a, entre autres fonctions, celle d'assurer la continuation des activités du défunt et d'opérer de véritables "concentrations" financières. Mais, comme nous le verrons, cette tradition est potentiellement génératrice de conflits entre l'oncle, devenu père, et le neveu, devenu fils.

Les mariages démultiplient ainsi les réseaux, ouvrent les possibilités d'échanges: ce type d'alliances en appelant d'autres, une toile d'araignée se tisse, qui change imperceptiblement à chaque génération. L'étude de quelques généalogies Lawbé permet de comprendre comment se fait la répartition des apprentis, comment s'établissent des rapports privilégiés entre deux individus et comme des réseaux commerciaux s'établissent.

Segmentation de Lignage et Choix du Gendre

Les trois généalogies Lawbé sélectionnées sur les soixante collectées,[7] ont toutes un lien direct avec le système commercial sénégalais en France. Le graphique 6.1 réalisé met toutefois en évidence l'extrême spécialisation professionnelle des différents segments d'un même lignage: les reconversions dans la sculpture moderne sont certainement beaucoup moins importantes que ne le laisse entrevoir cette sélection,[8] mais engendrent des stratégies matrimoniales tout à fait spécifiques. Il apparaît en effet que les descendants d'un Lawbé reconverti dans les productions modernes mènent des activités identiques à celle de leur père. On observe même une

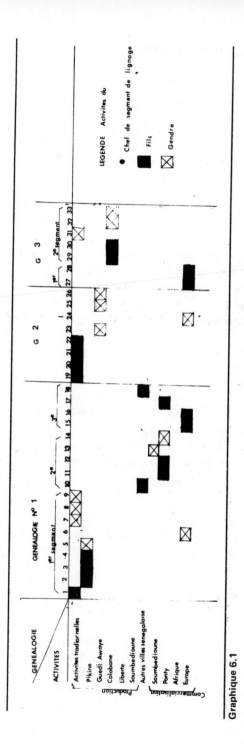

Graphique 6.1

229

spécialisation croissante dans le commerce proprement dit. Enfin, le choix des gendres se fait presque toujours dans le même domaine d'activités. A l'opposé, les groupes qui sont restés attachés aux productions traditionnelles n'ont que peu de contacts avec les groupes cousins reconvertis: les mariages sont lointains et le seul lieu réel est établi par les jeunes apprentis des ateliers de Guedj-Awaye, Pikine, et Colobane.

Le graphique suggère un très haut degré d'organisation et de spécialisation. Les exemples de Sadio Sow de Guedj-Awaye, de Yerim Sow de Grand-Dakar et d'Amadou Sow de Pikine sont éloquents.

Sadio Sow, des activités confinées dans le secteur artisanal. Sadio, doyen des Lawbé du Cap-Vert, est né vers 1890 à Pété Ouarak, dans la région de Louga. Il habite successivement dans les villages entourant Ndiakhaté et Ndiayène Bangouye (entre Kell et Louga), avant de s'installer à Saint-Louis, en 1920. Il rejoint à Dakar son fils Daouda (généalogie 6.1), en 1965.

Les enfants de Sadio sont occupés dans des tâches de production au Pack Colobane, Daouda (avec son fils) comme Mody l'était avant son décès. La situation est identique pour ses gendres Thierno et Balla. Faut-il voir l'explication de ce confinement dans le fait que les mariages des enfants ont été contractés à Saint-Louis, c'est-à-dire à l'écart des circuits commerciaux naissants? C'est ce que laisse entendre Sadio lui-même quand il précise

> On ne fait que des mariages entre Lawbé, pas avec les autres, jamais. Et entre Lawbé seulement quand le travail est le même. Avant, il y avait des mariages entre Lawbé Yett Ndiambour et Lawbé Yett Mbuki. Maintenant, les Mbuki sont devenus Dioula, c'est fini. C'est seulement quand la profession est la même [Sadio Sow, 1979].

Yerim Sow, une petite place dans les circuits de commercialisation. Yérim Sow (généalogie 6.2) a été un de nos informateurs principaux. Originaire de Diakhaté (Ndiambour), il a quitté son village natal en 1935, à l'âge de 21 ans. Nomade comme tous les Lawbé, il a habité une douzaine de villages entre Louga et Kebemer avant de s'installer, de façon définitive, à Dakar en 1946. D'abord sculpteur

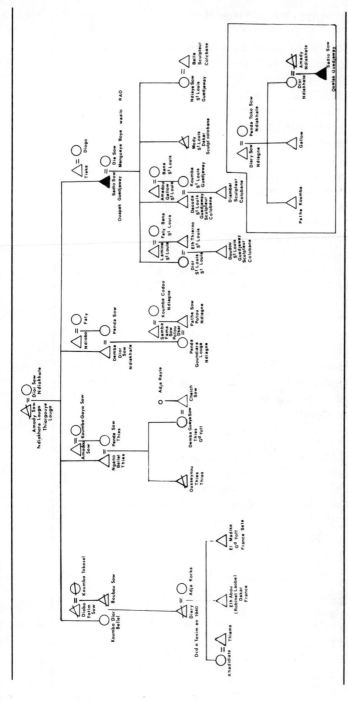

Genealogie 6.1   La première ligne indique le lieu de naissance, la seconde la residence

Généalogie 6.2

dans le quartier Tilène (Medina de Dakar), il s'est installé au village artisanal dès sa création. Maintenant retraité, il continue certaines transactions, mais ses enfants subviennent à ses besoins: Ablaye est commerçant en France, comme son frère Amadou, tandis que son premier gendre Abou a repris sa case au village artisanal, et que Samba et Oumou travaillent en étroite collaboration avec ses fils, en Europe.

Samba Toucouleur et Amadou Sow, une filière Saint-Louisienne. Venus de la région de Dagana, Samba Toucouleur Sow et son frère Amadou ont été les premiers Lawbé à s'installer dans le quartier Pikine de Saint-Louis (généalogie 6.3). Fabricants de pilons, mortiers et keul, Samba et son frère n'ont jamais fait de sculptures modernes. Cheikh Coumba Sow (second gendre de Samba Toucouleur) est à l'origine de la conversion professionnelle. Après le décès de son frère, Amadou a épousé Koumba, sa belle-soeur, pendant la période de Ndifftungu de Cheikh Coumba Sow. Amadou a ainsi hérité des alliances matrimoniales de son frère et — apprès le décès accidentel de Cheikh Coumba en France — des activités commerciales de son neveu/gendre par alliance. Ainsi ses neveux Amadou, Thiawa, Mamadou et son fils Babakar, tous commerçants en France, travaillent en étroite collaboration, entre Longwy et Perpignan, approvisionnés en marchandises par Daouda Sow du Pack Colobane (fils de Sadio Sow, cf. généalogie n 6.1). Cette filière originale reste Saint-Louisienne et se tient à l'écart des circuits dakarois: tous les investissements se font à Saint-Louis et il semble même qu'une chaîne d'ateliers modernes, directement greffée sur les packs de sculpture traditionnelle (quartiers Sor et Pikini), soit mise en place.

Les Stratégies Familiales, Matrimoniales, Économiques, et Résidentielles

Il nous a paru intéressant d'observer jusque sur les lieux de résidences, les stratégies familiales mises en place. Comme cela a déjà été signalé, l'accès à la propriété foncière constitue un enjeu central pour les néo-citadins, sans que la gestion de ce bien essentiel soit régie par des règles traditionnelles.

El Hadj Thiawa Sow, Président des Lawbé du Sénégal, fut un des premiers Lawbé a opéré une reconversion profesionnelle dans sa

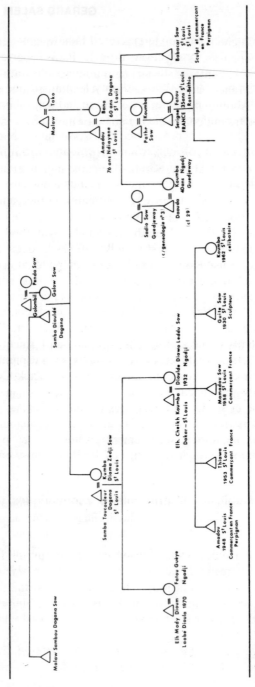

Généalogie 6.3

sculpture moderne. Aidé par son jeune frère Madiaw, il met en place de nombreux ateliers de production (dont le Pack Liberté) et se consacra très rapidement aux tâches de commercialisation. Propriétaire d'une échoppe avenue William Ponty, locataire d'une case au village artisanal de Soumbedioune, propriétaire du Pack Liberté dont il contrôle étroitement la production, El Hadj Thiawa Sow est aussi un transitaire important. La présidence de l'Association Nationale des Lawbé lui vaut, en outre, une certaine représentativité auprès des autorités administratives et politiques. Il a su, par un jeu commercial et politique habile et des alliances matrimoniales astucieuses, constituer un solide réseau qui en fait un des grands commerçants de la place.

Propriétaire d'une parcelle dans le quartier de Grand-Dakar, l'étude de l'occupation de la maison traduit l'efficacité de l'organisation commerciale mise en place (croquis 6.1 généalogie).

LES HABITANTS DE LA CONCESSION

Thiawa a eu deux enfants de son premier mariage, Fadel et Amadou. Fadel, son fils aîné, a la responsabilité de la case de Thiawa Sow au village artisanal, tandis qu'Amadou travaille avec son père Avenue William Ponty. Ses deux fils sont mariés et habitent la concession. Fadel est le gendre d'Abdou Sow de Pikine. Thiawa Sow a épousé la femme de son frère cadet Madiaw, décédé en 1973. Ce dernier avait six enfants: Diery, Faty, Malick, Thiema, Pape, et Diogo. Thiawa est leur père supplétif.

— Diery a été marié à Penda dont le père est grand commerçant en Gambie. Diery travaille avec Fadel au village artisanal dans la case de son oncle. Il loge avec sa femme dans la concession.

— Faty Sow a été mariée à Amadou Sow, commerçant avenue William Ponty, dont l'oncle, époux en lévirat de sa mère, est un associé de Thiawa.

— Les deux frères Malick et Thiema, âgés de 16 et 14 ans, sont respectivement apprentis à Soumbedioune et au magasin de l'avenue William Ponty.

Croquis 6.1 Residence EH Thiawa Sow Grand Dakar

Ce ne sont pas là les seuls habitants de la concession:

— Diouldé, fille de la première épouse de la soeur de Thiawa, a été recueillie par sa tante après le décès de ses parents. Thiawa l'a mariée à Mama Sow, commerçant en République Fédérale Allemande qui, quand il est au Sénégal, habite la concession de Grand-Dakar.

— Lamine Sow est le frère de Penda (époux du fils aîné de Thiawa): il est l'apprenti de son beau-frère au village artisanal de Soumbedioune.

L'OCCUPATION DE LA PARCELLE

La parcelle a été aménagée de telle façon qu'elle puisse héberger tous les enfants et alliés de Thiawa Sow. Elle fait, à chaque étape, l'objet d'un partage précis. En 1978, Thiawa partage la chambre F avec sa première épouse et la chambre C avec la femme de son frère (qui héberge également sa fille Diogo, la fille de Faty et Amadou).

— Fadel, Amadou et Diery occupent, avec leurs épouses et leurs enfants, les chambres A, E, et B. (Diery héberge son apprenti). La chambre D et le salon sont réservés aux gendres de passage.

La concession se révélant vite trop exiguë pour héberger tous les associés de Thiawa (et leurs descendants), les importants travaux entrepris en 1978 modifièrent la physionomie de la concession:

— L'avancée du salon et la suppression des pièces A et B individualisent deux cours, une première strictement interne et une seconde plus ouverte sur la rue;

— la construction d'un étage fait passer le nombre de chambres de 6 à 7, tandis que le salon et la véranda doublent de surface.

Ces aménagements ont pour but l'hébergement des épouses et des enfants encore célibataires.

Amadou Sow et Seydi Sow de Guedj-Awaye (croquis 6.2, généalogie) et leur famille habitaient le quartier Wakhinene-Baye Laye a Dakar avant d'être déguerpis en 1972, à Guedj-Awaye. Amadou est le fils aîné de Thiawa Sow, homonyme du président.

LES HABITANTS DE LA CONCESSION

Thiawa a eu cinq enfants avec Diogo Sow: Penda, Amadou, Faty, Diery et Malaw.

— Penda, fille aînée, est mariée avec El Hadj Ngoné Sow, commerçant Lawbé actuellement en Côte d'Ivoire. Penda et ses deux enfants vivent au domicile du mari, dans le quartier Ben-Tally de Grand-Dakar. El Hadj Ngoné a effectué sa période "probatoire" dans la maison de Wakhinane-Dakar.

— Amadou Sow Diogo, vit avec sa femme et sa fille dans la chambre E.

— Faty Sow, mariée à un Lawbé de Grand-Yoff, est séparée de son mari depuis peu. Elle est retournée dans la maison familiale et occupe la pièce D qu'elle partageait avant avec son mari.

— Diery et Malaw, respectivement apprentis au Pack Colobane et au village artisanal de Soumbedioune, se partagent la pièce C.

— Après le décès de son mari, Diogo Sow a épousé le frère cadet de celui-ci, Seydi Sow. Deux enfants, encore en bas âge, sont nés de cette union. Diogo occupe, avec son mari et ses deux enfants, les chambres A et B.

La répartition des pièces est, en fait, l'objet d'un compromis tacite et tendu entre Amadou Sow (chef de famille potentiel) et Seydi d'une part, entre Amadou et ses jeunes frères d'autre part. La parcelle de Wakhinane appartenait en effet à son père. Il devrait en hériter, selon les "règles musulmanes," c'est-à-dire divisée à raison d'une part pour les enfants de sexe masculin et d'une demipart pour les enfants de sexe féminin, la mère étant hébergée par le fils aîné. Le décès prématuré de son pére a fait de son oncle le nouveau chef de famille: c'est lui qui gère le magasin de l'avenue William Ponty, lui qui a organisé les mariages de ses neveux. Cette situation est à l'origine d'un conflit

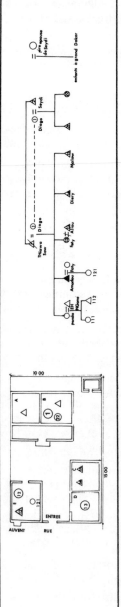

Croquis 6.2   Amadou (Thiawa) Guedj-Awaye

larvé entre Amadou et son oncle/beau-père, conflit largement amori toutefois, pour des raisons commerciales.

Il reste que le décès de Diogo retirerait à Seydi toute raison de rester dans la maison. En outre, Amadou semble décidé à mettre en place ses propres filières d'approvisionnement et à exclure, si cela se révèle nécessaire, ses jeunes frères de la maison pour y loger des apprentis.

Amadou Sow, quartier Djidda à Pikine (croquis 6.3, généalogie), anciens habitants du quartier Wakhinane à Dakar avec ses deux épouses ont devancé le dégeurpissement en s'installant à Pikine, dans le quartier Djiddah. La parcelle de grande dimension (17 × 12 m) ne comportait, en 1968, au moment de l'achat, que deux baraques, à l'emplacement actuel du garage. La maison a été construite en deux étages, construction des pièces A, B, C et D, en 1970, puis E et F en 1972.

LES HABITANTS DE LA CONCESSION

Amadou Sow, né en 1918, est commerçant en Côte d'Ivoire. Il a deux épouses, Awa et Aïssata, qui vivent toutes les deux dans la maison de Pikine.

Awa, la tante d'Amadou (soeur de même père et même mère de Diogo), est la première épouse. Elle a cinq enfants:

— N'Goné Sow, commerçant de l'avenue Georges Pompidou, qui vend en été ses marchandises à Sète. Il est en étroite relation avec son père (en Côte d'Ivoire) et son beau-père Aliou Sow, commerçant de Grand-Dakar, actuellement au Togo. Penda Sow, fille d'Aliou, vit avec son mari N'Goné et ses deux enfants à Pikine.

— Moktar Sow, partage le magasin familial de l'avenue Pompidou; il part tous les étés en Italie vendre ses marchandises. Il est en étroite relation avec son beau-père, Abdou Sow, gros commerçant de L'avenue Ponty et transitaire important. Niengoudy, la fille d'Abdou, vit avec son mari Moktar et sa fille à Pikine.

— Thiawa Sow, travaille lui aussi avenue Georges Pompidou dans l'échoppe d'Amadou (ego). Il part chaque été à Anemasse et Sète.

— Dienaba et Thiacka ne travaillent pas; ils logent également à Pikine.

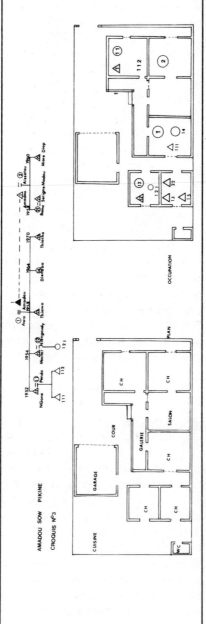

Croquis 6.3 Amadou Sow Pikine

Aïssata, la deuxième épouse d'Amadou, a deux enfants:

— Bana Sow, est l'épouse de Serigne Modou Sow, fils de Daouda Sow, commerçant ambulant à Dakar. Daouda Sow est le vendeur d'Abdou Sow (le père de Niengoudy). Bana Sow et son mari vivent dans la concession de Daouda Sow dans un autre quartier de Pikine. Serigne Madou Sow part six mois pour vendre ses marchandises à Longwy.

— More Diop Sow, âgé de 19 ans, est apprenti sculpteur dans un des ateliers de Pikine. More Diop vit dans la concession familiale.

L'OCCUPATION DE LA PARCELLE

Awa Sow, la première épouse, partage la pièce D avec Amadou Sow, son petit-fils et Dienaba, sa fille. Aïssata, la seconde épouse, occupe seule la chambre B, chambre qui sert souvent de salon de réception. N'Goné, fils aîné d'Awa, occupe la chambre A avec sa femme et son fils Ibra.

Ainsi définies les stratégies familiales lawbé aboutissent à un inextricable réseau d'alliances commerciales et familiales. Le tableau récapulatif qui suit limité à 3 familles, quand il en existe plusieurs dizaines, donne une idée de l'extraordinaire structuration des réseaux mis en place.

ÉLEMENTS DE CONCLUSION

A l'issue de cette étude nous pensons avoir montré que le secteur appelé couramment informel est un des plus fortement organisés qui soient. Cette organisation vise à une rationnalité économique qui extrait le profit d'une exploitation d'apprentis peu ou pas rémunérés. Cette exploitation est facilitée par les appuis divers qu'elle trouve dans le maintien de la famille étendue.

Ces conclusions nous poussent à nous inscrire en faux contre les hypothèses qui servent de fondement à nombre d'études. Ces hypothèses supposent en effet que la ville africaine serait le lieu d'élection de l'anarchie, de l'informalité, de la sous intégration. Il en

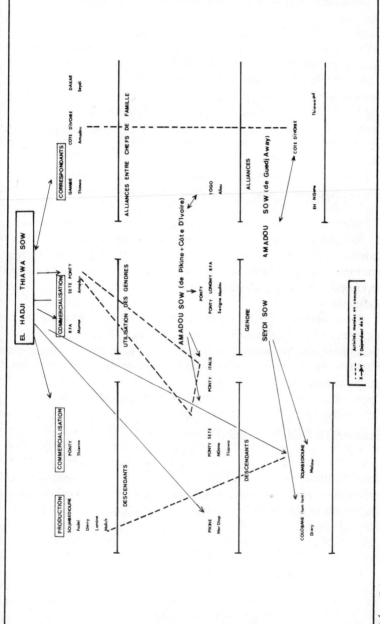

Schéma 6.1

243

est ainsi de la petite production marchande (informelle, non structurée, archaïque, etc.) et de l'urbanisation en général (anarchique, spontanée, sans logique etc.). Ces hypothèses en vaudraient d'autres si la méthodologie suivie un dérapage systématique vers la mise en place de postulats: le secteur informel est composé de mille et une unités anarchiques; on étudie isolemment ses milles et une unités; on fait ainsi la preuve de leur dispersion et que le secteur est "informel". On cherche à classer dans des catégories ethnocentriqus inopérantes les différents types de travail, et on prouve le caractère attardé de ces activités etc. . . . l'informalité de l'hypothèse est transposée dans la réalité.

Pour nous au contraire ce secteur dit "informel" est celui où se retrouvent le mieux dans le milieu urbain les systèmes sociaux et les rapports de production caractéristiques de la société considérée.

Par là même nous pensons qu'il faut rejeter toute opposition de type binaire entre milieu rural et milieu urbain, entre tradition et modernité ou encore entre société formelle et informelle, société structurée et destructurée. On peut bien entendu transporter de telles prémisses tout au long d'une étude et les retrouver sans surprise dans la conclusion.

Nos observations nous conduisent à insister au contraire sur la très fortes cohésion au sein de la ville des groupes sociaux qui sont nés et se sont développés dans le monde rural. Il y a un continuum entre le rural et l'urbain ou si l'on préfère un interprétation et une appropriation du milieu urbain par les groupes sociaux dont la cohérence est largement assez forte pour permettre l'adaptation à la ville.

En outre, en assimilant l'urbanisation spontanée au non respect des règles d'urbanisme, an expliquant le secteur artisanal par la négligence de la législation sociale, on n'explique pas ce que l'on devait précisément expliquer, on se place du point de vue des détenteurs de l'autorité que l'on conforte dans leur effort de nivellement, et on s'interdit de comprendre la stratégie des groupes qui sont tout simplement soucieux de leur survie.

NOTES

1. Avis de décès: Serigne Samb M'Backé, marabout d N'Doulo (Touba), El Hadj Ibrahima N'Daté Sow et sa famille à Marseille, El Hadj Mamadou Tokossele Sow et sa famille à Marseille, El Hadj Abdoulaye Diolgoti Sow et sa famille à Marseille,

Madame Hadewey, Post Peperstraat 4 Leewarden Hollande, Ali Faly Sow et sa famille à Longwy, El Hadj Papa Dieng et sa famille à Paris, El Hadj Ousmane Baye Fall Sow et sa famille à Mulhouse, El Hadj Cheikh Sow et sa famille à Mulhouse, El Hadj Abdoulaye Fall Sow de Mulhouse, Cheikh Diouga Sow de Mulhouse, Amady Magate Sow de Bordeaux, Adame Gueye de Bordeaux, Aliou Sow de Bordeaux, El Hadj Bara Diogo Sow de Bordeaux, El Hadj Cheikh Aïssata Sow de Bordeaux, leurs frères, leurs cousins, leurs camarades en France et ainsi que ses amis de Hollande font part du décès de Sidy Sow, fils de Diery Sow de Dakar et de Diery N'Dondy Sow, et transmettent leurs sincères condoléances à toute la famille au Sénégal.

2. Tout mouride qu'il soi, et quelle que soit sa proximité de la haute hièrarchie de la confrérie, un commercant forgeron-mouride reste un forgeron. Cette double identité, confrérique et de caste, permit a la confrérie d'assurer l'héritage de sa société "traditionelle" (cf. Salem, 1982).

3. Cette Association, qui regroupe essentiellement des Lawbé Ndiambour, est issue d'une scission de l'Union Nationale des Lawbé du Sénégal, presidée par El Hadj Ousmane Sow, Lawbé Sañaxor. Le conflit qui oppose les deux hommes est tant d'ordre politique (El Hadj Thiawa Sow était membre de la SFIO, El Hadj Ousmane Sow du Bloc Démocratique Sénégalais de L. S. Senghor) qu'économique. Thiawa Sow a su attirer à lui les Lawbé originaires du Ndiambour, presque tous spécialisés dans les sculptures modernes, tandies qu'El Hadj Ousmane Sow — dont l'Association est reconnue part le Gouvernement — regroupe des Lawbé Sañaxor et des Lawbé Guet et contrôle surtout les groupes bûcherons.

4. Les outils utilisés par les Lawbé sont d'une grande simplicité. Trois sont essentials: (1) le piegal, lame convexe d'une soixantaine de centimetres, fixée à un long manche, pour creuser en profondeur les tam-tam et les mortiers; (2) la serem, lame de 15 à 20 cm de long, droite, fixée a un manche de 30 cm, utilisée pour les travaux de sculpture; (3) la sawta, petite lame convexe et arrondie de 10 cm de longueur qui sert aux travaux de finition. Ces lames, qui coutent respectivement 500, 300 et 200 F CFA, sont toutes fabriquées par un forgeron de Pikine (Tally-Boubess) fournisseur attitre des Lawbé.

5. Pathé Sow a fait un premier voyage en France en 1968. Arrivé le 8 mai a Paris, il découvrit une France qui ne répondait pas exactement à l'idée qu'il s'en faisait. Ses parents à Paris on eu toutes les peines du monde à le convaincre que l'animation des rues ètait exceptionelle et qui'il fallait rester en France. Encore maintenant, il semble qu'un doute subsiste dans son esprit.

6. Il n'en est pas de même à l'aeroport international de Dakar pour El Hadj Ousmane Sow (President de l'Association de Lawbé) qui a réussi à obtenir un magasin. Les profits realisés sont très importants et ont financés le départ de ses enfants en France (Lille) et en Belgique.

7. Ces généalogies feront ultérieurement l'objet d'une étude spécifique. Signalons, dès maintenant, la reconversion massive des Lawbé Sañaxor dans les métiers "modernes" (gendarmes, comptables, enseignants).

8. Le recensement national de 1976 a classé les Lawbé parmi les groupes ethniques. Ces chiffres sont certainement très inférieurs à la réalité, les Lawbé se déclarant souvent membres de l'ethnie qui les accueille. Mais, même endessous de la réalité, ils montrent que la spécialisation dans la sculpture moderne est marginale. La région du Cap-Vert comprendrait 2,813 Lawbé, dont 632 hommes de plus de 15 ans, les recensement realisés dans les ateliers et commerces, au cours des enquêtes, n'indiquent que 200 artisans environ.

BIBLIOGRAPHIE

BOURDIEU, P., J. C. CHAMBOREDON, et J. C. PASSERON (1969) Le métier de sociologue. Paris: Mouton.

LENINE, V. (1974) Le développement du capitalisme en Russie. Paris: Editions sociales.

LY, D. (1938); "Coutumes et contes des Toucouleur au fouta Toro." Bulletin du Comité d'Etudes Historiques et Scientifique de l'AOF 28/2: 304-326.

MARX, K. (1960) Le Capital (Livre III, Tome I). Paris: Editions sociales.

SALEM, G. (1982a) " De la brousse sénégalaise au Boul'mich. Le système commercial mouride en France." Cahiers d'Etudes Africaines 81-83: 267-288.

———— (1982b) "Stratégie spatiale et stratégie familiale. La volonté de maintien en centre ville, exemples dakarois," en E. Leroy (ed.) Enjeux Fonciers en Afrique Noire. Karthala: ORSTOM.

———— (1981a) Grand-Dakar, un quartier charnière du Cap-Vert: Densification du bâti et organisation sociale. Dakar: ORSTOM.

———— (1981b) De Dakar à Paris, des diasporas d'artisans et de commerçants. Etude socio-géographique du commerce sénégalais en France. Paris: EHESS-ORSTOM.

SAMB, A. (1973) Matraqué par le destin de la vie d'une taalibé. Dakar: NEA.

SARR, M. (1973) Louga et sa région. Dakar: IFAN.

VERNIERE, M. (1978a) Dakar et son double: Dagoudane-Pikine. Paris: Ed. Imprimerie Nationale.

———— (1978b) Cartes du Cap-Vert in Atlas du Sénégal. (n.p.)

CITY, COUNTRY, AND CLASS

7

WORK, MIGRATION, AND CLASS IN WESTERN NIGERIA
A Reinterpretation

SARA S. BERRY

Since the early years of colonial rule, Africans have been leaving their farms in increasing numbers to work in industry or, more often, in trade, transport, or other tertiary activities. A good deal of research has been done on how occupational mobility has changed people's attitudes, knowledge, lifestyles, and social relationships, and on the implications of such changes for socioeconomic differentiation and forms of collective action in contemporary Africa. However, there has been relatively little discussion of how far occupational mobility has entailed changes in labor relations or how, outside of large-scale industry, the organization of work has affected the process of class formation or how class struggle has affected the organization of work. While it is clear that urbanization and the growth of nonagricultural employment have generally been associated with increasing differences in income and lifestyle among various social groups, there remains considerable disagreement over the extent to which these processes have created conditions of differential access to the means of production and, if so, whether and how those conditions are reproduced over time.

In the present chapter I shall use life histories of western Nigerians who moved from farming to nonagricultural employment (or self-employment) after 1950 to illustrate people's strategies of occupational mobility and accumulation and to explore the interaction between individuals' strategies and the conditions of production and accumulation in the regional economy. In particular, I shall try to show how accumulation and occupational mobility have affected and been influenced by the importance of descent as both an idiom and an instrument of Yoruba social interaction. The contradictions of accumulation in the cities of western Nigeria both reflect and reinforce those of class differentiation and communal affiliation in rural areas, a pattern that shapes the course of economic change in Nigeria as a whole. The argument of the chapter was developed from a case study of accumulation and social mobility among the descendants of one town, but it is consistent with a wider body of evidence on Yoruba economy and society, as I shall try to show.

OBSERVING CLASS FORMATION IN WESTERN NIGERIA: THEORETICAL AND METHODOLOGICAL ISSUES

Much of the literature on class formation in western Nigeria has been preoccupied with the structure of the regional political economy and people's perceptions of it. One argument is that, although western Nigeria has been characterized by growing inequality between rural and urban areas, salaried and self-employed workers, educated people and illiterates, and so on, Yorubas still believe that their society is relatively open and that individual effort is the key to upward mobility (Lloyd, 1974; Morrison, 1981). Hence, while the conditions for class formation may well be in the making, Yorubas do not yet identify or organize themselves or act primarily along class lines. Bienen and Diejomaoh (1981: 5) summarize this view succinctly:

> In objective terms Nigeria is forming a class structure, but most Nigerians do not perceive this. . . . Variations in perceptions of equity in society do not have any significant relation to a respondent's actual status. Survey analysis supports political and institutional analysis which argues that Nigerians are not likely to be mobilized widely on the basis of either class membership or status.

They later suggest that Nigerians are inclined to think and act in terms of communal rather than class criteria, basically because "it was easier for the elite to organize around communal — that is, language and ethnic-geographic — ties" (p. 159).

Others interpret similar evidence differently. Peter Gutkind (1974) regarded growing inequality, unemployment, and the restless anger of unemployed urban youth as harbingers of militant class action from below, while Beer and Williams (1976) have suggested that the Agbekoya uprisings of 1968-1969 manifested a growing sense of militancy among Yoruba peasants that might soon spill over into a form of class alliance with the urban poor. A strong current of opinion continues to emphasize the possibility of revolutionary upheaval emerging from widespread popular dissatisfaction with the corrupt, wasteful, and uneven ways in which the country's oil revenues have been spent by the state and its favored clients (Turner, 1978; Joseph, 1978; Barber, 1982).

Although reaching opposite conclusions, both these arguments employ a common approach: inferring patterns of behavior from evidence on structural parameters and people's perceptions of them. Since more than one course of action is possible in any given set of circumstances, both arguments are plausible — and inconclusive. Nigeria has experienced numerous instances of limited class action, including Agbekoya, in which farmers or workers have combined to seek immediate economic gains (higher crop prices, lower taxes, increased wages), but they tend to disband as soon as their immediate demands are met — even with token gestures of appeasement — and the revolutionary momentum forecast by radical observers has not so far materialized. On the other hand, Yorubas' stated perceptions of the structure of opportunities or of social divisions do not, by themselves, explain the process of differentiation. Aronson (1978a), for example, has questioned the importance of class in Yoruba society on the grounds that his informants tended to characterize people as either *akowe* (those who earn a living by writing things down) or *onisowo* (those who buy and sell). Since these categories embrace widely different levels of income and lifestyle, he argues that occupational differences do not correspond to differences in wealth as they would in a class society. He does not, however, explain the origins of his informants' categories or how their terminology is related to actual processes of differentiation. Thus, his argument shows only that the class structure in western Nigeria does not correspond exactly to that found in industrialized Western societies — not that such a structure is missing.

Similarly, Bienen's attempt to draw conclusions about class formation from survey analysis and the presumed rationality of individual actors does not explain *why* it should be easier for Nigerian leaders to mobilize support through communal rather than class identities. He asserts that the limited degree of class consciousness and the "weakness of class-based politics in Nigeria give leaders a great deal of political space" (Bienen and Diejomaoh, 1981: 18-19), but then goes on to show that those leaders have been virtually powerless to effect changes in income distribution. "Policies meant to bring about more equity in Nigeria had unintended consequences, unplanned effects on equity, and sometimes moved income shares in the wrong direction" (p. 19) Clearly, survey analysis of perceptions of equity cannot explain these contradictory results and Bienen makes no attempt to do so, thus illustrating the point that without marshaling some evidence on people's actions as well as on attitudes and structures it is difficult to go much beyond the truism that things are not always what they seem.

The relationships between sectional and class divisions or alliances in western Nigeria need to be examined historically. In a richly detailed study of one Yoruba kingdom (Ileṣa), John Peel (1980; forthcoming) shows how successive generations of emigrants from Ileṣa continued to maintain personal and political connections with their home community. Within Ileṣa, even the important instances of class-based mobilization and protest involve a communal dimension, for the ruling class was accused of failing to meet communal norms. Because wealth and opportunity, Peel argues, ultimately came from "foreign" sources — the slave trade, export produce markets, and oil — rather than from the exploitation of domestic resources, ordinary Ijesas had no direct control over access to wealth, but obtained it only through the local hierarchy, the gatekeepers to the outside world. A "class" demand — for a larger share of wealth — was actually a communal demand, for distribution to legitimate members of Ijeṣa community of the gains of slave trading, of cocoa marketing, or oil exports. In Ilesa, as in Nigeria generally,

> class action presupposes communal action, since the resources which are the focus of either action must first be acquired — and they are acquired from outside the highest-order community, the Nigerian state; on the whole the same applies to the various lower-order communities, down to units like the Ijesha divisions, Ilesha and the Ijesha towns and villages. The mass of the population is predisposed to accept the leadership of the elite, at each level of the communal hierarchy, since they depend on them in the initial acquisition from external agents of the resources that are critical for communal or individual aggrandisement at lower level [1980: 499].

Insofar as the ruling class actually does distribute goods along the lines of its community (or national) ties, the structure of the economy perpetuates the salience of communal ties in local (or national) politics.

Peel is quite right that oil has not reduced the Nigerian economy's dependence on foreign trade and that, both during and after the colonial period, the state has been able to exercise considerable control over some of the economy's principal sources of wealth.[1] However, it does not follow that all economic opportunity is exogenous (to Nigeria or to individual communities), or that collective action (on class or communal lines) is directed solely toward securing the redistribution of externally derived wealth. If that were true, it is not clear why anyone in Ilesa (or for that matter in Nigeria) should work at all. Yet people do work and work hard, many of them simply to maintain a very low standard of living. The question to which this essay is largely addressed is what difference this makes both for the growth and structure of the regional economy as a whole and for the form and historical significance of differentiation within it.

Adrian Peace's (1978) study of factory workers in an industrial estate outside of Lagos shows how both class and community-based ties and interests enter into the lives of young, urban, immigrant industrial workers. Personal ties and networks based on or patterned after relations of descent play a crucial role in young men's initial adjustment to the city: finding shelter and companionship, securing a stable job, and coping with local authorities. Such relationships also serve to constrain workers' upward mobility in the long run. Once a worker becomes established, he is expected to assist more recent urban arrivals and to take on greater family responsibilities. Often these obligations make it impossible for him to accumulate enough capital to enter self-employment, which most aspire to do. Hence, Peace concludes, the strategies young men use in seeking and securing wage employment tend to confine them to it, and thus contribute to the formation of an urban proletariat (c.f. Aronson, 1978b).

The closing down of opportunities to enter and succeed in self-employment, which Peace envisioned in 1970, was postponed by the inflow of oil revenue after the end of the civil war. The principal consequence of the oil money has been the rapid growth of the tertiary sector in Nigeria, and thousands of Nigerians have found new opportunities for self-employment, primarily in the distributive sector. Eades (1980) agrees with Peel that the process of tertiary sector growth has reinforced community at the expense of class identities and alliances, although his argument runs on somewhat different lines. For Eades, the structure of social relations is revealed by the strategies people pursue in seeking access to resources and opportunities. Thus, a person's position in the social structure is suggested by the identity of the people he or she turns to for resources or assistance. Among the Yoruba, he argues, communal or descent-based ties are more important to self-employed than to salaried workers because kin groups and home town networks are more effective than trade or craft associations in providing entrepreneurs with the means of mobilizing cheap labor and circumventing official controls over market transactions.

> Migrant entrepreneurs are likely to return to their home towns eventually, and building a house there is one of their highest priorities. The wealthy entrepreneurs — contractors, produce-buyers and the like — may decide to compete for titles at home. The support of the local branch of their home-town union may well be crucial in this. While many entrepreneurs do not have the time to participate regularly in town-union meetings, they are frequently invited to its functions as guests of honour, and they are expected to contribute generously. The wealthy entrepreneur, much more than the bureaucrat and professional, is concerned with this reputation at home and works hard to maintain it [Eades, 1980: 160-161].

However, oil has swelled the ranks of the salaried as well as of the self-employed in western Nigeria, and there is ample evidence that bureaucrats and professionals also build houses at home, compete for chieftancy titles, and play an active role in home town unions and community affairs. In my study of one small Yoruba town, where most of the economically active population lives and works outside the town, I found that the leadership of the town's progressive union was completely dominated by emigrant bureaucrats and professionals, who took the lead in persuading wealthy businessmen to contribute to local projects (cf. Berry, forthcoming; Aronson, 1978a; Imoagene, 1976). Moreover, a number of the town's wealthy entrepreneurs had begun their careers as salaried bureaucrats or professionals, jobs in which they had developed personal and political connections that enabled them to succeed as entrepreneurs. As one informant (a middle-level bureaucrat) explained, although the perquisites attached to civil service jobs are no longer so attractive as they were in the first years of independence, it is still advisable to begin one's career in the civil service. "Then, when you go out (into self-employment) you know where to lay your hand on things."

Over time, the lines between salaried and self-employed are not fixed in western Nigeria. People in both types of employment pursue class as well as community-based strategies, and may practice both types of occupation in the course of a lifetime. Thus, it is difficult to sustain the argument that the relative growth of the tertiary sector in Nigeria has tipped the balance in favor of "network" rather than "class strategies" (Eades, 1980) or that, therefore, class consciousness remains subordinated to descent-based forms of social identity in western Nigeria. To understand both the choice and the implications of people's strategies, we need to examine their histories of accumulation and mobility, not simply to classify them according to various socioeconomic characteristics. The question is not only to whom people turn for advice or assistance in different circumstances, but also what they do when they turn to them. The following sections will describe the practice as well as the aims of people's strategies, and discuss their implications for the changing structure of Yoruba economy and society.

STRATEGIES OF ACCUMULATION AMONG FARMERS AND THEIR DESCENDENTS

In undertaking the field research that informs the argument of this essay, I set out to discover what Yoruba cocoa farmers had done with the income they derived from cocoa production and how their uses of income have influenced their social position and that of their children. I began by interviewing residents of two cocoa farming villages southeast of Ife, which were founded around 1945 by migrants from Yoruba communities on the edge of the savannah (Berry, 1975; Olusanya et al., 1978). The migrants came to Ife to plant cocoa, acquired long-term rights to use rural land owned by Ife families, and built permanent villages near their cocoa farms. Although some farmers had thus lived and worked in the Ife area for thirty years or more, they continued to maintain close ties with their home towns on the edge of the savannah. They had also developed extensive linkages with the commercial and urban sectors of western Nigerian society through their own participation in commercial activity and through their descendants, most of whom had left farming for school or nonagricultural employment. In addition to recording the life histories of some sixty residents of the two cocoa villages, I traced their links with their home towns and with the nonagricultural sectors of the regional economy. To do this, I collected life histories from people in some of the occupations commonly pursued by farmers' children (namely, schoolteaching and motor repair) and also did a study of migration and community resource use in one of the villagers' home towns.

For most Yoruba farmers, cocoa production brought only modest increases in real income (Galletti et al., 1956; Essang, 1970; Clarke, 1978). Much of the increase was, however, invested in various undertakings designed to expand the future earning capacity of themselves and their descendants rather than absorbed in increased levels of consumption. Cocoa farmers are not unusual in this respect. The literature on Yoruba society is full of examples such as that of the elderly villager who asked a team of medical researchers from the University of Ibadan whether they could give her medicine that would enable her to conceive more children. When they replied in the negative, she thanked them for their answer: It would set her mind at rest and allow her to concentrate on making as much money as possible (Lambo et al., 1969). Similarly, when I asked a Yoruba mechanic in 1979 how he used the weekly proceeds of his enterprise, he replied, "I use about 35 for expenses and the remaining 15 for myself." He went to explain that his "expenses" involved providing food, shelter, clothing, and medical care for his wives and children; the money left over "for himself" was reinvested in his firm.

If individual Yorubas have proved to be enthusiastic accumulators, accumulation in turn accords well with culturally sanctioned values and aspirations. Both individually and collectively, Yorubas place a high value on hard work and on getting ahead in terms of influence and prestige as well as wealth itself (Aronson, 1978a: Barber, 1982; Eades, 1980; Fadipe, 1970; Lloyd, 1974; Peel, 1978). A person is respected and obeyed, in Yoruba society, in accordance with his or her skill in solving people's problems and ability to command the loyalty of others. Such attributes are presumed to increase with age, but they may also be acquired through marriage and child-bearing, through development of specialized skills or knowledge, and through accumulation of supporters and subordinates. Since all of these conditions for personal advance can be enhanced through appropriate uses of wealth, accumulation is central to building a personal reputation and assumes a prominent place in most people's personal goals. By the same token, the growth and commercialization of the Yoruba economy has served to expand the means for individuals to get ahead according to established definitions of status rather than introducing radically new criteria of ranking into Yoruba society. However, even if as individuals Yorubas often appear to personify Marx's stereotypical capitalist (see Akeredolu-Ale, 1975), for whom accumulation is "Moses and the prophets," capitalist values do not themselves make a capitalist economy.

The growth of agricultural production for foreign and domestic markets, which was the major form of economic expansion in the colonial period, did not create a proletariat (in the sense of a large class of people with only their labor power to sell), nor did it establish the conditions for significant development of the forces of production. Even under colonial rule, agricultural surplus was channeled either into increasing production of cocoa and food crops by existing methods of cultivation, or into expansion of the tertiary sector through the growth of the bureaucracy and the proliferation of small commercial and artisanal enterprises. Both in and outside the bureaucracy, money was made by facilitating or manipulating the traffic in imports and locally produced agricultural commodities rather than by increasing or diversifying production. The inflow of oil revenue after 1970 intensified the process, leading to an enormous growth in administration, education, and commerce, with relatively little industrialization.

Oil has also reinforced the colonial pattern of accumulation without proletarianization. In the colonial economy, both merchants and the state stood to gain from the growth and commercialization of local agriculture and hence had no reason to try to dispossess farmers or to prevent Africans from entering domestic trade and transport.[2] This was even more true of oil, which yields enormous wealth with very little input of labor. At the same time, colonial rule initiated a process of political centralization in Nigeria, which has been reinforced by the economy's orientation toward foreign trade. Through its ability to regulate foreign transactions and attract foreign capital, the state controls some of the most important resources of the Nigerian economy. Hence, for most Nigerians, access to wealth and economic opportunity is contingent on access to the state, and people tend accordingly to devote considerable time and money to developing good political and/or bureaucratic connections.

The significance of this point goes beyond the familiar complaint that corruption is a way of life in contemporary Nigeria (see, for example, Turner, 1978; Joseph, 1978; Akeredolu-Ale, 1975; and the Nigerian press in general). Access to the state is both an object and an instrument of accumulation. This fact has two major implications for the nature of economic development and social change. On the one hand, it constrains the development of the productive forces of the economy: People devote investable surplus, which might otherwise be available to expand productive capacity, to building relations of patronage and political influence: a process that affects the growth of output and productivity at the level of the enterprise as well as that of the economy, as we shall see. Second, because accumulation is often conditional on political connections, access to the state is potentially an important basis for differentiation. However, it does not follow that the process of class formation in western Nigeria consists simply of the division of Yoruba society into rulers and ruled, as is often suggested in the literature on the postcolonial state in Africa. Rather, people seek to acquire access to the state in a variety of ways and, in the process, help to generate multiple and sometimes contradictory forms of collective identity and action. The question is what kinds of strategies people used, with what success, and with what impact on processes of accumulation, class formation, and political action.

Strategies for gaining access to state-controlled resources were both individual and collective. Individuals often invest considerable sums in establishing personal relations of clientage with politically powerful people or, like the civil servant quoted above, seek to develop a network of contacts within the state apparatus by working for it. Establishing such contacts is often facilitated by having kinsmen in high places, but does not depend on it, nor is the fact of kinship itself a guarantee of effective clientage. People can attach themselves to patrons by offering loyal and/or lucrative service, regardless of kinship, while wealthy and powerful individuals are likely to do more for kinsmen who have actively served their interests than for those who have not. Access to the state may also be pursued collectively by descent groups and communities, or through political parties, trade unions, and so on. Collective strategies for gaining access to the state include efforts both to increase the power of one's community or profession as a whole and to advance one's individual standing within the group. In other words, people may seek access to the state through both class and community-based associations and, in fact, often pursue both simultaneously.

Such strategies may be observed among both rural and urban Yorubas. Farmers whom I interviewed in the cocoa villages had, for example, used surplus income from the sale of cocoa and other crops to expand their own enterprises, to train their children for nonagricultural employment, and to maintain or strengthen their position in their home towns by contributing to family ceremonies or community projects and often by building a house in the home town.[3] Investment in the farmer's own enterprise(s) usually took the form of planting or purchasing additional plots of tree crops and/or diversifying into trade. Several of my informants had learned a craft, such as tailoring or smithing, before they moved to Ife to plant cocoa, and sometimes practiced it in addition to farming. However, most of the men who pursued more than one occupation combined farming with trade: buying cocoa or other crops from their neighbors to sell to larger dealers, or retailing inexpensive tools and household goods in the village or nearby rural markets. During the 1950s and 1960s, cocoa production was expanding in the Ife area and rural trade offered opportunities for modest profits. By the 1970s farmers' purchasing power was being squeezed by inflation and rising labor costs (as people increasingly sought to take part in the expanding urban tertiary sector), and village traders who could afford to move to more prosperous areas did so. Farmers' wives followed a parallel course, working on their husbands' farms until the tree crops had matured and the farmer could afford to substitute hired labor for that of his wives and children; the wives then sought to establish their own business in food processing or rural trade. As schools proliferated in western Nigeria during and after the colonial period, children's labor was increasingly withdrawn from their parents' farms. Far from lamenting this development, however, Yoruba farmers actively encouraged their children to prepare for nonagricultural employment either through formal schooling or through apprenticeship, often at considerable expense. In short, cocoa farmers often used part of the proceeds of their farms both to secure better incomes for themselves and their children through commercial or other nonagricultural employment and to enhance their status within their descent groups or communities of origin (cf. Aronson, 1971, 1978a; Eades, 1979, 1980; Sudarkasa, 1979)

Farmers' collective activities reflected similar combination of class and community-oriented strategies. In the 1960s migrant farmers in the villages I studied had attempted to participate in political activities in the Ife area and had also organized cooperative marketing ventures designed to obtain better prices for their crops. One popular village resident was elected to the Local Government Council, although he was not of Ife descent, and held the office until the councils were disbanded by the military regime in 1966. The marketing cooperatives were organized entirely by farmers within each village and had no affiliation with the state-controlled Western Nigeria Cooperative Produce Marketing Union. Groups of friends within the villages decided to pool their cocoa in order to bypass local traders and sell directly to licensed buying agents of the state marketing board.[4] By doing so they could obtain a small premium offered by the licensed buying agents (LBAs) for bulk purchases and accumulate some surplus to make loans to their own members, thus relieving them of some of the hidden interest charges involved in obtaining crop advances from large traders. The village cooperative societies were never large and their membership did not extend beyond the residents of a single village. Nonetheless, they represented some effort on the part of cocoa growers to combine in pursuit of their mutual interest in securing a slightly larger share of the gazetted cocoa price. In these limited ways, the cooperatives can be seen as a form of class-oriented action aimed at gaining access to state-controlled resources.

During the 1970s, however, cocoa farmers abandoned even such limited efforts to organize around their common interests as agricultural producers. Declining incomes eliminated the tiny surpluses that the village cooperatives had managed to accumulate and they were forced to cease operations entirely. At the same time, migrants' efforts to participate in local politics disintegrated under the combined influence of military rule (when all overt forms of political mobilization were proscribed) and long-standing distrust of outsiders (cf. Oyediran, 1974; Berry, 1975; Clarke, 1978). By the late 1970s farmers had shifted their collective efforts to gain access to the state from the cocoa marketing system to their home towns. For similar reasons, the peasant militancy of the Agbekoya uprisings dissipated in the 1970s as oil eclipsed agricultural exports as the principal source of state revenue. Because the state no longer needed to exploit them, cocoa farmers lost what little leverage they had been able to exercise through concerted action before 1970. By 1978-1979, when the country was preparing for the return to civilian rule, it appeared more desirable to have kinsmen than fellow cocoa growers in high offices and farmers accordingly turned their attention homeward as the election campaign got underway.

In accordance with their parents' investment patterns, most of the children of my rural informants had left agriculture to seek education and/or employment in the tertiary sector. At the time of my survey, the majority of village residents' children were attending school while, among those who were gainfully occupied, only a handful were engaged in farming. Most were employed in relatively low-level civil service jobs (as clerks or teachers), or were self-employed as traders or artisans (see Table 7.1). While these categories correspond to Aronson's distinction between *akowe* and *onisowo,* the histories of individuals' careers show that people often moved between them in the course of a lifetime. Many of the motor mechanics I interviewed had chosen to learn that trade because they were unable to continue in school. Teachers and civil servnts, on the other hand, often aspired to self-employment, even those with relatively high levels of training and income (cf. Peace, 1978). The most successful of my informants — emigrants from the farmers' home town, Iree, rather than from the cocoa villages themselves — were entrepreneurs who had established their own businesses after a long period of employment with the government or a large expatriate firm. The contacts they had developed while on salary were, in all cases, crucial sources of capital and customers for their business ventures. Many had, however, originally obtained their salaried jobs because of their educational qualifications, which were, in turn, acquired with financial resources derived from their own or their parents' self-employment. In short, relatively successful careers (in terms of accumulation and upward mobility) were usually built through an adroit (or sometimes lucky) combination of education, commercial activity, and bureaucratic employment.

Just as their parents do, the children of farmers, village traders, and artisans also pursued descent-based as well as market-oriented strategies for getting ahead. Among my informants, people of all educational and income levels built houses in their home towns, participated in family and town union meetings, and even contested chieftancy titles in their home communities. These tendencies were manifested not only in the individual careers of my informants, but also in the history of emigrants' involvement in Iree. Not only traders and cocoa farmers, but also lawyers, engineers, and senior civil servants had built their houses in the town during the 1960s and 1970s. By 1979, the beginnings of an elite "suburb" were clearly visible on the west side of the town, and several young professionals were drawing up ambitious plans to expand it, with the help of the local Town Planning Authority (which was chaired by a son of Iree). Similarly, when a dispute developed in 1972 over the choice of a new *oba* (head chief), emigrant professionals were as closely involved in the ensuing struggle as were their less wealthy and educated relatives and neighbors. Emigrant professionals dominated the town's "improvement" societies during the 1970s and did not hesitate to mobilize the support of their fellow townspeople in pursuit of their own class interests, as well as vice versa. I shall return to this point below.

CONSEQUENCES OF ACCUMULATION:
MIGRATION AND PRODUCTIVITY

The simultaneous pursuit of class and community interests by people at all socioeconomic levels of contemporary Yoruba society has shaped both patterns of rural-urban migration and processes of accumulation in rural and urban enterprises. Rapid urban growth, declining agricultural output, and the rising cost of agricultural labor have all been frequently cited as evidence of massive rural-urban migration in western Nigeria (Adepoju, 1975; Caldwell, 1978; Essang and Mabawonku, 1974). Certainly a great many people have left comparatively rural for more urban communities in search of economic opportunity, although not all economic mobility has involved rural-to-urban migration. The spread of cocoa cultivation during the colonial period drew people from towns and cities into uncultivated forest areas (Berry, 1975; Olusanya et al., 1978), and

Table 7.1   Occupations of Farmers' Children

	Abakan		Abulemeji	
	Males	Females	Males	Females
Farming	3	12	8	22
Trade	2	11	1	20
School	45	29	120	102
Clerk, Teacher	3	1	13	7
Small-Scale Enterprise	20	2	36	9
Unemployed and Unknown	34	29	53	44
Total	107	84	231	204

SOURCE: Village censuses.

people have moved from agriculture into nonagricultural occupations within villages and even towns. As we have seen, however, whether migrants left villages for towns or vice versa, they have usually maintained a life-long association with their community of origin, a pattern which persists in the era of the petronaira.

In their efforts to avail themselves of new economic opportunities — in agriculture, trade, transport, crafts, or salaried employment — while maintaining or strengthening their ties with kinsmen and community of origin, Yorubas are continually on the move. People travel constantly, not only between workplace and "home," but also among an ever-expanding network of kinsmen, customers, creditors, patrons, clients, and friends, with whom the individual hopes to maintain potentially advantageous relationships. In a town such as Iree, where there are very few local opportunities for gainful employment, the majority of adult citizens live and work outside the town. In one compound, for example, out of 153 adult male members[5] only nine actually lived in the town. Yet people visit there frequently. Many of the farmers I interviewed went home several times a year, and some professionals traveled there every weekend, especially during the election campaign. People also change their place of principal residence more often than is usually implied in the literature on rural-urban migration. In one cocoa village, which I surveyed in 1970-1971 and 1978-1979, the total population remained constant during this period, but 60 percent of the individuals I enumerated in 1970-1971 had left by 1978-1979 and had been replaced by others.

As these examples suggest, the expansion of nonagricultural employment and the growth of urban population in contemporary western Nigeria has not led to the polarization of Yoruba society into privileged urban dwellers and "neglected rural majority" (Olatunbosun, 1975), or even into urban rich and urban and rural poor. Instead, it has engendered a kind of perpetual restlessness in which no one stays anywhere for very long lest he miss an opportunity somewhere else. The fact that the majority of migrants realize little at any point in their travels serves not to slow things down but to intensify the impetus to keep moving, if only to avoid falling further behind in the political and economic lottery of accumulating good connections.

Because Yorubas often invest in developing or maintaining descent-based relations as a potential channel of access to productive resources and profitable opportunities, relations based on or modeled after those of descent also enter into the process of production, particularly through the mobilization and control of labor. Except in large firms, most labor in both agricultural and nonagricultural enterprises is supplied by relatives or apprentices, who are not paid directly for their services in cash, but instead accumulate a claim on the employer's patronage that can, in principle, be used to establish an independent enterprise in the future. The prevalence of this practice is partly a consequence of poverty: for most farmers, artisans, and petty traders their receipts are too low and irregular to enable them to make regular wage payments, and employing junior kin or apprentices relieves them of this burden. (Hired labor did become fairly common in the cocoa growing sector partly because farmers were assured of a sizeable cash inflow at harvest time and workers knew it. Thus cocoa farmers were able to make wage payments after the cocoa harvest and were unable to deny the fact.)

In addition, because commercialization did not create a substantial number of dispossessed (and therefore proletarianized) people in western Nigeria, most Yorubas have been able to realize a measure of economic independence, if not prosperity, and thus have not been forced to anticipate a lifetime of working for others. Employers cannot hope to attract labor merely in exchange for daily subsistence. The thousands of petty traders, artisans, and casual workers who make up the bulk of the urban (and much of the rural) labor force act not so much as a "reserve army of the unemployed," but rather as a pool of would-be accumulators, who attach themselves to a particular master or patron only if he or she is likely to help them become economically independent in the long run. Wages are low, in other words, not because labor is in excess supply, but because it is not very productive. The reasons for low productivity lie, in turn, in the conditions of access to productive resources and the way they have shaped the organization of production and the forms of accumulation.

Accumulation in the tertiary sector has both facilitated the proliferation of small enterprise in western Nigeria and constrained growth of labor productivity. Relations of dependence and subordination between employers and workers entail a considerable measure of reciprocity. In Yoruba communities,

> any senior has a right to unquestioned service, deference, and submissiveness from any junior . . . in return for which (seniors) have their own obligations to lead, to teach and to aid any junior. . . . The importance of seniority has not diminished in new urban areas. . . . The uniformity that this code of authority imposes on wives, children, servants and employees alike constrains the common language often used for all these relationships: Yorubas speak in English of "sacking" (firing, divorcing) either a recalcitrant wife or a difficult employee [Aronson, 1978a: 94].

Similarly, Koll (1969) has pointed out that craft production in Ibadan is characterized by loose associations among autonomous artisans who may share tools or information but not customers or credit. "Since recruitment into a craft is no longer through kinship, such partnerships are apparently of a contractual nature; but in fact they have more in common with kinship relations . . . since prospective partners take years to judge each other's moral behavior and technical skills; once established, the partnership rests on mutual trust and understanding rather than on formalities" (p. 57). Thus, the organization of work is often patterned after relations among kin, not through force of habit or custom, but because "customary" labor relations have been perpetuated by the course of economic change itself.

The prevailing pattern of labor relations, in turn, limits both the harshness of exploitation and the productivity of work. Among the mechanics I interviewed and observed in their shops, labor discipline was a constant problem. Clumsy or careless apprentices could not be fined, since they received no wages, and if dismissed would have to be replaced with an untrained recruit, thus depriving the master of part of the returns to his own investment. Hence, labor discipline depended on the master's personal relations with his apprentices and required constant supervision. A successful master could demand more of his apprentices, since his future patronage would be of greater value to them. Success depended on developing and fostering a clientele of loyal customers, who, as one mechanic put it, "send for me when their cars break down in Ibadan." Cultivating customers (as well as creditors, suppliers of spare parts, and so on) also required personal contact and tended to take the master away from his shop, thereby reducing his ability to supervise his apprentices directly. This, in turn, affected productivity in several ways. For one things, masters rarely delegated authority to their apprentices, either to accept jobs or to handle money. While the master was away from the shop, work could not begin on jobs not already underway, nor could spare parts be purchased or payment accepted for completed work.

In addition, methods of production in most mechanics' shops were highly labor intensive, often requiring cooperation among the apprentices. One mechanic, for example, who specialized in repairing Volkswagens, owned one hand-operated hydraulic jack that was used principally for larger models. If a beetle needed to be raised when the jack was in use, four apprentices were mobilized to lift up one end, while a fifth pushed a discarded engine block under the axle. The time it took to organize such an operation was noticeably longer when the master was not around, at which time one or more of the apprentices required was apt to be building a fire, washing his clothes, transacting business with a passing food vendor, joking or wrestling with a fellow apprentice, or simply waiting for someone whom he considered suitably senior to himself to organize the undertaking. Similar delays often occur when a car breaks down on the road. Neither telephones nor towing services are readily available in western Nigeria. If a car breaks down and the motorist wants to reach his or her regular mechanic, he or she must usually go in person to the mechanic's shop and then find some means of returning to the disabled vehicle with the mechanic or a qualified apprentice to get it started again. If the master is not in th shop when the customer arrives, it may be necessary to await his return so that he can authorize an apprentice to leave. If the master himself accompanies the motorist, work in the shop will lag in his absence. In general, the larger the volume of business, the more time the proprietor must spend away from his shop and the less efficient the work which is done in his absence.

The observation that mechanics' strategies for pursuing commercial success tend to undermine the conditions for obtaining it applies not only to the labor process within the firm, but also to the structure of the market and the forms of accumulation arising from the growth of small-scale tertiary enterprise. The system of apprenticeship, which most mechanics adopted in order to avoid the financial burden of meeting a regular payroll out of their irregular earnings served to multiply the number of master mechanics over time, thus perpetuating risks and low returns to the individual firm by intensifying competitive pressure in the market as a whole. Similarly, mechanics' efforts to cope collectively with market uncertainty and competition sometimes conflicted with individual productivity. In Ife, the mechanics had formed an association that sought to maintain good relations with local authorities and to assist member mechanics to recover bad debts (by maintaining a blacklist of delinquent customers and sometimes by negotiating with them directly). The effectiveness of the association depended directly on its ability to command the support of all or most of the mechanics in the town, and much of its activities were directed toward reinforcing solidarity among the members. Though most mechanics attended the association's fortnightly meetings only when they had a particular grievance to discuss, they were expected to express their loyalty to the organization by refraining from work on alternate Friday mornings during the time when the meetings were held. In this case, collective efforts to protect mechanics' incomes conflicted directly with individual income earning activity.

Developing and maintaining a network of personal contacts to ensure the growth and viability of a business has not only undermined labor productivity in Nigerian firms, but also contributed to a high degree of mobility in western Nigerian society. Mechanics — like most self-employed Nigerians — travel frequently, between rural and urban areas as well as among towns, in a ceaseless quest for profitable contacts and reliable social relationships. Mobility has, in turn, contributed not only to the enormous growth of the transport sector in western Nigeria but also to a high rate of investment in housing. Most people rent or build a house in their home town (however distant from the workplace), as both a sign and an instrument of accumulation and prestige. The ability to accommodate relatives, clients, patrons, or business associates at a moment's notice reflects and reinforces a person's ability to develop such relationships; hence, the successful man often builds housing in excess of his regular needs. The storey house that stands shuttered and empty for most of the year is a familiar sight in rural towns and villages throughout western Nigeria, but even in the cities, prosperous men often keep empty rooms or whole buildings, which might be leased at high prices, to accommodate unexpected visitors. Thus, the conditions of accumulation foster unproductive uses both of investable surplus and the existing stock of durable structures.

CONSEQUENCES OF ACCUMULATION: DIFFERENTIATION AND CONFLICT IN IREE

Despite their considerable advantages over the majority of their fellow townsmen, the most successful sons of Iree tended, much as did their humbler relatives and neighbors, to pursue wealth and influence through a multiplicity of strategies partly in order to spread their risks. I traced a few of the town's wealthiest sons to Lagos in order to compare their life histories with those of their humbler compatriots. The men I interviewed included professionals (lawyers, architects, engineers) who were employed in the civil service or in parastatal or foreign-owned enterprises, and self-employed businessmen, who had spent a decade or more in government employment before establishing firms of their own. All had some form of postsecondary education, which had gained them entry to the middle or upper levels of the civil service (or to managerial jobs in large firms), but both promotion within salaried employment and the establishment of a successful private firm depended on the clientage relations a person was able to develop while in salaried employment. Characteristic examples were a former civil servant who, on his retirement, had obtained a large government loan to start a poultry business. Another was an entrepreneur who sold construction materials to customers whose loyalty he had cultivated while an employee of the United Africa Company and who "followed him" when he left the UAC to start his own firm. While these entrepreneurs used hired workers, their strategies of accumulation were directed toward reaping quick profits from the distribution or minimal processing of imported materials (including chicken feed).

However, their fortunes even at the highest levels of the state apparatus or the private sector, were as subject to fluctuation as those of the mass of small farmers and artisans; hence, even those at the top found it advantageous to keep their options open in an effort to maintain their privileged access to wealth and productive resources. During the election campaign of 1979, many of them made public contributions to projects in Iree, where the central thrust of the campaign was directed toward mobilizing community support for the Unity Party of Nigeria, which included a son of Iree on its slate of candidates. They also encountered contradictions similar to those facing the farmer or small urban entrepreneur. Sectional loyalties and conflicts weaken the power of the ruling class to implement self-aggrandising programs or to reproduce conditions for the smooth exercise of authority and the pursuit of state accumulation, just as the obligations of patronage undermine labor discipline at the level of the firm. At the same time, solidarity among persons of common descent is frequently undermined by differences in individuals' access to external sources of wealth and opportunity. These conditions constrain the elite's ability to consolidate its class position either by limiting elite recruitment to certain descent groups or by using class interests to override descent-based loyalties.

These processes are reflected in the history of collective projects of "community development" in Iree, as the history of the Iree Youth Movement (IYM) suggests. The IYM — an organization of university students and recent graduates — was founded in the mid-1970s largely in response to local political conflicts, which have been dominated by a pattern of religious polarization unusual in Yoruba society, but not surprising in this particular context. The principal agency of Christian proselytization in Iree during the colonial period was the American Baptist Mission in Ogbomoso. As in many Yoruba towns, foreign missionaries were received in Iree[6] with guarded politeness, but their early converts were looked upon with suspicion and hostility by local priests and diviners (babalawos) who feared that the new religion might threaten their own influence with the town's chiefs. During the colonial period, Islam attracted as many converts in Iree, if not more. By the 1930s, however, the spread of mission schools in western Nigeria and the growth of a western educated elite within the colonial framework was sufficient to give the educated Christians of Iree a decided advantage in terms of access both to education itself and to related forms of employment. Moreover, Iree's small size and out-of-the-way location meant that there was little development of commercial or administrative activity or employment opportunities within the town itself, which might have provided alternative channels of upward mobility. Thus the Baptist Mission remained throughout the colonial period the primary source of external resources available to the town and the local Baptists its principal beneficiaries. Their education and associated skills and contacts were both admired and resented by their relatives and neighbors. When the first Local Government council elections were held throughout the region in 1954, five of the six representatives elected from Iree were Baptists. On the other hand, mission-sponsored services and amenities actually brought to the town through the efforts of its Baptist citizens often became targets of jealousy and resentment among non-Baptists, who felt excluded from the management of such facilities, if not from their use.

In the 1950s, for example, the town decided to build its own secondary school to provide increased educational opportunities for local youths, jobs for local teachers, and prestige for the town as a whole. Money was raised from the whole community to erect the first block of classrooms, and members of all religious groups expected to share in the management of the school. However, the town was unable to meet the cost of teachers' salaries. When the school opened in 1959, it was staffed by teachers provided by the Baptist Mission and was officially named the Iree Baptist High School. The Muslims felt betrayed: Once again, it seemed, a community undertaking had been usurped by the Baptists, and the Muslims, in particular, deprived of the fruits of their own investment. Though there was little the Muslims could do at the time to change the finances or the name of the school, their sense of deprivation and antagonism toward the Baptists was greatly exacerbated.

Mutual suspicions flared into open conflict again in the early 1970s over the choice of successor to the *oba*, who died in 1972. Conflict crystallized around two rival candidates from the same house. One, a Baptist cabinet maker and contractor who had spent five years at a trade school in England, was favored by the town's educated elite and the majority of the Christians, both of whom considered his foreign experience and fluency in English to be proof of his ability effectively to represent the town's interests to the government. The other candidate, a Muslim who had spent many years in Ghana, was opposed by the elite and supported by a number of Muslims who felt that his opponent would allocate whatever resources he could gain for the town to the Christians, thus reinforcing their preferential access to externally derived benefits. The resulting controversy dragged on acrimoniously for three years until, at the behest of several prominent local sons, the Ministry of Local Government and Chieftaincy Affairs decided in favor of the Baptist and ordered his installation. Officially, this ended the dispute, but the antagonism between Muslims and Christians remained and continued to cast a pall over the community and efforts to mobilize support for local development projects.

The polarization of the townspeople into warring, ostensibly religious factions was deeply disturbing to a number of the town's educated youth, who regarded the chieftaincy dispute as anachronistic and the continuing religious factionalism as detrimental to the town's progress and prestige. Accordingly, they organized the IYM, dedicated to the promotion of communal progress and unity. Although the majority of its members were Christian, the IYM sought from the beginning to project a nondenominational image. Members exhorted their kinsmen and neighbors to religious unity; took care to include Muslims among their own officers; and sometimes voiced public support for suitable Muslim-backed projects, such as the idea of constructing a Muslim high school in Iree to equalize educational opportunities and power within the community. In 1977 they took a somewhat bolder step and launched a direct attack on one of the primary symbols of Baptist domination in Iree: the Baptist Welfare Center, a maternity clinic established in 1944 by the Baptist Mission at Ogbomoso, and run for 22 years by an American missionary. When the American retired in 1967, the Welfare Center was taken over by a relative of the locally born pastor of Iree's largest Baptist Church. He proceeded to make the Center financially independent of the mission by charging fees for consultations and medicines, a move widely regarded among the townspeople as yet another effort to turn a community facility into a profitable venture for a Baptist protege.

In 1977, the IYM stepped into the fray with a proposal that the Oyo State Ministry of Health be asked to take over the center, both to expand and upgrade its services and to forestall local coflict over its management. Several of the IYM's leaders had personal contacts in the Ministry of Health, and expected a quick and favorable official response to their suggestion. However, some of Iree's Baptists wished to retain control over the center and were also able to mobilize contacts in the Ministry. Months of correspondence and informal negotiations ended in stalemate and official indecision. For the time being, the IYM's efforts to use state intervention to rationalize the management of a community facility had foundered on the presence within the state itself of the very form of religious factionalism that they were trying to transcend on the local level.

By the end of 1978, the leaders of the IYM had turned their attention to the upcoming election and, specifically, to mustering votes for the UPN. In the campaign for the UPN, the IYM sought, characteristically, to appeal both to communal solidarity and to people's interest in upward mobility. In March 1979, for example, the IYM held a well-publicized ceremony in Iree to launch a new community development fund. They prevailed on several of the town's wealthiest sons and daughters (mostly emigrant professionals-cum-businessmen, like themselves) to attend and give generous contributions. During the ceremonies no explicit mention was made of any party platforms, but the coincidence between the achievements of Iree's educated sons and the UPN's platform of universal secondary as well as primary education was clearly implied.

Yet, the IYM's strategies for mobilizing popular support behind the party and program of their choice were grounded in appeals to sectional interests. The trump card in the UPN's campaign in Iree was the fact that the party's candidate for deputy governor of Oyo State was a local son. As one *omo* Iree (with a university degree) put it, in discussing the town's hitherto abortive efforts to get piped water and electricity installed by the state, "if a certain party (say, the UPN) should win the election, all the irregularities will be regularized." During the campaign, the leaders of the IYM worked openly with the UPN candidate and publicly urged the townspeople to support him. "Politics has come again," they reminded their kinsmen and neighbors, "and everyone must make his choice. You may vote for your native son, or you may vote against him." Similarly, although university students and young professionals considered themselves too enlightened to indulge in the religious factionalism that had so polarized their elders, they were just as anxious to master popular support for the new *oba* as were the staunchest of his Baptist supporters both to prevent local antagonisms from undermining support for the UPN, and because the *oba* was openly sympathetic to their interests. Having launched the development fund as a display of their own skill at mobilizing resources for community development, they decided to spend the money on the *oba*'s uncompleted palace. In local politics, as in the informal sector of the economy, pursuit of power and profit through both class and community ties often leads to the unproductive use of investable surplus.

CONCLUSION

Both under colonial rule and after independence, western Nigeria has been characterized by widespread, if often small-scale, accumulation; rapid occupational and social mobility; and a persistent tendency toward sectional mobilization and conflict at all levels of political activity. These characteristics have repeatedly been taken to mean that the equally evident patterns of growing inequality, lawlessness, and oppression somehow do not matter: people either don't perceive them or, regarding them as ephemeral or temporary, do not act on them. Instead, social behavior in western Nigeria is to be explained by the peculiar structure of the regional (and/or national) political economy, which must be deduced from exhaustive empirical research and description. This approach, which has been pursued by authors of widely differing ideological persuasions, has led to a proliferation of structural characterizations that tend to restate the contradictory nature of the evidence rather than to explain it.

In this essay, I have begun to explore one possible method for moving beyond the prevailing inconclusiveness of much of the literature on Yoruba economic and social change. My approach has been to collect evidence on actual patterns of accumulation, mobility, and collective action over time, and to use them as a basis for understanding not only the changing structure of economic and political opportunities and the strategies which people have used to take advantage of them, but also how strategies and circumstances have shaped each other and, in the process, given rise to the patterns of change described above. Specifically, I have tried to suggest how such an approach enables us to move beyond the question of whether class or community has exerted a predominant influence on the course of

Yoruba social history to a consideration of how they have interacted over time.

My examination of uses of surplus by cocoa farmers and their descendants suggests that in order to capitalize on the shifting and often unpredictable opportunities thrown up by the processes of commercialization and political centralization before and after colonial rule, Yorubas have typically pursued a variety of strategies that span village and city. They have frequently used available surplus to accumulate both capital (fixed and circulating) and social relations, which may facilitate continued or expanded access to capital and other productive resources. These patterns of accumulation have, in turn, given rise to differentiation in wealth and access to productive resources without transforming the labor process or the conditions of accumulation itself. Thus, the productivity of labor has not increased significantly, despite sometimes intense competition for labor supplies, and accumulation has led to the proliferation of tertiary sector proprietorships, rather than the expansion of directly productive capacity or the development of new forms of productive enterprise. At the same time, because descent-based social relations have been crucial to the process of capital accumulation, they have been reinforced rather than weakened by the changing structure of the regional economy, and continue to influence both patterns of resource allocation and strategies of collective action at all socioeconomic levels.

In this way, descent-based relationships not only persist in contemporary Yoruba society but have exerted an integral influence on the process of class formation. The frequent observation that kin and community ties cut across lines in Yoruba society is correct but it does not follow that they serve to diminish or offset the forces of polarization. Class formation is taking place within descent-based groups and institutions as well as around them. In consequence, those who would pursue their class interests (either individually or collectively) are obliged to dissipate a large part of their energy and resources in shuttling endlessly among an ever-widening network of contacts. Their restless mobility contributes to low labor productivity within Nigerian firms and to excessive investment in housing. In addition, the competitiveness of the economy increases the uncertainty of gain from any particular contact and thereby perpetuates the tendency to multiply them. This effect is manifested concretely in constant traveling by Yorubas of all occupations and income levels, and also in kind of collective inability to concentrate resources or authority, which tends to paralyze both the development of the forces of production and the consolidation of power, in urban as well as rural areas, and within the state as well as outside it. As we saw in the case of Iree, efforts to build collective solidarity — on *either* class or communal lines — tend to founder on the ubiquity of the opposing mode of collective identity and action. Thus, attempts by descent groups or communities to weld themselves into corporate agencies of progress or self-aggrandisement are often undermined by members' differential access to wealth and opportunities, while class alliances tend to break down under the pressure of sectional antagonism and conflict, even at the level of the state. As the history of accumulation, mobility, and conflict among the "children of Iree" reveals, the contradictions of class formation in western Nigeria as a whole not only parallel but also reciprocate the contradictions of accumulation in Yoruba households and enterprises in both rural and urban areas.

NOTES

1. It helps, of course, that Nigeria's foreign resources were increasing. State control over a dwindling stream of foreign credit and earnings is something of a paper tiger, as the Ghanaian experience shows (Chazan, 1981).

2. For a counterexample that reinforces the point, see Freund (1981). When British capitalists wanted a cheap labor force, as in the tin mines of the Jos Plateau, the colonial authorities did not hesitate to try to create one, by forcible means if necessary.

3. Such a house was available for the migrant's eventual retirement but, during his working life, was used only for occasional visits or by his kinsmen, free of charge. Thus it served not to enlarge the owner's current income, but rather to demonstrate his commitment to his community of origin and to provide a base there from which he could offer hospitality to visitors and kin: both a measure and an instrument of his personal reputation and status (cf. Eades, 1980).

4. All cocoa was required to be sold to the Marketing Board rather than exported directly by private firms. The board, in turn, issued licenses to private traders to purchase cocoa for the board at a fixed commission. Licensed buying agents (LBAs) in turn, purchased cocoa from a large network of private traders, who bore the risks of small-scale transactions and provided bulking services. To become an LBA, a firm had to meet a minimum working capital requirement; once licensed, they enjoyed a guaranteed market for their purchases and often developed other advantageous contacts with the state. Thus, the marketing system in western Nigeria was relatively monopsonistic and profits tended to be concentrated in the hands of the state and its agents (Essang, 1970; Helleiner, 1964; Bauer, 1963).

5. Defined as descendants of the house who had attended a family meeting at least once between 1976 and 1978.

6. My information on Iree history was obtained primarily from interviews with around ninety townspeople, both prominent and obscure. I also derived much useful information from unpublished materials in the library of the Baptist Theological Seminary in Ogbomoso; from Rev. E. A. Omilade, *Itan Ilu Iree* . . . (n.d.); the *Minutes Book* of the Iree Progressive Union; and from files in the Ifelodun Local Government Secretariat, Ikirun, and in the possession of M. O. Ajayi, secretary of the IYM.

REFERENCES

ADEPOJU, A. (1975) Internal Migration in Nigeria. Ife: University of Ife.

AKEREDOLU-ALE, E. A. (1975) The Underdevelopment of Indigenous Entrepreneurship in Nigeria. Ibadan: Ibadan University Press.

ARONSON, D. R. (1978a) The City is Our Farm. Boston: Schenkman.

—— (1978b) "Capitalism and culture in Ibadan urban development." Urban Anthropology 7: 253-269.

—— (1971) "Ijebu Yoruba urban-rural relationships and class formation." Canadian Journal of African Studies 5: 263-280.

BARBER, K. (1982) "Popular responses to the Petro-Naira." Presented to the annual meetings of the Canadian African Studies Association.

BAUER, P. T. (1963) West African Trade. Cambridge: Cambridge University Press.

BEER, C. F. and G. P. WILLIAMS (1976) "The politics of the Ibadan peasantry," in G. P. Williams (ed.) Nigeria: Economy and Society. London: Rex Collings.

BERRY, S. S. (1975) Cocoa, Custom and Socio-Economic Change in Rural Western Nigeria. Oxford: Clarendon Press.

—— (forthcoming). Fathers Work for Their Sons. Accumulation, Mobility and Class Formation in an Extended Yoruba Community. Berkeley: University of California Press.

BIENEN, H., and V. P. DIEJOMAOH (1981) The Political Economy of Income Distribution in Nigeria. New York: Holmes & Meier.

CALDWELL, J. C. (1978) Population and Growth and Socio-economic Change in West Africa. New York: Columbia University Press.

CHAZAN, N. (1981) "Development, underdevelopment and the state in Ghana." Presented to the Walter Rodney Seminar, Boston University.

CLARKE, R. J. M. (1979) "Agricultural production in a rural Yoruba community." Ph.D. dissertation, University of London.

EADES, J. S. (1980) The Yoruba Today. Cambridge: Cambridge University Press.

—— (1979) "Kinship and entrepreneurship among Yoruba in northern Ghana," in W. Shack and E. P. Skinner (eds.) Strangers in African Societies. Berkeley: University of California Press.

ESSANG, S. M. (1970) "The distribution of earnings in the cocoa economy of western Nigeria." Ph.D. dissertation, Michigan State University.

—— and A. F. MABAWONKU (1974) The Determinants and Impact of Rural-Urban Migration: A Case Study of Selected Communities in Western Nigeria. African Rural Employment Studies No. 10. Michigan State University.

FADIPE, N. A. (1970) The Sociology of the Yoruba (F. O. Okediji and O. O. Okediji, eds.). Ibadan: University of Ibadan Press.

FREUND, B. (1981) Capital and Labor in the Nigerian Tin Mines. Atlantic Highlands, NJ: Humanities Press.

GALLETTI, R., K.D.S. BALDWIN, and I.O. DINA (1956) Nigerian Cocoa Farmers. London: Oxford University Press.

GUTKIND, P.C.W. (1974) "From the energy of despair to the anger of despair." Canadian Journal of African Studies 7: 179-198.

HELLEINER, G.K. (1964) "The fiscal role of the marketing boards in Nigerian economic development." Economic Journal 74: 587-610.

IMOAGENE, S. O. (1976) Social Mobility in an Emergent African Society. Canberra: Australian National University Press.

JOSEPH, R. (1978) "Affluence and underdevelopment in Nigeria." Journal of Modern African Studies 16: 221-239.

KOLL, M. (1969) Crafts and Cooperation in Western Nigeria. Freiburg: Bergstrasser Institut.

LAMBO, T. A. and A. LEIGHTON (1963) Psychiatric Disorders Among the Yoruba. Ithaca, NY: Cornell University Press.

LLOYD, P. C. (1974) Power and Independence: Urban Africans' Perceptions of Social Inequality. London: Routledge & Kegan Paul.

MORRISON, D. G. (1981) "Inequalities of social rewards: realities and perceptions in Nigeria," in H. Bienen and V. P. Diejomaoh (eds.) The Political Economy of Income Distribution in Nigeria. New York: Holmes & Meier.

OLATUNBOSUN, D. (1975) Nigeria's Neglected Rural Majority. Ibadan: Oxford University Press.

OYEDIRAN, O. (1974) "Modakeke in Ife: historical background to an aspect of contemporary Ife politics." Odu (n.s.): 10.

PEACE, A. (1978) Choice, Class and Conflict: A Study of Southern Nigerian Factory Workers. Atlantic Highlands, NJ: Humanities Press.

PEEL, J.D.Y. (1980) "Inequality and action: the forms of Ijesha social conflict." Canadian Journal of African Studies 14: 473-502.

——— (1978) "Olaju: a Yoruba concept of development." Journal of Development Studies 14: 139-165.

——— (forthcoming) Ijeshas and Nigerians: A Sociological History of Ilesha, 1895-1975. Cambridge: Cambridge University Press.

SUDARKASA, N. (1979) "From stranger to alien: socio-political history of the Yoruba in northern Ghana," in Shack and Skinner (eds.)

TURNER, T. (1978) "Commercial capitalism and the 1975 coup," in S. K. Panter-Brick (ed.) Soldiers and Oil. London: Frank Cass.

Map 8.1   The Orange Free State, Showing Qwaqwa and Thaba 'Nchu

8

STRUGGLE FROM THE MARGINS
Rural Slums in the Orange Free State

COLIN MURRAY

INTRODUCTION:
TOWARD REGIONAL ANALYSIS

In recent years, the South African state has been engaged in an ambitious attempt to restructure the black labor force. Faced by the growing militancy of black labor in the 1970s and early 1980s, and by a resurgence of protest on other fronts across the country, the Botha regime's "total strategy" is intended to rationalize and coordinate otherwise haphazard and potentially contradictory responses by capitalist employers and by various agencies of the state to the changing requirements of capital accumulation and political stability. The regime's failure to manage the combination of repression and reformism that it explicitly espouses has been attributed to the "organic crisis" of South African racial capitalism (Saul and Gelb, 1981).

The growth of the independent black union movement is undoubtedly the most significant and hopeful manifestation of resistance to the apartheid state since the Soweto revolt of 1976. Painfully but persistently, these unions have sought to articulate the vital connections between issues of industrial strategy — union registration, employer recognition of workers' own organizations, wages, and working conditions — and the wider issues that affect whole communities: housing, the pass laws, transport, education, and political representation. This chapter does not, however, examine the causes

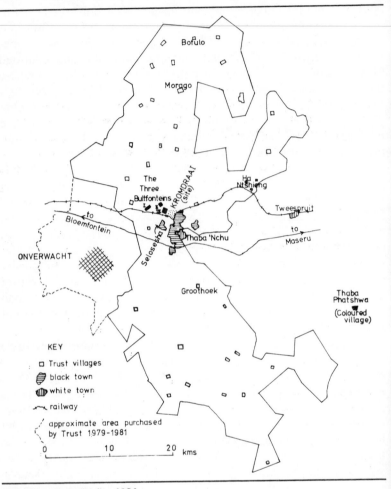

Map 8.2   Thaba 'Nchu, 1981

and consequences of the development of the independent black unions.[1] Rather, it is an attempt to illustrate another, less visible, aspect of the "struggle for the city": the predicament of South Africa's internal refugees who have been thrown to the periphery of the revolving wheel, so to speak, by the centrifugal force of the machinery of repression but who nevertheless continually exert a countervailing centripetal pressure toward the center, the urban core of "white" South Africa.

Three interrelated developments have worsened the predicament of the rural refugees. First, four of the ten Bantustans — Transkei, Bophuthatswana, Venda, and Ciskei — were made politically "independent" between 1976 and 1981, and all persons officially identified as citizens of one or other of these Bantustans, irrespective of where they live, were unilaterally deprived of South African citizenship. Second, the process of forced relocation has intensified in recent years. Many hundreds of thousands of black South Africans have been removed from white areas, both urban and rural, to new commuter towns and congested rural slums within the Bantustans, which are at the margins of the South African labor market. Third, the state has partially implemented a series of "reforms," based on the Riekert Commission recommendations of 1979, which are designed, above all, to reinforce the boundary between urban "insiders," with some rights to live and work in the white urban areas, on the one hand, and residents of the Bantustans: migrants, commuters, and the "economically inactive," on the other hand. These measures may marginally improve conditions for urban insiders; they also tighten influx control and facilitate the expulsion of "redundant" blacks from the urban areas.[2] Accordingly, they severely exacerbate the connected crises of poverty, unemployment, and repression in the Bantustans.

The administration of influx control against black South Africans is based mainly on the provisions of the notorious Section 10 (1) of the Black (Urban Areas) Consolidation Act of 1945, as successively amended by the Nationalist Government since 1948. The relevant subsections of this act provide that no African may remain for more than 72 hours in a "prescribed" (i.e., urban) area without proving that he or she

(1) has resided there continuously since birth; or

(2) has worked there continuously for one employer for ten years, or has resided there continuously and legally for fifteen years, subject to certain other conditions; or

(3) is a close dependent relative of, and ordinarily coresident with, an African who qualifies under (1) or (2), provided that he or she also entered the area lawfully; or

(4) has been granted special permission to be in the area. (Horrell, 1978; Davis, 1978).

Recent court cases have brought in question the practical interpretation of two of these subsections; but the vast majority of pass law prosecutions are undefended, and in any case the state has started deporting "illegal" blacks as aliens without any recourse to the judicial process at all (South African Institute of Race Relations [SAIRR], 1981, 1982; see also West, 1982).

The most ominous and comprehensive attempt to tighten influx control still further is the introduction by Minister Koornhof of the Orderly Movement and Settlement of Black Persons Bill at the end of the 1982 parliamentary session. This draft legislation abolishes the right to be in urban areas for up to 72 hours without permission and replaces it with an overnight curfew; it makes employers of illegal blacks liable to a fine of R5000 instead of R500 and those who accommodate illegal blacks in the townships liable to a fine of R500 or six months' imprisonment; it makes Section 10 rights conditional on the availability of "approved accommodation," and tightens up influx control in the rural (i.e., white farming) areas. Under this legislation, it appears, the dominant sites of influx control will be places of employment and accommodation rather than the open streets; and it will be enforced by fellow workers and neighbors as well as policemen (National Union of South African Students, 1982).

South Africa's internal refugees are thus caught between opposing forces: the centrifugal push outward of the state's repressive machinery and the centripetal push inward of the desperate search for jobs and housing in the white urban areas. The resolution of these opposing forces is neither uniform nor self-evident. Particular forms of struggle are defined by people's experience of harassment by diverse agencies of the central state and of the Bantustan governments; by local scarcities of jobs and housing; and by regional variation in the rigidity with which, in practice, the allocation of employment and unemployment is linked to the administration of residence permits and certificates of Bantustan citizenship. Forms of consciousness, likewise, depend on the developing nature of particular confrontations and modes of organization. The complexity and variety, in other words, of this aspect of the struggle for the city in South Africa require systematic and detailed regional analysis of a kind that has only recently begun to emerge.[3] This chapter is intended to illustrate, through the history of two large rural slums and the experience of a very few of the families who live there, the forms of struggle that have been taking place in one region, the Orange Free

State (OFS).[4] The term "rural slums" perhaps requires justification. The areas investigated are rural by virtue of the absence of urban infrastructure; but they are so densely populated, without grazing or arable land, as otherwise to qualify as urban. Housing consists overwhelmingly of self-constructed shacks made of corrugated sheeting alone or of combinations of mud brick and corrugated sheeting.

THE ORANGE FREE STATE: BACKGROUND

Reserves and Farms

Three Native Reserves within the OFS were "scheduled" by the Beaumont Commission under the terms of the 1913 Land Act: Witzieshoek in the Harrismith district, and Seliba and Thaba 'Nchu in the Thaba 'Nchu district (see Map 8.1). The history of these areas is briefly reviewed below. Together the scheduled areas made up less than half of 1 percent of the province. Beaumont also identified nineteen other scattered fragments of land as additional areas to be released in due course for African occupation. These latter recommendations were superseded, however, by those of the OFS Local Land Committee of 1918, which recommended that only two blocks of land in the Thaba 'Nchu district should be released for African occupation and consolidated with the two existing reserves there.[5] Legislative provision for this was not made until 1936, through the Land and Trust Act, from which date the South African Bantu Trust gradually acquired the designated areas and forced their inhabitants to move, under various schemes of betterment and rehabilitation, into newly established Trust villages (see Map 8.2).

Beaumont estimated in 1916 that there were about 24,000 Africans living in the Native Areas of the OFS — reserves, mission lands, and African-owned farms — out of a total rural population of 303,000, with 49,000 Africans living in the urban areas.[6] In the early decades of this century, then, the African population of the OFS was overwhelmingly concentrated on white farms. It is evident, in particular, that in the period following the Anglo-Boer War, when many white farms were undercapitalized and effectively rebuilding from scratch, the most important category of productive enterprise was African sharecropping on white-owned land (Keegan, 1979). These relations of production were, however, drastically restructured by the Land Act of 1913, which prohibited farming-on-the-half and whose immediate and tragic consequences were graphically described by Sol Plaatje in *Native Life in South Africa* (1916). It is impossible to estimate with any accuracy how many people were evicted from white farms as a result of the act in the OFS as a whole. The magistrate of Thaba 'Nchu reported to the OFS Land Committee of 1918 that about 1050 households were driven off farms belonging to Europeans in his district: perhaps as many as half of the total black population resident on the farms. More generally, the committee reported very wide variation in the estimates submitted by other magistrates of the numbers of people whose rights to land were "prejudiced" by the 1913 Land Act. It was reluctant to accept as valid a total estimate that emerged of about 5000 *families* affected in this way, about 25,000 to 30,000 people.[7] Whatever the actual numbers involved, it is clear that most black inhabitants of the OFS *initially* experienced the pressures of proletarianization on the farm through changing relations of production in the agrarian sector (Morris, 1976).

A steady drift to the towns took place in the twenty years after the passage of the 1913 Land Act. The population of the Native Areas — reduced in size through the continuing alienation of black-owned farms in the Thaba 'Nchu district — was recorded as 20,000 in 1936; that of other rural areas (almost entirely white farms) was 363,000 in the 1921 census and 449,000 in the 1936 census; while the urban black population of 104,000 in 1936 was approximately double that estimated by Beaumont in 1916.[8] These changes reflect a number of complex processes: a rapid increase in overall numbers; the partial enforcement of antisquatting legislation, which precluded more than five black families from living on one white farm; and the inexorable pressure of poverty, landlessness, and unemployment in the reserves.

Leo Marquard's report on agricultural recession and the conditions of farm labor in the OFS in the 1930s drew particular attention to a significant change in the racial balance of the rural population between 1921 and 1936: "The European population has declined by 4648 and the Native population has increased by 87,123," so that there were, on average in white farming districts, some four blacks to one white (SAIRR, 1939: 13). A continuing decline in the white population relative to the black population in these areas gave rise to acute political anxiety over the *beswarting* (blackening) of the platteland. The Du Toit Commission, which was appointed in 1959 to investigate this phenomenon, included in its report two maps that clearly demonstrated the extent of the "problem" in the southern districts of the OFS and in the OFS/Natal border region. In both areas many white-owned farms were either solely occupied or managed by Africans or abandoned and unoccupied altogether.[9]

Nevertheless, a striking trend within the republic as a whole since that time has been a decline in the proportion of black South Africans domiciled in rural (i.e., white farming) areas, from 3.76 million in 1960 (31.4 percent) to 3.83 million (24.5 percent), and 4.77 million in 1980 (22.7 percent; Simkins, 1981). It is impossible to present a systematic account of the patterns of movement these figures reflect, and their particular impact in the OFS remains to be investigated. In many areas, though not uniformly, farmers have been cutting down on their labor, expelling squatters and the few remaining labor tenants, and refusing to accommodate the families of farm workers whose sons have taken up contracts on the mines and elsewhere. Correspondingly, in response — first, to conditions on the farms, which vary a great deal but are for the most part appalling, and, second, to the prospect, which opened up in the 1970s, of employment on the mines for higher wages — many individuals and their families have decided to establish a home base in one of the reserves and to search for employment as migrant laborers in the towns. That they continue to do this in the face of very high levels of unemployment amongst the inhabitants of the reserves is an indication of the conditions from which they have come and of the desperate search for security.

Influx Control and Urban Relocation

The movement of Africans into towns has always been controlled with particular harshness in the Orange Free State. Until the Land Act was passed in 1913, the OFS was the only province that specifically prohibited Africans from acquiring freehold land in towns, despite the prevailing stereotype that they were temporary sojourners only in white urban areas. Again, at the turn of the century the OFS was unique in requiring women to carry passes as well as men: Bloemfontein passed its first municipal regulations for its black locations in 1893, which applied equally to men and women. According to Sol Plaatje (1916: 91), these measures of the old republic were applied with much greater rigor under the union: "no native woman in the Province of the Orange 'Free' State can reside within a municipality (whether with or without her parents, or her husband) unless she can produce a permit showing that she is a servant in the employ of a white person, this permit being signed by the Town Clerk." A determined campaign of passive resistance to passes was mounted by women throughout the OFS in 1913, and, in the end, forced the suspension of passes for women for thirty years. Julie Wells (1980: 30) concludes, "Legislators in 1923 were convinced, largely from the Free State example, that passes for women was too dangerous and volatile an issue to push. Consequently changes were made to guarantee women's freedom from passes in the 1923 Urban Areas Act. This freedom remained in effect until 1956 when the Nationalist Government began issuing passes for women." The immediate response — an angry mass demonstration by women in Pretoria — showed how dangerous and volatile the issue remained a generation later, although this time the women were not successful.

The pass laws have been repeatedly amended since 1923, particularly under the Nationalist Government since 1948, with a view to enforcing more and more rigorous control of the movement of black people into towns. Pass law contraventions nationally had soared to well over half a million per annum by the late 1960s (Wilson, 1972: 163). It is impossible to assess from the available official statistics how many people are forcibly relocated from the urban areas of South Africa. This is partly because of the confusion and overlap between different pieces of discriminatory legislation; partly because the number of pass law contraventions does not coincide with the number of people affected in these different ways; and partly because there is such a wide variety of forms of harassment available to the state: arrest and conviction under the 72-hour rule; "endorsement out" of people who fail to qualify under Section 10 of the Black (Urban Areas) Act as amended, for one reason or another; eviction of families from municipal accommodation when they are late in paying the rent or when the male breadwinner dies; and official refusal to register dependents. Furthermore, one of the Riekert recommendations was that the pass laws should be administered subject to the availability of "approved accommodation." Acute housing shortage thus now serves as a direct rather than an indirect (as in the past) mechanism of influx control. The elderly and unemployed, in particular, are immediately susceptible to this form of pressure when the old locations of white towns are "deproclaimed" and razed to the ground. Many of their inhabitants, disqualified from accommodation in the new planned townships, have been relocated to Qwaqwa and Thaba 'Nchu.

The overall strategy of urban relocation was spelled out in May 1979 in a sinister report of plans for a new South Sotho "city" outside Thaba 'Nchu, on the site of the present slum of Onverwacht (Map 8.2). According to the *Bloemfontein Friend* (17 May 1979), a spokesman for the Southern Free State Administration Board

> stressed that people would not be forced to leave their homes in Bloemfontein, the surrounding smallholdings and other Free State towns, but would move of their own free will. . . . Mr. Spies estimates that 30,000 people will be resettled from Bloemfontein, the smallholdings and country towns over a long term. . . . In Bloemfontein alone — where the housing backlog is currently 5000 — he expects more than 13,000 people to qualify for resettlement. These figures are made up of 2717 families who are mainly boarders and 717 families who must be rehoused because of poor housing. At an average of five a family, this means 13,585 people. The city's South Sotho population currently stands at about 37,000. There are about 40,000 South Sothos on the surrounding smallholdings. Of these the Administration Board estimates 3000 families or 15,000 people qualify for resettlement. There are another 372 South Sotho families or 1860 people in the Southern Free State who are unemployed. Mr. Spies did not foresee problems with job opportunities. Bloemfontein would be an important source, he said. The Free State goldfields would provide employment and the existence of the new city [Onverwacht] would create job opportunities. There was also the possibility of industrial development. He did not think transport for commuters between the new city and Bloemfontein would be a problem either.

The criteria of "qualification for resettlement" were not elaborated. The transport problem would be solved by the building of a double electrified, high-speed railway line from Bloemfontein to Onverwacht, Selosesha, and Thaba 'Nchu, which was announced in June 1981 (Bloemfontein Friend, 18 June 1981). The "problems with job opportunities" are the greatest single complaint of the inhabitants of the rural slums, as is evident below.

As for the Free State goldfields, there has been a particular squeeze on recruitment in recent years. The gold boom of the early 1970s induced a substantial increase in black wages and also a policy change in the distribution of recruitment by the Chamber of Mines to reduce the industry's dependence on foreign sources of labor supply

and to increase its dependence on South African labor. However, this
was also accompanied by a deliberate stabilization of the mine labor
force: not in the sense of phasing out the system of oscillating migration, but in the sense of increasing the proportion of skilled career
miners who return for further contracts on the basis of Valid Re-
Engagement Certificates (VRGs) administered by the individual
mines. Figures relating to recruitment from Lesotho during 1977-1980
show a steady increase in the length of the average contract and a
sharp decline in the recruitment of novices and of men with some
experience but without VRGs.[10] Figures collected from the TEBA
offices in Qwaqwa and Thaba 'Nchu for 1978 and 1979 are at least
consistent with this trend. There were 5300 recruits from Qwaqwa in
1978, of whom only 13 percent had VRGs; and 3936 in 1979, of whom
29 percent had VRGs. There were 4743 recruits through the Thaba
'Nchu office in 1978, 3168 in 1979, and 1212 in the first six months of
1980.[11] Significant numbers of men from the rural slums who could
have relied in the past on obtaining employment in the mines can no
longer do so.

Internal Refugees:
The Redistribution of
the "South Sotho National Unit"

One further way of understanding the mass population removals
that have taken place in the OFS within the last decade is to look at
the physical distribution at different points in time of the black population in terms of its ethnonational identity. The majority of the inhabitants of the OFS would identify themselves as descendants of the
various Sotho-speaking clans loosely aggregated as a nation under
Moshoeshoe I in the aftermath of the Difaqane wars of the early
nineteenth century. They are identified by the South African government as members of the South Sotho national unit whose official
homeland is Qwaqwa. However, according to the revised census
figures showing the de facto distribution of the 1.44 million people
comprising the South Sotho national unit in 1970 (Table 8.1), less than
2 percent were at that time resident in Qwaqwa. Substantial
minorities of South Sotho were found in two other Bantustans — the
Transkei and Bophuthatswana — than the one with which they are
officially associated. No fewer than 90 percent were in white South

Table 8.1   De Facto Distribution of the South Sotho
              National Unit, 1970

	Numbers	Percentage
Qwaqwa	25.2	1.8
Transkei	76.6	5.3
Bophuthatswana	25.6	1.8
Other Bantustans	21.6	1.5
White South Africa	1,290.0	89.6
Total	1,439.0	100.0

SOURCE: Adapted from Benbo (1979).

Africa, two-thirds of these in the OFS, one-third in the Southern Transvaal (Bureau for Economic Research, Bantu Development [Benbo] 1978: 22). Whatever the deficiencies of the 1970 census itself, statistical projections for later years that are based on the above distribution and that appear in official sources are quite unreliable, for they grossly understate the mass population movements that have taken place during the 1970s. For example, the state-sponsored research organization Benbo acknowledges the de facto population of Qwaqwa in 1977, in one source, to be about 200 000 (Benbo, 1978: 22). In another source it estimates the de facto South Sotho population of Qwaqwa in 1978 to be 94,400 (Benbo, 1979: Table 7). The 1980 census results, similarly, should not be accepted as definitive.

What follows here is an attempt to outline the most important of these mass population movements, with specific reference to the contradictions that have arisen out of the official identification of the South Sotho national unit with Qwaqwa.

First, the de facto population of Qwaqwa has increased *at least* tenfold since 1970. Approximately a quarter-of-a-million immigrants have poured into the already overcrowded and badly eroded territory, mainly from white urban and rural areas in the OFS. Many of them were evicted by white farmers or by municipal authorities. Many others came, apparently of their own accord, in a desperate search for security. Qwaqwa today is a rural slum, a dumping ground for South Africa's relative surplus population in the OFS. There is absolutely no prospect that jobs will be created for these people either locally or at a distance.

Second, perhaps 100,000 people, mainly but not exclusively Southern Sotho, came into Thaba 'Nchu during the 1970s, creating an intolerable strain on resources within this small reserve. Vicious conflicts developed along ethnic lines as a result of the South African government's insistence that people identify themselves either as Barolong and as citizens of Bophuthatswana, in which case they had a right to reside in Thaba 'Nchu, simultaneously renouncing their South African citizenship; or as Basotho and as citizens of Qwaqwa, in which case they had no rights in Thaba 'Nchu. By the mid-1970s the Basotho within Thaba 'Nchu vastly outnumbered the Barolong, by contrast with the distribution revealed in the 1970 census; and in due course the pressure was relieved by the relocation of the Basotho from Thaba 'Nchu to Onverwacht, which also became a repository for people expelled from towns and farms in the western and eastern districts of the OFS.

Third, the figure cited in Table 8.1 for South Sotho resident in Transkei in 1970 is a highly artificial one. It includes the populations of Glen Grey and Herschel districts, which were not part of the Transkei in 1970 but were ceded by the Ciskei to the Transkei in 1976, despite the results of an earlier referendum that clearly indicated that these people did not want to be ruled by Matanzima. The Sotho population of Herschel was 17,870 in 1970, according to a government ethnologist's survey (Jackson, 1975: 49). With independence for the Transkei imminent in October 1976, Chief Malefane and his Sotho followers fled from the Herschel district as part of a group of about 15,000 refugees from Matanzima's rule. Drawn by Chief Minister Lennox Sebe's promises of land and jobs, they went to the Ciskei, together with refugees from Glen Grey and other areas of the Transkei. The promises turned out to be false, and most of these refugees — about 50,000 people altogether — still live in terrible conditions at various close settlements in the Hewu district of the Ciskei (Development Studies Group, 1979: 94-96).

Fourth, following Transkei 'independence' particularly in 1978, there were rumblings of discontent amongst Sotho resident in the Maluti district: formerly Matatiele and Mount Fletcher districts (Map 8.1). This reflected their resentment of Xhosa domination in terms of the policy of ethnic nationalism, but attempts to give political expression to their secessionist impulse have been harshly suppressed. A number of prominent people have fled as political refugees from Maluti district to Qwaqwa (SAIRR, 1980: 318; Streek and Wicksteed, 1981: 50-56).

QWAQWA

From Tribal Reserve to Rural Slum

After the Difaqane, Witzieshoek was occupied by Chief Oetsi and his Kholokoe followers. However, the encroaching Boers complained of frequent cattle raiding by Oetsi's people, and the Kholokoe were driven out by a commando in 1856. In 1867 Moshoeshoe's half-brother, Mopeli, was given permission by the Volksraad to settle there with his Kwena followers as part of the initial peace dispositions of the second Sotho-Boer War. In 1873 a section of the Tlokwa under Koos Mota were also allowed to settle in the eastern part of the reserve.

The Africans who gave evidence to the Beaumont Commission in November 1913 complained that there was an acute shortage of arable land within the Witzieshoek reserve, and that many men and their families had been turned off white-owned land in the adjoining districts as a result of the 1913 Land Act, which prohibited farming-on-the-half. The white farmers who gave evidence — some of whom had been involved in sharecropping, others not — were uniformly opposed to the creation of another Native Location in or near the Harrismith district; they felt strongly that Africans should not be allowed to buy land; and they did not feel that the Witzieshoek reserve was already overcrowded.[12]

F.A.W. Lucas, in his dissenting Addendum to the report of the Natives' Economic Commission in 1932, pointed out that there was very considerable poverty and "a good deal of erosion" in Witzieshoek, and that "the general economic condition of the Reserve has gone back immensely in the past 40 years. The economic retrogression can be attributed to the fact that 30 years ago they were not so congested as they are today."[13] Witzieshoek was proclaimed a Betterment Area in 1939, and various measures were put into effect such as the fencing of arable and grazing areas and the culling of livestock.

Strong popular resistance to these measures throughout the 1940s culminated in the 1950 Witzieshoek Rebellion and violent retaliation by the state. Part of the terms of reference of the Commission of Enquiry into these events was to determine "whether the Reserve . . . is over-populated and over-stocked and, if so, what steps should be taken to remedy this." On the basis of its philosophy that the reserve should become a "self-supporting unit as soon as possible," the commission reported that "there is a considerable number of families in the Hoek who possess no lands"; that average production of grain in the 1940s was three bags per morgen; and that, even under the most favorable conditions, a possible production level of ten bags per morgen would not meet the requirements of residents. The commission argued that "detribalized Natives" who had left the reserve should not have later access to it, in other words, that proper provision should be made in the white urban areas for large numbers of Africans who were no longer attached to Witzieshoek. The commission concluded that

> even if provision is made for the abrogation of the rights of the detribalized Native and for the limitation of the population, with its natural increases, to those who reside in the Hoek or who do not remain absent from the Hoek for periods in excess of two years, the available agricultural land in Witzieshoek is not sufficient to ensure a decent livelihood to the Natives of the Hoek. If the position is left as it is at present, the number of able-bodied men leaving the Hoek to make a living elsewhere will increase from year to year, and only the aged, women and children, and those retiring on pension, or otherwise, will remain in the Hoek, and the position will deteriorate to such an extent that it will not be possible to rehabilitate the Reserve.[14]

This record of decline must be interpreted against the background of the population figures, tenuous as they are in many respects, relating to Witzieshoek reserve at different points in time: 4700 in 1911, 10,000 in 1932, 12,000 in 1950, and 24,000 in 1970.[15] It may be inferred that the situation in 1950, already very serious, was sharply exacerbated through the increase recorded in the following twenty years. Throughout this period the Witzieshoek reserve remained the same size as it was when originally demarcated in 1867. It was generally accepted for a long time to be 50,000 morgen in extent, but official sources now indicate 48,234 hectares (56,282 morgen).[16] The discrepancy probably reflects the difficulty of accurately surveying the extremely rough and steep terrain that makes up much of the reserve. According to the final consolidation proposals approved in 1975, the reserve will be enlarged by 13,766 ha to form one block of 62,000 ha through the compulsory purchase of adjoining white farms to the northeast (Benbo, 1978: 19). However, little progress has yet been made toward even this very limited objective.

The changes in political infrastructure over the years have, however, been extensive. Two Tribal Authorities were constituted in 1953, for the Kwena and Tlokwa tribes respectively, under the Bantu Authorities Act of 1951. A Territorial Authority was constituted in 1969 and a Legislative Assembly in 1971, and Qwaqwa was given limited powers or self-government in 1974 (Malan and Hattingh, 1976: 194). Elections were held in 1975 and 1980: In each case the Dikwankwetla party under Kenneth Mopeli won an overwhelming victory. However, only 20 of the 60 members of the legislative assembly are elected in this way. The other 40 members are nominated by the two tribal authorities, 26 by the Kwena and 14 by the Tlokwa. Constitutionally the cabinet must include both tribal chiefs. The chief minister himself is *rangoane* (father's younger brother) to the present Kwena tribal chief, Motebang Mopeli, who is also Minister of Health, so that the internal politics of Qwaqwa are dominated by the ruling Mopeli family. The elections of March 1980 were characterized by very low participation throughout the single twenty-member constituency that represents the South Sotho national unit and by subsequent allegations of corruption against the Dikwankwetla party (Bloemfontein Friend, 12 June 1980; Rand Daily Mail, 19 June 1980).

Since 1970 Qwaqwa has experienced an influx of refugees on a staggering scale. Its de facto population was estimated by official sources to be 200,000 in 1977, 250,000 in 1978, and 300,000 in 1980, although the 1980 census figure is given as 232,000.[17] If the highest estimate of 300,000 for 1980 is accepted as reasonably accurate for 1982, mean population density is now at least 1613 persons per square mile or 622 persons per square kilometer, compared with 54 persons per square kilometer in 1970 (Malan and Hattingh, 1976: 16). In fact, the population density in the settled areas is much higher than this, since many parts of Qwaqwa are too steep for grazing, let alone for human habitation. Residents describe the place as "one big location."

With some degree of understatement, Benbo (1978: 9) observed in 1978 that

> the country is over-populated in relation to available employment opportunities, is poorly situated with regard to the industrial areas and markets of Southern Africa, has no notable mineral or agricultural riches while a lack of capital and a topography which makes the development of infrastructure exceptionally costly and difficult are some of the most important factors retarding economic development. In spite of a limited tourism potential, the only possibilities to escape from economic stagnation, if resettlement continues, are development as a city-state or a considerable extension of the land area.

The latter option has been politically excluded. The former option, whatever it means, is entirely unrealistic: Benbo implicitly acknowledged this in noting that the city-state was likely to become a "haven for the wives of migrant workers, unemployed men, children and the aged."

There are no reliable figures to indicate where the immigrants into Qwaqwa have come from. Perhaps 60 percent have come off white farms, particularly in the northern, eastern, and northwestern districts of the OFS; and the remaining 40 percent are from the towns within an arc approximately described by Harrismith, Vereeniging, Klerksdorp, Wesselsbron, and Bloemfontein (Map 8.1). By 30 June 1976 the Department of Bantu Administration and Development had "assisted in resettling" 56,229 South Sotho in Qwaqwa (Benbo, 1978: 26); and, presumably, many more since then. Otherwise, probably the majority of people have moved voluntarily in the sense that they were not physically removed by GG (South African government) vehicles but made their own way to Qwaqwa. A shack in Qwaqwa, put together with corrugated sheeting at high second-hand prices, albeit with no arable or grazing land, with no urban infrastructure, no employment, and minimal social services (except schools, which are many and attract boarders from Kroonstad, Weldom, and other OFS towns), represents the first and only secure home that most immigrant families have experienced. However, there is no means of livelihood within the Bantustan, apart from employment in the Qwaqwa government service and a few jobs on construction and other projects in the capital, Phuthaditjhaba. The only real security that Qwaqwa offers is of a "place to die in" (Sunday Express, 14 September 1980).

Immigrants were also responding to a sustained campaign to encourage South Sotho to come "home." This was initiated in the early and middle 1970s by the Qwaqwa government together with Chieftainess 'MaMpoi, mother of Chief Motebang Mopeli. Since immigrants are directly incorporated into the existing tribal hierarchy and immediately subject to a network of bureaucratic controls connected with access to residential sites, to local jobs and services, and to the labor bureau, the effect of this campaign has been to establish hegemony over a political constituency that would otherwise have remained dispersed and fragmented and wholly out of reach of the Dikwankwetla party machine.

In 1978 Mopeli rejected the option of independence, but said that it might be considered if the size of the Bantustan were increased to half of the OFS (SAIRR, 1979: 295). He had earlier been quoted as saying that the ultimate aim of Qwaqwa was to "form a union with Lesotho which will include the South Sotho living in the Transkei and Eastern Free State" (Bloemfontein Friend, 14 September 1976). This aspiration is taken seriously neither by the South African government nor by the Lesotho government. Pending satisfactory settlement of its own claims to the Conquered Territory, which is quite unlikely at present, Lesotho will not find it attractive to absorb another 48,000 hectares, Qwaqwa's present land area, together with its resident population of nearly a third of a million people, since Lesotho already faces its own crisis of structural unemployment.[18] Having substantially failed in his bid for extra land in the OFS, Mopeli's strategy has been to articulate the grievances of South Sotho minorities in other Bantustans. For example, the Qwaqwa cabinet declared Transkei Independence Day, 26 October 1976, as a day of mourning for many thousands of South Sotho of the Herschel and Maluti districts who were not consulted about their future status and who felt directly threatened by the Matanzima regime.[19] Otherwise, Mopeli has taken a particular interest in the predicament of South Sotho immigrants into Thaba 'Nchu.

Peri-Urban Squeeze:
The Marginalization of Three Generations

In June 1980 SKM[20] was living with his family in a single shack, with unfinished extension, in the immigrants' section of an estab-

lished village on a windswept hillside in eastern Qwaqwa. They have
no land and no animals. They had moved in 1977 from smallholdings
near Evaton, northwest of Vereeniging, on the Transvaal OES border
(Map 8.1). His clutch of tattered but carefully folded documents
illustrates the extensive grip of several bureaucracies on the family's
everyday lives: a receipt for the compulsory contribution of R1 made
by every registered resident of Qwaqwa to the Mopeli Memorial
Fund; SKM's Qwaqwa citizenship card, which had just arrived, three
months after registration; a 1971 certificate to the effect that he was an
Elder in the African Presbyterian Bafolisi Church, Evaton; his new
reference book stamped March 1978 by the Qwaqwa magistrate; his
wife's old reference book stamped May 1957 by the Native Affairs
Department, Vrede district (OFS), where they were living at that
time, and her new reference book stamped April 1978 by the Bantu
Affairs Commissioner, Evaton; his wife's certificate from the Qwaqwa Registration office showing she was a registered voter for the
purpose of the Qwaqwa election of March 1980; his receipt for the
payment of R2 per annum to the Mopeli Tribal Authority for the
family's occupation of the site on which they live; a baptism certificate in respect of their youngest son born at Evaton in 1967; and a
police summons as witness in a trial at Residensia, north of Evaton, in
1974.

SKM, a Motlokwa, was born about 1925 on a farm in Warden
district, and moved with his mother several times from one farm to
another in the Warden, Harrismith, and Vrede districts. In the late
1950s he and his wife and children left the farms and settled in the
Evaton smallholdings, where they lived on three different plots over a
period of eighteen years. SKM had a series of unskilled jobs: Gras-
mere, Randfontein, and Park Station, Johannesburg, were three
places he mentioned. In the mid-1970s SKM and his wife were put
under pressure to leave the smallholdings (it is not clear by whom),
and told to go to the Evaton location. Despite the intervention of the
plot owner on his behalf, however, the municipal authorities would
not give him a residence permit for the location, presumably because
he did not qualify under Section 10 (1) (a) or (b). They were constantly
harassed: "That's when I saw this trouble, I'd run out of money
because sometimes, maybe, they catch you twice in a week and you
pay thirty [R30 fine] each time. Day and night! Day and night! They
catch you and you pay thirty and where do you get the money from?
That's when I left there and came to Qwaqwa to see about sorting
something out and to rest a bit." In Qwaqwa the real difficulties

started: "There's no work. We can't get jobs so that we can work for our children. . . . Work is the important thing. . . . When we do get work around here we can't get anything like enough money to look after our children. When you want work you go down to the office there [Phuthaditjhaba labor bureau] and hang around but there's nothing at all, you could wait a year without picking anything up. And the children are being killed by hunger. That's our difficulty in this place Qwaqwa." There was also an acute shortage of water in the village.

SKM and his wife have eleven children, of whom the five youngest are resident with them, and eight grandchildren, of whom five live with them. The thirteen de facto household residents in June 1980 are shown shaded in Figure 8.1, and the present tense in this account refers to this date. The eldest daughter (B1) used to live in Mabopane, north of Pretoria, but she was divorced or separated from her husband and came to Qwaqwa in 1979 with her two young children (C1, C2), who are now living with their grandparents. She works as a domestic servant in Phuthaditjhaba, and helps to support the household a bit on account of her children. The next daughter (B2) is also a domestic servant, at Vereeniging, where she has been working for many years. Her three children (C3, C4, C5) live in Qwaqwa with their grandparents and she comes home on annual leave at Christmas. Neither woman has an extant conjugal relationship. The eldest son (B3) has spent nine years employed at Lenz military camp, outside Johannesburg, "loading bombs and guns and all stuff like that." He stays in a municipal hostel for single men. He got married in 1979 and his wife (B4), several months pregnant, stays in Qwaqwa with his parents. Two bridewealth instalments — R70 altogether, the equivalent of three cattle — have been paid so far. The second son (B5) is a painter who works in Vereeniging. He used to stay on the smallholdings but when his parents left he was able to stay in Evaton township with his cousin. He and his wife (B6) have now been able to establish their own tenancy in the township where they live with their three children (C6, C7, C8). The next son (B7), unmarried, is in the second year of a contract at Sasol II (the oil-from-coal plant) at Secunda, Transvaal. He had been working in Vereeniging and renting a small room in Evaton; but after his parents moved to Qwaqwa his father asked him to move there also "because people just eat money up there," and his earnings would be more accessible to the family if his home base was Qwaqwa. If he got a contract from Qwaqwa his father would know where he was and be able to claim financial assistance

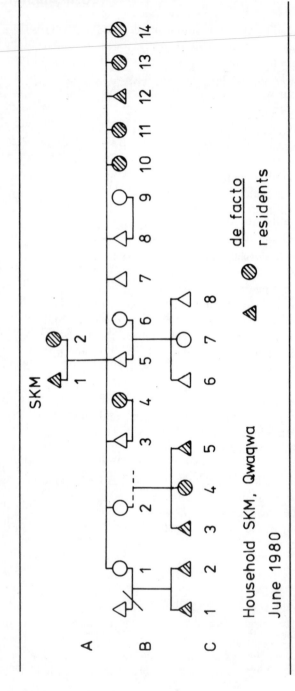

Figure 8.1 Household SKM, Qwaqwa, June 1980

the more readily. He comes home regularly, often every fortnight, and it is this son, according to SKM, who is the main support of the family. "The others have their wives to support." His younger brother (B8), aged 21 in 1980, had finished one mine contract of nine months at Welkom but was fed up with the deception and delays over further mine recruitment and had just taken up a contract for Sasol II. He eloped with a neighbor's daughter (B9) early in 1980, and she was temporarily absent from the household in June 1980 on account of her father's severe illness elsewhere in the village. Two younger daughters (B10, B11) had both left school because the family could not afford the fees, and one of them (B11) had recently eloped. The three youngest children (B12, B13, B14) attend school locally in Qwaqwa.

This family straddles the boundaries between residence in a Bantustan and the white areas and between the structural conditions of employment and unemployment. Remarkably, perhaps, no fewer than six adult sons and daughters are in wage employment: the two daughters in domestic service, one in Vereeniging, the other in Qwaqwa; the four sons distributed between relatively permanent employment and (albeit inadequate) accommodation in the white areas, on the one hand, and occasional contracts undertaken from the Bantustan, on the other hand. The family's move from Evaton to Qwaqwa, however, had the following effects. SKM himself, aged about 55 in 1980, was unlikely ever to be employed again, and his "voluntary" retirement to Qwaqwa (in the sense that he was not forcibly removed by GG vehicles) implied not only his own removal from the labor market but that his young dependants would have in the future only marginal access to the labor market. Two of his (then unmarried) sons were recent entrants to the labor market: one prior to the removal, who was persuaded subsequently by his father, for sound reasons from the latter's point of view, to take up contract employment from Qwaqwa of a kind that was thoroughly insecure (people in Qwaqwa remarked that, for security reasons, individuals were not offered second contracts at Sasol II); the other after the removal, who had no option but to take up a mine contract, which, however, he might be unable to repeat in the future. The younger children were now growing up at a much greater distance than their older siblings, both geographically and structurally, from access to employment and housing in the urban areas.

This case study also reveals three other features typical of the marginalized population of the rural slums: first, the vulnerability of people in a similar position to SKM, who had had a first career as a peripatetic farm laborer in the northeastern districts of the OFS and a second career in various unskilled laboring jobs in the peri-urban industrial areas of the Rand; second, the pattern by which "women's children" are reared by grandparents in the Bantustan in the structural absence of a husband/father and the physical absence of the women themselves at work elsewhere as domestic servants, dependent more or less exclusively on the appalling wages paid to this large and grossly exploited section of the labor force; third, the tight subordination of new immigrants into the Bantustan to the existing bureaucratic hierarchies established for many years within the framework of the Bantu Authorities Act.

THABA 'NCHU, ONVERWACHT

From Independence to "Independence": The Place of the Barolong

For three decades following the collapse of the Orange River Sovereignty in 1854, the Thaba 'Nchu area was effectively an independent chiefdom, occupied by Chief Moroka and his Barolong followers. They had settled there in 1833 as political vassals of Chief Moshoeshoe of the Basotho. Successive Sotho-Boer confrontations over land, however, undermined Moshoeshoe's control over the outlying areas west of the Caledon river, and Thaba 'Nchu was eventually surrounded by Free State territory. Moroka died in 1880 and there followed a bitter dispute over the succession. Its climax was the murder of the new chief, Tshipinare, by his rival Samuel in a dawn raid on Thaba 'Nchu in July 1884. President Brand of the OFS immediately annexed the territory to restore law and order.

In the following year the Gregorowski Commission confirmed the 95 land grants made by Chief Tshipinare to senior Barolong and appropriated the rest of the territory for the Free State government. Some titles were also registered in the names of individual whites. Two separate areas were set aside for occupation by Africans not otherwise accommodated: these became known as the Seliba location in the north of Moroka ward, consisting of seven farms; and the Thaba 'Nchu location, around the white village. Gregorowski recommended that the right of settlement in these locations be confined to bona fide members of the Barolong tribe. In the following twenty years many of the Barolong land titles were alienated to whites through the foreclosure of mortgages taken out by the farm owners. Moroka's territory, annexed as an integral entity in 1884, was effectively dismembered, and the distribution of this land in 1900 was as follows: 54 Barolong farms, some of which were mortgaged; 2 African reserves; 95 white farms; and 29 Government farms, many of which were leased to whites.[21] As Barolong farms were alienated to whites, many black families were evicted through antisquatting legislation that was designed to prevent more than five black families from squatting (i.e., paying rent in cash or labor for use of land) on white farms. Moroka's biographer Silas Molema (1951: 169-70) observed that "almost ten thousand — that is, half the population of the Moroka district of Thaba 'Nchu — went to live in Government and municipal locations in the various towns of the Orange Free State and elsewhere, and thus swelled the African urban population, which seems to be the problem of the twentieth mid-century in South Africa" (Molema, 1951: 169-70). It is clear that such movement was taking place well before the end of the century, but not whether Molema included in this estimate of the numbers of dispossessed all those who were later evicted from white farms as a direct result of the 1913 Land Act.

Alienation of black freehold titles in Thaba 'Nchu continued. F.A.W. Lucas observed in 1932 that 43 farms were leased by whites from blacks at that time; no additional land had been set aside for the Barolong; many Africans had been evicted from farms as they were alienated to whites; the two reserve areas were grossly overcrowded and overstocked, vegetation was scanty and land erosion very bad; "large numbers of Basuto and amaXosa have drifted into the district from time to time and have remained working on the farms"; and the Barolong tribal system was breaking down.[22]

Since 1936, the state has eliminated nearly all the "black spots" in the OFS, that is, African-owned land that was not immediately contiguous with or very close to existing reserves and that fell outside the limits of the "released" areas defined in the first schedule to the 1936 Land Act. The released areas have been gradually purchased by the South African Bantu Trust, partly from white owners and partly from black owners, and slowly consolidated with the two existing reserve areas of Seliba and Thaba 'Nchu. This newly consolidated territory, comprising not more than half of the original Moroka territory annexed in 1884, was incorporated as one of the seven separate fragments of Bophuthatswana on the attainment of its "independence" on 6 December 1977, under President Lucas Mangope. All its inhabitants, whether they live in the reserve areas, the remaining freehold farms, the Trust villages, the old Locations, the township of Selosesha, or new close settlements such as the Bultfonteins, are politically subordinate to the Barolong Tribal Authority, which was constituted in the 1950s under the terms of the Bantu Authorities Act. They are subject to the administrative and judicial authority of the new magisterial district of Thaba 'Nchu within Bophuthatswana (see Map 8.2).

Since Bophuthatswana became "independent" in 1977, the South African Bantu Trust has purchased many white-owned farms in a block immediately to the west of Thaba 'Nchu (see Map 8.2). The block was planned to consist of 25,000 hectares: 15,000 ha was for the enlargement of the Thaba 'Nchu enclave of Bophuthatswana (as part of a swap for land excised from other districts of Bophuthatswana); and the remaining 10,000 ha was to be made available for a new South Sotho city, which would service Bloemfontein from a distance convenient to the planners of separate development and which would in due course be taken over by the Qwaqwa government (Bloemfontein Friend, 3 February, 3 March 1979). The circumstances of this recent purchase are examined in detail below: It is the site of the huge rural slum of Onverwacht. Approximately 21,000 ha of land were purchased by the trust from individual white owners in the period from the second half of 1979 to the end of 1981, the bulk of the formal transfers taking place in September 1979.[23]

From Kromdraai to Onverwacht: The Place of Refuge

The 1970 census recorded an ethnically mixed population in the Thaba 'Nchu reserve: 24,300 Tswana, 12,000 South Sotho, and 3600 Xhosa in a total population of 42,000.[24] In the following years many more Basotho left white farms, the smallholdings round Bloemfontein, and the small towns all over the OFS, and drifted in to the existing Thaba 'Nchu Locations: Morolong, Mokwena, Moroka, Ratlou, Ratau, Motlatla; to the Bultfontein close settlements; and to the remaining Barolong freehold farms and Trust villages. A large concentration of illegal squatters developed in the bend of the railway east of Thaba 'Nchu station in an area that became known as Kromdraai (Map 8.2). It had been demarcated as grazing land, but thousands of people moved there apparently because plots had been fraudulently sold to them or because they had been led to believe that stands would be allocated to them. According to a press report, "It is the rejected who come to Kromdraai — those who can no longer work, those who cannot 'fix up their passes' — from the small dorps and farms all over the Free State. The Authorities of Thaba 'Nchu (in Bophuthatswana) do not want them and say they must go to their own place — Qwaqwa. But Qwaqwa is far away and over-crowded already" (Johannesburg Voice, 8 April 1978).

Initially, an attempt was made to deport the squatters to Qwaqwa. In 1974, for example, Mangope was reported to have made Bophuthatswana government vehicles available for this purpose (Rand Daily Mail, 21, 23, 30 October 1974). A reader of the *Bloemfontein Friend* (25 September 1976) commented on this:

When approaching Thaba 'Nchu by rail one is alarmed to notice the uncontrolled development of the squatter town now generally known as Kromdraai. For those who have the welfare of the Black people at heart, it was a great relief to see Government vehicles transporting these squatters to Witzieshoek. Black leaders in Thaba 'Nchu were happy to see one of their major problems so easily solved. . . . It is only hoped that the Sotho politicians using these squatters for their own political gains will realize what hardships they have caused and are still causing to innocent people and that they will have the courage to accept responsibility for the problems they are creating.

However, mass immigration continued, and the issue developed into a confrontation between politicians of Bophuthatswana and Qwaqwa, respectively. A Qwaqwa cabinet minister complained that South Sotho in Thaba 'Nchu were discriminated against in respect of work permits, residence rights, and language of instruction in the schools. In turn, he was accused of interfering in the domestic affairs of Bophuthatswana.[25] In 1978, the population of Kromdraai was estimated to be 38,000 people. They were living in poverty and squalor, in shacks roughly constructed from mud bricks and corrugated sheeting (Johannesburg Voice, 8 April 1978). They were regularly harassed by the Bophuthatswana police as illegal foreigners, and this pressure was intensified shortly after independence. Several massive raids took place in 1978. On 24 April, for example, 301 people were arbitrarily arrested, their children intimidated, their livestock dispersed and impounded; some people were shot, some women were raped. Those charged and convicted for squatting were fined R40 or imprisoned for forty days in Bloemfontein gaol by arrangement with South Africa. Another big raid on 21 December 1978 led to R60 fines or sixty days' imprisonment. The practice became lucrative for the Bophuthatswana authorities. On several occasions, indeed, the South African police intervened to persuade the Bophuthatswana police to behave more moderately. Basotho tenants in the Thaba 'Nchu Locations also complained of exploitation and harassment by Barolong landlords. In May 1978, Mopeli appealed to Mangope to leave South Sotho in Thaba 'Nchu alone until they could be resettled (Bloemfontein Friend, 13 May 1978).

During 1977 and 1978 negotiations took place between Bophuthatswana and Qwaqwa and the South African government over the provision of land for the relocation of Basotho from Thaba 'Nchu (Johannesburg World, 22 May 1977; Bloemfontein Friend, 19 September 1978). Removal of the Kromdraai squatters to the area known as Onverwacht (Map 8.2) began in late May 1979 — in winter — and was completed by December of the same year. Kromdraai itself reverted to bare hillside, scrub, and grazing. Only the graveyard remains, and rusting upturned vehicles are scattered across the veld. Basotho were also removed from the Bultfonteins, from the old Locations in Thaba 'Nchu, from freehold farms such as Ha Ntsieng near Waghorn station in the east of the reserve, and from Trust villages such as Paradys in the north and Dipudungwana in the south. People are still pouring into Onverwacht from elsewhere in the OFS. Many others are using Thaba 'Nchu as a staging post for being transferred to Onverwacht, so that the areas in the reserve from which Basotho have already been removed have rapidly filled up again. They qualify for residential stands in Onverwacht by producing a Qwaqwa citizenship card, a valid reference book, and a marriage certificate, and by paying R1 for the allocation. Chief Minister Mopeli, however, is acknowledged as not insisting on Sotho identity as a criterion of Qwaqwa citizenship, with the result that there is a significant minority in Onverwacht who are identified as members of the Xhosa ethnic group but as citizens of Qwaqwa.

Thus Onverwacht was barren veld in May 1979. Today it is a sprawling slum, also known as Botshabelo (Place of Refuge). It is extremely difficult to estimate its present population. All the Kromdraai people, numbering some 38,000 people at least, were moved there between the end of May and December 1979. The Department of Co-operation and Development only admitted that 6000 families had been moved to Onverwacht by the end of January 1980; but a year after the settlement's foundation, in June 1980, church workers informally estimated there were 100,000 people, and newcomers were arriving steadily. Thus official and unofficial estimates diverge considerably. A press report (Bloemfontein Friend, 31 March 1981) noted, "At present the official population of Onverwacht is 54,000 but the actual figure is closer to 100,000." Unofficial estimates for 1982 range from 160,000 to 200,000 (International Defense and Aid Fund, 1982). Eight sections of closer settlement are planned, eventually comprising about 50,000 residential stands.

People were allocated stands 30 m × 15 m in size, each consisting of a patch of bare ground with a tin prefabricated toilet (with bucket) whose number — painted on the toilet door — was the new address. They were provided with tents temporarily and told to build their own shacks. The price of second-hand corrugated sheeting immediately rocketed in response to the heavy demand, so that many families had the greatest difficulty in providing themselves with alternative accommodation. The tents, meanwhile, were bitterly cold, far too small, and a dangerous fire hazard. Possessions could not be protected from theft or damage. Some of the sites had large boulders on them, others were subject to flooding in the rains. The bucket toilet system was thoroughly inadequate, and there was an outbreak of typhoid early in 1980, denied by officials in Bloemfontein and Pretoria. Despite the provision of some piping and tap outlets, there was a severe shortage of water in most sections of Onverwacht throughout 1980 and 1981. By 9 July 1980 there were 258 adults' graves and 269 children's graves in the cemetery: a stark indication of high infant mortality. Despite all the difficulties, many people have shown remarkable ingenuity in building, improvising, furnishing, and decorating their tin shacks, which are uncomfortably hot in summer and very cold in winter.

Facilities are grossly inadequate for such a large concentration of people. One visitor at the end of 1981 observed one clinic, one police station, and one supermarket, no post office, and no electricity. There were nineteen schools, with nearly 20,000 pupils operating a double-shift system, which gives rise to acute anxieties for parents as young children return home in the dark. It was proving impossible to find qualified teachers to staff the two secondary schools.[26] Some building of brick houses took place in 1981, but these are available at a price of

R3000 or R4000, which, even spread over twenty years, very few people at Onverwacht can afford.

Onverwacht is administered by the Black Affairs Commissioner, Bloemfontein, on behalf of the South African Bantu Trust. Representatives of Dikwankwetla, the Qwaqwa ruling party, have an informal advisory function in the slum and purport to represent the South Sotho political constituency in its dealings with the South African authorities. For a short time it appeared that Chief Minister Mopeli of Qwaqwa had gained a considerable amount of political credit, particularly amongst the refugees from Kromdraai, for having led his people, as some of them expressed it, "from out of the land of Egypt into the land of Canaan," so that they were relieved from immediate harassment by the Bophuthatswana authorities. Mopeli's promises of land and jobs swiftly proved false, and support for the Dikwankwetla party, which seemed solid at least in the "singles" section in April 1980, shortly after the Qwaqwa election, has probably correspondingly evaporated. On 14 September 1980, two men were arrested by Bophuthatswana security police while Mopeli was addressing a crowd of 20,000 at Onverwacht, after rumors of a possible assassination attempt against him (Johannesburg Star, 13 September 1980). It is not clear why Bophuthatswana police should have been involved.

Frustration and anger have intensified during the three years of Onverwacht's existence. Unemployment is certainly very high, although it is impossible to quantify since the total population is unknown and since so many people experience difficulty in registering as work seekers. Particular focal points of frustration and anger are the forced auctions of livestock which have taken place; and the schools, which are overcrowded and where facilities are utterly inadequate: 600 students stormed the police station at Onverwacht on 11 July 1980 (Johannesburg Star, 11 July 1980). People also complain bitterly of the restrictions placed on informal sector activities: petty traders without licenses are constantly harassed, yet this is one of the very few activities open to someone with enterprise who must find a local source of income in order to look after a young family at Onverwacht.

The boundary between the black slum of Onverwacht and the black reserve of Thaba 'Nchu (Map 8.2), the areas respectively associated with Basotho and Barolong, is subject to continuing dispute, as is the boundary between black slum and white farming areas.

Examples of both sorts of dispute recur in press reports. In March 1981 Napoleon Khomo, national organizer of Dikwankwetla, warned of a "bloody confrontation" if the Bophuthatswana authorities did not stop impounding the livestock of Onverwacht people and auctioning them off without informing the owners. At about the same time, Dewetsdorp farmers vigorously complained of escalating stock theft in the Onverwacht area, attributed to the prevalence of unemployment there and the large number of "hungry Onverwacht dogs" (Bloemfontein Friend, 31 March, 20 April 1981). Onverwacht inhabitants had nowhere to graze the few animals they had been able to bring with them, partly because, despite compulsory purchase of other lands than those on which the settlement itself is concentrated, several farms which had been bought by the Trust had been leased to white farmers (Bloemfontein Friend, 24 July 1981).

"Seventh Hell": The Bureaucratic Nightmare

Again and again, Onverwacht residents complained of the ruthless and arbitrary bureaucratic obstruction they received at both ends of their desperate search for employment: at the Onverwacht office, an ex-farmhouse (ironically, that of Spes Bona) that also serves as a labor bureau, and the Bloemfontein offices of the Southern Free State Administration Board and the Black Affairs Commissioner. People pointed out that, in the first place, it was difficult to get a *soekwerk* (work seeker's) stamp at all: this was dependent on having Qwaqwa citizenship, having a valid reference book, and (sometimes) on being registered as occupier of a stand as opposed to being a temporary sojourner on someone else's stand, as well as being prepared to bribe the black office staff for access to the senior whites who controlled the use of such stamps. In the second place, the soekwerk stamp did not allow them to seek work but merely to compete with many others for the occasional unskilled laboring jobs for which requisitions came to Onverwacht. In the third place, even if individuals were lucky enough to find employment in this way, there was no guarantee that they would be paid even the very low wages they were promised; there was no effective means of redress if they were not. Many stories circulated of the utterly unscrupulous behavior of employers. These stories help to explain why people resist, when they possibly can, the most low-paid and insecure prospects of employment, especially seasonal

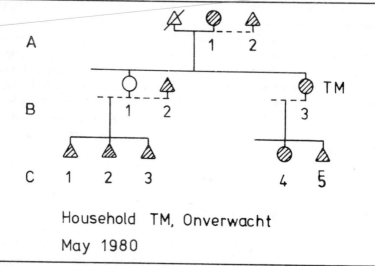

Household TM, Onverwacht
May 1980

Figure 8.2   Household TM, Onverwacht, May 1980

labor on the farms. They cannot afford to be absent from Onverwacht for two weeks and discover that they are only paid R5 for a week's work instead of, say, the R20 promised.

TM was born to Xhosa parents in 1952 in the Edenburg district. She went to Kromdraai on her own in 1974, leaving her mother and family on the smallholding near Ferreira station, outside Bloemfontein, where they had lived for many years. As TM put it, "the whites there didn't like it when I stood up for myself, they resented my behaving like a white madam." She rented a room at Kromdraai from a Basotho family already established there, and once tried to arrange (by night) for her elderly mother to move to Kromdraai with her young grandchildren and her belongings. But they were caught by Bophuthatswana police, who chased them away from Thaba 'Nchu. TM stayed in Kromdraai herself, however, giving birth to her second surviving child (three had died) in March 1978; and she was joined by her elder sister, who daily commuted to Bloemfontein as a domestic servant in the city, and the latter's boy friend, who was unemployed at the time. In 1979 TM worked as a domestic servant in Kempton Park, Johannesburg, for six months. When she returned in December, having been given a "back to" (return to place of origin) stamp in her reference book, the move from Kromdraai to Onverwacht had taken place. In May 1980 the family occupied two tents on a stand in the singles section (see Figure 8.2). TM's elder sister (B1) was the only member of the family in regular employment. She had to leave her three children in order to stay in Bloemfontein, visiting home once a month, because she could not afford the daily bus fare from Onverwacht, which took R12 out of a month's wages of about R30. Her boy friend (B2) had been in and out of various jobs in the middle and late 1970s: a Bloemfontein construction site; the bakery at Thaba 'Nchu; a mine contract at Carletonville; a garage at Pietersburg (northern Transvaal); and, illegally, the military base at Bloemfontein. As soon as the family moved to Onverwacht and he tried to regularize his reference book, he was repeatedly refused a soekwerk stamp because he allegedly owed two years of tax. How was he supposed to pay the outstanding tax if he could not get a job? No one explained. TM herself could not get a soekwerk stamp because she did not have her own stand, and they would not give her her own stand because she was an unmarried mother. She could not apply for a stand as a nominal dependent of her mother because the latter was already registered as a dependent of her elder daughter in whose name their present stand was registered. She was frustrated and outraged by the absurdity and injustice of such bureaucratic obstruction, and she used the phrase *diheleng tsabosupa* (seventh hell) to describe her experience of Onverwacht. The five children for whom, in her sister's absence, she was largely responsible, were all visibly undernourished.

Their mother (A1), who was born in Bloemfontein in 1910, had spent much of her adult life on the Ferreira smallholding, working on and off as a domestic servant. She moved to Onverwacht in July 1979 with the rest of the family. On her arrival she applied for a pension at the Onverwacht office but was told that she was "too young." So she returned to the Ferreira smallholding "where she had grown up," and enlisted the help of her daughter's employer in Bloemfontein in making a pension application there. By May 1980 they had received some papers that had to be completed at the Black Affairs Commissioner's office in Bloemfontein and then returned to Pretoria. This involved a further indefinite period of uncertainty and delay. Meanwhile the old woman returned to the Ferreira smallholding to await the approval of her application and had to beg the present owners for permission to stay with a black family employed by them. She was still waiting there in July. If her pension were to come through and she could then return to her family at Onverwacht, she would still have to travel from

Onverwacht to Ferreira to receive it every two months, since an attempt to transfer payment to Onverwacht would not be worth the further trouble and delay that they knew from experience would arise. Little as it is — R55 every two months at that time — her pension is a vital source of income for this family.

Family Life: A Variety of Experience

The circumstances of TM's family (above) illustrate extreme poverty and insecurity, conditions shared by many inhabitants of the rural slums. It would be misleading to represent the process of marginalization as if its consequences were uniformly distributed within the population of Onverwacht. All the refugees have been squeezed out of one means of livelihood or another, however tenuous, in another part of the country. All of them are on the wrong side of the line dividing urban insiders from migrants, commuters, and others domiciled in the Bantustans. The residents of Onverwacht are subject to similar conditions in their everyday lives: overcrowding, violence, and theft; an insanitary environment; acute shortage of water and other basic necessities; arbitrary oppression by South African officials. The experience of individual families is very diverse, nevertheless, in respect of the origins and background of their members, their access to various forms of employment, and their continuing links with the urban areas. The circumstances of two other families — one with a grossly inadequate but regular income from wage employment, the other relatively well off — are presented here in order to convey something of this diversity of experience.

In late April and early May 1980 MN was at home in Onverwacht, between annual contracts of employment as a *saakdraer* (unskilled laborer) in Klerksdorp, western Transvaal. He sees his family twice a year: on Christmas leave and when he returns to his "place of origin" to renew his contract. He wife, his mother, and the children moved to Onverwacht in September 1979 from Morolong Location in Thaba 'Nchu, and they occupy a two-room L-shaped shack in the dusty B section. MN was born in 1936 at Hennenman, a small town between Virginia and Kroonstad in the OFS, where his father worked for 25 years for the Anglo Alpha cement factory, and they stayed in the company Location. MN went to work in the cement factory in 1955; he got married in due course — his wife was also from that area — and they had their own place in the company Location. On his father's retirement with a lump-sum pension in 1964, his parents were no longer entitled to housing from the company, and they moved to Morolong Location, Thaba 'Nchu, where they built a house for themselves. Some time after 1964, however, MN lost his job as a result of a dispute with his employers, and came with his family to Thaba 'Nchu, where he picked up occasional bits of work for the municipality and in the town. He was often out of work and life was a real struggle, partly because the tribal labor bureau would not sort out his reference book. His wife worked for three years "in the kitchen of the commissioner" and she begged this official to arrange a job for MN. This contact helped for a while. However, MN was refused permission to build in Thaba 'Nchu on a site of his own. The old arrangement no longer applied, he was told, and Basotho were not allowed to build in Thaba 'Nchu any more. So the family stayed on MN's parents' stand. The authorities also refused to stamp MN's reference book to show that he belonged to Thaba 'Nchu. They said, "Go to your own place in Qwaqwa." MN went there in desperation, in the end, and they gave him a soekwerk stamp in Qwaqwa on 13 May 1974. Soon afterward he got fixed up with a job with a firm in Klerksdorp that hired labor in Qwaqwa. Meanwhile, his wife and the children stayed in Thaba 'Nchu. His father died in 1977, and the family was under pressure, with many others, from the Bophuthatswana authorities to leave Thaba 'Nchu. They did so in September 1979. By Easter of 1980 MN had completed six contracts for the same employer at Klerksdorp, on average earnings in that year of R26 a week.[27] He has to sign up for every new contract in Qwaqwa, involving an expensive and time-consuming triangular journey (Klerksdorp to Thaba 'Nchu/Onverwacht to Qwaqwa to Klerksdorp) whose minimum cost by train and bus worked out at R8.50.

The extremely cumbersome bureaucratic process involved in administering the pass laws may be illustrated through MN's "call-in-card" (in fact a long form), issued by the Western Transvaal Administration Board under the Bantu Labour Act of 1964. It consists of three sections. Part A is completed by the employer, who sets out the period, nature, and conditions of employment, with evidence of "approved accommodation," in this case an Administration Board hostel costing MN R4.50 a month for a room shared with two other men, without any form of heating supplied. The employer then certifies: "Please note that the holder of this card _____ was employed by me during the period _____ as _____. He desires to return to my service and I shall be pleased to re-engage him provided he reports to me within one month of the date hereof." Part B is completed by the Labour Officer of the Administration Board as follows: "I certify from my own records that the above-named Black was lawfully employed as indicated above. Suitable and approved accommodation is available. There is no objection to the attestation of a contract of employment provided this is done within one month of the date hereof." Part C is completed by "attesting officer or by tribal labour officer of labour bureau of area of domicile of worker" to the effect that the contract was attested on _____ (date), and the worker's reference book was endorsed accordingly. MN has not yet tried to transfer the office of attestation from Qwaqwa to Onverwacht: The latter office is so notoriously obstructive that he would not bother.

Before he set off again for Qwaqwa to renew his contract, MN was waiting to receive money for the journey from his eldest daughter SN, who had been working in a Qwaqwa government office at Wit-zieshoek since January 1977 (see Figure 8.3, i). She had passed Matric at a Roman Catholic secondary school in the Excelsior district, which she had attended between 1972 and 1976. Her salary was R152 a month in 1980, of which she sent perhaps R40 a month to her family in Onverwacht. She pays R2.50 a month to rent one room plus communal facilities (kitchen, toilet, backyard) in one of the municipal boxes in Phuthaditjhaba. She shares her room, approximately 5 × 3 yards — with her younger sister, who attends school in Qwaqwa because she had previously been to school in Thaba 'Nchu where only Setswana is taught; and with her close school friend for whom she had just been able to get a job as typist to the secretary of the Minister of Justice. SN has a Qwaqwa citizenship card, and the family stand at Onverwacht is actually registered in her name, since her father was absent at work at the time and her mother's reference book was lost. She had had to come down from Qwaqwa for the purpose. SN had a child in 1978 who now stays in the household at Onverwacht, which also contains a distantly related boy attending school in Onverwacht.

MM is the dominant figure in a household of refugees from Krom-draai who live in the singles section of Onverwacht. She was born in 1927 on a farm in the Zastron district, but the family moved repeatedly and she married her husband, born in 1922, at Dewetsdorp. She bore fourteen children, of whom seven died very young and seven survive:

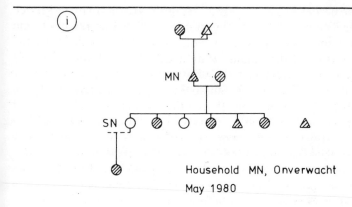

Household MN, Onverwacht
May 1980

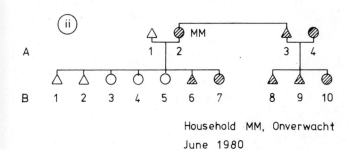

Household MM, Onverwacht
June 1980

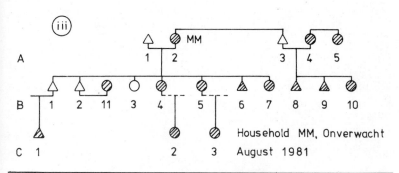

Household MM, Onverwacht
August 1981

Figure 8.3   i. Household MN, Onverwacht, May 1980
             ii. Household MM, Onverwacht, June 1980
             iii. Household MM, Onverwacht, August 1981

three boys and four girls. She is severely affected by high blood pressure. In a varied working life her husband has moved from farm work to mine work — three shaft-sinking contracts at Virginia, presumably at the time the OFS gold mines were being opened up after World War II — and back to farm work. Their last place was on a farm in the Wesselsbron district. The family spent about five years at Kromdraai but the move was a protracted one, with MM herself traveling frequently between Wesselsbron and Thaba 'Nchu. Initially her eldest daughter (B3) was living at Kromdraai on her own, while MM's husband was still working on the Wesselsbron farm. He finally left the farm in 1977 when a new owner expelled many of the old workers and their families. MM and her husband were arrested at Kromdraai during one of the raids by Bophuthatswana police in 1978, but were released after persuading the authorities that they did not intend to stay. Her husband found a cooking job later in 1978 but it did not suit him and he got another job at Welkom in February 1979. The family moved from Kromdraai to Onverwacht late in 1979 (see Figure 8.3, ii).

The two oldest sons both have jobs. B1, born in 1950, is a driver at Crown Mines, Johannesburg. He was married but his Xhosa wife deserted him and took their two young children to the Transkei. B2 works at Western Holdings gold mine, as a surface worker in the reduction plant, earning R194 a month. He did not join on contract but directly, he said, from the farm in Wesselsbron district. He would prefer to stay at home and "make a business," if he got the chance. The eldest daughter (B3) is a Moposetola — an adherent of an Independent (Zionist) Church — in Pretoria. The next two daughters (B4, B5) were both in school at Virginia and staying with their father's sister in the township. Their younger brother (B6) is at school in Onverwacht, as is the youngest child (B7).

MM's younger brother (A3), born in 1942, began his working life as a farm laborer, moving with his family from the Dewetsdorp district to farms in the Brandfort and Wesselsbron districts. At the beginning of 1974 he took a mine contract at Welkom, paying R14 a month to rent a place for his family to stay on a white farm outside the town. In addition, his wife (A4) had to work for the farmer without payment in the weeding and reaping seasons. At the end of 1975, through knowing some of the workers there, he was able to get a job with Boart Drilling for R120 a month, compared with his earnings at the mine of R70 a month at that time; and he was able to fix his pass accordingly. His family remained on the farm, his children unable to go to school, until December 1979, when they were evicted by a new owner who did not want to farm his land as a labor reserve. His wife and children were arrested and fined R90. He was eventually able to arrange for them to go and stay in Onverwacht where his brother-in-law was already established with his family. Their stand is intolerably crowded as a result, and he was anxious to register at Onverwacht so that he could be allocated a stand of their own. His wife could not do this in his absence because the office would insist on seeing her husband's reference book, and he could not risk remaining in his job at Welkom without this. So in February 1980 he gave up his job and came "home" where he was only able to find occasional piece work. They registered for a stand in June 1980 but were told, along with everyone else resident at Onverwacht already, that they were unlikely to be given a stand until August 1981, since the priority was to remove people from oppression by the Barolong in Bophuthatswana. It was now extremely difficult for MM's brother to find another job.

By August 1981, B1 had recovered one of his sons from his wife's family in the Transkei, and this boy (C1) was now living in the household (see Figure 8.3,iii). B2 had got married, while on leave, to a girl from the D section of Onverwacht who had just moved in with the family (B11). C4 and C5 had both returned from Virginia to Onverwacht where, within several weeks of one another in June 1981, they both gave birth to baby daughters by men who were working respectively at Welkom and Virginia and whose prospects were relatively good, although it was unclear at the time whether marriages would take place. A3 was away on a one-year contract on one of the new gold mines in the OFS. His wife's sister (A5) had been staying in the household for eight months. Thus there were fourteen de facto residents in August 1981, by contrast with eight in June 1980.

CONCLUSION

Mass population relocation in the OFS within the last decade may be understood in terms of two fundamentally interrelated processes. First, the central government sharply accelerated its attempts to squeeze black South Africans into the existing reserve areas. The flood of immigrants into Qwaqwa and Thaba 'Nchu reflected the acute insecurity people experienced on white farms and in black townships throughout the OFS. Second, conflicts developed within the reserves along ethnic lines because of official insistence that all black South Africans should be unequivocally identified as citizens of one or other exclusive ethnonational unit. The mass exodus from Thaba 'Nchu to Onverwacht reflected the facts that Thaba 'Nchu was defined as the land of the Barolong, and that here as elsewhere the Bophuthatswana government pursued a policy of strident Tswana nationalism in respect of access to very scarce resources of employment and accommodation.

Just as the hapless victims of the Bophuthatswana police in Thaba 'Nchu — the Kromdraai squatters — were being removed to Onverwacht in late 1979, it was rumored through a press leak that Thaba 'Nchu was excluded from the Van der Walt Commission's proposals to consolidate Bophuthatswana. The *Rand Daily Mail* (27 September 1979) commented, "The idea of surrendering Thaba 'Nchu is certain to bring heartache to the Bophuthatswana President, Chief Lucas Mangope, as it has been in the hands of the Tswana-speaking Barolong tribe for 150 years." Van der Walt's proposals have never been published, presumably because they are expected to exacerbate many controversial issues of precisely this kind.[28] Mangope's prospective heartache must not be understood, however, only as a tragic irony — the boot would be on the other foot — in the aftermath of the Bophuthatswana authorities' oppression of the South Sotho majority within Thaba 'Nchu. Nor should it be interpreted by reference to some gratuitous reconstruction of Barolong tribal history. It is clear, after all, that Moroka's territory was cynically dismembered after 1884 and only partially reconstituted, under very different social and political conditions, after 1936.

Rather, Mangope's anxiety over the future of Thaba 'Nchu must be interpreted within the framework of the South African government's insistence that particular ethnonational units belong exclusively to particular pieces of territory. The political process within which Mangope operates is about which unit properly belongs to which piece of territory. In the first place, the question of a transfer of Thaba 'Nchu to South Sotho political sovereignty would not arise outside the terms of reference of the strategy of separate ethnonational development. In the second place, by all accounts, relations between Basotho and Barolong in Thaba 'Nchu were notoriously harmonious for one hundred years, *until the 1970s*. A press report of

1977 commented, "There used to be a joke that the tiny dorp of Thaba 'Nchu was such a peaceful place that for many years the local police station was staffed by only one bored constable. He was eventually transferred because there was no need for him, there were certainly no 'tribal' differences between the local Tswana and the local Sotho."[29] On the contrary, there was much intermarriage and consequently much confusion — *when* it began to matter — about the identity of persons of mixed parentage.

There is no doubt, then, of the diagnosis of ultimate responsibility for the human misery and degradation caused by mass population removals in the OFS in the last ten years. The compelling force of the general diagnosis should not detract attention from the particulars of each case. In respect of the victims, the variety and complexity of the phenomenon of relocation even within a relatively small area such as Thaba 'Nchu is astonishing. One lesson of this investigation must be that the experience of relocated people is not necessarily a uniform experience. The rural slums have many features in common: overcrowding, high unemployment, grim poverty, and widespread malnutrition. There is a high proportion of marginalized people: women, children, the elderly, the unemployed, the sick, the "idle and undesirable." Despite their physical marginalization, their very survival depends directly or indirectly on the access of household members, however severely constrained, to one or other sector of the urban labor market. Nevertheless, the family case studies summarized above suggest considerable diversity of experience within huge slums such as Onverwacht and Qwaqwa. The wide range of places of previous residence and circumstances of relocation predispose to different forms of consciousness. Materially, there is a vast difference between a household with three migrant or commuter members in long-term, relatively well-paid employment on the one hand; and a household, on the other hand, in which an elderly evicted farm laborer or his widow struggles simultaneously to look after young grandchildren and to establish pension rights against a wall of mindless bureaucratic obstruction.

In respect of the beneficiaries of separate ethnonational development, there is a similar obligation to investigate the particulars of each case. Observations about the benefits to capital need not be made, and perhaps should not be made, at a highly abstract or rhetorical level. The regional investigations referred to in this essay presuppose that it is possible to generalize significantly from the analysis of concrete conditions in different areas. In the OFS, for example, capital injections into the economic infrastructure of Bophuthatswana and the proximity of Onverwacht have generated a major consumer boom for the dusty little white town of Thaba 'Nchu, which reportedly declared itself in an opinion poll in March 1982 in favor of incorporation into Bophuthatswana or Qwaqwa (Bloemfontein Friend, 28 February, 13 March 1981; Rand Daily Mail, 18 March 1982). Again, small black-owned trading enterprises have mushroomed throughout Qwaqwa, threatening the large white-owned monopolies.

More important, perhaps, partly in spite of and partly because of the changes that have taken place, there is a striking continuity in the political and economic domination of the black elites within the reserves. In Thaba 'Nchu the Barolong family names listed as private land owners in 1900[30] are the same names, by and large, that recur in the society gossip columns of the *Free State Advocate* in the 1930s and 1940s,[31] and that are prominently represented in the 1980s in the bureaucratic structures of the local state (Bophuthatswana) and in the management and share holdings of its new commercial enterprises. There is a local class, in other words, whose specific interests have been well served by the political and administrative superstructure of Bantu Authorities and the economic infrastructure of separate development: the tripartite business ventures, the access to Development Corporation loans, the patronage networks that dispose of jobs, pensions, residential sites, and trading licenses.

A similar point may be made about Qwaqwa. The Mopeli family name dominates the membership of the Qwaqwa legislative assembly and guarantees privileged access to the fruits — by no means petty — of self-government. The luxurious houses of Qwaqwa government ministers stand on a slope at Witzieshoek as offensive testimony to the chasm of aspiration, opportunity, and experience that divides the Bantustan leaders from the hungry refugees who are their political constituents. Qwaqwa's "greatest asset," in Chief Minister Kenneth Mopeli's view, is its human potential. He has recognized that "at present and in the distant future the people of Qwaqwa will be its main export. For that reason the quality of the article must improve so that there is a great demand for it among the industries of Southern Africa" (Informa, 1979: 1). This remark appears profoundly cynical in the light of the fact that *at least* nine-tenths of Qwaqwa's population have recently been imported into the territory and the majority are likely to remain quite out of reach of the major employment centres of South

Africa. Contrary to Mopeli's aspirations, mass removals to Qwaqwa and Onverwacht are a mechanism for the concentration of poverty and unemployment in remote and isolated rural areas. When he assumes direct responsibility for Onverwacht, Qwaqwa will consist of two entirely separate city-states: in fact, grotesquely overcrowded rural slums.

Mass relocation in the 1970s finally subverted — as manifestly absurd — the official pretense that the "homelands" would ever be "economically viable." Accordingly, the emphasis in policy has shifted away from the exercise in territorial integration represented by Van der Walt and towards a new strategy of regional development based on the recognition, in Prime Minister Botha's words, that "each black nation will exercise its political responsibilities in the economic field in that broader economic region of which it constitutes a functional part" (Johannesburg Star, 6 September 1980). The practical implications of this statement remain obscure. The rural slums investigated here fall within the recently defined Development Region C comprising "the Orange Free State/Qwaqwa/the district of Thaba 'Nchu of Bophuthatswana." A number of industrial growth points have been identified in this region: Bloemfontein, Harrismith, Selosesha (Bophuthatswana), Phuthaditjhaba (Qwaqwa), Onverwacht, and "a point near Harrismith (Qwaqwa)."[32] Meanwhile, population removals continue. There can be no prospect of improvement in the lives of the internal refugees in the OFS without a fundamental redistribution of land, repeal of the pass laws, and a clear recognition that South Africa belongs to all its people.

NOTES

1. The best single source on this is the South African Labour Bulletin (SALB), especially September 1981 and November 1981. See also Luckhardt and Wall (1981).

2. For analysis of Riekert and summary of measures already implemented, see SALB (November 1979), and SAIRR (1981, 1982).

3. See the five-volume report (1983) of the Surplus People's Project; recent issues of SALB, particularly (February 1982) on the Ciskei, and Work in Progress (Johannesburg); and Perlman (1982) on the Pretoria-Odi area.

4. This essay is based on a number of research visits to Lesotho and South Africa in 1980 and 1981.

5. *Report of the Natives Land Commission, UG 19-1916*, Vol. I, p. 45; *Report of the Orange Free State Local Natives Land Committee*, UG 22-1918.

6. UG 19-1916, Volume I, Appendix IV.

7. UG 22-1918.

8. For detailed analysis of the distribution and size of African Areas and of the African population as a whole between 1916 and 1936, see Lacey (1981: Appendix A).

9. *Report of the Commission of Enquiry into European Occupancy of Rural Areas* (Pretoria, 1960).

10. SALB (1980: vol. 6, no. 4: 58-61).

11. TEBA office, Qwaqwa, March 1980; TEBA office, Thaba 'Nchu, July 1980.

12. UG 19-1916, Vol. II, pp. 54-67.

13. *Report of the Natives Economic Commission 1930-32*, UG 22-1932, pp. 176-177.

14. *Report of the Commission of Enquiry into the Disturbances in the Witzieshoek Native Reserve*, UG 26-1951, p. 19.

15. UG 19-1916; UG 22-1918; UG 22-1932, p. 176; UG 26-1951, p. 17; Benbo, 1978: 21.

16. UG 26-1951, p. 16; Benbo, 1978: 18.

17. These sources are, respectively, Benbo (1978: 21-22); *Informa* (1979: Vol. 26, no. 9: 4); oral estimate from magistrate's office, Witzieshoek, March 1980; Development Studies Group (1981: 5).

18. SALB (1980: vol. 6, no. 4).

19. SAIRR (1977: 254); SAIRR (1980: 318); Streek and Wicksteed (1981: 50-56).

20. Initials only are used to disguise the identity of individuals interviewed.

21. *Report of the Land Settlement Commission, South Africa*, Part II, Documents, Evidence, etc. (HMSO, London, June 1901), Cd. 627, pp. 236-237, 244, 248.

22. UG 22-1932, pp. 178-180.

23. Information from the Deeds Office, Bloemfontein.

24. 1970 Population Census Report 02-05-10 (Pretoria: Department of Statistics).

25. See the correspondence that took place in September and October 1976 between S.O. Seata, representative of Thaba 'Nchu in the Bophuthatswana legislative assmebly, and J.R. Ngake, then Qwaqwa Minister of Education. *Bloemfontein Friend*, 27 September 1976; 5, 18, 30 October 1976.

26. See *Race Relations News* (1981: vol. 43, no. 11: 4).

27. The estimated Household Subsistence Level for an African family of six persons in Bloemfontein in October 1980 was R196 per month. SAIRR (1981: 84).

28. For example, the proposal to incorporate King Williamstown into the Ciskei provoked a storm of protest from white citizens and a referendum in April 1981 that decisively rejected this as a realistic political option.

29. *Johannesburg World*, 22 May 1977, cited in Rogers (1980: 64).

30. Land Settlement Commission, Cd. 627, pp. 236-237.

31. This was published as a supplement to the Maseru-based newspaper *Mochochonono*.

32. Supplement to *SA Digest*, 2 April 1982.

REFERENCES

Bureau for Economic Research, Bantu Development [Benbo] (1979) A Statistical Survey of Black Development. Pretoria: Author.

—— (1978) Qwaqwa Ekonomiese-Economic Revue. Pretoria: Author.

DAVIS, D. (1978) African Workers and Apartheid. Fact Paper on Southern Africa No. 5. London: International Defence and Aid Fund.

Development Studies Group (1981) Population Removals. Information Publication 3. Johannesburg: Author.

—— (1979) Control. Information Publication 1. Johannesburg: Author.

HORRELL, M. (1978) Laws Affecting Race Relations in South Africa, 1948-1976. Johannesburg: South African Institute of Race Relations.

International Defence and Aid Fund (1982) Removals and Apartheid. Briefing Paper No. 5. London: Author.

JACKSON, A. O. (1975) The Ethnic Composition of the Ciskei and Transkei. Ethnological Publications No. 53. Pretoria: Government Printer.

KEEGAN, T. (1979) "The restructuring of agrarian class relations in a colonial economy: The Orange River Colony, 1902-1910." Journal of Southern African Studies 5: 234-254.

LACEY, M. (1981) Working for Boroko. Johannesburg. Ravan.

LUCKHARDT, K. and D. WALL (1981) Working for Freedom: Black Trade Union Development in South Africa Throughout the 1970s. Geneva: World Council of Churches.

MALAN, T., and P. S. HATTINGH (1976) Black Homelands in South Africa. Pretoria: African Institute.

MOLEMA, S. M. (1951) Chief Moroka: His Life, His Times, His Country and His People. Cape Town: Methodist Publishing House.

MORRIS, M. (1976) "The development of capitalism in South African agriculture: class struggle in the countryside." Economy and Society 5: 292-343.

National Union of South African Students (1982) Riding the Tiger: Reform and Repression in S.A. Cape Town: Author.

PERLMAN, J. (1982) "The state and the African working class in the Pretoria-Odi area: population relocation, state management and class restructuring." Southern African Research Service Dissertation Series No. 1. Johannesburg.

PLAATJE, S. (1916) Native Life in South Africa. New York: Negro Universities Press. (reprint 1969)

ROGERS, B. (1980) Divide and Rule: South Africa's Bantustans. London: International Defence and Aid Fund.

South African Institute of Race Relations [SAIRR] (1982) Survey of Race Relations in South Africa 1981. Johannesburg: Author.

—— (1981) Survey of Race Relations in South Africa 1980. Johannesburg: Author.

—— (1980) Survey of Race Relations In South Africa 1979. Johannesburg: Author.

—— (1939) Farm Labour in the Orange Free State. Johannesburg: Author.

SAUL, J., and S. GELB (1981) The Crisis in South Africa: Class Defense, Class Revolution. New York: Monthly Review Press.

SIMKINS, C. E. W. (1981) The Distribution of the African Population of South Africa by Age, Sex and Region-Type, 1960, 1970, and 1980. SALDRU Working Paper No. 32. Cape Town: South African Labour and Development Research Unit.

STREEK, B., and R. WICKSTEED (1981) Render Unto Kaiser: A Transkei Dossier. Johannesburg: Ravan.

WELLS, J. (1980) "Women's resistance to passes in Bloemfontein during the interwar period." Africa Perspective 15: 16-35.

WEST, M. (1982) "From pass courts to deportation: changing patterns of influx control in Cape Town." African Affairs 81: 463-477.

WILSON, F. (1972) Migrant Labour in South Africa. Johannesburg: South African Council of Churches and Spro-Cas.

About the Contributors

SARA S. BERRY teaches economics and history at Boston University. She has just completed her second book, *Fathers Work for Their Sons: Accumulation, Mobility, and Social Transformation in an Extended Yoruba Community.*

FREDERICK COOPER has written two books on agricultural labor in coastal Kenya and Zanzibar, and is writing another one on urban labor and disorder in Mombasa. He teaches history at the University of Michigan.

JEFF CRISP was educated at the University of Wales and the Centre of West African Studies, University of Birmingham. He has lectured at Coventry Polytechnic, and is the author of *The Story of an African Working Class: Ghanaian Miners' Struggles, 1870-1980.*

COLIN MURRAY lives in Liverpool. The results of his extended fieldwork in Lesotho on migrant labor in the 1970s were published in *Families Divided* (1981), and he has been working recently on a regional study of the eastern Orange Free State, South Africa. He teaches mainly in the sociology of development and underdevelopment and the sociology of race and racism.

JEANNE PENVENNE recently completed her Ph.D. dissertation at Boston University on "A History of African Labor in Lourenço Marques, Mozambique, 1870 to 1950."

GERARD SALEM is an anthropologist and research scientist with the Office de la Recherche Scientifique et Technique Outre-Mer in Dakar. He has written a doctoral thesis and numerous articles on the social and commercial networks linking artisans in Senegal with markets in France.

LUISE WHITE's research is on the history of prostitution in Nairobi, Kenya, from 1900-1952. She has taught African history and women's history part-time in the Los Angeles area and teaches African history at Rice University.

WILLIAM WORGER recently completed his Ph.D. at Yale University with a dissertation on the South African diamond industry, and he is currently a Killam Postdoctoral Fellow in African Studies at Dalhousie University.